Stringed Ins
of the Midc
An Illustrated History Guide

by H. Panum & J Pulver

Published by Fairhaven Press &
The String Music Archaeology Project

A detailed and comprehensive history, with illustrations, of the evolution of the medieval stringed musical instruments from their first appearance in the records of the earliest civilizations, through their gradual development in the Greek, Roman and Christian eras down to more recent times.

First published 1940. Revised and Republished in 1971 & 2015.

Forward by Michael J. Hollis, Ph.D.

ISBN: 978-1-62992-015-3

Published in the US and UK.

Fairhaven Press Publishing Headquarters:

PO Box 49947
Austin, Texas 78765, USA

www.fairhavenpress.com

Table of Contents

Hollis Preface (2016)

Music is perhaps the world's only truly universal language. There is no society on Earth that doesn't have it and there are commonalities throughout. Tracing the evolution of music and musical instruments over time however can be a difficult task. As instruments spread and change, they are absorbed into the local communities and made their own.

Over thousands of years, many instruments have been created and discarded but some have stood the test of time. What is it about these instruments that have such universal appeal? What other instruments along the way helped them become the instruments they are today? What impact did these instruments and the music they produced have on shaping the cultures of the past? The only way to answer these questions is to study the art and writings of the past; to trace how music and other forms of culture spread around the world.

This is why I have focused on String Music Archaeology as my field of study. I have sought to answer some of these questions that we can only begin to speculate about at the present. The first step in the research process is to gather and analyze all existing information in the literature before it is also lost to history.

This text is a reproduction of the original Panum & Pulver (1940) text. The reason why it keeps being brought back is because it is the most important study to date on stringed instruments of this period. Since the original sources are long lost, it has been scanned and images modified and improved as much as possible. I'm afraid it is not a technically perfect reproduction but is as high quality as reasonably possible with technology today.

There are areas in the text, which we now know new information about, but by and large, most of what the author's proposed is still true, today. This text is an important primer for students of string instrument history. It categorizes instruments per physical characteristics and what loose instrument families they belong in. It is a strong reader and reference text for students in this field and all of those who are simply interested in the topic.

A word of warning is order here. Like most fields of archaeology and history there is quite a bit of subjection involved. The study of the evolution of stringed instruments is still in its infancy and a number of educated assumptions need to be made. It is up to the individual student or researcher to compare all of the available sources of information and make their own decisions accordingly.

There are many time periods that are of interest to those doing research in this field. The first is early prehistory. There is evidence in German cave paintings of music bows in use as many 17,000 years ago. This actually predates hunting bows by several thousand years and shows us how long stringed instruments have been in existence. Prior to modern languages first appearing, these forms of art and the few relics left behind are our only ways of knowing what instruments existed and what their cultural implications were for most of human history.

When the first written languages began appearing nearly 6,000 years ago, there were already substantial references to harps and lutes and similar instruments already well established in culture. How they came to this point is still a mystery.

The next great leap forward occurred during the days of the Silk Road and Byzantine Empire. In 1066, we see written accounts of the guitar fiddle, a bowed instrument that is a strong candidate for the common ancestor of both the modern guitar and violin families. It was between that period and the Renaissance that most stringed instruments of today began taking their modern forms.

That is also the value of this particular text. With illustrations and explanations, the authors of this text illustrate how stringed instruments of the Middle Ages came to be and took their form. This is an important era to study for all of those interested in learning more about the history of stringed music.

-- Michael J. Hollis, Ph.D.
String Music Archaeologist

Pulver Preface (1940)

The Middle Ages, so often and so undeservedly called the Dark Ages by many whose study of the period has not taken them far below the surface of the subject, comprised an era of great activity. Between the collapse of the Roman Empire and the Renaissance a great task had to be completed. Many of the arts lost during the Germanic migration into, or conquest of, the Roman provinces had to be revived, in many cases, renewed, strongly influenced by the manners and customs of the Teutonic peoples. A new civilization, a new political science, a new art had to be built up on the ruins of the old; the spread of Christianity left its traces everywhere, in music as in pictorial art, politics and sociology; the minds of the slowly blending Germano-Romanized peoples had to be re-accustomed to the arts of peace. This was the work of the Middle Ages.

The art of the Renaissance did not spring forth fully grown and equipped, like Minerva, in a miraculous manner. The medieval craftsmen and artists experimented ceaselessly; and their period, far from being an age of barbaric crudity and intellectual stagnation, was one of constant development and progress. Such a work as is contained in the following pages will possibly help to bring home this truth with more force than many a work of general history. For while the historian supplies us with the information we need on the development of governmental theories, the codification of laws and the evolution of the legal systems of Europe, the effects of the struggle between the Papacy and the Empire, and the results of the feudal system, such a work as this affords us an insight into the social life of the people, their art, their pleasures, and their relaxations, of which far too little is known.

Although our authoress merits great praise for her indefatigable researches into medieval art and literature after references to the instruments of music already so well known to most of the expert musical historians, she is entitle to our special gratitude for the information she gives us on a group of instruments far less familiar to the readers of our standard works of reference.

-- Jeffrey Pulver

INTRODUCTION.

The features which characterise stringed instruments are the strings, the sound-box, and the means by which the strings are made to vibrate.

The strings. The invention of the stringed instrument was due to the entirely accidental discovery that a stretched sinew or gut-string produced a sound when thrown into vibration.

According to the Greek legend it was the twang of the bow-string that first made Apollo aware of the musical properties of a vibrating string. An Helleno-Egyptian legend credits Hermes with the discovery. One day, as he was walking along the bank of the Nile, his foot chanced to strike against the shell of a dead tortoise, causing its dried sinews to vibrate. An Irish tradition maintains that it was the play of the wind on the dried muscle-fibres of a dead whale that presented man with the first idea of a stringed instrument. And there are many other legends of equal value.

Whether the note produced by a string is high or low, depends upon the rate at which it vibrates. The rapidity of the vibrations is further governed by the nature of the string—its length, thickness, weight, and tension. The shorter, thinner, and lighter the string is, and the greater its tension, the more rapidly does it vibrate, and the higher is the pitch of its note; the longer, thicker, heavier, and slacker it is, the more slowly does it vibrate and the deeper is its note.

A critical examination of the vibrational possibilities of each of these categories gives the following results :

a. *Length.* If two strings are struck, one of them being half as long as the other, the shorter, in the same period of time, will vibrate twice as rapidly as the longer, and will give a note an octave higher than the latter. If the short string measures only one-third of the length of the longer, it will vibrate three times as rapidly and will produce the twelfth above the note emitted by the long string. If the ratio of the two lengths is as 1 : 4, the short string will vibrate four times as rapidly as the long one and produce the double-octave of the note given by the long string. If the fifth of a string divided into five equal parts is sounded together with the whole undivided string, we hear the third of the double-octave; a sixth gives the fifth of the double-octave, a seventh the seventh of the double-octave, an eighth the triple-octave, a ninth the second of the triple-octave, and a tenth the third of the triple-octave.

b. *Thickness.* If two strings, one of them half the thickness of the other, are sounded, the thin string will vibrate twice as rapidly as the thick one and will give the octave of the note produced by the latter. If the thin string be only one-third of the thickness of the other, it will vibrate three times as rapidly and produce the fifth of the octave above the note of the thick string, and so on as above.

c. *Weight.* This depends upon the material of which the string is made. The heavier this is, the lower is the pitch of its note. As metal strings are heavier than gut, two strings of equal length and equal thickness, but one of which is metal and the other gut, will consequently produce notes of different pitch; and, being the heavier, the metal string will give the deeper note. To avoid the use of gut strings that are inconveniently thick, the method now adopted is to increase the weight by over-spinning the gut with metal. The ratios between the vibrations of a string and its weight are as follows: a string weighing one-fourth of another of similar length and thickness will vibrate twice as rapidly; if the lighter string is only one-ninth the weight of the heavier one, it will vibrate three times as rapidly; if it is one-sixteenth the weight of the heavier one, it will vibrate four times as rapidly; if a twenty-fifth it will vibrate five times as rapidly, and so on. The intervals will then be the octave, the fifth of the octave, the double-octave, the third of the double-octave, and so forth.

d. *Tension*. In order to gauge the tension of the string the physicist stretches it by attaching a metal weight to it. The heavier the weight, the greater will be the tension of the string and the higher its note. If we compare two strings, one of which supports a four-pound weight and the other only one pound, we will find that the former vibrates twice as many times as the latter in the same period and gives the octave above. If the first string supports a nine-pound weight and the second a one-pound weight, the former will vibrate three times as rapidly as the latter and the notes of the two strings will be a twelfth apart; if the former supports a sixteen-pound weight, it will vibrate four times as rapidly as the one with only one pound attached, and so on. The weight of the load and the number of vibrations thus correspond relatively to one another as weight and vibrations did in strings of unequal weight.

The Sound-box. The sound produced by the vibrating string alone, is too weak to be heard at any distance. If the sound is to possess a greater carrying power, the string will have to be connected with a sound-box. Among peoples in a primitive stage of civilisation the very simplest of means were employed for this purpose. Certain savage tribes, whose only stringed instrument was the bow, made use of the open mouth as a sound-amplifier (Fig. 1); others employ a hollowed-out fruit, such as a calabash or the like (Fig. 2).

Most civilised races, on the other hand, concur in the use of a closed sound-box. If the vibrations are communicated

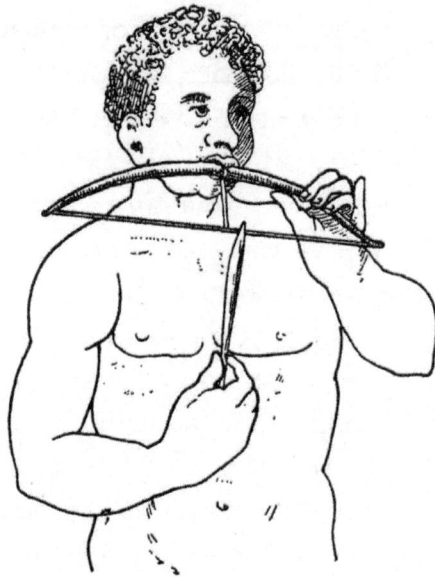

Fig. 1.

to the inside of this cavity, they become concentrated and are thus increased in volume when they make their way out through the openings in the sound-board. The sound-box is the central feature in the organism of all stringed instruments.

The volume and timbre of the tone are essentially dependent upon the material of which the instrument is made, its shape, and the manner in which the sound-board is connected with the strings.

The character of the tone is also governed by the means whereby the strings are set in vibration. If the strings are plucked by the fingers or a plectrum, or if struck by a hammer, a short, sharp note is produced; if they are stroked by a horse-hair bow or a wheel rubbed with resin, the sound is singing and sustained.

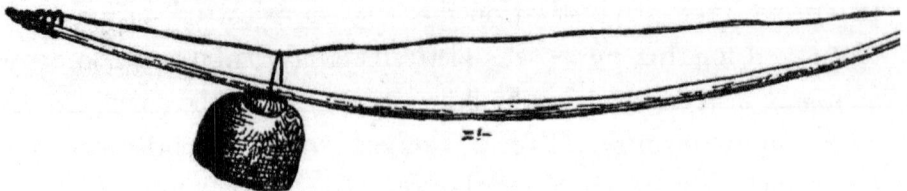

Fig. 2.

The strings and the sound-box form the fundamentals of the stringed instrument, but these elements contain the possibility of many variations; and in the course of time man has succeeded in creating a multitude of different stringed instruments based upon the lessons he has learned by observation and experiment.

CLASSIFICATION OF STRINGED INSTRUMENTS.

Stringed instruments can be divided into two main classes.

The first of these contains all the instruments played with open strings. This class can be divided into two families, viz. :

(1) The lyre family, in which the strings are of equal length but of varying thickness and tension.

(2) The harp family (harps and psaltery), in which the strings are of differing length and so placed that they gradually increase in length.

The instruments of the first main class are played either with the fingers or with a plectrum.

The second main class contains those instruments whose strings are stopped (divided) so that each string is used to produce several notes. The stopping of the strings is performed by the fingers of the left hand (or in rare cases by means of a short staff), pressed tightly against the string, thereby shortening its length more or less and thus raising its pitch. In most cases the strings on such instruments have a finger-board; but on a certain group of mediæval instruments the strings are stopped by directing the pressure immediately against the open springs. In this second class of instruments the strings are set in vibration either by plucking with the fingers of the right hand or a plectrum, or by bowing (with a bow or a wheel covered with resin).

BOOK I

STRINGED INSTRUMENTS WITHOUT FINGER-BOARD.

The instruments played with open strings (i.e., the lyre and the harp families) occupied so prominent a position in the ancient civilisation, that in order to understand their development it will be necessary to follow them from their very origins. Not to disturb the general impression by constantly returning to the early conditions, all the instruments belonging to this class will first be examined in their antique state. The discontinued threads will then be taken up again and brought down to the Middle Ages.

PART I

ANTIQUITY.

I. THE LYRE FAMILY.

The sides of the lyre are formed by two arms proceeding from a sound-box, connected at the top by a cross-bar called the yoke. Between the sound-box and the yoke, a greater or lesser number of strings are stretched which, in consequence of their passing freely through an open space, may be plucked

Fig. 3. Assyrian symmetrical lyre. Bas-relief from Khorsabad.

Fig. 4. Hittite symmetrical lyre (Hermann und Puchstein, "Reisen in Klein-Asien u. Nord-Syrien").

Fig. 5. Phœnician symmetrical lyre. Bronze statuette in the Louvre (Paris).

8

from either side. In most cases the strings are of equal length, and their differing pitch is the natural consequence of their varying thickness and tension.

The lyre type is first found in western Asia, in the land lying between the Euphrates and the Tigris. Thence it made its way to the Nile country and to Greece, where it was quickly adopted as the national instrument and where it reached the zenith of its artistic career.

(1) THE LYRE IN WESTERN ASIA.

The west Asiatic lyre occurs in two forms being found either symmetric, with arms of equal length and a straight yoke, or unsymmetrical with one arm longer than the other and consequently with an oblique yoke. In this lyre the yoke is always placed across the arms like a bridge and is never intersected by them, nor do the arms extend beyond it as in the case of the majority of the Greek lyres. In those cases where the sound-box is visible it is found to be square. In playing, the base of the western Asiatic lyre either rests directly against the breast of the player or is held flat under the left arm. In most cases it is carried in a sling.

There is not much to be said of the details connected with the symmetrical lyre of western Asia, as they show only the outlines of the instrument and give no indication of its construction (see Figs. 3-5). In Fig 3 the player is plucking the strings with his fingers, one hand playing on each side. The reproductions of the unsymmetrical or oblique lyre are far more complete. On this, the attention is first attracted to the oblique yoke which served to stretch the strings. Tied to the lower end of the yoke, the strings were pushed by the hand, one by one, along the oblique bar until they were in place and in tune. In its simplest form the oblique lyre is found in two Assyrian bas-reliefs in the British Museum, one of which is reproduced here as Fig. 6. From the profile of the player

Fig. 6.   Oblique lyre on a bas-relief in the British Museum (Kouyunjik, 9th century B.C.).

protrude two rod-like arms, of which the upper one is somewhat longer and more oblique than the lower. At the end of these arms the yoke is fixed, both ends terminating in a carved goose-head. The shape of the sound-box cannot be determined as the base of the instrument is hidden behind the body of the performer. As this lyre is carried by captives, it can scarcely be assumed that it is an instrument originating in Assyria. Most archæologists believe that in these prisoners they recognise Hebrews. Engel, on the other hand, takes them to be of North African origin and points to the striking likeness existing between the type of lyre depicted here and the lyre which, under the name of *Kissar*, is still used by several North African peoples (see Fig. 20).

Of much more decorative appearance is the oblique lyre to be found on an Assyrian bas-relief, in the hands of a native eunuch (see Fig. 7), and in another relief manipulated by a Philistine. In these examples the lyre-arms are elegantly shaped and the broad yoke is prolonged at the top, to project from the instrument like a horn. The photograph shows clearly how the strings were tied to the yoke in the manner described above. In the right hand of the player is a pointed plectrum.

Fig. 7. Assyrian harp and oblique lyre. Bas-relief in the British Museum (Kouyunjik Collection).

A third oblique lyre of which only the outlines are reproduced and which, unlike the last-named specimen, is plucked by the fingers, can be seen in Fig. 8. If the drawing is correct this lyre is without any kind of sound-box, and the strings are apparently attached to the frame.

Quite unique is the archaic Chaldæan lyre depicted in Fig. 9, which in respect of age is said to exceed by far the

Fig. 8. Assyrian oblique lyre Bas-relief (Bonomi, "Nineveh and its Palaces," third edition.).

oblique lyres hitherto mentioned, archæologists dating it back to the second millennium B.C. Its square form recalls the symmetrical lyre reproduced above, while in its colossal size and upright position it is quite distinct both from this lyre and from the Assyrian oblique lyres described earlier. What attracts the eye most of all, however, is the tail-piece of entirely modern appearance at the base of the sound-box, and the peculiar tuning mechanism placed above the smoothly forward-sloping yoke. The placing of the tail-piece close to the longer arm of the lyre has the effect of making the strings appear to fill only the foremost half of the open space between the arms, or the outermost string rises vertically to meet the yoke exactly at the middle, while the other strings are drawn one by one across the oblique yoke to the point where the latter and the longer arm meet. The tuning device to be observed bears a surprising resemblance to the one which is seen now and then —on Pompeian mural paintings—on Greek lyres, and which likewise occurs on one of the Ethiopian examples of the North African *Kissar* (see below, Fig. 37). An explanation of this tuning method will be given when we deal with the Greek tuning mechanisms.

Fig. 9. Archaic Chaldæan oblique lyre from Tello. Second Millennium B.C. (De Sarzec, "Decouvertes en Chaldée.")

(2) THE LYRE IN EGYPT.

The earliest Egyptian representation of a lyre comes from a tomb at Beni-Hassan (XII Dynasty). Among a walking group of men of foreign appearance—whom the archæologists take to be immigrating Asiatics—there is, in the painting, a man playing a lyre. The instrument, which has a square capacious sound-box, is carried horizontally so that its base is placed against the breast of the player. Exceedingly strange is the stringing of this lyre. All the strings proceed from the base of the sound-box and then divide into two groups, the eight or nine lower strings going directly to the yoke, while the higher ones (to all appearances three or four) are carried downwards in an oblique direction to disappear beneath the other strings soon after leaving the sound-board. In two of the modern reproductions it looks as if the oblique set of strings were carried beneath a finger-board which, in the form of a support for the straight strings, accompanies them up from the sound-box to the yoke; for here the colour of the sound-box beneath the strings is carried to their upper ends on the yoke (see Fig. 10). That this finger-board is only an optical illusion, however, appears to be certain from a third copy, where the straight strings are placed against a white (empty) background and from the fact that the left hand on all reproductions is visible behind the strings. It cannot therefore be decided where the oblique strings actually end, or how they were used. All that is certain is that they were present in the original for they recur consistently in all the drawings that were made while the details of the old painting could still be made out. According to Professor V. Schmidt, the original is now so faded that it would be fruitless to re-examine it for details. As to the mode of playing, the painting only shows that the right hand plucked the strings with a plectrum from the front, at the point where they passed over the sound-box, while the fingers of the left hand twanged the strings from the back, in the open space between the arms.

Fig. 10. Lyre on a sepulchral painting from Khnum-hotep's tomb at Beni-Hassan. XIIth Dyn. *Ca.* 1800, B.C.

14

Even after the lyre had—from the XVIII Dynasty—
gained a permanent footing in Egypt, it is still mostly people
in Asiatic dress who carry this instrument in the pictures. In
a sepulchral painting with an exceptional number of lyres, at
El Amarna (see Fig. 11), the interior of a harem is repro-

Fig. 11. Tomb-paintings at El Amarna. XVIII Dyn. ("Archæol.
Survey of Egypt.")

duced, where native and foreign slave-women, in a number of
rooms, large and small, are being instructed in singing and
dancing. The two long locks of hair worn by several of the
women depicted here are—according to Griffith ("Arch. Survey of Egypt")—said to indicate Syrians or Hittites. They
are accompanied by harps, lyres, and lutes. Two types of
lyres are reproduced. One is comparatively small, and when
played is carried horizontally; while the other is as high as
a man and is stood upright on the ground when in use. Both
are remarkable for their slender spiral arms and large sound-
boxes. As far as can be seen, both these lyres are symmetrical.

The same two types of lyres are found in two mural paintings on Ay's tomb, dating from the reign of Amenhotep IV,
and they are here carried by persons whose clothes again characterise them a strangers. In all probability they are foreign
musicians who belonged to the royal household of the dowager-

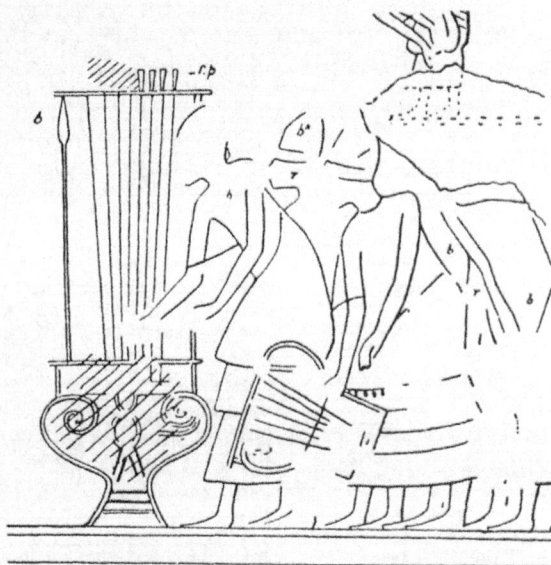

Fig. 12. Lyres in a sepulchral painting on Ay's tomb. (Reign of Amenhotep IV, 1383-1365 B.C. " Arch. Survey.")

Fig. 13. From the same tomb.

queen Tiis. According to museum-inspector Blinkenberg, the dress here reproduced was used at that time in several countries near the eastern part of the Mediterranean, and during that period Egypt really was in communication with these parts of the world, especially with Asia Minor and Crete.

From the yoke of the large standing-lyre in the picture (Fig. 12) will be seen a number of pins which call to mind the tuning mechanism used in the archaic Chaldæan lyre from Tello (Fig. 9). In Fig. 13 two persons are plucking the strings of this enormous lyre at the same time.

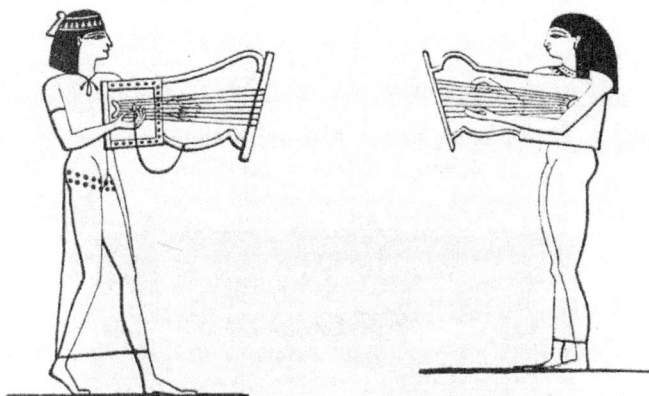

Fig. 14. Oblique lyre in a mural painting at Thebes. (From a drawing. Wilkinson.)

Fig. 15. Oblique lyre with straight yoke in a mural painting on Rat-eser-kasenb's tomb. (" Memoires publiées par les membres de la Mission arch. franc. de Caire.") Photo.

Egypt provides only two examples of the ordinary western Asiatic type of lyre with oblique yoke; both are reproduced in Wilkinson's " Manners and Customs of the Ancient Egyptians." Wilkinson informs us that he found them in a mural

Fig. 16. The same type of lyre. Mural drawing from Thebes (Champollion). From a drawing.

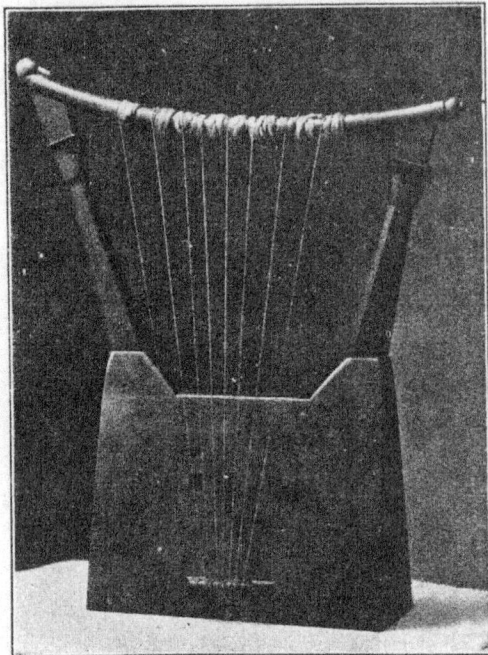

Fig. 17. Modern copy of the ancient Egyptian oblique lyre in the Museum at Cairo. Made for the collection of instruments in the Brussels Conservatoire.

painting at Thebes, but unfortunately does not give the precise source.

In all the other oblique lyres found in the Egyptian mural pictures, the unequal arms are always bent so that the yoke is parallel with the upper edge of the sound-box and consequently lies squarely over the strings (see Figs. 15 and 16).

That the oblique yoke in Wilkinson's copies may be quite correct is proved by three original examples of the ancient Egyptian lyre, one of them preserved in the Museum at Cairo and the other two in the Old Museum in Berlin.

There is a correct modern reproduction of the Cairo lyre in the collection of instruments in the Brussels Conservatoire and shown here in Fig. 17, from a photograph sent me by M. Victor Mahillon, Director of the Museum. Two arms, of which one measures 31 cm. and the other 26, rise from the two sides of a square sound-box, the front and back of which are connected by wedge-shaped side-pieces, thus providing a broad supporting base. Across the arms lies the oblique yoke, the top end of which ends in a carved goose-head, while the other end terminates in a rounded button. On the sound-board at the very base of the sound-box is a tail-piece for fastening the lower end of the strings, and from this the strings radiate upwards to the yoke.

Fig. 18. Original ancient Egyptian lyre in the Berlin Museum.

Fig. 19. Copy of the Berlin lyres on a mural painting from Thebes (Wilkinson; drawing).

In the two lyres at Berlin, of which only one is reproduced here (Fig. 18), both of the unequal arms end in carved horse-heads, and the bridge-shaped tail-piece is replaced by a large square box projecting out of the base of the sound-box. At the upper edge of this box, as well as on the yoke, the furrows cut by the strings into the wood are still to be seen. On the superior edge of the chest thirteen strings may distinctly be counted, and these, according to the varying distances between the grooves, must have been arranged in pairs, so that a long and a short string were always adjacent. In all probability this lyre, as is the case with the earlier Greek examples, produced a scale of seven notes of which six were produced by double strings and the seventh by a single string.

A lyre which exactly resembles the two examples in Berlin was found by Wilkinson in a pair of Theban mural paintings. In his copy the arms are, however, equally long, and the projection is not placed at the base of the sound-box, but midway up its sound-board (Fig. 19). From this reproduction it will be seen that the Egyptian lyre was carried upright and was plucked with the fingers from both sides—i.e., without a plectrum.

Besides the three original lyres described above there are, according to Wilkinson, Fétis and Engel, two more, one of them belonging to the Museo archeologico in Florence, the other to the Egyptian collection in the State Museum at Leyden. A letter to the directors of these museums, however, brought me this negative result: that, according to a photograph sent me, the Florentine "lyre" is not a lyre but a harp (cf. below, Fig. 63), and that the Leyden lyre is made of three fragments which originally belonged to three different instruments: one arm being borrowed from a small lyre, the other from a large one, and the sound-box with its ring-shaped tailpiece originating in a third instrument. The oblique lyre thus produced may therefore be described as a forgery.

By examining the ancient Egyptian pictures we thus arrive at this conclusion : that the lyre in the Nile valley never was so popular as the harp, for in the pictures we find but one lyre to every twenty harps, and nearly a half of the number playing on lyres are foreigners. (Note: An account of the Leyden "lyre" mentioned above may be read in: P. A. A. Boesser, "Beschreibung der aegyptischen Sammlung des Niederländischen Reichsmuseum der Alterthümer in Leiden. Die Denkmäler der Zeit zwischen dem alten u. mittleren Reich und des Mittelreiches. Zweite Abtheilung," p. 7.)

(3) THE LYRE IN GREECE.

Literary testimony. The earliest evidence of the existence of a stringed instrument of the lyre family is to be found in Homer (ninth century B.C.), who sometimes calls it *phorminx*, sometimes *kitaris*, but who evidently means the same instrument in both cases. From a philological point of view *phorminx* is considered to be of Hellenic, and *kitaris* of Asiatic origin.

As to the nature of Homer's *kitaris alias phorminx*, the "Odyssey" and the "Iliad" only contain scattered and incomplete references. Achilles' *phorminx* is described in the "Iliad" (IX, 185 *ff.*) as a stately and beautiful instrument with a silver yoke :

"And they came to the huts and the ships of the Myrmidons, and found him delighting his soul with a clear-toned lyre, fair and richly-wrought, whereon was a bridge of silver." (Trans. by A. T. Murray.)

In the "Odyssey," moreover, he speaks several times (17, 261; 22, 340; 23, 143) of the vaulted *phorminx*, at the same time giving the impression that the instrument was comparatively small and light, so that during the banquet the *phorminx* of the blind Demodokos was hung on a peg above his head in order that he might feel his way to it with his hand and take it down to play ("Od.," 8, 67 *ff.*):

"And he hung the clear-toned lyre from a peg close above his head, and showed him how to reach it with his hands." (A. T. Murray.)

As to the strings, it is said ("Od.," 21, 404-9) that they were made of gut, and were tuned by means of the so-called *collopes*.

"So spoke the wooers, but Odysseus of many wiles, as soon as he had lifted the great bow and scanned it on every side—even as when a man well-skilled in the lyre and in song easily stretches the string about a new *kollope*, making fast at either end the twisted sheep-gut—so without effort did Odysseus string the great bow." (Trans. A. T. Murray.)

Concerning the use to which Homer's lyre was put, we learn that it was played during meals and banquets and to accompany songs on the deeds of the heroes and songs for dancing. In one case, indeed, "the clear-toned lyre" was the only accompaniment of "a gladsome dance" ("Od.," 23, 133 *ff*).

The *phorminx* alias *kitaris* is described far more thoroughly in the Greek legend of Hermes than is the lyre in Homer. This story was first narrated in a hymn to Hermes which was once ascribed to Homer, but the genesis of which has been placed by modern investigators some time between the fortieth and the twenty-sixth Olympiads, i.e., at the end of the seventh century B.C. In the hymn the legend is related in this strain: Only a few hours after his birth Hermes climbed out of his cradle to find and steal Apollo's cattle. In crossing the "sill of the grotto" he met a tortoise shuffling along in the long grass. Delighted with his find, he took the animal into the grotto and with a chisel bored out the "marrow" of the "mountain toad." He then cut sticks to measure which he inserted into the holes he had made in the carapace of the tortoise, stretched an ox-hide over it, and set the arms, which he connected with a yoke. He finally strung the instrument with seven strings of sheep-gut. When the lyre was ready he tested each of the strings with a plectrum, and "it sounded mighty under his hand when he improvised and tried to sing a beautiful song to its music."

If we compare the evidence given by Homer and the Hermes legend regarding the lyre, it will be seen that it was an instrument of vaulted shape and with strings of gut. Homer's description of Apollo's *phorminx* as a beautiful instrument provided with a silver yoke, on the other hand, does not fit into the description in the myth of Hermes' *phorminx* as a wholly primitive and crudely-made instrument. The age of the literary sources and the logical place of the instruments as dictated by their development, are in this case reversed, for the later source (the Hermes hymn) describes a primitive type, while the earlier one (Homer) describes an instrument which implies a long anterior development.

As the Homeric poetry originated in Asia Minor, it is to be supposed that the lyre mentioned by the poet was an Asiatic instrument; its apparent completeness is also an argument in support of this theory, for, as we know from the illustrations in western Asia, the lyre may be traced there farther back than in any other part of the world. Asia is also indicated by the statement in the "Iliad" that Achilles took his *phorminx* from the spoils when he plundered an Asiatic town ("Iliad," IX, 185 *ff.*). Even if we may assume that the Hermes hymn also came into existence in Asia Minor, it does not preclude the possibility that the legend it recounts may have been borrowed from Hellas, for here an Hellenic god appeared as the inventor of a stringed instrument of a type not hitherto found outside of Greece. Neither in Asia nor Egypt does antiquity offer an example of a lyre with a tortoise-shell sound-box. Consequently this type may for the present be characterised without hesitation as Hellenic. By making Hermes present his lyre to the Thracian Orpheus, a later legend even points to the country where this category of lyre came into existence.

As a special Greek type we shall now subject the lyre of Hermes to a close literary examination, for the description given in the Hymn is illustrated by evidence which rests partly upon more recent observation, but in the main is to be deduced from other testimony found in ancient literature on Hermes' instrument. Of these the most important are Appolodorus (III, 10, 2), Diodorus (V, 75), Lucian ("de Deor.," 7, 4), Philostratos ("Imag.," I, 10), Pausanias (V, 14, 6, and VIII, 17, 4), and Eustathius (574, 36, 1913, 38).

The Hermes hymn gives the components of the tortoise-lyre as: (1) the tortoise-carapace and the ox-hide in conjunction, (2) a number of reed sticks placed in the carapace, (3) the arms of the lyre, (4) the yoke connecting them, (5) seven gut strings, and (6) a plectrum for plucking the strings.

1. The tortoise-carapace and the ox-hide. Among peoples of primitive culture we still find stringed instruments the sound-box of which, as in this case, is made of nature's materials: a fruit or the like. Tht hide-diaphragm, too—which, by the way, is not mentioned in any Greek sources other than the Hermes hymn, and which in time was replaced by a thin wooden sound-board, cf. below—is found rather frequently in primitive instruments. In a way it is interesting to compare the Hermes lyre with the modern Arabian *Kissar*, which often has half of a large gourd covered with a piece of undressed leather as its sound-box (see Fig. 20).

The two arms of the lyre—which both begin at the very base of the sound-box and under the leather sound-board—gradually separate, pierce the sound-board and, having passed the upper edge of the sound-box, continue to the point where the yoke is laid across to connect them. The manner in which the yoke is connected with the arms will be described when the different modes of joining the arms and the yoke in the Greek lyre are dealt with. At the same place a picture of another north African (Nubian) lyre will be found, the shape

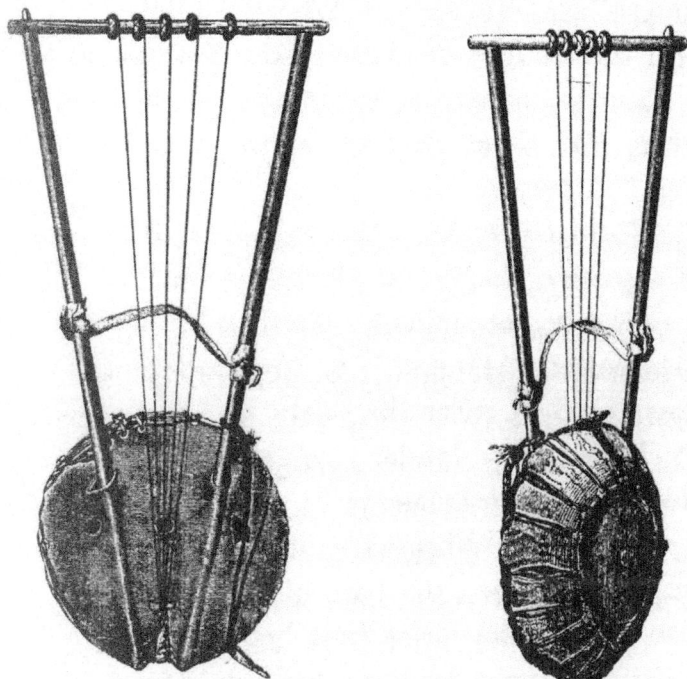

Fig. 20. Arabian Kissar. (From "Description de l'Egypte, Etat moderne.")

of which differs to some extent from the one described here, the yoke being oblique. The five strings, made of camel-gut, are connected at the lower end by a knot, and fastened to the sound-box. After passing over a small bridge, they are carried through the open space between the arms of the lyre up to the yoke, where they are fastened and tuned according to a method which will be explained later.

The tortoise-carapace is mentioned late in Greek literature as a suitable foundation for the lyre. Thus Pausanias (ca. 175 A.D.) states that the oak forests of Arcadia were full of wild-boars, bears, and large tortoises of which lyres could be made of a size equal to those supplied by the Indian tortoises. The carapace is also indicated by the frequent use of the name *Chelys*, i.e , tortoise (Lat. *Testudo*) by the poets, for this type of lyre. In the absence of real tortoise-shells an imitation made of wood was used, as appears, for example, in

Philostratos' description of a lyre illustrated, "the sound-box of which is exactly reproduced after Nature, and is covered round about with flat-vaulted scales, of which one overlaps the other, and of which each carries a golden-yellow eye" ("Imag.," I, 10).

2. The reed sticks. We do not find these sticks mentioned anywhere but in the Hermes hymn, so that their real object cannot be determined. Matthiæ ("Animad.," p. 220), and Baumeister ("Hymni," p. 193), are of the opinion that they were used to cover the cavity of the carapace and were placed immediately under the sound-board. Jan ("Die Griechische Saiteninstrumente"), on the other hand, sees in these reed sticks a likeness to the sound-post which violin-makers place between the back of the body and the table in order to prevent the latter from breaking under the pressure of the strings on the bridge. Reinach (Daremberg et Saglio, "Dic. des Antiquités Grecques et Romains," s.v. Lyra) finally suggests that they may have served to stretch the leather sound-board just as tent-poles are used to tighten the tent canvas.

3. The arms of the lyre (*pecheis, keras, ancones*). We are not told in the Hermes hymn of what material these arms were originally made. But we have a number of later pieces of evidence. First, Herodotus (fifth century B.C.), who, when mentioning the animals native to Lybia, refers to a kind of gazelle "the horns of which were used as arms for a stringed instrument." Sophocles refers to gold-mounted horns when he undoubtedly means the arms of a lyre; and this is confirmed by Pausanias' description of a contemporary painting (by Polygnot in the Assembly-hall at Delphi; X, 30), in which Thamyris is depicted with a lyre, one arm of which is broken off and the strings of which are snapped. Mention should also be made of Philostratos' comparatively late statement that the musician borrows the horns of his lyre from the leap-

26

ing ibex, and the poets' frequent use of the word *Kerata* (i.e., horns) for the arms of the lyre.

4. The yoke. Nothing definite is stated in the Hermes hymn as to its construction or material. A later source (Theophrastus, fourth century B.C.), on the other hand, states that as a rule it was made of the hard wood of the holm-oak.

5. The strings. According to the Hermes hymn the strings were made of sheep gut, according to Appolodorus of ox sinews. This conforms with the application of the ox hide as sound-board in the Hermes hymn. Appolodorus, presumably for this very reason, prefers not to allow the lyre to be invented until the theft of the cattle has taken place. The fable recounted by Philochoros, to the effect that the lyre at first had strings of flax and that Linos was the first to use gut, is not to be trusted. It is probable that ox sinews designate a later stage than gut strings. Scholiasts writing on Aristophanes's " Frogs " say: " The sinew strings are to this day still called gut strings, because they were *formerly* made of gut " (italics by the author). While the Hermes hymn and a few other sources (Lucian, VIII, "Dial. deor," 7, 4; Hor., " Carm.," 1, 15) all give the lyre seven strings, there are some traditions—in Strabo, Boëthius, and others—which, from the beginning, give it only four and ascribe the invention of the seven-stringed lyre to Terpander. One tradition perpetuated by Diodorus Siculus even says that the lyre began as a three-stringed instrument.

6. The Hermes hymn does not mention where he secured the material for the plectrum with which he finally tested the strings. In other places, however, this implement is described as "a thorn" made of a hard material, sometimes wood, sometimes horn, ivory or metal. Besides Hermes, Sappho is also mentioned as the inventor of the plectrum. The strings and the plectrum complete the list of the parts of the lyre mentioned in the Hermes hymn. Our sources of knowledge

concerning the parts that still remain must therefore be sought elsewhere.

In regard to the placing and fastening of the strings at the top and bottom, Aristotle (fourth century B.C.), states that they began at the tail-piece *(chordotonon)* and ended on the yoke *(zygon)*. According to Lucian and Philostratos (second century A.D.), the tuning mechanism (the so-called *kollopes*) were also placed on the yoke. The bridge *(magas)* mentioned by Lucian and Philostratos, and described by Hesychios and Photius as a small, somewhat vaulted, four-sided board supporting the strings, served to raise the strings from the sound-board. Ancient literature provides no further information as to how the tailpiece was devised. Concerning the tuning apparatus, however, a mediaeval author—Archbishop Eustathios in his commentary on the twenty-first song of the " Odyssey " (twelfth century A.D.)—repeats a rather interesting statement, which he says he found in old dictionaries. " In ancient Greece," he writes, " they used the so-called *kollopes* or, as they termed them later, *kollabos*, the thick hide from the back of the neck of an ox or sheep. This hide itself was called *kollops*, and glue *(kolla)* was also made of it." One of the same sources also says that a little fat was usually allowed to remain on the hide. Hesychios (fifth century A.D.), when mentioning the tuning instruments, also says that the back and neck of the ox were called *kollops* (from *kolla*, glue) because they were used for making glue. Involuntarily one's thoughts are led to a tuning method still used on the Nubian-Arabian kissar (see above, Fig. 20). Before the ends of the strings are wound round the yoke, the Nubian packs under each of them a scrap of cloth, into which they cut so that they are kept in place and prevented from gliding back (Carsten Niebuhr's " Reisebeschreibung," I, 179). The Greeks, then, used the fresh sticky hides of the ox or sheep in the same manner. Once the string was tuned to the proper pitch, they pressed the square of skin together with the fingers so that it was literally glued in position.

While the oldest literary sources used only the names phorminx and kitaris, two new terms come into fashion in the seventh century B.C.—*lyra* (mentioned for the first time in Margites, seventh century) and *kitara*. To all appearances phorminx and kitaris, which now gradually disappear, had been synonymous. In the later literature, on the other hand, lyra and kitara are so consistently placed in opposition to each other that they necessarily must have belonged to different instruments. Both Plato ("Republic," III) and Pollux (IV, 8) mention the lyra and the kitara side by side among the stringed instruments. Pausanias states that in Olympia Hermes and Apollo had one altar between them, because Hermes had invented the lyre and Apollo the kitara; Aristides Quintilianus says: "The sound of the kitara approaches that of the lyra, but is less deep and virile," etc.

The fact that the old name kitaris and the new one kitara recall one another might lead us to suppose that these two names belonged to the same instrument; but against this view we have Aristoxenos's statement that "kitaris and kitara are not the same" and that "the lyra is a kitaris." If the lyra is a kitaris, and if besides, the lyra is the instrument that was invented by Hermes, it is thereby established that by this name the Hellenes understood the ancient national tortoise-lyre. The kitara placed in opposition to the lyra must therefore have been an instrument introduced into Greece at a later time. Whence this instrument came will be seen from Plutarch's "De Musica," Chapter 6, where it is stated that they called the kitara *Asias* "because it was mostly used by the Lesbian singers, who live over in Asia" and that it was Kepion, a pupil of Terpander, who first determined the form of the kitara. The reason for the introduction of the new instrument was evidently the insufficiency of the lyre, when the games at last compelled the production of more artistic lyre playing.

Aristotle points expressly to the kitara as the instrument which belongs primarily to the games and the virtuosi, and which is consequently not adapted to the general education of youth. Procles's "Chrestomatie" even mentions the Cretan Chrysothemis as the person who at an Apollo festival at Delphi used the kitara for the first time instead of the lyre (Photios, "Bibl." 239).

In our enquiry as to the nature of the new type of lyre, the designation "Asiatic" makes it probable that what took place was a definite transfer of the elegant Asiatic type of instrument already mentioned by Homer, from Asia Minor to Greece, where the tortoise-lyre had until then alone prevailed. In order to distinguish between the earlier and the later types, the lyre introduced from abroad was given the Asiatic-sounding name of *kitara*, while the national tortoise-lyre was given another title—the *lyra*.

The old literature gives no definite information on the form of the *kitara*. A few quotations from Cicero ("De Nat. Deor.," II, pars. 144, 149) lead us to suppose that the arms were hollow and, together with the sound-box, helped to increase the volume of the tone: " . . . . that is why," he writes, "tortoiseshell or horn gives resonance to a lyre, and also why winding passages have an echo which is louder than the original sound." In another place he says that "my school is fond of comparing the tongue to the quill of a lyre, the teeth to the strings, and the nostrils to the horns which echo the notes of the strings when the instrument is played." To intensify the tone it seems as if certain parts of the sound-box were covered with horn or metal. Theophastrus (89, 10) writes: "For the instrument which at its base is covered with horn or metal will give a fuller tone, as the sound is called forth all over the instrument in the same fullness," and Aristotle mentions ("De Audobilibus," 801) that by adding their sound the metal plates and the arms make the tone of the instrument clearer. Pollux (IV, 62) also mentions metal and horn plates as elements of the stringed instrument in addition to the strings, arms, etc. Otherwise we learn only that the new instrument gradually made use of more and more strings, and thereby now and then gave offence to people who demanded that Terpander's classical number—seven—should be held in respect. The Spartans especially protested against this increase in the number of the strings.

Plutarch says that when Phrynis showed his nine-stringed *kitara* in Sparta for the first time, the Ephor Ekprepes without hesitation cut away two of the strings, saying: "Do not ill-treat music, I beg of you."

As the favourite festive instrument the *kitara*, like its Homeric predecessor, was frequently noticeable on account of its costly material and elaborate decoration. Lucian tells us of a certain Evangelos who, at the Pythian games, used a *kitara* of pure gold adorned with pearls and carved stones.

The evidence of the pictures. With the literary sources as our starting point it will be comparatively easy to understand the lyre as it is presented to us in the pictures.

Under the name "lyra" we first find two instruments which coincide, feature for feature, with the description of Hermes' tortoise instrument as it is found in literature, and which is to be seen so often in pictures that this fact alone points to its importance as one of the chief national instruments (Fig. 21, and the vignette at the end of the section). This instrument was chiefly found in domestic settings and where the subject is the musical instruction of the young (Fig. 22). On the other hand, it is never found in the hands of players who by their surroundings, dress, etc., are characterised as performers of artistic lyre-music.

In festive scenes, and in the hands of the virtuosi, we find quite another type of lyre, which is evidently made to supply a tone of far greater carrying power, and which is consequently, both in regard to acoustics and equipment, far superior to the

31

Fig. 21. Terpsichore with lyre
(O. Müller, "Denkmäler d. alt.
Kunst").

Fig. 23. The type of lyre used
at the Games: Kitara. (E. Gerhard, "Auserlesene Vasen-
bilder.")

Fig. 22. A Lesson on the Lyre. (Furtwängler, "Griechische Vasenmalerei," Ser. II.)

tortoise-lyre. On the coins of the Lycian Union this instrument bears the name of Χιδαρηφόροι (see Fig. 23).

The first lyre-like instrument of all those occurring in the
Greek pictures dates from about 1500 B.C., and was found in
Haghia Triados' palace, excavated in Crete about thirty years
ago. But this lyre, of which there exists one fairly well-pre-
served drawing (on a painted sarcophagus) and another very
defective one (on a wall found near the palace), is so different
in appearance from the lyres known from other pictures, and
divided chronologically by so great a gap from the period at
which the pictures render a survey of the Greek lyre-types possible, that it would be too speculative from this one source to
infer anything as to the general type and construction of the
prehistoric Greek lyre. It must therefore suffice to reproduce
the best of these two pictures and by its aid analyse as far as
possible the composition of the instrument (see Fig. 24).

Fig. 24. Prehistoric seven-
stringed lyre on a Cretan
sarcophagus, ca. 1500 B.C.
("Monumenti antichi,"
XIX.)

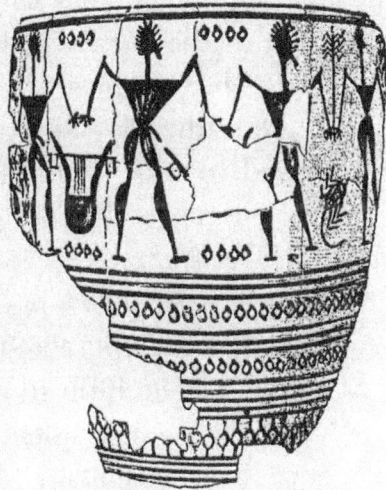

Fig. 25. Four-stringed tortoise-lyre
on an Etruscan vase of the 9th-8th
cent. B.C. ("Jahrbuch des Kais. deutschen arch. Inst.," 1899.)

The most striking feature is the total absence of a sound-
box. The arms, formed like bent swans' necks and both ending at the top in a small pointed head, merge below into a

round and comparatively narrow frame. Where the swans' heads bend in towards each other there are on the necks two low columns which apparently make their way through the rather clumsily built cylindrical yoke on which seven strings, spread fan-wise, terminate. How the strings were fastened to the lower part of the lyre-frame does not appear from the picture; nor is it possible to discover the means of tuning on the yoke. From the attitude of the player it would appear that the instrument was heavy. The hands pluck the strings at different heights and without the aid of a plectrum. It must certainly be due to the faulty drawing that in the picture the hands are both placed behind the arms of the lyre, and the manner in which the black ribbon that decorates the dress of the player is passed through the instrument is also rather unnatural. The seven strings of this lyre are interesting, for they show that eight hundred years before tradition allows Terpander to "invent" the seven-stringed lyre, examples of an instrument with this number of strings were already to be found in Greece.

As early as the ninth-eighth century B.C. the pictures already afford two examples of the national Greek tortoise lyre which are unmistakable; and in both cases the lyre has four clearly-marked strings. One of the pictures is on an Athenian vase in the antique collection at Copenhagen, and the other, reproduced in Fig. 25, is to be seen on an Etruscan vase from Amyklaion in Laconia, now in the National Museum at Athens.

An almost contemporaneous picture (seventh century; see Fig. 27) exists of the form in which the *kitara* became typical and which probably was identical with the final form which Kepion gave this instrument. Yet a whole century before this, there is another in which the form of the *kitara* appears to be in its embryonic form; at least the upper part of the instrument with its pillared arms and the large knob which ends the yoke to the right, points much more to the *kitara* than to the *lyra* (see below, where the two types are more clearly distinguished). The rounded lower part, on the other hand, still unquestionably recalls the tortoise sound-box. Oddly enough, this pre-Terpander lyre also has seven clearly-marked strings (see Fig. 26).

Fig. 26. Transitional form between lyre and kitara. Vase-painting from Melos, 8th-7th cent. B.C. (Conze, "Melische Thongefässe.")

If after having made the acquaintance of these earliest representations, we would now investigate the entire Greek pictorial material in order more exactly to define the difference between the *lyra* and the *kitara* of ancient literature, it will soon be realised that it is the form of the sound-box and of the arms that more than anything else distinguishes the two types from one another.

As a natural consequence of its traditional tortoise origin the sound-box of the *lyra* is vaulted and round. In the pictures we often recognise the scales of the tortoiseshell lying like tiles beside each other and partly overlapping (see Figs. 22 and 39). In the sound-board which, according to the Hermes hymn, originally consisted of ox-hide, but which was later made of a thin wooden plate, small perforated sound-holes are often to be detected in the pictures. The arms are slender and through their curved form and outline, confirm the evidence of literature that they were originally made of horns (gazelle or ibex; see Figs. 29 and 35). At the same time we must note, in Fig. 28, a *lyra* of the early sixth century which still appears to have an ox-hide tympanum.

The sound-box and the arms of the *kitara*, however, are of an entirely different nature. The former appears as a square

Fig. 27. Kitara on a breastplate of the 7th cent. B.C. (Found in a Greek river; "Bulletin de Correspondence Hellenique," 1883.)

box with sides sloping evenly outward. The front, where the strings are attached, is flat and devoid of sound-holes; the back, on the other hand, is often very vaulted (see Figs. 30 and 31). The base is in most cases flat so that the instrument can stand without support. The apparently hollow lower parts of the slightly convex and strongly-built arms merge into the sound-box and form part of it. Above, they form perpendicular angular pillars projecting somewhat above the yoke and, judging by the somewhat lighter colour which they are often given (see Fig. 32), seem to have been made of a material different from that used in the lower parts. On their inner side the arms are often decorated with fretwork and inlaid woodcarvings.

Apart from the sound-box and the arms, the two types of

36

Fig. 28. Sixth-century lyre (with leather sound-board?) in the Museo Archeologico in Florence. (Furtwängler, "Griechische Vasenmalerei," Ser. I.)

Fig. 29. Lyra with bridge and tail-piece. (Panofka, "Cab. Pourtales.")

lyre appear in the pictures to be similar in all other respects. Thus the use of a tail-piece is common to both kinds of lyre. Sometimes this only appears as a fillet. glued to the sound-board as, for example, is the case in the modern guitar (see Fig. 28). In other instances it consists of a small board which projects from the edge of the sound-box a little over the sound-board, like the modern violin tail-piece. On both types of instrument a bridge is also seen in most cases (see Figs. 29 and 30).

Fig. 30. Kitara seen from the front. Greek coin from Mytilene, 350-250 B.C. (British Museum).

Fig. 31. Kitara seen from the back. Greek coin from Methymna, ca. 330-240 B.C. (British Museum).

The principles applied in the construction and manipulation of the Greek lyre-instruments differed very widely, especially in the connection of the yoke with the arms and the tuning of the strings.

Concerning the connection of the yoke with the arms of the lyre, it appears in some of the pictures as if the yoke were passed through the arms from the side so that it could be turned with the hand by means of one of the large knobs which usually terminate it at both ends. In this connection the observation made by Hermann Smith ("The World's Earliest Music") is interesting, viz., that the knobs are often of different size, and that the larger in such cases is always placed on the right to serve as a handle for turning the yoke. The movable yoke, which permits a simultaneous tightening or slackening of all the strings was, in Smith's opinion, for the purpose of preserving the strings, which were inclined to snap when constantly kept at a high tension. When the instrument was laid aside, the strings were loosened by turning the yoke one way; when it was needed again they were tightened by turning the yoke in the opposite direction. The tuning of the individual strings, which was regulated independently of this turning by means of the special mechanism placed on the yoke (see below), was not thereby disturbed, because all the strings had their tension increased or diminished to the same extent by the turning of the yoke. Fig. 33 shows the method in practice.

Fig. 32. Kitara with white arms and black body, and with *kollopes* on the yoke. The right hand tunes the strings. (Gerhard,, "Auserlesene Vasenbilder.")

Fig. 33. Turning the yoke (T. Hope, "Costume of the Ancients").

Some lyre remnants in the British Museum acquaint us with another method of connecting the arms with the yoke. The latter is split at both ends so that it may be pushed down over the pointed lyre-arms until it reaches a notch into which it slips and is held fast. A similar procedure is still followed in the Nubian lyre in Fig. 20, where, however, only one of the arms and the yoke are connected in this manner; on the other side the yoke rests on the end of the arm, as will be seen in the picture. In Fig. 34 an example of another Nubian lyre will be seen, in which the cleft yoke is apparently replaced by one that is perforated at both ends by the arms.

In antique Greek pictures the yoke is sometimes seen behind, and sometimes before the arms of the lyre; this may be due to the employment of one or other of the methods described above. If the yoke is behind, it may be assumed that it passes through both arms and may consequently be turned; if it is in front, the lyre-arms probably pass through the yoke, thus making it immovable.

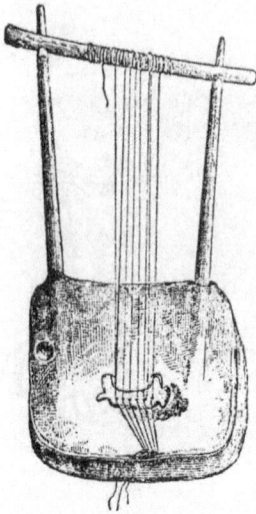

Fig. 34. Nubian lyre (South Kensington Museum).

Fig. 35. Lyre with *kollopes* (Gerhand, "Anserl. Vasenbilder.")

On the evidence of the pictures, one method of tuning the strings appears to have been used more than any other. On the yoke there are what appear to be beads (see Figs. 32 and 35) and we often see the hand of the player grasping one of them as if he were on the point of turning it or securing it (see

Fig. 32). In these beads we have without doubt an instance of the *kollopes* so often mentioned by the old writers (Homer, Lucian, Philostratos, Phrynichos, etc.) and of which Eustathios gave an explanation (p. 30) the correctness of which can scarcely be doubted since a similar procedure is actually still followed on a modern African lyre (see Fig. 20). The explanation of another tuning-principle which is also shown in the pictures (see Fig. 36) and of which I consider we already

Fig. 36. Pompeian wall-painting (fragment). Photograph.

have an instance in the archaic Chaldæan lyre in Fig. 9, was found by Victor Mahillon, director of the Instrument Museum in Brussels. In the Trocadero Museum in Paris, Mahillon found an Ethiopian lyre on which exactly the same method is used (see Fig. 37). In this, each string was tied to a short cylindrical stick, and was then once wound round the yoke so that the stick was made to stand perpendicularly in front of it. By pushing the stick forwards or backwards, the string was tuned up or down respectively. In order to test the utility of the method, Mahillon transferred this tuning apparatus to a copy of the kitara played by the Vatican Apollo (see Fig. 38), and it then appeared that the strings when tuned in this manner really kept their pitch as well as when tuned by pegs. A third method appears to be quite primitive: criss-cross grooves were cut into the yoke, through which the strings were carried in order to be stretched and fastened.

Only in a single example did Dr. Karl von Jan, who more than any other has endeavoured to discover (in "Die griechische Saiteninstrumente," Leipzig, 1882) the ancient methods of tuning, find a piece of apparatus which looked like a tuning-screw; but the absence of further evidence renders it impossible to establish anything definite. It may be that behind the "screws" which are illustrated, quite a different means of tuning is concealed. One of the two original lyre-yokes, together with other fragments of lyres in the British Museum, seem to have been adapted for *kollopes*, for the wood still bears traces of the strings that were wound round it. The other yoke, however, proves the existence of another very strange and hitherto unknown antique tuning mechanism. Eight separate cylindrical joints which were turned from the side by means of small levers, formed the yoke-bar. In each joint was a round hole, and in each hole was a lever—one of them being still in position. Probably the levers served for fastening the strings, but their object was also, without doubt, to stretch and slacken them as the hand moved the levers forwards or backwards, thus turning the cylinder on its hinge. How this hinge was finally secured so that it could not slip back, does not appear clearly from the descriptions of the yoke given by Jan (op. cit.) and Hermann Smith ("The World's Earliest Music"); but unfortunately I have not had an opportunity of examining it myself.

While the Asiatic lyre and the majority of the Egyptian examples were played in a horizontal position, the Greek lyres

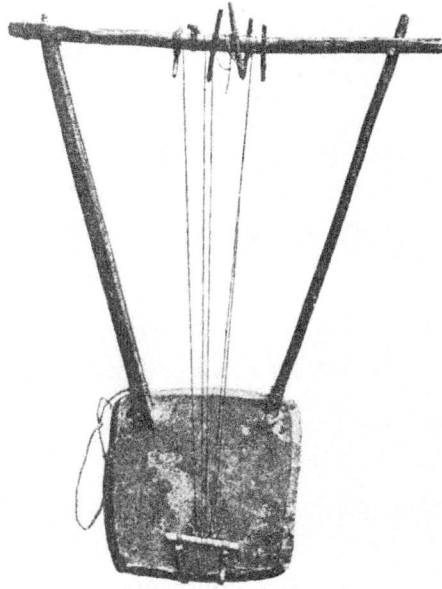

Fig. 37 Ethiopian lyre (Mission Duchesne Fournet, "Travail sur l'Anthropologie et l'Ethnographie de l'Ethiopie" (Verneau).

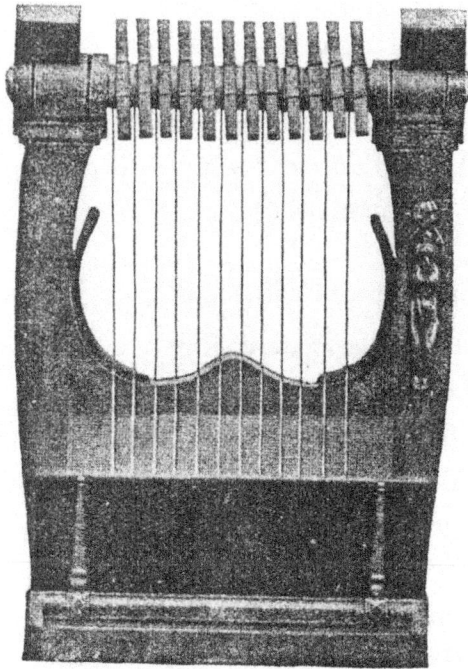

Fig. 38. Copy of the Greek Apollo-lyre (in the Instrument Museum of the Conservatoire in Brussels).

were in most cases carried vertically, i.e., with pendent sound-box. A sling was seldom employed; but in both lyres frequent use was made of a band looped on to the left wrist of the player and drawn tightly to a button on the farther arm of the lyre, from which the ends, embroidered and provided with fringes, hang down as ornaments. In the same manner the virtuoso often hung an elegantly embroidered cloth on the nearer arm of the kitara. While the lyre was often played in a sitting position, the kitara-player generally stood. On both instruments, playing was divided between the left hand, the fingers of which plucked the strings directly from the back, and the right hand, placed before the instrument and generally using a leaf or heart-shaped plectrum. Consequently the left-hand technic was, in Rome, called *intus canere*, and that of the plectrum *foris canere* ("to play on the inside" and "to play on the outside"). For plectrum-playing the Greeks used the terms *plessein, krekein* or *kruein* (i.e., to beat), whereas finger-plucking was called *psallein* (i.e., to snap one's fingers or to harp).

Together with the genuine lyra and kitara, the pictures portray some lyre-types which may best be characterised as transitional or intermediate forms, for it is often difficult to classify them as belonging absolutely to one or the other of the two forms.

Most closely related to the lyra is an instrument, occurring frequently and of very peculiar form (see Fig. 39). From the rounded sound-box on which the tortoise-shell scales often appear quite clearly, two slender and lengthy arms rise and on their way to the yoke gradually increase the space between each other, and suddenly turn inwards again just below the yoke. In the ordinary lyre the arms are most convex near the sound-box, and thence slowly turn towards one another (see Fig. 25), curving outward above the yoke. In this type of lyre Jan considered that he recognised the barbiton, distin-

Fig. 39.   Barbiton (Gerhard, " Auserl. Vasenbilder ").

Fig. 41. The same, back view (Trojan coin in the Brit. Mus.).

Fig. 40.   Kitara; variant form, seen from the front.   "Bulletin de Corresp. hellénique, XII."

guished by its deep sound, and introduced, as some say, by Terpander, and according to others, by Sappho.

On the other hand, the two lyre-types reproduced in Figs. 40, 41 and 42, which likewise appear rather frequently, must be placed in the kitara family. The first (Figs. 40 and 41) is relatively small and by its simple construction rather recalls the primitive Asiatic type known to us from Syrian, Assyrian

Fig. 42. Kitara variation: Apollo Citharœdus (Smith and Percher, "History of the Discoveries at Cyrene").

and Egyptian pictures (see Figs. 3-5, and Fig. 10). In this the arms do not divide as in the large concert kitara into upper and lower parts, but rise like straight columns directly from the sound-box, the cross-section of which is triangular, as the back bulges outwards to a sharp vertical edge. The other type can compare with the kitara in size. The sound-box, which in this case rests on a broad base, has a very vaulted back, and as a continuation of its curve the heavily-built arms rise, bend forward, and hold the yoke. The strings reach the yoke from a box-shaped tail-piece projecting from the base. By being thus stretched between two projecting points, the strings are kept out of the ordinary plane between the lyre-arms, and are held away from the instrument, as the bow string is kept from the bow.

Having now utilised the ancient literature and the pictures for the examination of the lyre-types supplied by Ancient Greece, the next step will be to examine the literature dealing with the compass of the Greek lyres and their musical properties and potentialities. We have nothing but uncertain traditions to guide us. As to the compass of the three-stringed lyre, for instance, we have only Diodorus's vague statement that one of the strings gave a high note, the second a deep one, and the third a note of medium pitch. According to Boëthius ("De Musica," lib. 1, cap. 20) the four-stringed lyre is said to have been tuned as follows:

but at another place in the same work it appears that prior to this tuning there was another as follows:

i.e., to the Dorian tetrachord.

Statements in reference to the seven-stringed lyre are somewhat more definite; and according to the tradition so often cited, it is said to have been invented by Terpander, though it was demonstrably used before his day. Concerning this pre-Terpanderian tuning, Aristotle's "Problems" (XIX, 7, 24, 44,

47) contain the statement that its seven notes gave two similar four-note groups which, by means of a note common to both— the *mese*—were connected with one another. In accordance with this rule, however, the old authors give two different scales: both Aristotle and Nicomachos ("Harmonices enchiridon," cap. 3) give this seven-note scale, in which two Dorian tetrachords are connected:

Hagiapolites's fragment (printed by A. J. H. Vincent in "Notices et Extraits," 1847, p. 270), on the other hand, maintains with Philolaos the Pythagorean as his authority, that the central note of the pre-Terpander lyre was a fifth from both outer strings, so that in each of the two connected tetrachords one note was skipped:

In the ninth chapter of "Harmonices," Nicomachos, under Philolaos's name, gives a third tuning which, however, does not follow Aristotle's precept, as the middle note there connects two differently constructed tetrachords:

As the earliest of these sources, Hagiapolites's fragment, no doubt, deserves most respect. As the Auletean Olympos, who lived before Terpander, is said to have invented a flute-scale which is in close agreement with the lyre-scale mentioned in Hagiapolites's treatise, it is an obvious assumption that this broken-note series, which in the case of the flute arose in all probability for purely technical reasons, was borrowed from the flute practice.

There is also a skipped note in the heptachord which is said by Aristotle and Nicomachos (cap. 5) to have been invented by Terpander: "It is because," writes Aristotle, "the notes were originally seven in number, and Terpander took away the *trite* and added the *nete*." As Aristotle supposed that the pre-Terpander lyre gave a Dorian heptachord (see above), he consequently arrived at this scale, which distinctly reminds us of the third of the above pre-Terpander scales:

According to some traditions it was Pythagoras, according to others, Lichaon of Samos, who at length thought of filling the gaps in these lyre-scales and thus reaching the eight-stringed lyre-tuning in which two Dorian tetrachords were placed side by side, separated by a whole note:

With the eighth string, which it is supposed first occurred on the kitara, it became possible to use different keys by retuning one or other of the strings of the instruments. By raising C and F to C sharp and F sharp, it was possible on the original Dorian lyre to play in the Phrygian mode. By further raising D and G a semitone it was made possible to play in the Lydian mode also:

As a practical means of passing from one key to another without re-tuning, a ninth string was introduced later. It was placed between the old *mese*, A, and its neighbouring note, B, and made an interchange between the Dorian and the Hyperdorian (Mixolydian) modes possible:

Nine Strings.   Dorian Mode.

Mixolydian mode (Hyperdorian):

Later the kitara was given first one and then two more strings for the higher notes:

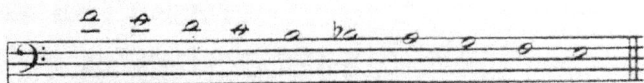

and thus it was possible to play in the Lydian:

Hypolydian:

Phrygian:

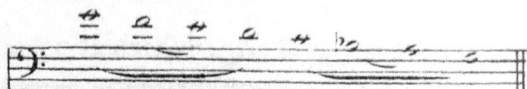

and Hypophrygian modes:

By raising one or two of the eleven strings a semitone, other transpositions were again obtained, e.g.:

Hypodorian: Hypophrygian:

Mixolydian: Hypodorian:
Dorian:

Phrygian: etc.

Fragments of a few vocal melodies are the only examples left of the music which had these numerous modes for bases. As to instrumental music we are reduced to what the authors have to relate. We know from them that the lyre and the kitara were used from the beginning for the accompaniment of song only. Concerning the nature of this accompaniment, Apuleius states that it was performed by the fingers of the left hand only, while the instrumental interludes which now and then interrupted the song, were played with the plectrum held by the right hand. "L'attitude est exactement celle d'un jouer de cithare," writes Apuleius, " . . . sa cithare est etroitment assujettie au baudrier grave qui la soutient; ses mains sont delicates et allongées: la gauche, les doigts ecartés, se pose sur les cordes; la droite, faisant le geste du musicien qui joue, approche l'archet de la cithare, comme prête a en frapper l'instrument dans les intervalles ou la voix se repose" (Florida, XV, xx; on the statue of the beautiful Bathyllus in the Temple of Hera on Samos. Time of Pindar. Quoted for the first time by Jan and translated by Paul Vallette). In this description we find a reason for the right hand of the kitara-player, holding the plectrum, being so often in an extended position before the instrument (see Figs. 23, 35 and 36). As to the musical nature of the accompaniment there is a statement by Plutarch which created a great stir among musical experts. "It is a widespread assumption," writes the Greek author, "that Archilochos invented instrumental music for use in song; the old played everything in unison." Westphal and Gevaert saw in these words a proof that harmony was already known to the Greeks in the form of a contrapuntal combination of two melodies, of which one was sung while the other, lower in pitch, was played, most probably extempore. In refutation of this conception, however, is the striking fact that no such harmony is mentioned anywhere in ancient literature. Not even such an eminent musical scholar as Aristoxenos refers to it with a single word. Hugo Riemann ("Handbuch der Musikgeschichte," I,

Pt. I, pp. 14-16) is therefore of opinion that Plutarch's note was wrongly translated by Westphal and Gevaert, as it should not read that Archilochos invented the playing of the instrumental music below the song, but rather together with or interspersed in the song. Even this translation leaves some doubt as to whether by this interspersed instrumental playing in the song is meant the plectrum-playing which, as mentioned above, came in every time the song paused, or whether the instrumentalist, while otherwise playing in unison with the melody, here and there inserted harmonising notes in the shape of ornaments. Archilochos also is contemporaneous with the earliest use of the kitara as a solo instrument. The first masters of this art mentioned are the Argives Aristonikos and Lysander of Sicyon; but what the nature of this solo kitara playing *(Psile kitaros)* may have been—whether it used both plectrum and fingers, or only one or the other, is not clear from the literary allusions.

4. THE GREEK LYRE AND KITARA IN ITALY.

By settling colonies and founding towns, Greece at an early date extended her territory in a westerly direction to the south of Italy *(Magna Græca)* and Sicily; and thus Greek culture and Greek art made their way to the Italian peninsula very early. For a long period—almost from 600 to 300 B.C.— Etruscan art was also under Greek influence, and the kitaras and lyres found on Etruscan vases are therefore in the main copies of the Greek pictures. When Greece came under Roman sway, Greek music and Greek stringed instruments, primarily the kitara and the lyre *(Testudo)*, also came into fashion in Rome. From the reigns of Nero and Domitian we have evidence of Greek *agones*, including musical competitions. According to Ovid, it was considered good form in Roman society for young ladies to sing and play on a stringed instrument. At the same time he was of opinion that playing the lyre and kitara and singing were effeminate; while St. Hieronimus says in plain words that a Christian maiden should not even know what was understood by a lyre or flute, or for what purpose they were used.

The ancient Greek traditions were finally destroyed completely at the time of the Great Migration. When from the beginning of the eighth century the lyre-type of instruments appear again on the monuments, their sphere of action had been removed to another part of the world, far away from where they achieved their greatest triumphs in antiquity, under the ægis of classical poetry.

II. THE HARP FAMILY.

Strings of unequal length, graduated according to their size, give all the instruments of this class a more or less irregular form. The semicircle or bow-shape seems to have been the original type, and from this the triangular and trapeziform types were gradually developed.

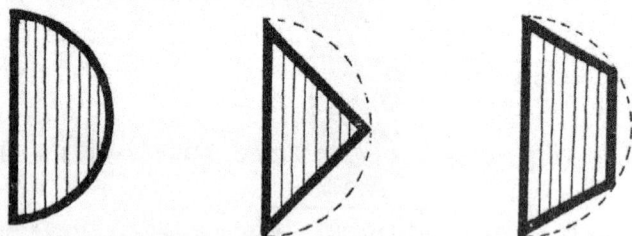

By bisecting these shapes we obtain the following forms which were equally well known to the ancient world and in the Middle Ages:

The harp family is divided into two branches: (1) the Harp Proper, in which the strings are stretched freely so that the hands may reach them from either side, and (2) the Psaltery, in which the strings are extended over a sound-board so that they can be twanged from one side only.

1. THE HARP PROPER.

The harp of antiquity did not use the front pillar which in the modern harp stays the string-frame, and the longest string was at the open side. Moreover, the frame of the ancient harps to which strings of unequal length were attached, took the form of a semicircle or of an angle made of two staves.

The bow-shaped harp. The bow-harp is chiefly known from the Egyptian mural drawings in which it may be found as early as three to four thousand years B.C. It may accordingly be considered with some probability as the original type out of which all the harps were evolved. By means of the Egyptian pictures it is possible to follow the development of the bow-harp almost step by step from its very origin to the time when, under the New Empire, it appeared fully developed as a musical instrument which is surprisingly like the modern harp in many respects.

Fig. 43. Egyptian bow-harp; IVth Dyn. (*ca.* 4000 B.C.).

In the earliest known picture the bow-harp only takes the form of a somewhat more amply-strung counterpart of the bow-harp still in use among some of the north African tribes (cf.

above, p. 4; and see Fig. 43). On a slightly curved and apparently still quite solid stick, which is of equal thickness from end to end, six strings are stretched. It cannot be seen how these strings were fastened below, but at the top they run to a corresponding number of studs which protrude at the back of the harp stick, and which to the spectator look like tuning pegs. In reality they seem to be only wooden pegs driven into the arm to prevent the frame to which the strings were attached from gliding on the polished neck (Curt Sachs, " Musikinstr. d. alten Aegypten," Berlin, 1921). As this harp still wanted

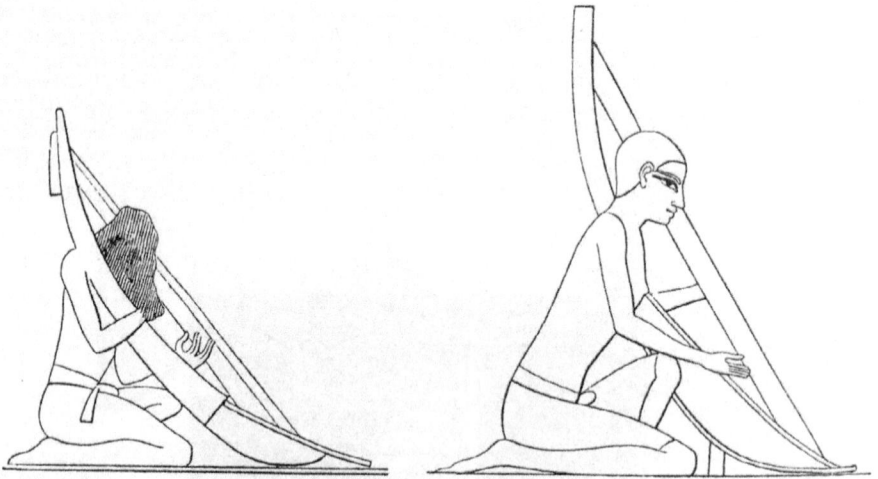

Figs. 44-45. Egyptian bow-harps with concave sound-box (IVth Dyn.).

a sound-box, its tone must have been very small, and therefore only suitable for use in the home.

For banquets, at which the larger rooms used needed louder instruments, a sound-box was indispensable, and the majority of the harps dating from the IV to the VI Dynasty were therefore already thus provided. As is natural, the base of the sound-box adapted itself to the arch in which it was placed and thus became concave. In consequence of the slim build and slight convexity of the earliest harps, the depth of the sound-box was not great (cf. the two profile pictures in Figs. 44, 45). On the other hand, we find that it was fairly broad, which appears from Fig. 46, where the sound-box is turned so that the sound-board faces the observer, while the upper part of the harp is seen in profile—a twisted method of illustration not uncommon in early art.

Fig. 46. Bow-harp in which the surface of the sound-box is turned forwards, while the harp-stick is seen in profile. From Imai's tomb, Gizeh (IVth Dyn.).

The sketchy nature of the pictures only gives an incomplete idea of the construction of the bow-harp. Along the surface of the sound-board we notice a slip of wood, the end of which extends a little beyond the extremity of the frame. It will be seen from other pictures that this baton was intended to hold the lower end of the strings. In Figs. 45-6 only the outer strings are drawn, but this at least gives us an idea of how large a space the strings occupied in the harp-bow. The projections at the upper end of the harps in Figs. 44 and 46 are of the same width and mark just as sketchily the place where the strings were fastened and tuned by means of a hidden contrivance.

Fig. 47. Bow-harp sculptured on the tomb of Ka-Em-Nofer. Dyn. IV. From a drawing.

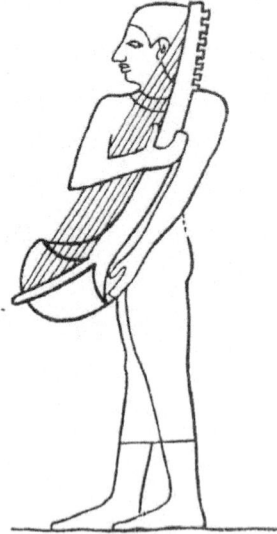

Fig. 48. Restoration of the same with strings added.

These details are more elaborately illustrated in Fig. 47, where a smaller specimen of this harp-type is cut in stone, thus making the form clearer. Here the tail-piece is clearly adapted to the concave front of the sound-box, and the contrivance for tuning is plainly seen to consist of seven studs inserted in the back of the frame. On the other hand, the seven strings which correspond to the studs have been erased. Two short lines seem to me to be the last traces of these, both running towards the tail-piece. One of them reaches from the neck of the player to his right elbow, while the other appears under the right wrist and runs up to the frame. As the outlines of the sound-box are effaced in the original on one side of the tail-piece, a modern artist has attempted a reconstruction by continuing the first of these strings, under the elbow of the player, in a downward dotted line, which first runs outwards and later turns in towards the tail-piece; but by so doing he has given the sound-box an entirely unsymmetrical shape that is quite out of place. My reconstruction seems more reasonable (Fig. 48), for it makes the harp quite symmetrical and closely in agreement with other reproductions of these earliest of Egyptian bow-harps. The picture does not show how the tail-piece was fastened to the harp-frame; but in the British Museum there is an original Egyptian bow-harp, from which this point may be made clear. The sound-box in this example is of a different type, it is true, and the tail-piece is lost; but the bed in which it rested is so clearly marked that it is possible clearly to recognise both the character of the missing tail-piece and the manner in which it was fastened. The lower open end of the slightly bent cylindrical and hollow harp-frame is, in this harp, used as a sound-box, shaped like an oval and rather flat spoon. In its hollow there is a deep longitudinal groove, in which the slim tail-piece apparently rested, the upper extremity being most probably inserted in the open end of the hollow frame, while the lower end extended a little beyond the point of the spoon (see Fig. 49 and compare it with Fig. 47).

It is not possible to decide whether the cavity in these oldest of the bow-harps was covered with a sound-board. In the case of the harp in Fig. 49 this is probable; at any rate in the negro states west of Bahr-el-Abiad there is a harp of similar appearance in which the sound-box is covered with a sound-board of parchment (Fig. 50).

From the XIIth Dynasty onwards we observe practical improvements in the Egyptian bow-harp. In the larger specimens the lower part of the bow is now often flattened, so that the instrument may stand on its base. The position of the strings is thereby made perpendicular, thus causing them to be easier to manipulate than before, when the harp rested in an oblique position in the arm of the player. The tail-piece which before ran towards the base of the sound-box, is now raised above it and is placed so that its centre is free while the two ends only are attached to the sound-box. In order to make room for a greater hollowing of the sound-box, the frame was given a more pronounced curve, thus making the instrument both broader and rounder (see Fig. 51). The sound-box was especially deep in the knee-harp so often illustrated, the lower

Fig. 49. Original Egyptian harp. British Museum. Photograph.

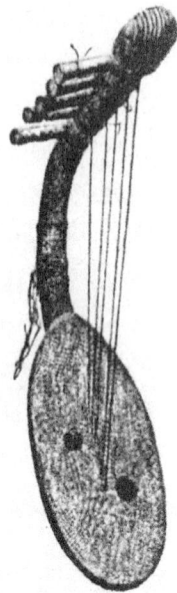

Fig. 50. Negro harp from Bahr-el-Ábiad (A. Hammerich, "Catalogue of the Mus. Hist. Museum in Copenhagen").

part of which was broadened out so much that it resembled a small drum. To prevent the instrument from slipping off the lap of the player, it was provided with a long leg, the upper bent end of which was fastened to the front edge of the drum, from which it sloped down to the ground. A small fork pro-

truding from the base of the drum was intended to hold this
leg in position (see Fig. 52).

In the small shoulder-harp which accompanies the drum-

Fig. 51. Bow-harp. XIIth Dyn.

Fig. 52. Drum-harp (right) and shoulder-harp.

harp in Fig. 52, and which is played standing, the slim shape
favoured during the Old Empire is still retained. As there are
several original examples of this type in the British Museum,
its arrangement is quite clear (see Fig. 53). About half-way
down, the harp-frame bends into the broad end of the sound-
box, the shape of which may be compared with the cut-off stem
of a narrow canoe; it then closely follows the base and finally
protrudes in a point from the rounded stem of the sound-box.
A sound-board of parchment perforated with small sound-holes
is stretched over the cavity of the sound-box, and lengthways
runs a rod-shaped tail-piece which rests on the underlying
harp-frame throughout its length. The instrument as a rule
has only four strings.

While the Egyptian bow-harps of the Old Empire as well
as of the Middle Empire were, with few exceptions, all played
in a kneeling posture, we find several harps in the New Empire
played in a standing position. Foremost among them are the
large harps in which the frames and the sound-boxes merge so

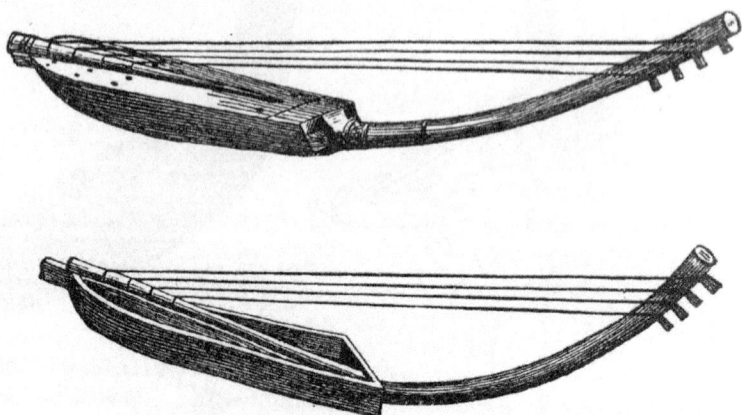

Fig. 53. Original Egyptian Shoulder-Harps. (British Museum.)

imperceptibly into each other that it cannot be decided with
certainty where the former end and the latter begin. Some of
these harps still retain the slightly curved form of the Old
Empire (see above, Figs. 15, 16). In others the upper and
lower parts of the bow extend farther forward so that the string

space is increased, providing room for a comparatively much larger number of strings than before. Good examples of this are to be seen in the two huge temple harps discovered in the latter part of the eighteenth century by James Bruce, in a tomb-painting on a royal tomb at Thebes, and since copied innumerable times : by Champollion, "Monuments de l'Égypte et de la Nubie," Roselini, "I Monumenti dell' Egitto," Wilkinson, "Manners and Customs of the Ancient Egyptians"; but the reproductions do not quite agree, the number of strings in particular being shown differently.

Fig. 54.   Egyptian Temple harps, painted on a Royal tomb at Thebes.

Especially noteworthy in both these harps is the very large sound-chest extending from the foot of the frame, and providing space before the strings for an artistically decorated sphinx-head, which clearly indicates the environment in which these instruments belong.   A festive effect is produced by the artistic inlays of polychrome mosaic which ornament the whole of the body and which bear witness to the strikingly high standard reached by the Egyptian artists and craftsmen.

Still stranger than these harps are two bow knee-harps which Dr. Flinders Petrie recently found painted on a royal tomb in Abydos (see Fig. 55). Like our modern grand piano-fortes, these instruments have two sets of strings crossing each other. Unfortunately, neither of these instruments is shown being played; but as the strings of the harp are plucked from both sides as on the lyre, the obvious assumption is that each of the hands plucked its own set of strings. The pictures do not show how the strings were fastened or how they were tuned; all that we see is that both sets of strings pass before the upper part of the frame. At the same time we note that despite the double stringing only a single row of tuning-pegs is inserted into the frame. As in the case of the drum-harp, these instruments were also supported by "legs." Curt Sachs believes that the cross-stringing was the result of an error.

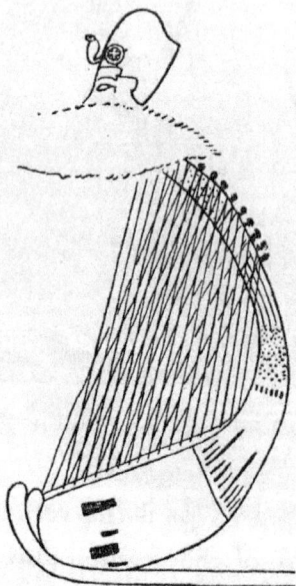

Fig. 55. Cross-strung bow-harp from a royal tomb, Abydos.

Fig. 56. Hand-harp on a bas-relief from Philæ.

To the bow-harp class belongs also a small hand-harp which is to be seen in bas-reliefs at Philæ. In spite of its small size this harp was played standing, being placed on a low table so that the upper part of the frame, generally ornamented with a carved sphinx, slopes forward. The left hand then fingers the lower strings while the right plays on the upper (see Fig. 56).

Outside of Egypt I have only succeeded in discovering a few sporadic instances of the bow-harp, one of which, found in a painting on a Pompeian wall, is reproduced in Fig. 57.

2.   THE ANGLE HARP.

To support the strings in this type of harp, a frame was used, made of two staves forming an angle.   The arm to which

Fig. 57.   Mural-painting at Pompeii (Mus. borb., I, 30).

one end of the string was fastened was hollow and spacious enough to form a sound-box; the upright arm to which the string was carried for tuning was slender and solid, and formed the yoke of the harp.   The Greek writers declared western

Asia to have been the home of this type of harp, and it is certainly to be first observed in the west Asiatic pictures of the Assyrians.

A. IN ASSYRIA.

On the Assyrian monuments two stringed instruments are to be seen which, by their form and arrangement, may be considered angle-harps: in one of them the strings proceed from a horizontal, wedge-shaped and very long sound-box, and are drawn forwards and upwards to an arm which is fastened perpendicularly to the end of the resonance-chamber. When in use, the broad end of the sound-box rested on the hip of the player, while the tapering end carrying the arm pointed away from the body. The strings were thus made to run parallel with the player's extended fingers and could therefore only be plucked with difficulty. It was on that account played with a plectrum held in the right hand, and the strings, which were stretched one above the other, were struck upwards from the right side. On the opposite side of the strings the left hand acted as a damper, the palm being placed against the strings which were either not to sound or were to be damped quickly (see Fig. 58). The manner in which the ends of the strings were fastened to the upright arm was very strange; and it was a method used in all the angle-harps of western Asia. Just as the ends of the strings on the antique lyre were often packed in a sticky piece of skin, over which they were fastened to the yoke, so the ends of the strings in the west Asiatic angle-harps were continued in braids tied to them, which, after having been wound round the harp-arm a few times, hang down in long fringes, each ending in a tassel. The pictures do not show how the strings were fastend to the sound-board. They only make clear that the broad end of the sound-box acted as a base for the longest and heaviest strings, and that from there the sound-box gradually narrowed as the length of the strings decreased. The significance of the small upward-pointing hand

Fig. 58. Assyrian horizontal Angle-Harps. Bas-relief from Nimroud (Brit. Mus.).

placed on the top of the perpendicular arm is not clear. As the instrument is mostly seen in use at religious ceremonies, the hand may have had some symbolic meaning.

The other Assyrian angle-harp had a less strange effect because, like the Egyptian bow-harp and the frame-harp of the

Middle Ages, it was carried in an upright position and was plucked by the fingers from both sides. The strings were in this case taken from an oblique sound-box perpendicularly downwards to a horizontal arm and were tuned in the manner described above, by winding them round the arm; the ends of the strings provided with braids and tassels fell as a decorative fringe far below the instrument (see above, Fig. 7). When played, the harp rested with the angle on the player's hip, while the top reached far above his head. As to the mode of playing, it is noted that the thumb and the three middle fingers of the right hand pluck the bass strings near the harp-arm, where the little finger supports them by being placed in an extended position against the lower side of the arm. The left hand, which from the opposite side twangs the shorter treble strings, touches them higher up.

Whether he carried one or other of these two types of harp, the Assyrian player is always shown standing or walking. The harp was at no time frequently used in a horizontal position, and two of them were generally played in consort. On the other hand, the upright harp, which occurs most often in processions, is generally the commonest and is always placed in the van. Such a procession is reproduced in a giant bas-relief in the British Museum, and is placed by archæologists in the reign of Saos-don-Khin (i.e., 667 B.C.). At the head of the body of soldiers forming the king's escort there is a crowd of twenty-six musicians made up of seven harpers, two flautists, one psalterist, one drummer, and fifteen singing women and children. The cold sculpture probably gives only a slight idea of the reality. Only by allowing the imagination to add colour and sound to it, is it possible to imagine the magnificence displayed on such occasions. The harpers especially must have been a wonderful sight at the head of the procession, garbed in multi-coloured festive dress and playing their many-stringed instruments.

While the horizontal angle-harp is only known to us from

Assyrian pictures, it is possible by means of these reproductions, to follow the upright harp far beyond the frontiers of Assyria. It is to be found in Babylon not so far away, in Egypt, and in Greece. In the Middle Ages it even made its way as far as Spain. In a Spanish manuscript of the thirteenth century it is reproduced for the last time—as a nun's instrument (see Fig. 59).

Fig. 59. The West Asiatic upright harp in the Middle Ages. Spain, 13th century.

Fig. 60. The god Bes playing the "World Harp" in the temple at Dakkeh (Rossellini).

B. IN EGYPT.

The angle-harp which appears in the Egyptian tomb-drawings of the XVIIIth Dynasty had so much in common with the Assyrian harp that its Asiatic origin can scarcely be doubted. Like the upright Assyrian harp, it was so turned that the arm stretched in a horizontal direction from the base of the sound-box, which sometimes projected obliquely above

it so that the strings fell perpendicularly down to the harp-arm
(see Figs. 60 and 61); sometimes it stood perpendicular,
making the run of the strings oblique (see Fig. 62). The

Fig. 61. Angle-harp (on the left) in
a tomb-drawing on Paranefer's tomb
at Tel-el-Amarna. XVIIIth Dyn.
("Archæological Survey of Egypt.")

Fig. 62. Angle-harp in a
tomb-drawing from Thebes
(Wilkinson).

strings were thus tuned from below in the Asiatic manner, while
in the national Egyptian bow-harp they were tuned from the
top. The method of tuning also resembled the Asiatic procedure, according to which the ends of the strings were tied
to the harp-arm (see the oblique lines traversing it in Fig. 62),
and, prolonged in braids and tassels, hung loosely below the
instrument (see Figs. 60 and 62).

Two originals, one in Florence ("Museo Archeologico")
and the other in Paris (Louvre) offer an opportunity of examining the Egyptian angle-harp more closely. It is a question,
however, whether the Florentine harp (see Fig. 63) is a trustworthy example, as several circumstances indicate that, like
the Egyptian lyre at Leyden, it has been made of two fragments which originally could scarcely have belonged together.

Fig. 63. Original Egyptian harp in the Museo Archæologico in Florence. Photograph.

Thus in the Florentine harp the slimness of the arm compared with the large opening through which it is carried into the sound-box is striking, and in order to steady the arm it was found necessary to fill up part of the hole with wood (see Fig. 63). There is a further discrepancy between the number of string-holes in the sound-box and the number of pegs inserted into the arm to which the strings pass. On the sound-box there is provision for twelve strings, on the harp-arm only ten. As the harp was found without strings, the Museum—according to a written statement from Mr. L. A. Milani, Director of of the Museum—strung it at random in order to emphasise the triangular form of the harp. The Florentine harp therefore gives no reliable information on the original method of stringing.

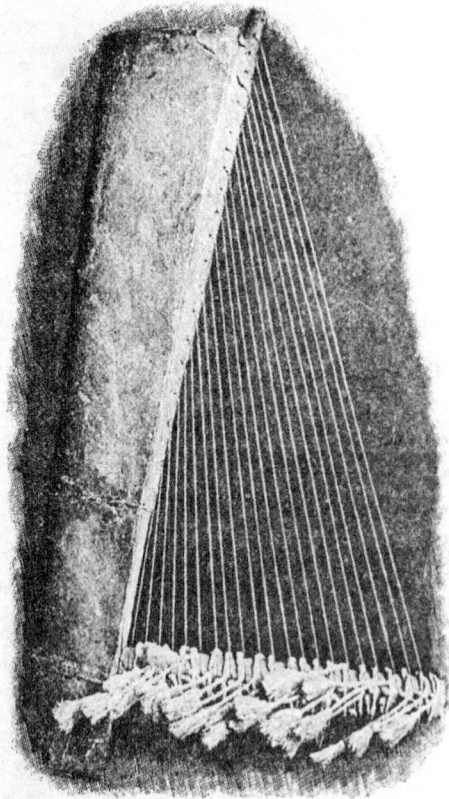

Fig. 64. Original Egyptian harp in the Louvre Museum. (Photo.)

The Louvre harp is a much more reliable example (see
Fig. 64). The upright Assyrian harp may without hesitation
be singled out as its model. From an oblique sound-box the
strings are drawn perpendicularly down to a horizontal arm
to which they are fastened. For securing the upper ends of
the strings there is a raised perforated border on the inner surface (sound-board) of the sound-box, and through the holes
the strings are passed forward after having been secured by
knots at the back. This manner of fastening the strings appears on the Florentine harp also. Strange to the true Asiatic
harp, too, are the sprigs which look like tuning-pegs and which
have been inserted into the arms of both the Parisian and the
Florentine harps. They were, in fact, considered as such in
Florence (see Fig. 63), whereas in Paris the sprigs were only
used for twisting the lower ends of the strings, which were then

prolonged by adding braids and tassels in order, in imitation of the pictures, to wind them further round the harp-arm and allow them to hang down below the instrument. The English musicologue, Engel, maintains that the harp, at the time it was found, still had a few strings which were actually fastened in this manner. Charles Boreux, of the Egyptian Department of the Louvre Museum, knows nothing of the existence of these original strings, and maintains that all of the strings are at most a hundred years old and in all probability were added by the Egyptologist, Champollion, editor of the monumental work, "Monuments de l'Égypte et de la Nubie."

Fig. 65. The Assyrian (West Asiatic) upright angle-harp on a bas-relief from Heliopolis in Southern Egypt, now in the Museum at Alexandria. Photograph.

An interesting explanation of the mode of manipulating the Louvre harp is given in an Egyptian tomb-drawing of the Saïte period. The instrument is there played by a sitting performer and is held so that the harp-arm throughout its length rests in his lap, while the upward sloping sound-box projects far above his head (see Fig. 65). Of the strings only the outermost one which outlines the form of the harp is seen. All the others are erased, but their existence is disclosed by the position of the hands. The fingers of the right hand pluck the longest and deepest strings from the back while the left hand, placed before the instrument, twangs the treble strings. The pendent ends of the strings will be recognised in the oblong block hanging below the harp-arm.

C. IN GREECE.

On Greek territory the angle-harp may be followed in the pictures as far as the pre-Hellenic cultural period. In a tomb on the island of Keros, together with two female idols, two statuettes were found in the eighties, one of which represented a harper and the other a flautist. As the archæologists see in the idol representations of the Phœnician goddess, Astarte (identical with the Assyro-Babylonian goddess, Istar), it has been assumed that the statuettes represent her servants which were placed beside her as attributes. The small sculptures are very roughly made. The figures have neither mouth nor ears, and the nose is indicated by a projection in the middle of the perfectly flat face (see Fig. 66). Surely just as naïve are the instruments which the figures hold in their hands and of which only the harp interests us now. At first glance it looks like a closed triangular frame from which the strings had been omitted; but this explanation does not fit in with our previous experience, that the triangular harp of antiquity was as a rule open on the side accommodating the longest string. In my opinion the oblique front beam is only a clumsy imitation of the outermost and longest string, which the sculptor was obliged to give in order to indicate the form of the instrument; for it would have been difficult to reproduce all the strings in detail. That it is a string and not a side of the frame appears, (1) from the manner in which the left arm of the player is bent forward as if the missing left hand were plucking the string, and (2) from the beak-like projection at the top of the triangle which in all probability formed the end of the right-angled frame. The manner in which the supposed string is inserted at the base in the horizontal arm of the angle, inclines me to explain it as a correspondingly crude method of reproducing the manner of fastening the string to this side.

Fig. 66. Prehistoric Greek angle-harp. Statuette found in a tomb on the island of Keros (Perret et Chipiez, " L'Art dans l'Antiquité "; Tome VI).

Fig. 67. Prehistoric Greek angle-harp. Statuette found on Thera. (Walz, " Über die Polychromie der antiken Skulptur," Tübigen, 1853.)

There are two interesting parallels to the harp-playing figure from the tomb in Keros, which were found forty years earlier on a neighbouring island (Santorin, the classic Thera). There the harp has the same form and arrangement, but the beak which in the Keros harp most probably forms the end of the frame, is lacking. On the other hand, these figures confirm the assumption that the oblique side of the frame is a string, as the player who in this case has retained both his hands, resolutely plucks it with the fingers of his left hand (see Fig. 67). The Phœnician idols found together with the Keros harp make it presumable that this type of harp originates in Phœnicia, which is expressly mentioned in Greek literature as one of the countries which in ancient times used triangular stringed instruments. In order to find an angle-harp of the same form it will be necessary to go as far as Egypt (see above, Fig. 62), but the type may nevertheless be Phœnician, for in

Fig. 68. Greek angle-harp. On a vase from the days of Alexander the Great, now in Munich.

ancient days Egypt and Phœnicia were in close connection, and it has been proved above that the angle-harp was not an instrument originating in Egypt.

On the sculptures and vase-paintings belonging to the classic era of Greece, the large harps have a form which de-

cidedly leads the thoughts to the upright Assyrian angle-harp
in Fig. 7. Here, as there, the strings from the spacious sound-
box, which bends forward, are drawn to a horizontal arm to
which they are secured for tuning, the ends of the strings falling in a fringe below the instrument (see Fig. 68). Far more
frequent than these large harps in the Greek pictures is a small
hand-harp of nearly the same form (see Figs. 69-71). In some
of these hand-harps a decoration (a bird, scroll, or the like) is
placed outside the longest string and connects the ends of the
sound-box and the harp-arm, recalling the pillar which characterises the framed harp of the Middle Ages and the present
time (see Figs. 70 and 71, and the vignette at the end of this
section). But whether this pillar, as is now the case, was
added for practical reasons (in order to increase the resisting
power of the frame) cannot be determined; for in the large harps
where such a support might be considered more necessary, we
do not find it anywhere. The neat form of the pillar makes

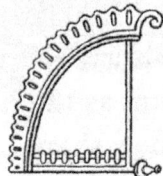

Fig. 70.

Fig. 69.

Fig. 71.

Greek hand-harps. (Figs. 70 and 71 with decorative pillar.) Gerhard,
"Vases Grecs relatifs aux Mystères."

me believe rather that it is only decorative, which is here so
much more likely since these small harps are also in other
respects noticeable for their strikingly ornate appearance.

Another peculiarity of these small harps is that some of
them have a sub-arm parallel with the harp-arm, which in Jan's

opinion has the same object as the *capo tasto* of the guitar and the pedals of the modern harp—namely, to raise the pitch of the strings a semitone (see Fig. 70 and the vignette at the end of this section). A corresponding device is now and then to be seen on the Greek lyre-types of the Roman period, especially on the wall-paintings of Herculaneum, but on these it was placed near the yoke.

The large harps as well as the small ones in the Greek pictures were played in a sitting position. Most often they are seen in the hands of women; in isolated cases only is one of the small harps handled by a man. The harp-arm generally rested throughout its length in the lap of the harper, the sound-box leaning against her left shoulder.

3.   THE PSALTERY.

Owing to its strings of unequal length, this type of instrument has the same irregular form as the harp proper; but while the harp varies between the bow-shape and the triangle, the psaltery is fundamentally a triangular instrument. The triangle may be either equilateral or right-angled, but it is often reduced to a trapezium by the removal of one of its corners. Thus the three most common types are:

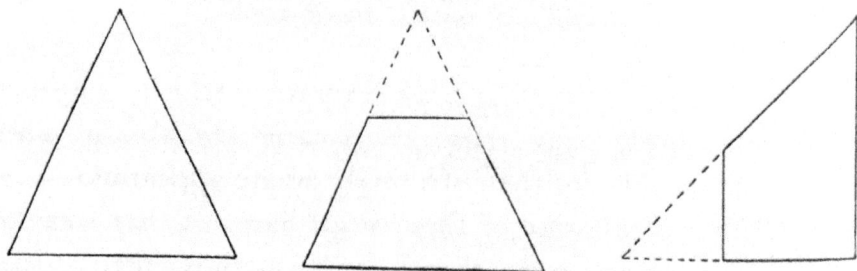

The psaltery, however, differs from the harp proper chiefly in that the strings can be plucked from one side only, for they are not stretched across an open frame, but lie closely above the irregularly shaped sound-box, which is generally composed of a back, either flat or convex, a table (the sound-board), and the ribs which connect them.

Antique reproductions exhibit only one instance of an instrument which may be placed in this category. It is found on the above-mentioned gigantic Assyrian bas-relief in the British Museum, but as a piece of historical evidence it is quite unreliable, since the part of the relief in which it appears is broken and therefore it is seen only in a restored state (see Fig. 72). As the instrument appears in the picture, it is at any rate without meaning. Above a sound-box with vaulted back, extended horizontally, ten strings are stretched forward and end in bows,

Fig. 72. Supposed psaltery on the large bas-relief in the British Museum (Kouyunjik).

one above the other, falling in a decorative fringe far below the instrument. A plectrum carried in the right hand plucks the strings, which are again damped with the palm of the left hand. The most curious feature is the curvature of the strings and their being placed one above the other. A string cannot sound when it is curved. The curve can therefore only be explained by the supposition that the strings were tightened across a bridge at the end of the sound-box, which either the Assyrian sculptor or the unskilled restorer has simply omitted. The reason for the strings being placed one above the other may be that the artist desired to show them all, and was consequently forced to raise them in this manner; for had they followed the plane of the sound-box they would have appeared as a single line to the eye. There is the possibility, however, that the so-called psaltery is entirely the result of a faulty reconstruction, and is nothing but a bungled reproduction of the horizontal angle-harp shown in Fig. 58. The strings which are tightened forward, the hanging ends of the strings and the mode of playing it are in any case points of resemblance calculated to arouse such a suspicion. On the Oriental santir and kanun, from which the European psaltery is said to have been derived, the strings never run forward from the body of the player, but always transversely. In the pictures therefore the existence of the psaltery in ancient times can only be proved by means of a unique example of an extremely unreliable nature; and even if we turn to literature we do not, as will appear from what follows, find anything to prove that this type of harp was used by the civilised peoples of antiquity.

4. HARP-TYPES IN GREEK LITERATURE.

Of the Greek instruments the *Sambuka* (*Sambyke*, or the Chaldæan *Sabka* or *Sabeka* mentioned by the prophet Daniel), the *Psalterion* (in all probability synonymous with the *Psanterin* of the prophet Daniel), and the *Trigonon* (i.e., triangle) are directly connected with the stringed instruments of a triangular form, and are thus undoubtedly to be placed among the harp-types, i.e., either as real harps or as psalteries. In addition to these instruments there are the *Magadis* and the *Pektis*, described as forerunners of the *Sambuka* and the *Psalterion*, and must consequently have been triangular too. Menaichmos and Aristoxenos (Athenæus, XIV, 635) maintain that these two names were synonymous; the tragic poets, Diogenes and Phyllis of Delos *(Id.)* declare that they belonged to different instruments. Pindar emphasises as a peculiarity of the *Magadis* that it reproduced at the same time the melody in the pitch of grown men's and boys' voices, and, confirming this, Phyllis of Delos writes that the instrument called *Magadis* had, besides the strings that harmonised with the pitch of the singing, other strings in the octave. To judge from these statements, two strings must have been used for each note on the magadis, the one being the octave of the other, and therefore the twenty-stringed magadis would in reality have had a range of only ten notes. The pektis is also indicated as a double-stringed instrument : " Thou tookest the gorgeous double-toned pektis in your hands," writes the parodist Sopatros (Athenæus). Euphorion *(Id.)* states that the magadis in the course of time was changed, and was called sambyke. The instrument of this name is generally given as a triangular instrument with very short strings of high pitch (Aristides Quintilianus, II, 101). Another descendant of the magadis, according to Appolodorus in his reply to Aristotle's letter, was the psalterion. " The magadis," he says, " is the instrument which is now called the psalterion."

The magadis, pektis, sambuka and psalterion, to judge by these statements, would be branches of the same stem, and the use of double strings by the two first-named instruments, together with the psalterion, quite naturally leads one's thought to the definite type of harp which in the Middle Ages was called *psalterium*, and which in fact had two or three strings for each note (see later the stringed instruments of the Middle Ages). Neither the double strings nor the name are complete proof of the accuracy of this supposition, for in the Egyptian pictures we find instances of both lyres and harps with double strings (see Figs. 10 and 55), and in a painting from Herculaneum the name psalterion is connected with a stringed instrument which is not triangular, but longish, and which in its whole design is definitely distinct from the harp family.

We are on quite uncertain ground when we consider the fifth name, *Trigonon*, for the explanation given by one author is only that it was a triangular, deep-pitched stringed instrument, the opposite of the high-pitched sambyke. Here again it becomes a question of choosing between the harp and the psalterion. None of these triangular instruments was a native of Greece; the magadis and pektis are stated to have been Lydian instruments, the trigonon was Phrygian according to Sophocles, and Syrian according to Jobas. The sambyke is alternately called Syrian and Phœnician, while the psalterion is stated to have been Hebreo-Assyrian.

Conclusions. As far as the Greek harp-types are concerned, the pictures are in reality our one reliable support, and on them, strangely enough, we do not find a single instance of the type of harp which now—according to mediæval usage—is called the psalterium. All the stringed instruments which by their design must be placed in the harp-family have, in the pictures, free strings and are consequently harps proper. Those harps which are of large size fit in with the description given of the trigonon as a low-pitched instrument. The small ones, on the other hand, lead us to think of the short-stringed, high-pitched sambuka. Both in Greece and in Rome the sambuka is said to have been the instrument generally played by the *hetairai*, and curiously enough it is indeed women who everywhere in the pictures hold the small harps, and especially women who, by their motley dress, do not give the impression of belonging to respectable society. On the whole, it seems as if the instruments of the harp-type were held in scant esteem in Greece. Even if some authors, among them Sophocles, called their tone beautiful, the philosophers considered them ill-sounding and—on account of their effeminate and sensual character—they deemed them injurious to the morals. Plato and Aristotle placed a veto on them, and they were entirely excluded from the public contests. The Romans held the same view and declared "the oblique strings" (i.e., the harps) to be actually indecent in respectable families (Scipio Aemilianus in Macrobius, *Sat.*, 3, 14, 7. Juvenal, 3, 63).

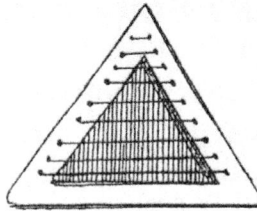

PART II.

THE MIDDLE AGES.

INTRODUCTION.

<small>MEDIÆVAL PICTURES AND ARRANGEMENT OF THE MATERIAL.</small>

Strictly speaking, the Middle Ages in musical history commence with the spread of Christianity; for under its influence the art developed along different lines. It was in the Christian Church that the artistic music of Europe was born, and it was in its shade that from the beginning it grew so strong that after a time it was able to detach itself from its protector to extend its activities independently and find occupation in a wider field.

Although song was the only form of the art that the Church took under its care at first, and although in consequence of this, ecclesiastical vocal music provides our main sources for the study of mediæval musical development, the Church has also yielded a relatively generous supply of pictures for the study of the musical instruments that bear witness to the fact that instrumental music was also performed. In the Middle Ages this took place outside the Church, among the people as well as among those in a higher station.

Both as symbols and in virtue of the part they played in the records of the Old Testament, musical instruments acquired an important place in sacred illustrations—in the carvings on the doors, in the paintings on the ceilings and walls, in the miniatures of the Missals, and on the hewn tombstones—in which the Church represented the persons and events treated of in the Holy Writ and in the legends.

During the first period, when the Christians still frequented the catacombs for fear of persecution, it is solely the pagan instruments of antiquity—the pan-pipe and the lyre—that are depicted. In order to avoid making the transition from the old doctrine to the new one too sudden and noticeable, the Fathers of the Church allowed the elements of the antique heroic age, which were explainable from a Christian point of view, to appear in Christian pictures. Thus it was that both Hermes with the ram and Orpheus with his lyre appear on the ceiling-paintings of the catacombs as symbols of Christ in the rôle of the Good Shepherd and in that of the Saviour triumphant over Sin. For Orpheus, like Christ, descended into Hades, and Orpheus by his lyre-playing tamed the fierceness of the animals, just as Christ through His doctrine curbed the evil passions of man. As a Christian symbol Clemens of Alexandria had the antique lyre engraved on the rings worn by the believers.

Obvious occasions for depicting musical instruments were, first and foremost, the numerous scenes in which instruments were used in accordance with the Old Testament precepts. One of the favourite subjects was King David and his family. Thus from the very first days of Christianity up to the fourteenth century, the vision of Isaiah takes a leading place in the pictures of the Church. In the lower part of the picture a gigantic Isaiah is generally seen in deep slumber; from his side grows a mighty tree, on the branches and twigs of which kings—including King David—are placed, who in most cases hold instruments in their hands, and who sing in concert a hymn of thanksgiving to Jesus, the last divine descendant of Isaiah's kin (see the frontispiece). Most often, however, King David is depicted alone surrounded only his permanent staff of four musicians, Asaph, Heman, Ethan and Jeduthun. By means of these David pictures alone it is possible to observe how, in the course of time, one instrument succeeded the other. In the earliest days of Christianity it was still the antique lyre—in the pictures of David as well as in the reproductions of Orpheus— that was used. After that—in the seventh and eighth centuries—the mediæval successor to the lyre, the north European round-lyre, came into its place. In the ninth and tenth centuries the Anglo-Saxon framed harp came to the fore, and at the time of the Crusades the psalterium, introduced from the Near East, was enthroned as the natural instrument of the Psalmist. For some time the small portable organ was fashionable, until finally the former tradition prevailed again, and the harp was definitely made the permanent attribute of King David.

Next to the pictures supplied by the Old Testament, those of the saints are found to include instruments, and from the fourteenth century Saint Cecilia appears prominently as the patron saint of music.

Instruments finally played a prominent part in the allegorical church-pictures, of which the Dance of Death, prevalent around the fifteenth century, is of interest on account of the copious and extremely instructive reproductions of instruments it exhibited.

From the moment at which the Crusades began in the twelfth century, a new wave of culture rolled from the Orient into Europe. In the Near East the crusaders made the acquaintance of a new and strange culture which quickly encouraged imitation; and before long Oriental art, industry and science began to make their impression on Europe, and automatically new material was thereby brought to the study of musical history. Through the crusades Europe gained the finger-board instruments headed by the lute; and at the same time the psaltery and several new instruments of percussion and wind-instruments were acquired. This movement had its repercussion on the pictures, which from now on are enriched from another quarter as profane works also came under its spell : the romances of chivalry, the troubadour poetry, etc., were embellished with miniatures, a type of picture which hitherto had been confined to the ecclesiastical manuscripts. In these pictures it is not King David or the holy representatives of the Church who carry the instruments, but the motley crew belonging to the gay life of the court; the troubadours, minstrels, jugglers and players. The aristocratic stringed instruments of the Church pictures therefore, the round lyres, harps and psalteries, now find rivals in the popular instruments of the wandering musicians : the lute, fiddle, gigue, flute, drum, etc., and soon afterwards the religious pictures do not hesitate to make use of them. As early as the twelfth century all the instruments are found in motley profusion on the entrances of the French and Spanish churches, which, by their representations of large orchestras, become from now on one of the main sources of information for the history of mediæval instruments.

If the pictures have been dealt with in the foregoing with some elaboration, it is mainly because they give us such an excellent guide to the chronological order of the instruments. By means of the pictures it is possible not only to observe how the fashions changed, so that now one instrument, now another, was placed in the foreground, but to see in each kind of instrument the results of the experiments which in the course of time were made to improve the different categories. A natural consequence of this desire to improve was the vast number of varieties created during the Middle Ages within each group of instruments. The stringed instrument in particular was made the subject of innumerable experiments in the Middle Ages. In the early part of the period the instruments of the lyre and harp type were especially dealt with; but later on the fingerboard instruments had their turn, and the number of musical instruments from now on increases, so that for a time a complete survey is almost impossible. It is only when, at the beginning of the Renaissance, the instruments were used in artistic music, that there was a reaction; for it was then that those which could be employed in the service of art were selected from each group of instruments, while the remainder were set aside as superfluous. Some of the discarded instruments were taken up by the masses and were for a time used as popular instruments, while others were gradually and completely discarded never to be taken into favour again.

While the lyres and harps of antiquity (the lyre-type, the harp proper, and the psaltery) had a common birthplace, viz., the vicinity of the eastern Mediterranean, the mediæval representatives of this class of instruments lead us first as far as the north-western corner of Europe (for the lyre and the harp proper) and to the Near East (for the psaltery).

As a natural consequence this investigation—as far as the Middle Ages are concerned in this book—falls into two parts, the first of which will deal with the lyre and the harp proper, while the other will be devoted to the psaltery. This is also justified on chronological grounds, for the lyre and the harp in Europe belong to a much older culture than the psaltery. In round figures the development of the former falls between the eighth and the fourteenth centuries, while the psaltery does not make its way into European music until the twelfth century, reaches its zenith between the fourteenth and the sixteenth centuries, and finally disappears from the scene in the seventeenth century, i.e:, well within modern times.

THE LYRE AND THE TRUE HARP ON THE MONUMENTS.

A. THE LYRE.

When the glory departed from Greece, the antique lyre was, as previously stated, inherited by the Romans; and it seems to have been by them that it was carried in time to Gaul (for on two Gallic coins of the time of Caesar—found in Auvergne and Bretagne respectively—lyres of pure Greek form are depicted), and to the British Isles, where in its antique shape it may be followed sporadically in the pictures as far back as the tenth century (see Figs. 73 and 74). In the northern half of Europe a new type of lyre comes to the front in the ninth century and before long it completely supplants the antique lyre. In its soft outlines it differs decidedly from its sharply cut predecessor, for in it the arms and yoke are fused into a hoop, giving the instrument a certain resemblance to a padlock. From a narrow tail-piece fastened to the base of the sound-box, the strings proceed to the pegs which are placed at wide intervals in the curve of the hoop. From its shape this lyre must, to differentiate it from the antique form, be characterised as the *round lyre*.

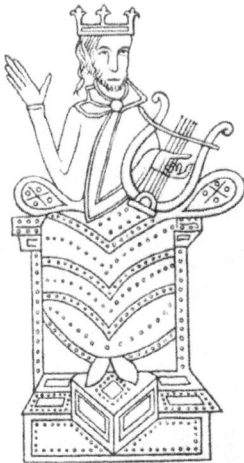

Fig. 73. Antique lyre of the 9th-10th cent. From an Angers MS. Didron, " Annales archéol." III.)

Fig. 74. Antique lyre. (MS. in the British Museum, " Cleop." C. 8.)

The round lyre on the German monuments. In Gerbert's " De cantu et musica sacra " (II) may be seen a round lyre taken from a Black Forest MS. of the twelfth century, now destroyed. It is called the *cythara teutonica*, i.e., the German stringed instrument (see Fig. 78). The fact that the lyre was considered to be a German instrument in the twelfth century makes it natural for us to attempt to discover by means of the pictures whether the German stringed instrument was in any way connected with the antique type.

As a first possible link in such a development I shall refer to a prehistoric lyre, a picture of which Oscar Fleischer discovered on an Hungarian tomb ("Musikinstrumente aus deutscher Urzeit," in the "Allgemeine Musikzeitung," 1893, Nos. 30-32). At Marz near Oedenburg in Hungary, i.e., immediately to the north of the Greek peninsula and in the vicinity of the supposed home of the antique tortoise lyre, Thrace, an urn which is now in Vienna was unearthed in the nineties. On it we see a man handling a lyre-like stringed instrument, which, like the earliest Greek lyre, has but four strings (see Fig. 75). The urn is said to date from the period between the eighth and fifth centuries B.C. Whether or not Fleischer is right in concluding from the place at which it was found that this lyre is Germanic, is not for me to decide. I suppose that the utmost one can maintain is that the occurrence of the lyre in a prehistoric central European race makes it probable that it was introduced into Germany at an early age.

Fig. 75. Lyre-player on an urn in the Nat. Hist. Royal Mus. in Vienna. 8th-5th cent. B.C.

The first remains of a lyre which may with complete justification be described as Germanic was found in the year 1846 in a warrior's grave at Oberflacht in Tuttlingen, in the Wurtemberg Black Forest (see S. Dietrich and Wolfgang

Menzel, "Die Heidengraeber in Lupfen bei Oberflacht"; for the Wurtemberg Archaeological Society). Another find has quite recently been added from the same locality (see Oscar Fleischer, "Die Musikinstrumente des Alterthums u. Mittelalters in germanischen Ländern," in O. Paul's "Grundriss der germanischen Philologie," III, 567). In a warrior's grave in the neighbourhood of Lupfenberg the skeleton of a man was found in whose arms was a complete and quite well preserved lyre (see Fig. 76). Like the Greek lyres, this Germanic specimen is provided with both bridge and tail-piece. As will be seen from the six pegs in the yoke, it was six-stringed and was carried by a ribbon round the neck, for the two wooden pegs inserted into the yoke on each side of the six tuning pegs

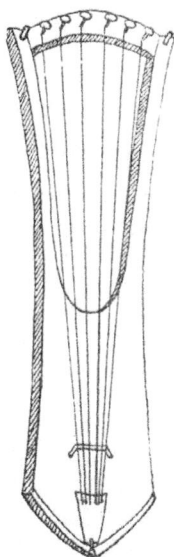

Fig. 76. Germanic lyre, 4th-7th cent. A.D. In the Museum für Völkerkunde in Berlin.

Fig. 77. Lyre similar to the Germanic warrior's instrument. 10th cent. In "Cod. lat.," 343 (Royal Libr. in Munich).

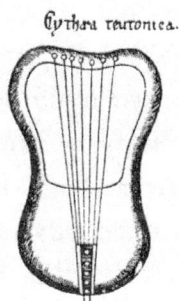

Fig. 78. German stringed instrument. Cythara teutonica, twelfth cent. (Gerbert, "De cantu et musica sacra.")

evidently served to fasten the ribbon. Archaeologists estimate the period of these discoveries to lie between the fourth and seventh centuries A.D. I found a comparatively late example of this Alleman warrior's lyre in a north Italian manuscript from the neighbourhood of Milan (tenth century). The instrument, which in this case has only five strings, is played by King David, whose left hand is tuning one of the strings at the top with a massive wrest, while his right thumb and middle finger test the tuning below by vibrating the string (see Fig. 77). From this lyre, which with its definite yoke still points back to the antique lyre, we will return to the *cythara teutonica* (twelfth century) which, as I have said before, was found by Gerbert in a manuscript written in Germany (see Fig. 78).

On this round lyre, which has seven strings and quite a violin-like tail-piece, the curved form of the antique lyre-arms is still clearly preserved in the curves of the frame on both sides of the strings; and these wave-like outlines may be observed in most of the German round lyres that I have seen. Next to the *cythara teutonica* special interest attaches to the following: (1) A five-stringed round lyre in the same manuscript, complete with bridge and a wrest tied to the frame with a ribbon. On this instrument the tail-piece is taken down from the sound-box and projects like a shaft from its base. (2) A five-stringed round lyre from a manuscript in the Royal Library in Munich, twelfth century. With his right hand the harper (King David ?) grasps the upper part of the frame as if in some way or other screwing up the string, at the same time endeavouring to counteract the pressure by grasping the lower part of the frame with his left hand from behind (see Fig. 79). (3) An exceedingly beautiful picture of a German round lyre on a portable altar at Welfenschatz near Vienna, about 1130 (see Fig. 80).

The round lyre on the Anglo-Saxon monuments. Still earlier than in Germany, the round lyre may be found among the Anglo-Saxons, for the oldest reproductions there originate as early as the seventh and eighth centuries. The Anglo-Saxon round lyre only exceptionally has the undulating outlines of the German type, the sound-box and frame being most frequently continuous. On the whole it is oblong in shape with

Fig. 79.   Round lyre in a Munich
MS. of the 12th century.

Fig. 80.   Round lyre on a portable
altar in Welfenschatz, in Vienna.
(Falke and Frauberger, "Deutsche
Schmelzarbeiten des Mittelalters"),
12th century.

Fig. 81.   Anglo-Saxon round lyre. MS. in the British Museum, Cotton,
"Vesp.," A. I; 7th century.

rounded corners, in the upper part of which an oval opening is cut to make the strings accessible from both sides. The strings stretch from the base of the sound-box across the sound-board and then through the open space to the pegs in the upper part of the frame; the right hand is placed over the sound-board while the left hand plucks the strings from behind, playing in the frame where the strings are open (see Figs. 81 and 82, showing both sides of this round lyre). It is strange to observe the double string in Fig. 82 which shows the original, gener-

Fig. 82. Anglo-Saxon round lyre; 8th cent. (from Westwood, "Palæographia sacra pictoria").

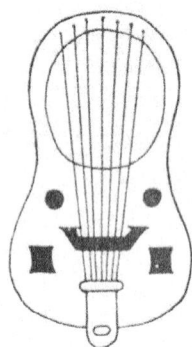

Fig. 83. Anglo-Saxon round lyre; 13th cent. Brit. Museum, MS. Harl. 2804. Drawn from the original.

ally completely effaced border line between the arms and the yoke. Closer akin to the German round lyre is the comparatively late Anglo-Saxon lyre in Fig. 83 of the thirteenth century, for on it we recognise both the curving outlines of the German round lyre, its violin tail-piece and its flat bridge, to which are added, as a novelty, two round and two square sound-holes which are cut symmetrically in the sound-board.

The round lyre on Nordic monuments. A Norwegian

stringed instrument which was found some years ago in Kravik in the Nume valley, and now preserved in the State Museum at Oslo, is closely related to the *cythara teutonica*. Compared with its German and Anglo-Saxon relatives, this round lyre is comparatively young; Norwegian archaeologists are of opinion that it can date from a period not earlier than the fourteenth century, probably even still later. On the other hand, I have heard opinions inclining in the opposite direction. As a type the Norwegian instrument comes close to the ordinary round lyre, and the deviations in form look rather like approximations to the Germanic and antique Greek lyre than to a younger invention (see especially the yoke definitely separated from the arms). The Norwegian round lyre is seventy centimetres long over all, and about twenty-five centimetres broad. When it was brought to the museum, it was broken lengthways and part of the yoke was wanting. The instrument was therefore glued and the missing part replaced by another. Nevertheless the instrument is not complete, for only the vaulted trough-like back remained of the oblong sound-box, the sound-board having disappeared. It still bears traces of the nails that once held it together. The nature of the sound-board may therefore only be inferred by an examination of the Anglo-Saxon and German round lyres. In all probability it was provided with sound-holes and formed the support for a bridge to carry the strings and to transmit their vibrations to the sound-board. Clear proof of the instrument having been provided with a tail-piece is seen in the rounded projection which terminates the sound-box flush with the back, and the large cut right across this button indicates that, like the end button of the violin, it was intended for fastening the tail-piece. From the tail-piece the strings were probably stretched like a fan to the pegs placed in the six round holes in the yoke. One of the pegs is still in place (see Fig. 84).

Besides this type of lyre Norway possessed another. It is possible to find it represented three times on Norwegian wood.

Fig. 84. Original Norwegian round lyre; 14th cent. (?). The State Museum, Oslo.

Fig. 85. Fragment of the Austad gate. Photograph.

Fig. 86. The church-door of Hyllestad. Photograph.

carvings, and also on a Norwegian stone font, all four examples illustrating the Gunnar legend. This instrument is portrayed clearest and most beautifully on two church-doors,
which belonged originally to the Hyllestad and the Austad
churches, in the Saeter valley, but which are now in the State
Museum at Oslo. On the Austad lyre there are two bent arms
which meet at the top, closing like a frame round the strings
which are apparently free. Below is the surface of the circular
sound-box. Where the arms meet at the top is a crown, which,
literally speaking, lends a royal appearance to the instrument.
It is possible that this crown was only a decoration, but it was
possibly also the place where the perpendicularly stretched
strings were fastened (see Fig. 85). Gunnar's stringed instrument on the magnificently carved church-door of Hyllestad
has exactly the same characteristics. This instrument is here
seen in a reversed position, so that the sound-box points upwards, and the crown, which is here replaced by a round
button, downwards. As Gunnar's feet in both carvings pluck
the strings in the broad part of the pear-shaped string-opening,
his position in the Hyllestad representation is much more com-
fortable than in the Austad example, where, in order to pluck
the strings at the proper place, he is obliged to lie with his
head down and his feet up (see Fig. 85). Much more incom-
pletely designed is Gunnar's instrument in the last two reproductions, one of which is found on an arm-chair from Hitterdal
church in Telemark (now in Gols church, Bygdo), and the
other on a stone font in Norum church, in Bohus county (now
in the Historiska Museum in Stockholm (see Figs. 87 and 88).
After having considered the two previous pictures from Austad
and Hyllestad it is easy to recognise the same instrument, which
is here lying on its side, while Gunnar is shown standing, and
in the first instance full face, perhaps because the carver was
not able to reproduce his profile in the difficult recumbent position. We readily recognise the same outlines with the pear-
shaped string-opening; even the button or crown which con-

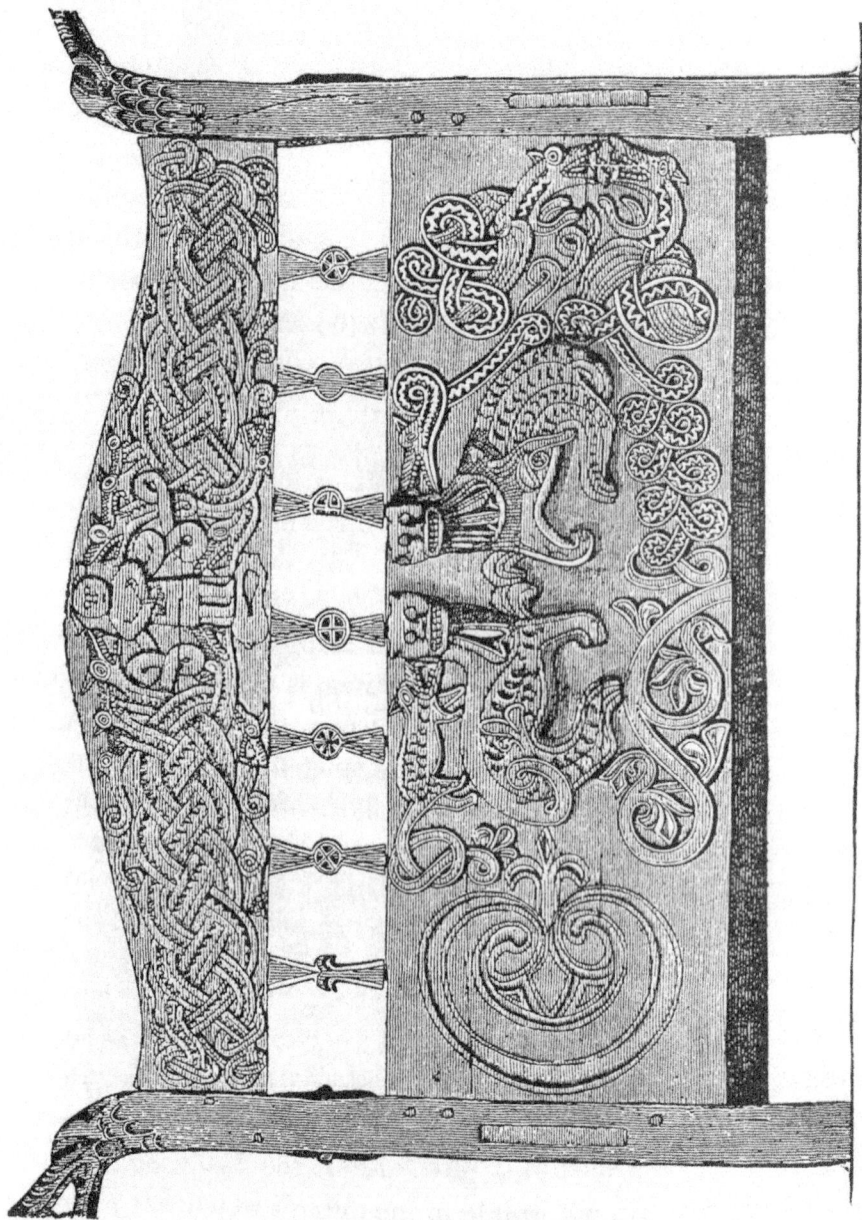

Fig. 87. The back of an armchair in Hitterdal Church. (L. Dietrichson, "Norwegian Stave Churches.")

nects the arms at the top may be vaguely seen in this otherwise crude design.

Fig. 88.   Baptismal font in Norum Church, in Bohus county.

Unfortunately it has not been possible for me to find more than these four reproductions of this strange variety of the lyre.   The only example of a similar instrument I have found outside of Norway was in a Slav manuscript and was copied by its owner for the collection of pictures connected with the instrument museum of the Brussels Conservatoire (see the vignette below).   The instrument, which belongs to the thirteenth century, has three distinct strings, but is in other respects so simply drawn that it is impossible to form any clear idea of its details.

B. The True Harp.

While the antique harp which originated in the Near East was peculiar in having the outermost and longest string open, the European mediæval harp was a closed instrument, the frame carrying the strings being supported by a pillar placed outside the longest string and enclosing the strings in a frame, the form of which is always triangular with an angle at the base.

This is found at an early stage in the British Isles. Whether it was native there is another question, for in this connection there is considerable difference of opinion. Galpin, in 1911 (" The Origin of the Claveach or Irish Harp," in the Report of the Fourth Congress of the International Music Society), advanced the opinion that the frame harp originated in all probability in the Scandinavian countries and was brought to Britain by the Vikings. He based his theory on the fact that the frame harp on the Scottish stone crosses appeared at the very moment when the Angles, Saxons and Norwegians set foot for the first time on the East Coast of Scotland.

Cythara anglica.

Fig. 89. English harp, *Cythara Anglica*; 12-13th cent. (Gerbert, " De cantu et musica sacra.")

Nevertheless it is a striking fact that on the Nordic monuments we have to wait another two centuries before we find the first reproductions of the frame harp, and that in the Nordic saga literature we do not find descriptions of it until the fourteenth century. If the Nordic Vikings in foreign lands immediately began to cut their supposed national instrument on fragments of rock, why did they hesitate so long before portraying it in their own country where they had the same material to work upon? As a proof of the Norsemen's predilection for the frame harp, Mr. Galpin also refers to the frequent mention made of the harp in the earliest English song, "Beowulf." But can it be taken absolutely for granted that the harp there spoken of was a *frame harp?* To the Norsemen, whose achievements are the principal theme of the song, the word "harp" in those dim distant days (sixth-seventh centuries) meant a lyre, to which instrument, in fact, the plectrum (*hearp*, Nails) with which the harp in the song is played, was applied. In antiquity the cithara (which was a lyre) was in Greece and Egypt mostly played with the plectrum; in my opinion a plectrum-twanged harp, on the other hand, never occurs in antiquity, and even in the Middle Ages it would look like a unique phenomenon. The statement made by Otto Anderson ("The Bowed Harp," London, 1930) to the effect that the plectrum in the Middle Ages was sometimes—especially in the northern countries—used to indicate a bow, even admits the possibility of the instrument in "Beowulf" having been a bowed lyre.

In 1915, when publishing the first volume of this work in Danish, I advanced another hypothesis without knowing anything of Canon Galpin's idea at the time; namely, that the frame harp may possibly have been created by the attempts of the British Celts to make a more complete stringed instrument of their inherited national lyres and quadrilateral instruments. They were thus creators of instruments, some of which strikingly recall the frame harp (see below, Irish transitional forms between lyre and harp).

While seeking instances of the frame harp in antiquity, reference has been made to the Greek *sambyke*, which in the ancient pictures is now and then represented with something like a pillar (see Figs. 70, 71); but the arm supported by this pillar and serving to fasten the ends of the strings, is there formed by a horizontal rod from the left extremity of which proceeds the forward-bending arm. The result is therefore a type of harp the outlines of which deviate so much from those that typify both the mediæval and the modern frame harp, that it seems to me to be rather far-fetched to indicate the sambyke as its origin. More weight must, in my opinion, be given to the statement made by Curt Sachs, that a triangular harp with a pillar, and of exactly the same form as the mediæval European frame-harp, is actually still used by the eastern Yakuts living in north-west Asia. But in this connection we must put the question: when did the East Yakuts first use the pillar? Was the idea conceived by them in times immemorial, or was it borrowed from some European nation which in the course of time influenced their culture? The questions of the provenance, the true age, and the evolutionary changes of the European frame harp still remain open. All that we know for certain is that this instrument, in the Europe of the tenth century, was for the first time found on Scottish stone crosses and in English manuscripts, and that in a German manuscript of the twelfth century it was expressly characterised as *Cythara Anglica*, i.e., English harp.

The harp among the Anglo-Saxons. While the harp on the Scottish stone crosses was only roughly reproduced, it is possible to examine all the details of its arrangement in the English manuscripts. In the first clear picture of the frame harp (in an Oxford MS.; Bodl. Libr., Junius XI; and cf. Galpin, "Old English Instruments," first edition, p. 11, Fig. 2) it looks like a comparatively small and slenderly-built instrument which reaches from the knee of the sitting performer to the crown of his head. In the sound-box, which is rather spacious and which broadens gradually towards the top, there are three round sound-holes. Where the sound-box ends at the top, its right side turns abruptly to the left and thereby

102

prepares the way for the forward-bending and slender arm which, together with the chest, forms the frame in which the strings are stretched; finally, to support the frame, there is the thin rod-like pillar which, in order to stand at some distance from the strings, turns outwards at the top and thence descends perpendicularly to the foot of the sound-box, where it is fastened just outside the longest string. In another English manuscript in the University Library at Cambridge (eleventh century), the harp has already attained a more elegant appearance, the arm there ending in a carved animal's head while the bend of the pillar has disappeared, so that it is brought down in a graceful curve to its termination (Galpin, Plate III, No. 1). With this the Anglo-Saxon harp was given its definitive plastic form in which it is already presented in the twelfth century as *Cythara Anglica* in a German manuscript, and in which it is reproduced in English manuscripts so frequently up to the fifteenth century that it must suffice here to refer to the pictures in English works that are easily accessible: Strutt, "Manners and Customs of the Old Anglo-Saxons," "The Sports and Pastimes of the People of England," and Westwood, "Palæographia sacra pictoria," etc.

In Ireland. When the English harp was taken up by the Irish in the eleventh century, they immediately began to improve it. While the strings of the Anglo-Saxon harp were of twisted horse-hair, those of the Irish harp were made of metal (gold, silver, or brass). At the same time the sound-box was enlarged and the number of strings increased. In other words, the harp was there developed into a much more sonorous instrument.

The earliest picture of a harp in Ireland decorates one side of St. Mogues' reliquary (Fig. 90) preserved in the Museum in Kildare Street, Dublin, and dates as far back as 850. The reproduction, however, is not so old, as the plate on which it is carved has been proved to be an addition of later date (eleventh century). It is also possible that the carving was done by an English artist, as the harp shown closely agrees, both as regards form and design, with the Anglo-Saxon harps of the same period.

Fig. 90. Harp on St. Mogues' Reliquary. Ca. 850. Dublin.

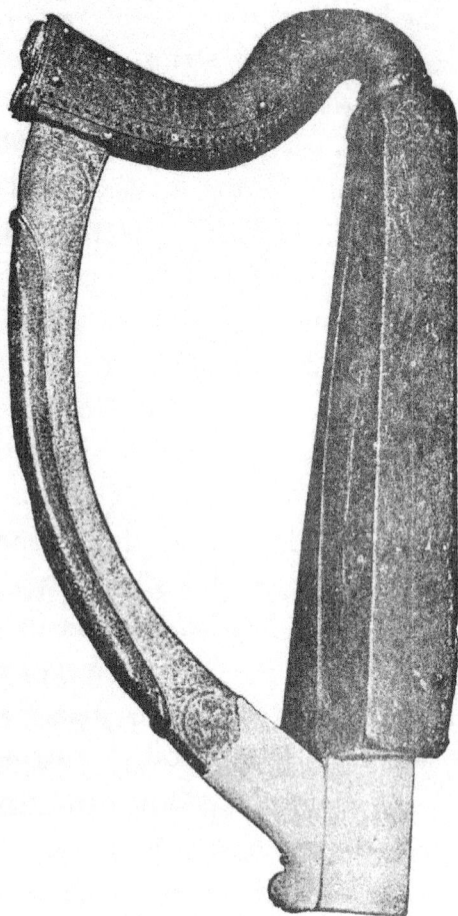

Fig. 91. Brian's Harp. Trin. Coll., Dublin. 13th-14th cent.

The instrument shown in Fig. 91, on the other hand, is typically Irish, and of this type an original example is preserved in Trinity College, Dublin. According to tradition it is said to have belonged to the Irish king, Brian Boiroimhe, who at the end of the tenth century made his name famous as the conqueror of the Danish Vikings. Irish archæologists, however, are of opinion that it does not date earlier than the thirteenth century, possibly even the fourteenth (Bunting,

" Ancient Music of Ireland "), at which time a harp of exactly the same appearance is found on a Scottish monument (see Fig. 92; the Trinity College harp is now assigned to the King of Thomond, ca. 1220, who sent it to Scotland as a pledge— which may account for similar instruments appearing in Scotland.—ED.)

Brian's harp is only thirty-two inches high but had thirty strings, for in the arm there are thirty pegs and along the sound-box thirty string-holes may be counted. The sound-box is made of oak, the sound-board of willow. The pillar is partly inlaid with silver and on the outer side it carries a large crystal set in silver; below it there was once another stone. The string-holes in the sound-board are all decorated with engraved and gilded metal settings. The four sound-holes were without doubt also decorated with silver ornaments, but in the course of time they have been stolen. The lower part of the harp is wanting, but has been restored with plaster of Paris (see Fig. 91). On the Irish crosses we already see harps of a similar shape. Several of them are so large that they reach from the head of the sitting player to his foot. As instruments, some of these harps apparently left much to be desired In some of the reproductions they look as if they were quite roughly made of a simple triangular, completely solid, wooden frame, without, as far as can be made out, the slightest trace of a sound-box (Fig. 93); in other cases they appear as comparatively highly developed instruments of plastic form and with a very large sound-box which narrows at the top (see Fig. 94). One particular form of the Irish harp was blunted at the lower end, so that it was something between the ordinary triangular harp and the Celtic square instrument which will be dealt with below. The earliest example is found on the stone cross at Monasterboice (ca. 800). See Figs. 95 and 96. A later example belonging to the latter half of the eleventh century is to be seen on a cross in the Isle of Man (for the probable age of this cross cf. S. Bagge, "Aarboger for nordisk Oldkyndighed," 1900; see Fig. 97). The cross has an inscription in runes and in Norse: "Malumkum raised this cross to Malmuru, her foster-mother, Dufgal's daughter, the wife of

Fig. 92. Harp on a stone monument in Kiels; 14th century. (From "Sculptured Monuments in Iona and the Western Highlands.")

Fig. 93. Harp from a stone cross at Monifieth. Photograph.

Fig. 94. Fragment of a monument at Nieg (Scotland); 11th century.

Adisl." The names show that the stone belongs to a people of purely or partly Celtic race. The harp is clumsily made and tells us nothing of the details of the instrument, such as the number of strings and the like. Judging by its shape it belongs decidedly to the British Isles. A third instance of this blunted tringular harp is perhaps seen on an ancient Irish manuscript-cover of the eleventh century, but the picture is drawn in so few strokes that as historical evidence it is of somewhat doubtful value. It is therefore only for the sake of completeness that it has been mentioned and illustrated here (Fig. 98).

In Wales. The Welsh harp is reminiscent of the Irish harp both in its size and in its large resonance-chamber. An outstanding feature is the great length of the pillar; but strangest are the large square openings that are often cut at the back of the sound-box and give access to the cavity. Presumably these openings were originally covered with doors or

Fig. 95.   The cross at Monasterboice
(before 830).   Photo.

Fig. 96.   The harp
on the same cross.
Enlarged.

Fig. 97.   Harp on a
stone cross on the
Isle of Man; 11th
c e n t.   (Cummings,
"Runic and other
Monumental Remains
of the Isle of Man.")

Fig. 98. Harp on an
old MS. cover. Be-
fore 1064 (O'Connor,
"Rerum   Hiberni-
carum Scriptores
Veteres").

shutters; for a harp with sound-holes in front and such large openings at the back could not possibly have given any tone worth mentioning (see Fig. 99). All the Welsh harps which now exist, however, belong to recent times. One of the oldest specimens is that owned by the Dublin Museum, and is said to have belonged to a bard of the O'Neill family. According to the Catalogue, however, it is not more than 250 years old. The obvious resemblance to the apparently large harp at Nieg, on the other hand, tells in favour of its representing, in its outward form, a very old type of harp.

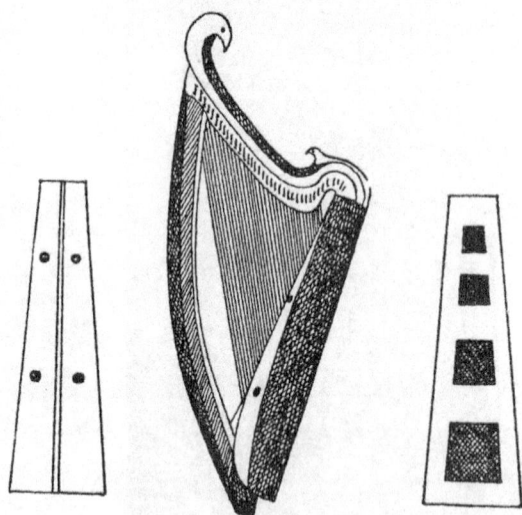

Fig. 99. Welsh harp in the Dublin Museum; about 1650. (From "A Descriptive Catalogue of the Antiquities in the Museum of the Royal Irish Academy," by W. R. Wilde, Dublin, 1863.) The two drawings at the sides represent the front and back of the resonance chamber and are added by the author.

The construction of the sound-box prevented the Welsh harp of earlier days from standing unsupported. As the pillar is usually very much worn, Mr. Armstrong, whose close studies of the old British harps makes him an authority on the subject, has come to the conclusion that when the harp was not in use the Welsh harper placed the instrument in a corner with the pillar turned towards the wall. Sometimes the harp-pillar is also provided with a supporting rod, sometimes not. In the more modern examples the lower part of the sound-box is altered, so that the harp can stand without support. Mr. Armstrong supposes that this alteration took place about the year 1784.

The arrangement of the numerous strings on the Welsh harp is peculiar, for they are grouped in three rows—two outer groups and an inner one between them. Each of the two outer groups gives a diatonic scale; the right row manipulated by the right hand extends from A to a''', while the left group begins with c, and rises like the right one, the strings tuned in unison lying immediately above each other. While the two outer rows are plucked by the hands, the thumbs act on the middle group, beginning from C sharp opposite the C of the right group, rising thence and giving the chromatic semitones D sharp, F sharp, G sharp, and so on. This triple stringing, however unpractical it may have been, was used in Wales up to the nineteenth century. According to Edward Jones ("Musical and Poetical Relicks of the Welsh Bards," London, 1794) it cannot, however, be older than the fourteenth century. If we disregard this peculiarity, which thus does not seem to belong to any very early age, the Welsh harp must in other respects be considered as a lateral offshoot of the Irish harp. Its most characteristic feature, the high pillar, is also sometimes found in Ireland (see Fig. 94) or territory influenced by Ireland.

In the Scandinavian countries. The oldest Nordic representations of a harp is found on the above-mentioned stone cross in the Isle of Man (*ca.* 1050). To judge by his language, the rune-carver was a Norseman (Norwegian), but the harp belongs to a peculiar group of the Irish harps and has no counterpart in the Scandinavian countries.

The triangular harp is very rarely found on the Nordic monuments, which is true until well into the Middle Ages. It is first found well and clearly reproduced in two carvings, of which one (in Norway) is in the Opdal stave-church at

Numedal. L. Dietrichson says ("Norske Stavkirker") that the period of the picture is the end of the thirteenth century, but I know that other Norwegian archæologists are of opinion that it dates from the tenth or eleventh century. The other is on a baptismal font from Lockne church in Jemtland (now in Nordiska Museum in Stockholm). In both places the Nordic mythical hero-king, Gunnar, is connected with a type of harp which seems to come near to the Irish Brian harp. The arm and the pillar in both cases have the very bent form of the Irish harp. Apparently the Norwegian harp had thirteen strings, the Swedish specimen only five. Unfortunately it is impossible to form any idea as to the breadth and volume of the sound-box, as both instruments are seen from the side (see Figs. 100 and 101).

The third example to follow is a large and strikingly generously strung harp on a fresco in Roda church in Vermeland. It is played by King David, and by its outlines decidedly recalls the Opdal harp, except that all the curves are more emphasised; I am almost tempted to call this harp a caricature of the Irish Brian harp (see Fig. 102).

The reproductions of early harps found in Denmark are only of small interest. Roughly carved in stone as they are, they give only the outlines of the instrument and no details. The first is a representation of Saul and David on the north door of Vejlby church, near Randers. David's instrument is there shown as a small heart-shaped hand-harp with comparatively few strings (five or six; see Fig. 103). The second is on a roughly-made stone baptismal font in Lille Lyngby church near Arresoe (see Fig. 104). A third example is on a tombstone in Vinderslev churchyard (see Fig. 105). On all three only the outlines can be made out, and consequently it is difficult to define the type.

On the Continent. From the British Isles the harp in both of its principal forms reached the Continent at a comparatively early date. The earliest instance is the *Cythara*

Fig. 100. The harp-playing King Gunnar in Opdal Church, Numedal. From a drawing in Oslo in the archives of the Foreningen til Bevaring af norske Fortids-Mindesmaerker.

Fig. 101. Fragment of a wooden baptismal font from Lokne church in Jemtland. Nordiska Museum, Stockholm.

Fig. 102. Harp on a fresco in Roda Church in Vermeland. (Mandelgren, "Monuments scandinaves du moyen-âge.")

111

Anglica, already mentioned several times, which Gerbert found in a twelfth-century manuscript from the Black Forest, and which, in form and design, resembles the Anglo-Saxon harp so often reproduced in English manuscripts. The manuscript used by Gerbert was formerly erroneously placed in the

Fig. 104. Harp on a stone baptismal font in Lille Lyngby Church; 12th century. (Drawn from the original.)

Fig. 103. King David as a harper, on the north door of Vejlby Church near Randers. Photograph.

sixth, eighth, or ninth century, due to a misinterpretation of the misleading mode of dating employed by Gerbert. Instead of stating the date of the manuscript, he used to give its age at his own period. *DC annorum* thus does not mean, as may be supposed, the sixth century, but six centuries ago, i.e., the twelfth century, since Gerbert wrote in the eighteenth century. A descendant of the *Cythara Anglica* is evidently the small song-harp which in the days of chivalry appears in the hands of the German minstrels and the French jongleurs, and at the same time also plays an important part in the private performance of music for the nobility. The Irish harp, too, at an early

Fig. 105. Harp on a Tombstone in Vinderslev Churchyard (from "Aarbog for Nordisk Oldkyndighed," 1888, II, 3).

Fig. 106. The Irish harp on a German coat-of-arms; 14th century.

Fig. 107. The Irish harper, Denis a Hempson (died 1807). From "The Irish Harp," a lecture by S. Shannon Millin, Belfast, 1898.

date travelled far with the harpers of that country. A descendant of it is clearly enough the harp which is shown on a German coat-of-arms of 1372. As late as the sixteenth century the Irish harp was praised by Italian musicians as the best in Europe. In his "Dialogo della musica antica e moderna" Galilei wrote (1581): "Among the stringed instruments which are at present used in Italy, the harp ranks first. This ancient instrument was, according to Dante, brought to us from Ireland, where it is excellently made and very frequent, for it has been played by the inhabitants of that island for many years. They even place it in the coat-of-arms of the kingdom, paint it on their public buildings and stamp it on their coins." In Ireland itself the native population has loved the harp as long as history records. When in the days of James I (1603-1625), Barnaby Rich visited Ireland, he stated that the Irish had their own harpers whom they held in such esteem that in times of insurrection nobody dared touch them or their property. Almost at the same time (about 1636) we read in a manuscript, "History of Ireland," in the library of the Royal Irish Academy in Dublin, that among Irishmen there were but few men or women who did not know how to play the harp. There was no house of any size that did not possess one or two of these instruments or which had not its regular harper to play during meals and on other occasions when the master of the house wished to regale himself or his friends with music. At a still later date we have many proofs of the marked predilection of the Irish for the harp and its music. Like a mediæval troubadour, the blind Irish harper, Turlogh O'Carolan, went from one manor to another at the beginning of the eighteenth century in order to entertain the Irish nobility with his music. He did not play for money, but was received everywhere as a friend, his visits being even considered an honour to the house. When he died at a great age, while a guest of one of his distinguished patrons, the rumour of his death called together people of all classes, among them sixty priests. The whole population of Ireland strove to honour the dead minstrel. A memorial tablet to the memory of "the great Carolan," the last of the Irish bards, has since been placed on the wall of St. Patrick's Cathedral in Dublin. After Carolan's death several vain attempts were made to revive the national music of Ireland. In order to save what was possible, of the old Irish harp-music a public appeal was made from Belfast in 1792, requesting all the harpers of the country to appear on a certain day to show a committee of experts and musicians what they still possessed of the Irish melodies. Ten appeared, all of them old men and six of them blind. The most interesting was Denis a Hempson, ninety-seven years old, and who lived another fifteen years after that. The day before he died, in 1807, he was visited by Sir Harvey Bruce, an Irish clergyman, who took a great interest in the old man and his art. The more than centenarian asked for his harp, but after having plucked the strings for a moment, fell back in his chair quite exhausted, his vital forces spent. With good reason the harp is still retained in the coat-of-arms of Great Britain as characteristic of the Irish people. ·

C. IRISH TRANSITIONAL FORMS. (FROM LYRE TO HARP.)

The Irish stone crosses exhibit a small group of stringed instruments which, on account of their strange appearance, have puzzled the historian. Their regular quadrilateral form reminds us of the square lyre, while other features argue that they are transitional forms between the lyre and the frame-harp. The fact that they occur only on very early monuments, and especially in Ireland, may indicate that they were produced at a time when attempts were being made to discover the most convenient form for the plucked instrument—attempts which perhaps ended in the frame-harp which was so strongly developed acoustically.

The first examples are to be found on the stone crosses at Ullard and Castledermot, in the counties of Kilkenny and Kildare respectively. These two stone crosses belong in all probability to the same period, in the opinion of archæologists about the year 800. It was the Irish musical historian, Edward Bunting, who, in the year 1845, drew attention for the first time to the Ullard cross and its strange harper. In his book, "The Ancient Music of Ireland," he gave a drawing of the type reproduced on the left arm of the cross, in his opinion a unique European instance of the harp without a pillar. As

Fig. 108. The Ullard harp in Bunting's "Ancient Music of Ireland."

this pillar is indispensable on the ordinary European mediæval harps, but is lacking in the harps of antiquity, Bunting saw in the Ullard harp a striking proof of the old tradition concerning a prehistoric contact between the original inhabitants of Ireland and the ancient Egyptians.

In the autumn of 1902, while in London, I had an opportunity in the library of the British Museum of comparing Bunting's drawing with another in O'Neill's "The most Ancient Crosses of Ancient Ireland." It then appeared that the so-called "harp" which in Bunting's book is reproduced as a square instrument without a pillar, is in O'Neill's book shown as triangular with a distinct pillar. Both drawings are given here (Figs. 108 and 109). The strange difference between the

Fig. 110. The Castledermot Cross.
Photograph.

Fig. 109. The Ullard harp in O'Neill's "The most Ancient Crosses of Ancient Ireland."

Fig. 111. The left arm of the cross.

two reproductions made me go out to see the old cross for myself while visiting Dublin. After having borrowed a ladder at a neighbouring house so that I could reach the picture, I did my best to make it out; but unfortunately did not succeed in obtaining any positive result, for my eyes were not sharp enough to discern all the details of the half-obliterated stone-carving. It was the eminent English musical historian, the Rev. Canon Francis W. Galpin, who about ten years later, by means of rubbings and photographs, succeeded in making out all its lines, and thereby producing a trustworthy copy. From this it may now be established that the Ullard harp did in reality have a pillar (see Galpin, " Old English Instruments ").

Still more clearly than on the Ullard cross, this instrument is reproduced on the Castledermot cross a few miles from Ullard. The latter is shown in the photograph (Fig. 110) which I received from the director of the archæological department of the Dublin Museum after returning to Denmark. In this case it is clearly seen that the strings were surrounded on all sides by a frame, so that in my opinion it is proved beyond question that Bunting's discovery of an Irish harp without a pillar was partly imaginary, in consequence of the rough design at his disposal.

We find an entirely unknown instrument on the high stone cross at Durrow. For a long time it was wrongly described by the archæologists as a harp, and the obliterated outlines of the stone-carving explain the misunderstanding. In order to discover the faint lines giving the shape of the rare old instrument, it was necessary to exert the greatest care. Together with Mr. Hipkins and some other musical experts, Miss Margaret Stokes succeeded finally in making a true copy of this ancient stone monument. We are accordingly now able to ascertain that the instrument shown resembles a harp in certain points, it is true; but in other respects it exhibits a hitherto unknown transitional form between the lyre and the harp (see Fig. 112). The large square sound-box from the base of which six strings rise, is quite lyre-like. On their way across the sound-board the strings pass over a bridge placed obliquely, and through the open space between the lyre-arms they finally reach the bar on which they are tuned. The tuning, however, is not effected on an independent yoke as in the ordinary lyre, but on the left arm, for the latter bends forward across the strings until it meets the right arm, which in this case is quite straight. It was this left lyre-arm, formed like a bow-harp, which at first glance, in combination with the pillar-like straight arm, gave the instrument the above-mentioned resemblance to a harp. The similarity between the Durrow lyre and the archaic-Chaldæan lyre from Tello (cf. *sup.* Fig. 9) is interesting. The latter was in its main features a huge lyre, with two arms rising from the sides of a large square sound-box and connected above by a yoke; but while the strings of the ancient lyre ascend, as a rule, perpendicularly from the sound-box to the yoke, and are generally divided equally over the open square string-space, they ascend fan-like from one corner of the frame in this case, just as in the Durrow lyre.

Fig. 112. Miss Stokes's reconstruction of the stringed instrument on the Durrow cross. (M. Stokes, "The High Crosses of Castledermot and Durrow," 1898.)

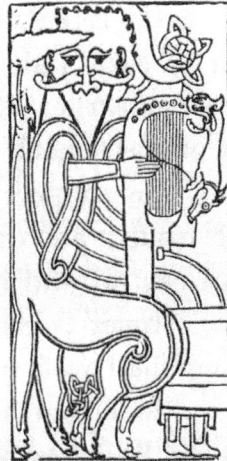

Fig. 113. Westwood's reconstruction of the harp in MS. Vitellius, F. XI; British Museum, 10th century.

Closely related to the strange instrument which Miss Stokes found on the cross at Durrow is evidently the stringed instrument which Westwood, with the aid of a magnifying glass, reconstructed from a charred manuscript now in the British Museum. In this picture, which is often used in historical works, the instrument has a greater number of strings than the one found by Miss Stokes; they are also perpendicular and lack the support of the bridge mentioned above; but the form of the instrument, the large sound-box, the bent arm and the pillar, which in this case is artistically carved, are elements which all occur in the Durrow lyre (see Fig. 113). In another manuscript in the British Museum ("Harl.," 3240, f. 22) are two instances of stringed instruments which stand more clearly than any others I have hitherto seen, on the border-line between lyre and frame-harp. On them the left lyre-arm is shortened to a minimum, so that the highly-developed sound-box and the yoke almost meet. By this means the right arm completely assumes the character of a pillar. One even hesitates between calling this instrument a lyre or a harp. The manuscript which, according to the language, is English, belongs to the fourteenth century, and shows that the attempts to combine the lyre and the harp, which in ancient Ireland were made at an early date, were continued in later days, and that then, just as earlier, they led to interesting new forms in the domain of instrument making (see vignette, p. 123).

With the support of the monuments the following provisional results are obtained: the only stringed instrument which in central and north Europe may be followed back to prehistoric times is the lyre. A form of the lyre closely approaching the Greek type occurs in the last millennium before Christ, on the Danubian plain, and, in the days of the Migration, in the Rhine countries. A derivative, the round lyre—in the twelfth century designated as *Cythara Teutonica*—occurred as early as the eighth century among the Anglo-Saxons, and finally is also one of the chief instruments on the oldest of the Nordic pictures (in the Stave-churches).

The harp proper is first found in the British Isles. The hypothesis that it was of German origin has no support from the monuments. Its first occurrence among other nations shows—wherever it is possible to examine it—British influence. In Germany it was called *Cythara Anglica*. The oldest Nordic picture of a frame-harp is found among the half-Celtic Norsemen in the Isle of Man, and it displays the peculiar form unquestionably to be found only in Ireland. Besides the far more frequent round lyres, the harp is later found twice in the Scandinavian Gunnar-pictures, in a short heavy form recalling the harp of the wandering Irish minstrel. Later information also suggests British influence.

In the British Isles themselves the harp occurs frequently among both the Irish and the Anglo-Saxons. With the Anglo-Saxons it always takes the same form, and is a slender hand-harp of easily recognisable shape. Among the Irish, on the other hand, it is possible to observe numerous variations. There the triangular harp occurs in both the large and small forms, with large sound-box, etc. At the same time we meet with harps in which the regular triangular shape is replaced by other forms. In some the lower point of the triangle is blunted to a level base; others are square and have the pillar that is peculiar to the frame-harp; others are again hybrids between the lyre and the harp. The Irish thus experimented clearly enough, and it is therefore possible that it was their experiments which at length created the frame-harp. In face of this hypothesis there are, as stated above, others quite as justifiable; and of these the greatest credence must undoubtedly, at the present moment at least, be given to that made by Curt Sachs. It is, however, best for the present to allow the question of the origin of the frame-harp to rest as it is until further examination will, it is to be hoped, some day produce the proofs which will render all conjecture superfluous.

THE NAMES OF THE INSTRUMENTS AND OTHER LITERARY EVIDENCE RELATING TO THE LYRE AND THE FRAME-HARP.

(THE CHROTTA BRITANNA OF FORTUNATUS AND THE CRUIT OR CRWTH OF THE CELTS.)

In Fortunatus's well-known poem (sixth century: "Venantii Fortunati Poemata," Ed. 1617):

> Romanusque lyra plaudat tibi, Barbarus harpa,
> Graecus Achilliaca, Chrotta Britanna canat

the harp is stated to be peculiar to the barbarians, and at the same time another instrument, called *Chrotta Britanna* is mentioned. As Fortunatus lived at Poitiers, he probably referred to a stringed instrument used by the neighbouring Celtic Bretons and scarcely to a British instrument. The name of an instrument which is etymologically identical with Fortunatus's Chrotta is actually to be found in the Celtic language. In his book, "Altkeltischer Sprachschatz," Holder gives the name in the following terms: old Irish *crot* for cithera, Welsh *crwth* for fidicula, old English *crûdh*, English *crowde*, *crowd*, or *croud* for violin. We first meet with the name in the old Irish manuscripts which must be dated immediately before the coming of the Vikings. The *cruit* is there given as the oldest of all stringed instruments. While in the old Greek legends dealing with the discovery of the stringed instruments and their wonderful power, it is always the lyre which plays the chief rôle, among the Irish it is the cruit which takes the legendary place in the pedigree of the stringed instruments.

Once upon a time there lived a husband and wife, runs the Irish tradition; Cuil Midhuel's son was the husband, Canochiach Mhor his wife. And the wife nourished hatred for her husband and fled through the woods and through desolate and uninhabited places, and her husband pursued her incessantly. And one day when the woman came to the shore of Camas and walked along the beach, she found the skeleton of a whale. And she heard the sound of the wind blowing through the sinews of the dead whale, and fell asleep to the monotonous sound. Her husband overtook her and heard what had made her sleep. And he went into the woods and made the frame of a cruit, and he made strings of the sinews of the whale, and this was the first cruit ever made.

The reference to the cruit found in the ancient description of Tara's Hall is also interesting. Written in the sixth century, it mentioned the places assigned in the king's hall to all the guests, including that of the *cruitire*, the players on the cruit.

The literary sources alone give little information as to the nature of the old Irish cruit. The Irish traditional version of the instrument's origin resembles that of the antique plucked lyre so closely, however, that we may be permitted to draw the conclusion that the name means a stringed instrument played by plucking. From the fact that Daghda found his cruit hanging on the wall in the camp of the enemy, it is moreover possible to assume that the instrument was not very large.

Thanks to the classic authors who wrote of the Gauls, we have more ancient particulars of the stringed instruments used by the Celtic peoples. Thus Diodorus Siculus ("Bibliotheca historica," Lib. 5), who lived at the time of Cæsar and Augustus, wrote that the Gauls had their lyric authors whom they called bards, and who sang "one song for praise and another for mockery" to instruments "resembling lyres." A still earlier author, Posidonius (Arbois de Jubinville, "Littérature celtique," I, Intro., p. 50 *ff.*), describes how a Gallic bard ran beside the carriage of the king, reciting a poem. This source does not tell us whether he had a stringed instrument in his hand; but as Diodorus Siculus considers the stringed instrument an indispensable accessory to the public appearances of the bard, it may be supposed without much doubt that one who appeared before the king to sing his praises must have had such an instrument. The continued use of this instrument by the bards of later days supports the assumption. As *crot* or *cruit* was the only name for a stringed instrument used by the Celts, it must have been an ancient possession of theirs, and may therefore be inserted in these old Gallic stories. That the instrument was small will, as suggested above, be seen from the Irish legends, and is confirmed by Posidonius's narrative of the running bard.

Bearing all this in mind, it may perhaps seem strange that the name of the Welsh form of the crwth is not associated in

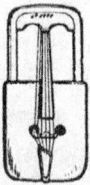

Fig. 114. Welsh crwth. (See also Book II.)

modern Wales with a plucked instrument but with a bowed one. This bowed instrument, which is said to have been known earlier in Ireland and which, according to Welsh belief, is very ancient, possesses, however, properties indicating that it was not destined from the beginning to be played with a violin-bow. The flat bridge carrying the strings over the sound-board made it almost impossible to bow the strings of this instrument separately—a manner of manipulation which is also prohibited by the straight sides of the sound-box; i.e., they lack the indentations necessary to permit the stroke of the bow (see Fig. 114). If we examine it closely, however, we shall see that this bowed instrument greatly resembles a round lyre in shape. Like the latter it has two arms which are fused into a yoke at the top. Properly speaking, the only novelty is the fingerboard, which on this crwth divides the open space between the lyre-arms in two. This fingerboard may well, however, be an addition of more recent date. When, in about the year 1000, the violin-bow was brought to Europe, it was for a time used experimentally on nearly all the existing stringed instruments, and the experience gained gradually modified some of them as occasion required. In this manner the Welsh crwth may at some time have been given a finger-board, the existence of which would otherwise be difficult to explain on an instrument of the lyre-type. A number of repro-ductions of the twelfth century, which were recently found in environments where Celtic influence is probable, allow us to presume that the bowed Welsh crwth actually had ancestors which, to judge by their appearance, closely resembled the round lyre; and the assumed descent of the crwth from such a source is thereby made almost certain. In literature, too, while it was once considered possible to trace the Welsh crwth back to the fifteenth century at the earliest (Edward Jones, "Musi-cal and Poetical Relics of the Welsh Bards," 1784), there are now proofs that it was already used in Wales in the twelfth century (J. F. W. Wevertem ("Zwei veraltete Musikinstru-mente," in "Monatshefte für Musikgeschichte," 1881). As the bowed Welsh crwth was a fingerboard instrument, and will consequently be dealt with in Book II, the presentation of these discoveries must be left until we reach it. Suffice it now to note their existence.

The Celtic peoples thus used *cruit* as the name of a stringed instrument in the remote past. All we know of the instrument itself is that it was played with the fingers, and that in most cases it was small and light. It cannot be decided whether in the earliest times several different instruments did not con-ceal themselves behind this name. Later on the crwth (cruit) was re-discovered in Wales as a bowed instrument; but the bowed crwth now used undoubtedly gives the impression of having originated in a plucked instrument—the lyre.

THE ROTTA OF THE TEUTONS.

Rota, rote, rotta, rotte, and in the older language, *hrota* and *hrotta*, connote in the Germanic and Romance languages linguistically with *crot* and *cruit* in the Celtic. In a manuscript in the Vatican, Fortunatus's poem has *Rotta Britanna* instead of *Chrotta Britanna*. In originally calling the instrument of the Bretons *chrotta*, Fortunatus was in accord with the pronunciation of the Franks; in the Celtic form the word should be crotta: for the Germanic *h*, formerly *ch*, corresponds to the Celtic *c*. The existence of a special Germanic form of the word may, in the opinion of philologists, indicate either that it had, from an early date, been common to both Celts and Teutons, or that in some prehistoric time it was borrowed from the Teutons. This conclusion, however, is not quite satisfying. The complete absence of the word in the northern and Anglo-Saxon countries and its frequent occurrence in the Roman (originally Celtic) countries, make its Germanic source improbable. Moreover, in the oldest sources *rote* appeared more often in connection with convent-schools and the like than with national art.

The most ancient definitions of the word unanimously describe the *rote* as an instrument with plucked ("harped") strings. In a Munich manuscript quoted in Schmeller's "Bayerisches Wörterbuch" under *rotte*, we read: "Als her David sein Rotten spien, wan er darauf herpfen wolt." Likewise a letter from an eighth-century abbot to a colleague in Germany (published in "Epistolæ St. Bonifacii Martyris," Mainz, 1629): "Delectat me quoque cytharistam habere, qui possit cytharisare in cythara quam nos appellamus rottam." For a time the term *rotta* seems to have been the common name of several kinds of plucked instruments. Notker, of St. Gall (tenth century), states somewhere that the *rote* was handled as a lyre and, like the latter, had seven strings. "Fóne díu sínt ándero lîrûn únde rótûn iô síben síeten, únde síbene gelîcho geuuerbet" (quoted in Gerbert, "Scriptores ecclesiastici de Musica sacra potissimum," Vol. I, p. 96, St. Blasius, 1784).

In the St. Gall manuscript version of Notker's psalms, *rotta* is explained as an improvement on the old psalterium (see *inf.*, p. 168). Later, in the Romanesque-Germanic Middle Ages, *rote* seems to be the name of a particular stringed instrument which is described in literature as "a small harp decorated with jewels," and very often used as a social instrument side by side with the harp to accompany song. Gottfried von Strassburg in "Tristan" (thirteenth century) says: "Über sinen Rücke fuort er / eine Rotte, diu was kleine / mit Golde und mit Gesteine / Geschoenet unde gezieret / Ze Wunsche gecordieret." In practice the round lyre, i.e., Gerbert's *Cythara Teutonica*, seems to have been the nearest to it. In the thirteenth century it happens as an exception that the *rote* is now and then described as a bowed instrument; thus, in a note by Aloise de Lille (thirteenth century: "De planctu naturæ"): "Lira est quodam genus cytharæ vel fitola, alioquin de Roet," and in a vocabulary of 1419 where we read: "Rott, Rubeba est parva figella" (*Fitola* and *Figella* are late mediæval Latin for "fidel"). De Lille thus gives *lira, cythara*, and *de Roet*, as bowed instruments. Similarly Gerbert found in a Latin manuscript (which he placed in the ninth century but which is no doubt less ancient), a one-stringed *gigue* designated as *lyra*. In a similarly figurative sense *harp* was sometimes used of a bowed instrument in the Scandinavian countries.

THE HARP OF THE TEUTONS.

As "harp" in the earlier Middle Ages was common to the Germanic peoples and occurred only among them, the name may without hesitation be considered to have originated with them. The etymological meaning of the noun has not yet been discovered (S. Kluge, "Etymologisches Wörterbuch der deutschen Sprache," 1899). But the verb "to harp" (from which "harper," i.e., "fiddler"), derived from the noun, occurs in several Germanic languages, and was used in the sense of "to play a stringed instrument." Thus, in the above quotation, "Als her David sein Rotten spien, wan er darauf herpfen wolt." In England, Chaucer's mendicant friar of the fourteenth century is found "singing to the rote and harping." In the Middle Ages it was applied exclusively to the plucked instruments, but later it was sometimes used to indicate bowed instruments also. Peder Syv, in "Proverbs" (I, 373) has: "A bad harper always scrapes on the old string." In Sweden the name *Nyckelharpa* is still used for the old *Schlüsselgeige* introduced from Germany. It is thus probable that the word "harp" first indicated a stringed instrument, the strings of which were "harped," i.e., plucked.

THE HARP AMONG THE ANCIENT GERMANS.

In old literature the harp is mentioned for the first time in the poem of Fortunatus, already quoted: "Romanusque lyra, plaudat tibi Barbarus harpa," but no description of this so-called barbarian harp is given. All we see is that Fortunatus considered the harp as peculiar to the barbarians, and the connection shows that by barbarians he meant the Germans, or more precisely, the Franks living in Gaul. Information on the use of stringed instruments by the Germanic peoples, dating from still earlier times, is available. Jordanes (*ca.* 5) wrote: "that thus the mighty deeds of their ancestors were praised at the court of the Gothic kings to the *Cythara*." Procops ("De bello Vand.," II, 6) stated of Gelimer, king of the Vandals (533), that, shut up in the Numidian mountain fortress of Pappua, he asked the besieging captain, Belisarius, for a loaf of bread to satisfy his hunger, a sponge to bathe his eyes, which were red with weeping, and a stringed instrument in order that he may accompany a song composed by himself. In Cassiodorus ("Var.," II, 40 *f.*) we read that Chloderich, the founder of the Frankish Empire, asked the Ostrogoth, Theodoric, to send him "a cythara-player" to entertain him at his meals. It does not appear, however, whether he meant a Gothic or a Roman artist.

Concerning the nature of these instruments we have no particulars. As the word "harp" is the only one to occur in the earliest Germanic manuscripts, it must be supposed that both Goths and Vandals used it as the generic name for their stringed instruments. All that we can gather is that the instrument was used for accompanying songs, and that it was played not only by professional singers, but also by kings. Its rôle as a domestic instrument, as will soon be seen, was common to the harps of the Teutons in the earliest times.

THE ANGLO-SAXON HEARP.

Called poetically the "joy-wood," this instrument was already mentioned in "Beowulf," the genesis of which has been placed in the eighth century. With the "joy-wood" in his hands the Anglo-Saxon gleeman struck up the songs in which he lauded, now the achievements of the heroes to fire the warriors to noble deeds, now the beneficence of the Creator. To the notes of his harp he was often heard bewailing the transient nature of human life. It was not only the gleeman who plucked the "twisted strings" of the harp. In "Beowulf" we also hear of the king, old in the experiences of life, plucking the "joy-tree" or improvising an artistic song (see Grein, "Dichtungen der Angelsachsen," I, 2105, 2260, 3020). There can be no doubt that this Anglo-Saxon *hearp* was the instrument to which allusion is made in Bede's Latin church-history (seventh century), where it is related that at the banquets of the Anglo-Saxons the *Cythara* passed from hand to hand so that all the guests in turn could sing a song to its accompaniment. It was a disgrace for a man to be unable to take part in this diversion. Ashamed, Caedmon left the banqueting-hall and the house, every time the *Cythara* approached his seat. Every Anglo-Saxon who had received good training was expected to know how to touch the harp and possess one. This instrument was the only article of his property that even his creditors were not allowed to seize.

From the Anglo-Saxon poem, "On the fate of man" (Grein, op. cit., II, 158, 80), we learn that the harp was played with a plectrum—in Anglo-Saxon the *Hearp Nägel*. "With the harp many an one shall sit at the feet of his master and receive the treasure; he shall quickly make the strings vibrate and bring forth a merry note; he who wields the stick with ability while performing music, displays his zeal."

Conclusion: the Anglo-Saxon harp was sometimes played with a plectrum, and was small and light, so that during a banquet it could be passed from hand to hand.

THE HARP AMONG THE NORSEMEN.

In the ancient literature of the North the name *harp* was mentioned for the first time in the Edda songs (Vóluspă, Atlakvidha, tenth century; Atlamâl and Oddrûnagràtr, beginning of the eleventh) in which it occupied an important place in the legends of king Gunnar, who played the harp in the snake-pit. When king Atle threw Gunnar alive into the pit with his arms tied behind him, Gunnar touched the harp:

> " hraerði ilkvistum :
> slá hann svá kunni,
> at snótir grétu,
> klukku þeir karlar,
> er kunnu görst heyra."
>
> (Otto Andersson, " Strakharpan," page 158.)

The Edda songs attribute such strength to Gunnar's touch on the harp, that Oddrun, his former love, hears it far away on the Isle of Laesö, whither she had gone to prepare the banquet for king Geirmund:

"Nam ek at heyra
ór Hléseyju,
hve par af striđum
strengir meltu."

(Otto Andersson, page 159.)

The "Völsunga saga" (C. 37; thirteenth century, but narrating older legends) states that it was the sister Gudrun, the wife of king Atle, who sent the harp to Gunnar, and that he played until all the snakes slept with the exception of one which crept up to him and bit him. Thus ended Gunnar.

Long after Christianity had displaced paganism, the memory of king Gunnar and his harp lived on in Iceland, Norway and Sweden, as we shall soon see from fourteenth-century sources.

Apart from the Gunnar legend, the harp was also mentioned in Voluspa:

"Sat par á haugi
ok sló hörpu
gýgjar hirđir,
glađr Eggper."

(Otto Andersson, page 158.)

In ancient Nordic literature we do not find any mention of the instrument having been used to accompany song. For this information, as well as for several other particulars, I am indebted to Prof. Axel Olrik, who, by examining the literary sources of antiquity and the Middle Ages in the north, has been of great assistance to me. Singing and harp-playing are always mentioned separately. Just as swimming, archery, ski-ing, etc., playing on the harp and scalding, were individual occupations in which high-born youth had to be proficient. Ragnvald Jarl, in the Orkneys, who in the middle of the twelfth century is mentioned as a Crusader, boasts of knowing nine forms of sport, viz., board-game, runes, to read a book, forging, ski-ing, shooting, rowing, harp-playing and scalding.

As to the arrangement of the "harp" in Nordic antiquity, the songs thus tell us no more than that it was a stringed instrument plucked with the fingers. We see that professional harpers are never mentioned, but that the harp was always played by laymen and especially by kings, in the same way as among the Teutons of antiquity and the Anglo-Saxons.

THE HARP AMONG THE MEDIÆVAL NORSEMEN.

From the ancient Norse songs (*anno* 900-1100) we will now pass to the time of the legendary literature of the North (*ca.* 1150-1350), which is treated separately because it contains several strange features that do not appear in the songs.

In mediæval literature we must, in the first place, reckon the legend of Aslog in the "Völsunga Saga." This dates from the thirteenth century. According to information given me by Prof. Axel Olrik, the legend of Aslog is mentioned for the first time in a poem of *ca.* 1150, but is hardly much older (cf. Olrik, "Sakses Oldhistorie," II, 95). From this Saga we learn with certainty that Heimer's harp had a very capacious sound-box, for it would not otherwise have concealed a child and many costly clothes and jewels of gold and silver. The same narrative also gives an idea of the height and weight of the harp; for when Heimer visited the old peasants, Aage and Grima, on the farm in Spangareid, he placed the harp beside him, and when the people had murdered him, Grima took the harp and ran away with it. Thus the instrument was not very high and comparatively light.

In the "Saga on Nornagest" (fourteenth century; "Nornagestspáttr," *k.* 2; 52, 8-11) we hear for the first time what kind of music was performed on this harp. The saga relates how the wandering singer, Nornagest, arrives at Olaf Trygvasson's at Trondhjem. In the evening he entertains the king and his men with the harp; he performs " Gunnar's Touch " and the ancient piece called " Gudrun's Trick," " which had not been heard there before and which is pleasant to the ears of all." The titles " Gunnar's Touch " and " Gudrun's Trick " again point back to the Gunnar legend, and the saga-teller evidently believes that it was with these pieces that Gunnar attempted to charm the snakes. Whether this was but an invention of the saga-teller as scholars assume, or not, it gives us the interesting information that during that period they had pieces of music with definite titles, sometimes named after the persons who were supposed to have played them. In this respect the saga gives evidence of a rather well-developed musical culture judged by the standards of the time.

In form, Nornagest's harp evidently resembled the one described in the Aslog legend, for in the great cavity of the instrument Nornagest carries the large wax candle which is mystically connected with his life. Thus, by reason of its capacious volume, the body of the harp served as a receptacle. In the saga it is therefore called the stomach of the harp, as in the somewhat fanciful " Herroed and Bose Saga " (fourteenth century) in which the " stomach " of the harp is described as being so large that a man could stand erect in it. Bose also used the harp as a hiding-place for the gold-embroidered white gloves which he wore when performing one of his highly effective pieces of music at the wedding banquet of the king's sister. From a musical point of view the description of these pieces is of great interest. The very titles " Gygeslaget " (the " harp-touch of the giantess "), " Drombud " (the " boasting piece "), " Hjarranda-hljöd " (" Hjarranda's song "), " Faldafeikir " (the " head-kerchief stormer ") arouse our interest and disclose the intention of the Nordic composer to describe some definite action or situation. Peculiar also is the effect of these pieces on the audience. When Bose tunes the harp for the first time, the knives and platters begin to dance and the listeners to leap up from their seats and dance; the second time he plays so loudly that it resounds all over the hall. All, with the exception of the bride, the bridegroom, and the king, rise and move round the hall. This having gone on for some time, the king asks whether he knows any other tunes, and is told that he does, but that he wishes the guests to rest first. When "Faldefeikir" is played, the head-kerchiefs fly off the women and twine round the beams; men and women jump up, nobody can sit still, etc.

In the Nordic, especially the Danish, folk-songs the "harp" is frequently mentioned, often while emphasising how magically impressive is the playing. It is still a private instrument, played by both men and women of the nobility (cf. many passages in the old Danish folk-songs, e.g., Nos. 65, 73, 265, etc.). Several times it is given as having been small in size—e.g., in "Little Kirsten." In the rose-grove Mr. Tönne meets the daughter of the dwarf king, and "she had the golden harp in her hands."

Results. The most noticeable feature distinguishing the use of the harp in the Middle Ages from that of antiquity, was that in the Middle Ages it was played by professional wandering harpers. We can also identify the instrument they played. It had an exceedingly large sound-box, very elongated in form, for it was said to have been large enough to contain a taper, a child, and even an adult, and in the latter case the instrument must have been taller than a man. These details correspond exactly with what the monuments tell us of the Irish harp. The possibility that these were instruments of the lyre-type is absolutely precluded. The older custom, that princely and other private persons practised the playing of the harp, on the other hand, seems to have disappeared or to have been forced into the background. The domestic harp of the folk-songs differed essentially from the harp mentioned earlier in the sagas; but it resembled the harp of Nordic antiquity in being a domestic instrument, used especially by the nobles and in being used only for solos and not for accompanying song.

THE IRISH CLARSETH AND THE WELSH TELYN.

Clarseth, alias *clarseach*, is the Irish name for the triangular frame-harp. How old this name is, can only be arrived at with difficulty. In old Irish literature it does not seem to occur, for there the *cruit* appears alone. Mr. Conran ("The National Music of Ireland," 1850) states, without giving any proof, that it was already known before the twelfth century. It is possible that the name in Ireland is as old as the frame-harp itself; at any rate it is certain that the latter instrument never bore the name of "harp" in Ireland. The Irish language has only two terms for the old stringed instrument, i.e., *cruit* and *clarseth*. Armstrong ("Gael. Dict." and "Dict. Scoto-Celticum") supposes that the ancient *cruit* and the possibly somewhat less ancient *clarseth* were used side by side for a time, and that *cruit* meant a harp with gut-strings, while *clarseth* designated a harp strung with metal. Both Mr. Conran and Mr. J. Walker ("Historical Memoirs of the Irish Bards," London, 1786) give the names of four harps used by the ancient Irish: (1) *clarseth* (i.e., the triangular harp), (2) *keirnine* (an unknown instrument), (3) *cionar cruit* (also unknown), and (4) *creamtine cruit* (i.e., the six-stringed Welsh crwth).

The old Irish bard played the *clarseth* with his nails, and there is an old legend of a bard who, to atone some offence or other, was punished by having his nails cut, so that he was debarred from playing until they had grown again.

Telyn, telen, were the names of instruments native to Wales and Brittany respectively; and, like the *clarseth*, they both mean a triangular frame-harp. The telyn is already mentioned in the so-called "Leges Wallicæ," of which a part is to be dated as early as the tenth century. A distinction was here drawn between three kinds of telyn—namely, the King's telyn, the telyn of the music master, and the nobleman's telyn. The first two were valued at 120 pence each, and the last at 60 pence. Consequently the harp must have been played in the olden times in Wales both by musicians and amateurs. These sentences from the same source bear witness to this: "Three thing are indispensable to a nobleman or a baron, viz., his telyn, his cloak, and his chess-board," and "Three things are necessary for a man to have in his house, viz., a virtuous wife, a cushion in his chair, and a well-tuned telyn."

It appears from a paragraph in the "Leges Wallicæ" that a telyn strung with horse-hair was used in the twelfth century by the lower class telyn players, and that the master player was entitled to receive twenty-four pence from every minstrel who changed his hair-strung telyn for a better one in order to become a fully qualified performer. As the horse-hair harp is used to this very day by many primitive peoples, it may perhaps be taken as a proof of its having belonged to a primitive culture.

As late as 1581 a Welsh bard still referred to this primitive harp:

> "If I have my Harp, I care for no more;
> It is my treasure, I keep it in store;
> For my Harp is made of a good mare's skin,
> The strings be of horse-hair, it maketh a good din.
> My song and my voice, and my Harp doth agree,
> Much like the buzzing of a humble bee."

It is recorded that about the year 1100 the Welsh had their musical canon regulated by Irish harpers, and Caradoc states that the Welsh received the harp from Ireland. It was evidently the introduction of the Irish harp which at length brought the old horse-hair harp into contempt, so that it became the instrument of the lower class musicians. Thence onwards only its name, *telyn*, was held in honour for it was transferred unchanged to the newly introduced and more complete instrument.

In the twelfth century Giraldus Cambrensis said—unfortunately in Latin—that a *cythara* was to be found in every home in Ireland and Wales and was played by everybody; the stranger who entered a house had to deliver up his weapons at the entrance, and was then offered water to wash his feet. If he came rather early in the day, he was entertained the whole evening by conversation, by the young women and by cythara playing. This "cythara" was undoubtedly the frame-harp, i.e., the instrument which in Ireland was called *cruit* or *clarseth* and in Wales *telyn*.

The results. If we finally compare the literary evidence with the monuments, we find: That the name "harp" from the beginning was never connected with any definite form of instrument, but often covered several. The most striking proof of this comes from Norway; where, according to literary evidence spread over the period between the tenth and the fourteenth centuries, it was "a harp" that King Gunnar played in the snake pit. The monuments, however, teach us that only in one case out of five did Gunnar's instrument take the form of a triangular harp; in four cases it was a round lyre. Those who carved the monuments therefore, in the greater number of cases, called the round lyre a "harp." Among the Anglo-Saxons we find something of the same kind. Literature gives us only the one name "hearp"; from the monuments we learn that two kinds of stringed instruments were used together: i.e., the round lyre and the frame-harp. This uncertainty remained clinging to the harp for a long time. "Das, welches einer ein Harpffen hat genennet, das heisst ein ander ein Leier," wrote Sebastian Virdung as late as 1511. In conformity with this the noun "harper" is still used by Peder Syv to designate a fiddler (v. sup. page 130). The word "harp" was undoubtedly used by the Germanic peoples in prehistoric times, and it is very probable that it was their only name for a "stringed instrument." To this must be added the circumstance that on the monuments we can only follow one stringed instrument back to prehistoric times. Consequently the lyres in the tombs of the Germanic warriors must in the German language have been called "harps." At a time when only instruments of the lyre type existed, "harp" thus meant lyre. It seems to have been a survival of this primordial circumstance that Gunnar's harp as a rule took the form of a round lyre, and only in two cases did it appear as a harp introduced from Ireland. Only one name can be considered to be old German—"harp"; only one old Celtic —"cruit." No wonder that all the languages had to be content with one name, for in all other essentials there existed, as far as we can see, only one instrument, i.e., the lyre in its different forms. As "harp" was preferably used on our oldest monuments to indicate the lyre, so does it seem to have been with the *chrotta*. The Welsh crwth was originally—i.e., before it became a bowed instrument—a lyre. *Rotta* seems especially to have been the name of a kind of lyre—the round lyre. "Chrotta" and "harp" were the names by which the barbarians (Teutons and Celts) designated the lyre borrowed from the culture of Greece.

The oldest records of stringed instruments (Irish, Gothic, Anglo-Saxon and Nordic, to which must be added the evidence of the Nordic folk-songs) give no details; but on the other hand they give us a rather eloquent picture of the use made of these instruments, which seems to have been strangely similar everywhere. The instrument was in the first place carried by the high-born warrior; it was small and was hung on the wall (see the Irish legend and the Nordic folk-songs), or it was carried on a ribbon by the armed warrior (Allemanni); and it often followed him to the grave together with his weapons (Allemanni, Swedes). In a few cases the harp was also seen in the hands of other free and independent men (Anglo-

Saxons). In the vast majority of cases, but not in the ancient north, the instruments were used to accompany song and thus had no independent importance. This earliest period had as yet no professional harpers, nor instruments of large size; neither the sound-box nor the other parts of the instrument seem to have enjoyed much development as yet.

The stringed instrument reached a higher standard during the succeeding period, when the professional harper acted as the most important cultivator of music, and the frame-harp came to the fore. A glance at the monuments causes us to look upon the British Islands as the home of this harp. It first made its appearance there, and thence also was the provenance of the large number of strange forms which reveal the persevering endeavours of those islanders to find the best form of stringed instrument. The British Isles had no particular name for the frame-harp, but the Irish had one (*clarseth*), the Welsh and the Britons another (*telyn*). Thus the philological facts support the hypothesis of the late and Celtic origin of the harp. In addition, the literary records of the musical life of the Celts, of the value they attached to proficiency, and of the alterations and improvements made by the Irish and the Welsh, support the theory that here was the centre where the frame-harp was perfected. The literary information has moreover confirmed that it was essentially instruments of the Irish type that reached other countries. Quite a number of Nordic mediaeval legends treat of harps which serve as hiding places and which must therefore have had the capacious sound-box peculiar to the Irish harp. The harp from the Isle of Man and the Gunnar harp from Opdal were evidently also of western origin. At the same time we obtain a clearer notion of the manner in which the word "harp" was used. In old German territory it first designated a lyre or, generally speaking, a stringed instrument. The Anglo-Saxons kept this inherited name and used it to indicate their chief instrument, the new British triangular harp. From the Anglo-Saxon name for the harp the word then spread together with the Celtic type of instrument to the Romance and Germanic countries. It was in itself quite natural for the Anglo-Saxons and not the Celts to name the new instrument in the musical language of Europe. "Clarseth" and "telyn" sounded strange, and the Celtic peoples did not agree in their names. "Harp," on the other hand, was already a well known word and easy to incorporate into Latin and the Romance languages. Gradually the old meaning of the word was forgotten, and it became attached solely to the particular instrument which came from the British Isles. This designation, however, took a long time to make headway against inherited usage; in Germany it was still opposed in the sixteenth century, and in Sweden it was still fighting with the popular designation in the nineteenth.

The literary records thus in no way overthrow what the monuments teach us, but on the contrary support and complete their information. And the result has in addition an inner probability, as it corresponds in all essentials to what we know of the ways of cultural development in other directions. The harp of German antiquity was not a special barbarian instrument, but was actually only the Greek lyre, received at a time when the southern culture, on the whole, set its mark upon central and northern Europe. The arts of antiquity and the Middle Ages thereby prove that they are closely connected.

It is otherwise with the triangular harp. To guide us to its origin we have nothing more than supposition, the correctness of which is in no case proved by positive evidence. In this respect we have in reality only the monuments, and according to them it is the British Isles that show the first example—the slender Anglo-Saxon harp of the tenth century. A much more perfect instrument in respect of tone is the Irish harp, which from the thirteenth century was general in Ireland, Scotland and Wales, and which had a capacious sound-box and a large number of strings. It was preceded in Ireland by the variously shaped square harps appearing on the earliest Celtic stone crosses, which were at one time connected with the round lyre and which point forward to the frame-harp. Whether or not the frame-harp had its prototype in antique culture, or was connected with it or with the *toro(go)-jux* recently found among the East Jakuts, is still obscure.

THE PSALTERY.

This kind of harp did not make its presence felt in European art until the twelfth century, and was originally borrowed from the Orient. Instruments of this kind may be followed far and wide, and in the eastern countries were considered to be of ancient origin. They therefore appeared in many forms in their native lands.

A. THE PSALTERY IN THE NEAR EAST.

The European mediæval psaltery may with certainty be followed back to two primitive forms which are still used in the East. One is called the *santir* in Persia and Arabia, the other the *kanun*.

The oriental santir normally had the outlines of an equilateral triangle, from the apex of which a smaller or larger piece had been cut away (see Fig. 115 and cf. with No. 2 of the psaltery types given on page 80). Sometimes the santir took the form of an oblong, so that it was only by means of oblique bridges that the length of the strings was regulated. Twenty-five groups *(Chor)* of strings, each of them containing four steel strings, are stretched across the sound-box, and under them small bridges or trestles are placed alternately on the right and left, limiting the central sounding part of the strings. The wooden pegs are placed at the edge of the sound-box (see the description of the psaltery on page 80) on the right of the sound-board. In the latter there are three decorative sound-holes (or "roses"), one of which is placed in the narrow end of the sound-box, midway between the two series of bridges, while the other two are placed at the broad end of the instrument, one on each side of the bridges. On the modern instrument illustrated here the strings are played with small hammers, but in an old Persian picture of this type of psaltery two curved plectra are used instead of the hammers, being of a type also seen in mediaeval European reproductions of psalteries (see Fig. 116).

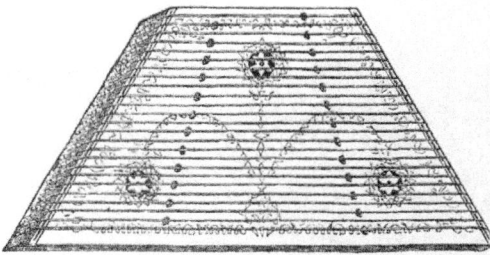

Fig. 115. Oriental Santir. South Kensington Museum.

Fig. 116. Santir in an old Persian picture (Engel, "A Descriptive Catalogue of the Musical Instruments in the South Kensington Museum").

The Perso-Arabian kanun is a trapezium similar to the third of the psaltery types reproduced on page 80. In this the tuning pegs are inserted in a special peg-board following the oblique side of the sound-board. While in the santir described above each of the groups of strings rested on a bridge of its own, and the bridges there were placed one to the right and one to the left alternately, the groups of strings on the kanun are supported at both ends by a moulding glued to the sound-board and running under all the strings. One moulding runs parallel with the oblique side of the sound-box close to the peg-board, while the other runs along the opposite straight side, the intervening sonorous part of the strings thus becoming gradually longer and the pitch lower as the two mouldings

Fig. 117. Perso-Arabian kanun. (Engel, "S. K. Museum Cat.")

move farther away from one another. On this type of psaltery the twenty-five strings are generally trichord and made of gut, being played with small plectra attached to the forefingers of the performer.

B. The Psaltery in Mediaeval Europe.

(A). On the Monuments.

Mediæval forms of the psaltery which may be followed back to the oriental kanun and santir. As the introduction of the psaltery into Europe coincided with the time of the Crusades, it may be assumed that it was brought to the west by returning pilgrims. This may have been the cause of the surprisingly rapid popularisation of the instrument in all the European countries.

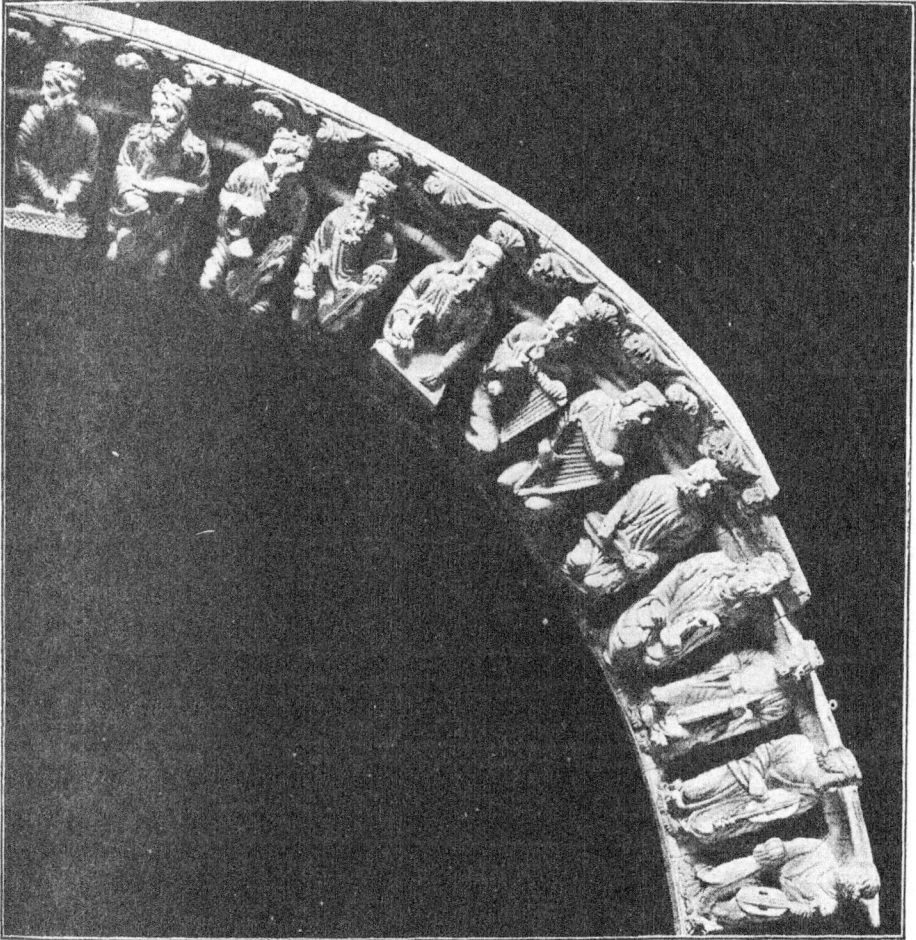

Fig. 118. The right half of the arch over the church door of S. Iago. 11th-12th century.

In mediæval pictures the psaltery appears in countless forms; but if we examine them more closely we find that they are chiefly variations of the two main oriental forms described above: the kanun and the santir. Only in a few cases does the method of pictorial reproduction leave us in any doubt as to what kind of psaltery is meant. Thus, on the famous church door of S. Iago (Spain) there is among the twenty-four performing figures of the Revelation of St. John, one who twangs a flat horizontal stringed instrument with his left hand; an instrument that belongs decidedly to the psaltery family, though its true outlines cannot be made out since the arm of the performer covers part of the sound-box (see Fig. 118, fifth figure from the top).

Fig. 119. Fourteenth century Kanun. Painting by Francesco Traini.

We recognise without hesitation, however, the oriental kanun type in Francesco Traini's famous painting, "Il Trionfo della morte" (fourteenth century) in the Campo Santo at Pisa (see Fig. 119). The kanun described by Jean de Muris (circa 1300) in "Musica speculativa," and by him treated with the musical scientific apparatus, had clearly enough the same form: "This instrument has nineteen strings and comprises a double octave and a fifth. The two sides form a right angle, the third passes through three points (i.e., forms an obtuse angle so that the outline of the whole instrument is a trapezium); it may, however, also have other outlines and be either round or concave. This instrument, so to speak, comprises in itself all others." In the Traini picture we are surprised only at the position of the instrument. When this type of kanun was played by the Arab in Fig. 117, he had it flat on his lap; the mediaeval European painter on the other hand had it played in an upright position, the longer of the parallel sides running horizontally beneath the chin of the player, while the opposite short side of the instrument rests on her knees. In all other respects the instrument agrees with the model. The tuning pegs are placed in the oblique side of the sound-box and the strings are arranged in groups, fifteen in all, each with four strings. This kanun has five sound-holes, a large "rose" in the centre, three small roses along the upper edge of the sound-box, and a fourth immediately below the central rose. The horizontal instrument in Fig. 120 is also decidedly a kanun. In this case the noticeable features are the shortness of the strings and the placing of the pegs on the straight side of the sound-box. Like the oriental kanun, this instrument was played with both hands; but whether the forefingers were armed with the above mentioned plectra cannot be seen. I am inclined to consider the instrument reproduced in Fig. 121 as a modified kanun. The sharp corner which generally separates the oblique side of ·the trapezium from the shorter of the parallel sides, is here rounded off, so that the sound-box has the form of a segment. The strings are arranged in groups (four by four) and are twanged with the fingers of the right hand, while the left merely holds the instrument.

Compared with the kanun the variations of the santir occupy a far more prominent place in the mediaeval pictures. In some of these varieties the sides of the sound-box are so slightly oblique that the outline approaches the oblong rather than the blunt triangular form. Such an oblong psaltery is seen in Fig. 122, which gives another of the numerous instances of the mediaeval psaltery being placed on edge and played from the side. One of the shorter sides of the instrument is pressed

Fig. 121. Rounded Kanun (13th cent. From the same MS.)

Fig. 120. Spanish Kanun (13th cent. MS., " Cantingas di Santa Maria," Madrid).

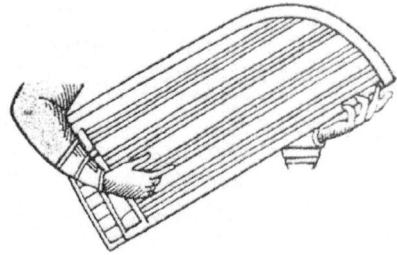

against the breast of the performer, while the opposite side with the pegs points forward. The right hand plucks the strings with a small plectrum which is tied to the instrument by a ribbon, while the left arm, supported by the drawn-up left knee, holds the psaltery in position. This santir has five sound-holes—the large central rose and four small ones placed in the four corners of the sound-box. The psaltery shown in Fig. 123 has almost the same form and design. It is somewhat larger in size, it is true; but the pegs are placed on the same side, the sound-holes are arranged in the same manner, and it is played in the same way. In this case the larger size of the instrument obliges the player to sit, so that one edge of the sound-box rests on his knees. The instrument rises like a wall before the body of the player and is held by his left hand on the top edge. The square psaltery reproduced in a twelfth-century Danish manuscript is very small, and is shown in Fig. 124. The small size of the picture has, of course, prevented the artist from including all the details. Of the sound-holes only the usual large central rose is seen, and of the strings only

Fig. 122. Square Psaltery in an ivory painting belonging to the Chapter at Würzburg, 12th-13th cent.

Fig. 123. Square Psaltery in "Cantingas di Santa Maria," 13th cent.

seven single ones are included. The model for this square psaltery was without doubt the larger and more richly strung instrument seen in Fig. 125, which represents a regular santir-type, the shortest straight side being scalloped decoratively.

The psalteries fashionable during the Middle Ages, and which for a time displaced most other forms, were of a highly ornamental type. Fundamentally it was a triangular instrument with incurved sides. In 1620 Prætorius stated that its popular name in Italy was *Istromento di porco*, and in Germany "*ein Sau- oder Schweinekopff*"; Ludovico de Victoria calls it *Istromento di Laurento*, and Guiseppe Zarlino refers

Fig. 124. Small square Psaltery (?). MS. in the Thott Collection, fol. 143. 12th cent. (Royal Library, Copenhagen.)

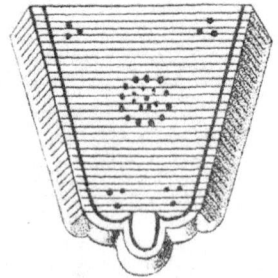

Fig. 125. Santir with rounded point. MS. in Nat. Libr., Paris.

Fig. 126. Istromento di Porco. British Museum MS. Add. 30045. 11th cent.

to it as *Istromento di alto basso*. I found the earliest example of this type in an eleventh-century manuscript in the British Museum (Add. 30045; see Fig. 126). This instrument has nine strings and is provided with two large and two smaller sound-holes. It rests in the lap of a king (David?), who blows a horn and at the same time plays with a staff on a number of

150

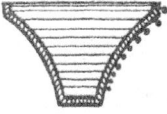

Fig. 127. *Istromento di porco* in Add. MS. 16975, British Museum, 12th cent. Drawn from the original.

Fig. 128. Sculpture on the great gate of Amiens Cathedral. 13th cent. (Didron, " Annales archéologique," IX.)

Fig. 129. Relief by Lucca della Robbia in the Opera del Duomo in Florence. 14th cent.

bells hung from a stand. Here the sides are evenly rounded inwards near the blunt point of the triangle, while they are generally sharply concave after having first been drawn somewhat forward in a straight or oblique direction from the broad end (see Figs. 127-129). In Fig. 126 the narrow end of the sound-box is drawn out so much that the instrument almost has the shape of a top hat. In its more normal form, i.e., as it is most commonly drawn, the *Istromento di porco* is shown in Fig. 129, where five of them are used to accompany the singing. The psaltery is here played with both hands: three of the figures support it against the breast, the fourth allows it to hang downwards, while the fifth places it in the Oriental manner flat on the lap. The first mode seems to be the one most commonly used, and in most cases the hands then pluck the strings with two plectra (see Fig. 130). A late instance of this *Istromento di porco* is shown in Fig. 131, taken from Prætorius's "Syntagmatis Musici" (*Tom. Sec.*, 1618). It is here called "ein gar alt italienisch Instrument," and strangely enough, it still has the same shape as when it first made its appearance in the eleventh-century pictures (see Fig. 126), except that the sound-holes are here reduced to a single large rose in the centre of the sound-box. Prætorius's description of the instrument, which in his time was obsolescent, runs thus: "In the curves there are pegs at both sides; on one side they are made of white bone and are somewhat longer than the iron pegs used in the clavicymbalum. In the middle of each of them is a hole through which the string passes. On the other side the pegs are made of wood. There are generally thirty strings, each longer than the other."

In its regular form, as a triangle with a truncated point, but with straight sides, the santır-type may be traced in Europe up to the seventeenth century. From the fifteenth century onwards this type was taken up especially by amateurs, and it was very fashionable throughout Europe. While the psalteries in the older mediæval pictures were everywhere played with the fingers or with bent plectra, it gradually became usual to use small hammers or beaters. The hammer-heads were generally covered with felt on one side in order to vary the tone. When playing *forte* the strings were struck with the

Fig. 130. *Istromento di porco*, played with two plectra; Ely Cathedral. 14th cent. (Carter, "Specimens of Ancient Sculpture and Painting.")

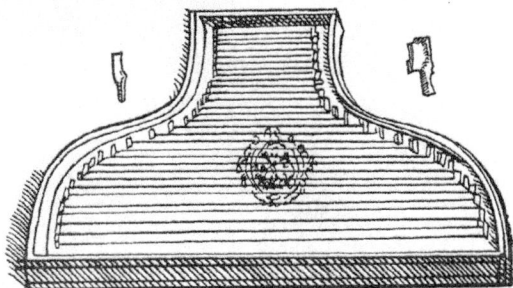

Fig. 131. *Istromento di porco*. Prætorius, "Syntagmatis Musici," 1618.

hard side of the hammer, and when playing *piano* the other side was used. Here it seems that Germany took the lead. In Italy, where both methods of playing were in .vogue, a distinction was made between the *Salterio tedesco* (German psaltery), which was played with hammers, and the ordinary *Salterio* which was played with plectra. In Germany the hammer-psaltery was called the *Hackbrett* (owing to the sound-box being treated like a chopping-board); in England it was called the dulcimer. Nowadays the use of the psaltery, played with beaters, is confined to gipsy bands.

As a late example of the mediæval triangular psaltery (santir-type) I reproduce (Fig. 132) a French specimen from Mersenne's "Harmonie Universelle" (1636), as still used in France in the seventeenth century. According to this picture

the instrument had the normal santir form : a triangle with a
blunt point; but Mersenne indicated the constant fluctuation
in the shape, saying that "the triangle may be equilateral,
isosceles, or how you like." The figures seen on the right of

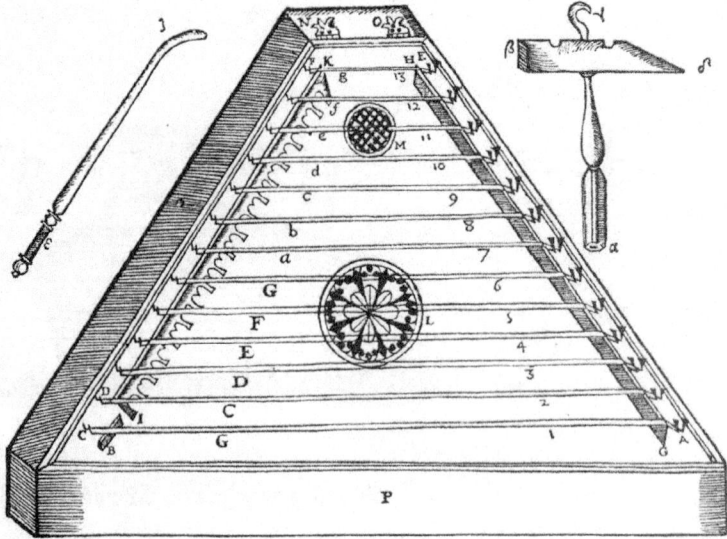

Fig. 132. French triangular psaltery, 17th cent. From Mersenne,
"Harmonie Universelle."

the picture, on the sound-board, number the strings (which are
bichord, in unison): G, c, d, e, f, g, a, b, c′, d′, e′, f′, g′.
The string of lowest pitch rests on a bridge of its own on the
left, indicated in the picture by B; on the right it passes over
a long fillet—G-H—which on this side runs paralled with the
side and beneath all the strings, having its counterpart in
another fillet—I-K—which runs below the strings c to g′ on the
left. All the strings are attached to iron nails on the left side,
while on the right they are inserted into pegs which, like the
tuning-pegs of the pianoforte, are tuned by means of a tuning-
hammer (seen on the right of the instrument). The two longest
pairs of strings are of brass, the rest of steel. M and L show
the two sound-holes cut into the sound-box. The instrument
is played with two beaters like the one shown on the left of

the instrument. The hand holds the shaft and strikes the strings with the bent end, "which must fall lightly on the strings so that it springs, thus producing a pulsating tone." Mersenne is therefore of opinion "that the instrument in a way may be placed among the instruments of percussion, although it may be played with a feather or with the fingers like the harp, the mandora, or the cittern." The letter P indicates the depth of the instrument. It was made in all sizes, "but is generally only one foot each way, so that it may be portable." The lid is attached to the two small iron nails N and O, and with it the psaltery was covered when not in use.

Before leaving the mediæval triangular psaltery, I should draw attention to a few mediæval variations which arose by halving the original shape and which explain the meaning of

Fig. 133. Spanish demi-santir, 14th cent. (Juan Riano, " Notes on Early Spanish Music.")

Fig. 134. *Demi-istromento di porco.* 13th cent., Naples. (Serout d'Agincourt, 'Histoire de l'Art.")

the affix *demi* often used in literature, such as *demi-kanun.* The first of these varieties is seen in Fig. 133, showing the right half of an ordinary santir. All explanation of the design is rendered superfluous by the extraordinarily careful drawing. In order to keep the three strings which formed a group in tune, the oblique side of the triangular sound-box is stepped, so that the three tuning-pegs belonging to each note form a group on their own step.

Fig. 134 shows one-half of the incurved *Istromento di porco*, and it is of interest only because we recognise in it the origin of the modern grand pianoforte. Unlike the example in Fig. 133, which is played with a plectrum, this psaltery is plucked by the fingers only.

The Harp-Psalteries. In the mediæval pictures we often find a stringed instrument which has the shape of the harp, is held like a harp, but is arranged as a psaltery with a sound-box under the strings.

Early instances of the harp-psaltery are, in my opinion, included on the church-door of Sant' Iago (see Fig. 118) and on a door of St. George's Church at Bocherville, Normandy. In the former the instrument takes a place between a horizontal santir and a real harp, and in reality seems to be a hybrid between these two instruments. In common with the harp, it has the perpendicular strings, while the outline rather recalls a psaltery of the santir type. In the latter, too, where the presence of the sound-box under the strings is clearly indicated by a number of round sound-holes, the instrument at first glance resembles a santir placed on edge so that the strings are perpendicular. Nevertheless this confirms my assumption that in both of these cases they are harp-psalteries. In the Bocherville relief the perpendicular position of the strings cannot, I am sure, be accidental, for the instrument is being played and is therefore held in that position intentionally. As we have seen, the psaltery, whether it was held erect or flat, was always held so that the strings were horizontal in playing.

The first two undoubted examples of the harp-psaltery appeared in a German manuscript, now destroyed: Herrad v. Landsperg's "Hortus deliciarum," of the twelfth century.

The original was owned as late as 1870 by the University Library of Strassbourg, but was burned during the Franco-German war. Consequently only two copies exist now. One of them was published in 1818, together with explanatory

Fig. 135. Harp-Psaltery in Herrad v. Landsperg's "Hortus Deliciarum," 12th cent.

comments by C. M. Engelhardt, who still had the original at his disposal, while the other, partly from Engelhardt's copy and partly from a number of still existing drawings, was published in 1878 by Keller and Straub. Both the form and position of the harp are wholly preserved in the picture reproduced as Fig. 135. In this a harpy is playing a harp, the eleven strings of which are completely backed by a sound-box which renders it impossible to manipulate from more than one side. While the right hand plucks the strings from the front, the left merely holds the instrument by the back. The side of the harp which generally forms the sound-box, rests in the right arm of the performer, while the side carrying the tuning-pegs, and which represents the harp-arm, lies against her chin. The wrest hangs by a long ribbon beyond the longest string.

Fig. 136. King David with a Harp-Psaltery. From H. v. Landsperg's "Hortus Deliciarum," 12th cent. MS.

In Fig. 136 the same instrument is seen in the hands of King David: "David Rex, Psalterium dodeca cordum" being inscribed in the picture. In this case the psaltery is not being played, but only tuned; and that is why it is held in a position different from the normal. One long side of the instrument rests on the knees of the performer, so that the board (harp-arm) leans perpendicularly against his body. In this position he can handle the wrest more easily with the right hand. In his new edition of the manuscript, it is true, Straub maintains that the appliance which David holds in his right hand is not a wrest, but a metal grip, fixed to the soundbox and serving only to keep the instrument in position; but in my opinion this explanation is contradicted by the very manner in which the instrument is placed. When the harppsaltery was played, it was invariably held as in Fig. 135, i.e., as a harp, nor is the plectrum carried in the left hand, but in the right. That the appliance is a wrest is proved by the circumstance that the left hand with the plectrum is actually testing the tuning of the string against the peg of which the tool is directly applied. Finally, there is a striking resemblance between this supposed "metal grip" and the tuning-hammer which hangs from the harp-psaltery in Fig. 135. As Straub only had Engelhardt's older copy for this picture, his assumption rests in reality on an unsafe basis. Engelhardt (Herrad v. Landsperg's "Hortus Deliciarum; ein Beitrag zur Geschichte der Kunst u. Wissenschaft," etc., 1818), who still had the original picture before him, sees in the article a tuning-hammer, as I do. As will appear from the copy of Engelhardt's reproduction, the pegs on this harp-psaltery were arranged in two series, which indicates a bichord stringing. Judging by the legend *dodeca cordum* there should have been twelve pairs of strings, but on the design we find only twice ten strings plus one—twenty-one in all.

From the thirteenth century onwards the harp-psaltery is also found in Spanish and French pictures. Figs. 137 and 138 are again taken from the Spanish manuscript, "Cantingas di Santa Maria," mentioned earlier; and both show the same harp-psaltery possibly viewed from both sides. At any rate, one performer has the right hand and the other the left hand on the strings. In both instruments we see a large round sound-hole in the centre of the sound-box, and round the edges a quantity of fine decoration, crosses and curves. In Fig. 137

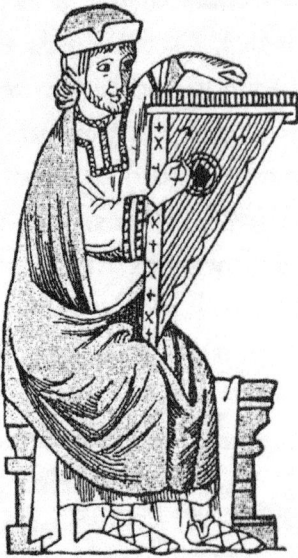

Fig. 137. Harp-psaltery of the 13th cent. From the Spanish MS., "Cantingas di Santa Maria."

Fig. 138. The other side of the same instrument.

the instrument is being tuned. A tuning-hammer is applied by the left hand of the player to one of the tuning-pegs, probably the one belonging to the string being struck by the fine plectrum in the right hand. In Fig. 138 the harp-psaltery is being played; and as the left here carries the plectrum and the other is hidden behind the instrument, it is probable that the sound-box in this case is strung on both sides, so that one hand can pluck the strings on each side. In this manner the instrument resembles the harp in a still higher degree. This finds further support in Figs. 139 and 140, reproducing two French harp-psalteries, each showing a different side. These two instruments exhibit a striking resemblance to the harp, for the side holding the tuning-pegs is bent like a harp-arm in both pictures. Fig. 140 even looks exactly like a harp with an inlaid sound-box, as the latter, the harp-arm, and the pillar, are all clearly separate from the underlying sound-board, which, moreover, only partially fills the string-space and is quite devoid of sound-holes. In Fig. 139, where the sound-board entirely fills the frame, there are four roses of equal size.

Fig. 139. French Harp-Psaltery (in MS. 9025; Royal Library, Brussels).

Fig. 140. French Harp-Psaltery (in MS. 9002; Royal Library, Brussels).

An unusual example of the harp-psaltery is seen in Fig. 141. It appears to have been an attempt to create a psaltery out of one of the above transitional instruments between the lyre and the harp.

A late descendant of the harp-psaltery was the "wire-harp" which was fashionable in the seventeenth and eighteenth centuries. The form resembled that of a kanun placed on edge, so that the point stood upwards. Like the kanun, it was played with small plectra attached to the fingers. The wire-harp had two sound-boards, one of which had steel strings, the other brass; and the strings were generally arranged in groups of two or three. When played, this harp, which was about three feet high, was placed on a table so that the sound-board carrying the steel strings (the treble) rested against the right hand of the performer, while the opposite side bearing the brass strings, was to the left (see Fig. 142).

Fig. 141. Unusual intermediate form between lyre, harp and psaltery (Welislavian Bible; Prince Lobkowitz Library, Prague).

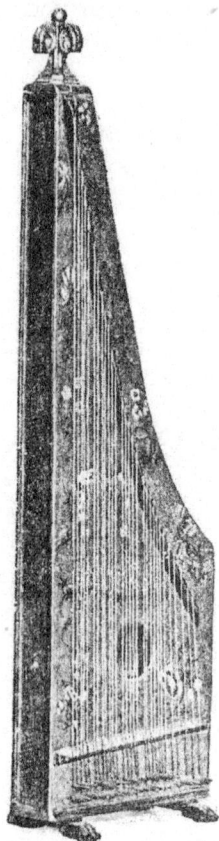

Fig. 142. Wire-harp in the Mus. Hist. Museum, Copenhagen. (A. Hammerich, Catalogue of the Museum.)

In the fifteenth century an attempt was made to attach a keyboard to the psaltery, thereby providing the basis of the *clavicembal*, one of the keyboard instruments preceding the pianoforte, alias the Hammer-spinet. The other ancestor of the pianoforte, the clavichord, was developed from the monochord, which, belonging to the finger-board instruments, will not be dealt with in this section. Only a very small part of the history of the keyboard instruments belongs, strictly speaking, to the Middle Ages Nevertheless, as obsolete forerunners of the modern pianoforte, both the clavicembal and the clavichord deserve to be remembered in this work, and they will therefore be treated in a supplementary chapter later on.

As a stringed instrument played by plucking, the name of the Psaltery, as mentioned above, is already present in the old Greek literature; but it does not appear with certainty whether it applied in antiquity to a special type of instrument or was used as a generic name for several kinds of stringed instruments (see p. 83). The word is explained in somewhat more definite terms by the earliest authors of the Christian era. Both St. Augustine and St. Hieronymus were of opinion that the difference between the psaltery and the cythara of antiquity lay in the fact that the sound-box of the psaltery was over the strings, but under them in the cythara. At the same time Hieronymus explained the psaltery as a square stringed instrument, and looked upon its four corners and ten strings as symbols of the four evangelists and the Ten Commandments ("Epist. ad Dardanum"). Cassiodorus and St. Isidorus ("Origines"), on the other hand, like the majority of the ancient Greek authors, give the psaltery the shape of the Greek △.

In Latin manuscripts dating from the ninth to the twelfth century we repeatedly find under the name of *psalterium* a kind of triangular or square instrument which gives a curious impression of being unfinished, but which on closer examination sometimes fits in with one, sometimes another, of the descriptions already given of the psaltery. The comments attached, moreover, leave no doubt whatever that these pictures of instruments were merely based upon tradition, and are consequently quite worthless from an historical point of view. Foremost among "these lucubrations of the imagination of the mediæval monks" (Ambros) is a reproduction of a psalterium in a French manuscript at Boulogne-sur-Mer (ninth century). Under the title "Hic est David, Filius Jesse, tenens

Psalterium in Manibus suis, hæc est Forma Psalterii," we find a square instrument which evidently consists of an open frame and which, according to the recipe of St. Augustine and St. Hieronymus, is built with a large sound-box over it and has ten strings. It rests on a frame, and is manipulated with both hands (see Fig. 143). Two instruments of the same kind are reproduced in a manuscript in the Royal Library at Stuttgart (tenth century). One of them is seen in Fig. 144.

Fig. 144. Similar instrument in a MS. at Stuttgart.

Fig. 143. So-called *Psalterium* in a MS. at Boulogne (9th cent.).

In the so-called Emmeraner Codex (tenth century) the "psalterium" is seen both in the square form and as a right-angled triangle; and with the latter is the inscription, "alii psalterium sic pingunt in modum Deltæ litteræ." There is also a twenty-four stringed instrument of the same form entitled "Cythara ut Hieronymus dicitur in Modum deltæ litteræ cum XXIV cordis."

Further reproductions of triangular and square psalteries with similar titles are to be found in the twelfth-century Codex of St. Blasius (Gerbert, "De Cantu et Musica Sacra"; see Figs. 145 and 146); and a Delta-shaped "Psalterium" in an English manuscript (Edwin's Psalter in Cambridge; same period) must, I am sure, be referred to the same category of reproductions (see the vignette on p. 85).

Quidā pſalreriv̄ imodū delte·
litere   ſic pingunt

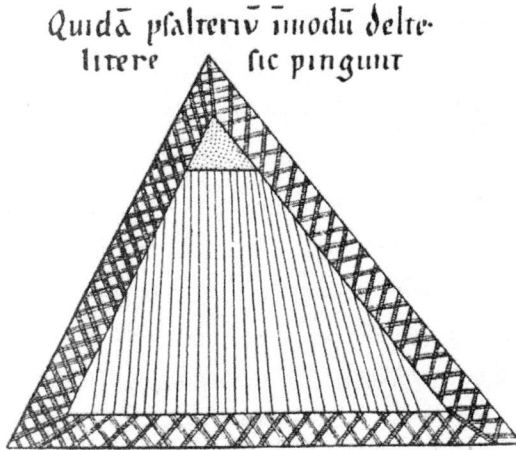

Fig. 145.   Delta-shaped "Psalterium" in a MS. at St. Blasius. Gerbert, "De Cantu et Musica Sacra."

pſalreriv
decacord   imodū
vm   clypei
              q̃dran.

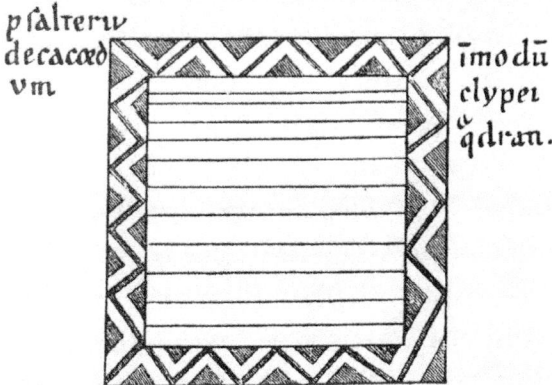

Fig. 146.   Square Psalterium. From the same source.

Some of the earlier musical historians have accepted these fantastic pictures in spite of everything. The beginning was made by Sebastian Virdung who, *ca.* 1511, in his "Musica getutscht," copied St. Hieronymus's instruments which he had seen in a large parchment "which his teacher, the late Johannes de Zusato, D.M., had written and composed." Prætorius took the pictures from Virdung into his "Syntagmatis Musici" (1618), and thence they wandered into the "Musurgia" of Athanasius Kircher, and Forkel's "History of Music," etc.

The next question is what was actually the nature of the stringed instrument which was used in the tenth century in the convent-schools under the name of Psalterium. The common-est source of information on this head, and the one most fre-quently quoted, is the one which occurs at the end of a copy of the hymns of Notker, written at St. Gall: "Sciendum est quod antiquum psalterium, instrumentum decachordum utique erat in hac videlicet deltæ literæ figura multipliciter mystica. Sed postquam illud symphoniaci et ludicratores ut quidam ait ad suum opus traxerunt, formam utique ejus et figuram commodi-tati suæ habilem fecerunt et plures chordas anectentes et nomine barbarico rottam appellantes, mysticam illam trinitatis formam transmutando."

This passage, which thus explains *rotta* as an improved edition of the old Biblical psalterium, is generally ascribed to Notker himself by those who quote it, but a closer examination led to the assumption long ago that this description was a later addition made by another. My source of information here is the article already quoted, by I. F. W. Wewerten in "Monats-hefte für Musikgeschichte," XIII, 1881; "Zwei veraltete Musikinstrumente." For in another copy of the same work at Vienna, the quotation does not appear. As both the hand-writing and the colour of the ink on this last leaf of the copy match the rest of the manuscript, and as this final sentence has no logical connection whatever with what goes before, it is sup-posed that it was the twelfth-century copyist who used the last blank sheet for noting down a conception which was either his own or was possibly current at the time. The other rather numerous passages in the manuscript where *Psalterium* and *Rotta* are identified, also give the impression of being later additions. Wherever Notker in his translation of the psalms mentions the psalterium, we find written in parenthesis above the text the word "Rotta." There remains only one sentence which is really placed in the body of the text and in plain words says: "Das Saltirsanch heizet nu in dutiscan rotta" ("The psalterium is now called rotta in German"), and here there is, it is true, a basis for the hypothesis advanced by Wewertem, that the copyist, by a mistake in this case, allowed the explanation to slip into the text when logically it ought to have been placed above it. If this supposition is correct, there remains only one authentic piece of information from the hand of Notker himself; for to the twenty-second verse of Psalm LXXI, where we read: "I will also praise Thee with the psaltery, Even Thy truth, O my God," he adds the traditional explanation: "*Psalterium* habet obenan buh, dannen gânt nider die seiten quasi cœlestis prædicatio, áber *Cythara* hábet nidenan bûh." But this information again applies clearly to the Biblical psalterium, as word for word it repeats the description given by St. Augustine and St. Hieronymus. This exhausts the evidence hitherto used in defence of the assumption that the *psalterium* and the *rotta* were the same instrument; and I fear that we shall have to give up all hope of learning anything from a contemporaneous source, as to the nature of the instrument which before the introduction of the Oriental *psalteria* was known in the convent-schools by a name inherited from antiquity. Not until the moment at which the Oriental forms of the psalterium—santir and kanun—were introduced into Europe at the time of the Crusades, does the name "psalterium" become an established term. The resemblance between the traditional antique Græco-Latin name and that of the Oriental santir was probably the reason that the old familiar classical name was transferred without further ado to the new instrument, and thus *psalterium*, through the variants *salterium*, *salterion*, *saltère*, *salteire*, in common with the kanun and the demi-kanun, acquired the definite meaning of a harp-instrument with a sound-board under the strings. Fétis in his "Recherches sur la musique des rois de France au Moyen Age" ("Revue Mus.," 1832, No. 25, *f.*) stated that the French kings had special musicians to play the strange Oriental instruments, *psalterion, canon*, and *demi-canon*. While the new instrument in the David pictures replaced the so-called Biblical psalterium, it was from now onward inseparable in literature from the lists of names belonging to the instruments used by minstrels and jongleurs. From the pens of the troubadours, Guirault de Calanson, the king of Navarre (Thibaut), the Spanish poet, Juan Ruiz (Archbishop of Hita), and Eberhard Cersne (author of the celebrated rules of the Minnesingers, 1404), there are such lists of jongleurs' instruments (see Vol. II, p. 98, Ambros, "Gesch. d. Mus."; II, Supplement). That the psalterium was also brought to the Scandinavian countries by the minstrels, is proved by the following quotations from the later Scandinavian saga-literature.

Gangerolf's saga (in the opinion of Prof. F. Jonsson not much later than 1300) has: "Many kinds of stringed instruments were heard; harps and gigues, sinfon and salterium; drums were beaten and whistles were blown." In Sigurd Jorsalfar's saga we read: "They use fireworks partly learnt by witchcraft; they also use all kinds of instruments: organ, simfon and salterium, harps and gigues, and all sorts of stringed instruments." Jókul Bue's saga contributes: "Marcibilla was brought into the hall with all the entertainment possible in this country," a statement expanded in later manuscripts by the list of instruments: "Psalteria, flutes, gigues, symfons, lutes and harps, organs and drums." The psalterium referred to in the sagas is, of course, the instrument used all over Europe at that time by the wandering minstrels.

From another Nordic literary source, on the other hand, we have a description of a psalterium which was evidently somewhat removed from the ordinary European orchestra. This psalterium is the *Kantele*, the ancient Finnish national instrument, the invention of which is placed by tradition in legendary times. While the psalteria described above could only be explained by the pictures, it is solely on the evidence of the legends that we must find our way to the details of the mediæval kantele. Our chief source here is the great Finnish folkpoem, "Kalevala," for the original examples of this kind of psalterium still existing, are comparatively late, the oldest of them being dated 1600. "Kalevala" consists of a number of ancient popular poems, which were collected at the beginning of the nineteenth century among the Finnish peasantry by whom they had hitherto been handed down verbally from father to son. According to expert opinion, this series of songs accumulated in the course of six hundred years. The earliest specimens date back, it is thought, to the eighth century, the latest to the fourteenth. As the kantele is not mentioned until the fortieth of the fifty songs, it is thought that its invention or introduction into Finland may be placed in the twelfth or thirteenth century.

The kantele in the "Kalevala" songs plays a similar part as the lyre in ancient Greek legend, and the cruit in old Celtic history; for popular superstition allows all stringed instruments to arise from it.

When the three Kalevala heroes, Wäinämöinen, Ilmarinen and Lemminkäinen, were sailing to Pohjola in order to steal the *Sampo quern*, the boat was stopped by the "mighty pike" which Wäinämöinen killed and cut to pieces. While looking at the teeth and jaws of the monster and considering to what use they could be put, he exclaimed:

> "Might a magic harp be fashioned,
> Could an artist be discovered
> That could shape them to my wishes."

(J. M. Crawford, "The Kalevala," New York, 1889.)

Wäinämöinen then fashioned the harp himself:

> "Set himself at work designing:
> Quick became a fish-bone artist,
> Made a harp of wondrous beauty,
> Lasting joy and pride of Suomi.
> Whence the harp's enchanting arches?

From the jaw-bones of the monster.
Whence the necessary harp-pins?
From the pike-teeth firmly fastened.
Whence the sweetly singing harp-strings?
From the tail of Lempo's stallion."

"and," the poem adds, "thus was born the harp of magic."
People of all ages and both sexes came to see the stringed instrument. Wäinämöinen offered them the pike-bone instrument to try:

"Wäinämöinen, ancient minstrel,
Let the aged try the harp-strings,
Gave it to the young magicians . . .
When the young men touched the harp-strings,
Then arose the notes of discord;
When the aged played upon it,
Dissonance their only music."

Lemminkäinen mocked them and said:

"Hither bring the harp of fish-bones,
Let me try my skilful fingers."

Nor could he make the harp sound better. Then Wäinämöinen said:

"Let us take the harp to Pohya,
There to find a skilful player."

The harp is then sent to Pohjola, but even there they did not
succeed in playing it properly:

"Could not find the notes of joyance,
Dissonance their only pleasure;
Shrieked the harp-strings like the whirlwinds,
All the tones were harsh and frightful."

A blind old man lying on the stove in the corner of the room
leaped to his feet and complained of the awful sounds. He
counselled them either to throw the harp into the sea or to hand
it back to the master. The harp was then taken back to Wäinämöinen:

"Wäinämöinen, ancient minstrel,
The eternal wisdom-singer,
Laves his hands to snowy whiteness,
Sits upon the rock of joyance,
On the stone of song he settles,
On the mount of silver clearness,
On the summit, golden coloured;
Takes the harp by him created,
In his hands the harp of fish-bone,

With his knee the arch supporting,
Takes the harp-strings in his fingers,
Speaks these words to those assembled :
' Hither come, ye Northland people,
Come and listen to my playing,
To the harp's entrancing measures,
To my songs of joy and gladness.'
Then the singer of Wäinola
Took the harp of his creation,
Quick adjusting, sweetly tuning,
Deftly plied his skilful fingers
To the strings that he had fashioned.
Now was gladness rolled on gladness,
And the harmony of pleasure
Echoed from the hills and mountains ;
Added singing to his playing,
Out of joy did joy come welling,
Now resounded marvellous music.
Every creature in the forest
Came to listen to his playing,
Came to hear his songs of joyance."

The poem then alludes to all the animals of the forest, the air, and the water. Even the sea-king, Ahto, rises from the depths to listen to the music. But, says the poem, all—both men and women—wept, so wonderful was the song and so beautiful the playing of the old man. Wäinämöinen himself was moved to tears; they fell into the sea and were transformed into pearls "shining and clear." When the "Kalevala" heroes finally reached Pohjola, Wäinämöinen took out his pike-bone harp and sat down to play. All listened and fell asleep. The heroes then stole the quern and started homewards. But on the voyage a storm overtook them, and the kantele fell out of the boat and sank. Wäinämöinen looked in vain for his lost harp in the water. Wandering full of sorrow through a grove, he heard the wailing of a birch-tree. Wäinämöinen consoled the birch, saying :

" I will turn thy grief to joyance,
Make thee laugh and sing with gladness . . .
Then the ancient Wäinämöinen
Made a harp from sacred birch-wood,
Fashioned in the days of summer,
Beautiful the harp of magic,

> By the master's hand created . . .
> Fashioned from the birch the archings,
> And the framework from the aspen."

Later on he asked:

> "Whence the hooks and pins for tuning,
> That the harp may sing in concord?"

> "Near the wayside grew an oak-tree,
> On each twig an acorn growing,
> Golden balls upon each acorn,
> On each ball a singing cuckoo.
> As each cuckoo's call resounded,
> From each throat came liquid music,
> Gold and silver for the master.
> Thence he took the merry harp-pins,
> That the harp might play in concord."

> "Spake again wise Wäinämöinen:
> 'I the pins have well completed,
> Still the harp is yet unfinished;
> Now I need five strings for playing,
> Where shall I procure the harp-strings?'"

He goes into the grove to seek the strings and finds a maiden.

> "In the hope that her beloved,
> Would the sooner sit beside her."

Wäinämöinen steals upon her barefoot and asks her for a lock of hair:

> "Give me, maiden, of thy tresses,
> Give me of thy golden ringlets;
> I will weave them into harp-strings,
> To the joy of Wäinämöinen.
> Thereupon the forest maiden
> Gave the singer of her tresses,
> Gave him of her golden ringlets,
> And of these he made the harp-strings,
> Sources of eternal pleasure
> To the people of Wäinola."

So Wäinämöinen obtained his harp, his new kantele made of birch:

> "Thus the sacred harp is finished,
> And the minstrel, Wäinämöinen,
> Sits upon the rock of joyance,
> Takes the harp within his fingers,
> Turns the arch up, looking skyward;
> With his knee the arch supporting,
> Sets the strings in tuneful order,
> Runs his fingers o'er the harp-strings,
> And the notes of pleasure follow.
> Straightway ancient Wäinämöinen,

The eternal wisdom-singer,
Plays upon his harp of birch-wood.
Far away is heard the music,
Wide the harp of joy re-echoes,
Mountains dance and valleys listen,
Flinty rocks are torn asunder,
Stones are hurled upon the waters,
Pebbles swim upon the Big Sea,
Pines and lindens laugh with pleasure,
Alders skip about the heather,
And the aspen sways in concord " . . .

" All the daughters of **Wäinolo**
Straightway leave their shining needles,
Hasten forward like the current,
Speed along like rapid rivers,
That they may enjoy and wonder.
Laugh the younger men and maidens,
To enjoy the common pleasure."

In these extracts from the " Kalevala " the kantele first appears as the primitive natural instrument, made of natural materials accidentally found, namely, the jaws of the great pike (for the sound-box), its teeth (for the pegs) and the mane or tail-hair of the horse (for the strings). When this first kantele was lost, Wäinämöinen made another which already possessed more of the character of an artistic instrument, and it is therefore probable that this part of the poem dates from a period when culture was in a more advanced state. The sound-box was this time made of birch, the pegs were fashioned of the gold falling from the tongue of the cuckoo, the five, six, or seven strings were braided out of a maiden's hair. It is also interesting to collect what was said in the two periods on the manner of playing the kantele. The performer sat down and placed the instrument across his knees, under his hands and finger-tips. From this it appears that in the "Kalevala " it was a psalterium lying horizontally, with strings which were plucked from above, and not a harp in the modern sense of the word. Before Wäinämöinen began to play, he carefully tuned the strings and brought them in accord with one another; he then placed his fingers in position and moistened his two thumbs. While playing, he allowed his "ten nails, five of his finger-tips," to touch the strings and run up and down the "harp." He played with a light touch, the fingers being actively lifted and the thumbs bent outwards.

Bearing the evidence of the legend in mind, let us now proceed to examine the kantele, which in modern Finland is identified with the stringed instrument invented by Wäinämöinen, and which on several important points (such as the number of strings, the material of the sound-box, etc.) actually agrees with the description given in the saga of the composition of the original kantele.

The shape of this musical instrument reminds us of the Oriental kanun in so far as the sound-box of birch or pine is cut off obliquely at the end which carries the pegs. The fewness of its strings, however, causes the sound-box of the kantele to be relatively narrow and more oblong in form, while the fan-like arrangement of the strings results in the instrument being narrower at the base than at the upper, or peg, end. Strangely enough, this form is repeated in the ancient Chinese psalterium—*Kin*—which, like the oldest Finnish kanteles, has only five strings, "the symbol of the five fingers of man." One of these instruments is in the ethnographic department of the National Museum, Copenhagen. In a discourse on the amusements and pastimes of the ancient Finns, Jacob Tengström said in 1795 that the old Finnish kantele was "nearly three hands long and one hand broad at the lower end, but somewhat less at the upper end, and as thick as an ordinary violin."

In the sound-board five round sound-holes were formerly arranged in the form of a cross (see Fig. 148); in later examples they were replaced by a cut cross, and in the latest by a large round rose and a small heart-shaped hole at the narrow end of the sound-box. In the oldest specimens (in the Museum at Helsingfors) the sound-box itself is hollowed out of one piece of wood, and is open (see Fig. 147); later the hollow was covered with a thin wooden plate (see Fig. 148); finally, the modern kantele is, like the ordinary psalterium, made of a table and back, with broad connecting ribs. The strings, which are of brass and arranged in the order of their decreasing length, were formerly, when the kantele had five strings, tuned to g′, a′, b flat′, c″ and d″, "but with the B flat slightly flatter than the true minor third of G minor" (Tengström). As the

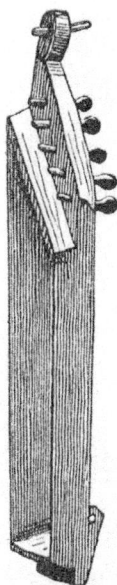

Fig. 147. Oldest type of Kantele with five strings, but without table. From the district of Ilomants in Karelen (one-ninth natural size).

Fig. 148. Kantele with five strings and table. From the same neighbourhood. One-ninth natural size. (Gustav Retzius, "Finska Kranier.")

kantele later acquired more strings (six to thirteen) the sound-box was made broader. A modern example, which I received from Uleåborg has thirty-one steel strings and has the shape of a harp.

In the "Kalevala" the kantele is chiefly used as a solo instrument; but that the Finns used it to accompany their singing also appears from the records of the traditional Finnish "Rune-song." "If there was a clever player," writes Tengström, "he was always ready to support the singer with notes and chords, and sometimes he took the place of the regular accompanist."

In modern Finland the kantele is extremely rare, at any rate, in its genuine old form. Gustav Retzius travelled all over Finland forty years ago in the hope of finding it, but not until he reached Ilomants in Karelen did he hear of an old man who still owned such an instrument and knew how to play it (Fig. 149).

Fig. 149. Kantele Performer at Ilomants. Photographed in 1873. (Retzius, "Finska Kranier.")

From the statements of more modern writers, we learn that the ordinary European psaltery was a very melodious instrument. Both Mersenne and Athanasius Kircher praise its silvery tone above that of all the other stringed instruments.

Mersenne had no doubt that as much—or perhaps more joy— might be derived from the psalterium as from the spinet or harp, if the same trouble were taken to practise it as was bestowed upon the keyboard instrument. On the other hand, he recommends it as an instrument easy to play; "the psaltery," he writes, "takes precedence over other instruments, as you may learn to play it in the course of an hour or two, and consequently it is suited to those who have no time for practice" ("Harmonie Universelle," 1636). Kircher was of a different opinion; he maintained that great skill was necessary to play the psaltery, because the performer was obliged to use his fingers for damping, in order to prevent a clashing of dissonant notes, while at the same time using two plectra.

CONCLUSIONS.

The harp-instrument now called Psaltery did not attract notice in Europe until a comparatively late date. It was, it appears, not until the time of the Crusades that it was brought from the Orient, and it cannot, in any case, be found in the West before the eleventh century. It quickly made its way into every corner of Europe. In Spain, France, and the British Isles, in Germany and Italy, it was in the twelfth century one of the instruments most frequently depicted. In the thirteenth century the new instrument had already gained a permanent footing among the instruments of the jongleurs and minstrels. In the Nordic saga it appeared another century later, and was described as being one of the instruments used at court, at marriages, and other important festivals. The popularity enjoyed by the psaltery during the Middle Ages is proved by the variety of forms in which it was found. Most of these forms were variations of the Oriental psalterium types, the santir and the kanun. Foremost among these variations were the *Istromento di porco* and the harp-psaltery used every-where from the eleventh to the fifteenth century. The harp-psaltery shows that the experiments made by the Irish with the plucked stringed instruments were continued on the Continent, where the frame-harp was developed into a psalterium, which then resolutely contested for pride of place with the mother-instrument and quickly grew in popularity everywhere.

Standing strangely alone is the type of psalterium repre-sented by the Finnish national kantele, which is considered by popular superstition to have been an instrument originating in Finland and invented by a local semi-divine musician. There is no trustworthy evidence as to the historic past of the kantele, and it is only possible to assume, on the strength of the supposed age of the Finnish legends, that the instrument was known in Finland as early as the twelfth or thirteenth century. But whether it was an original Finnish instrument, as the legend claims, or whether it was an Asiatic instrument brought to Finland by an unknown route, we cannot say.

While the psaltery was, from the very outset, either plucked with the fingers or a plectrum, it was, in the sixteenth century, customary to use beaters instead of the plectrum in Germany. From that moment a distinction was drawn be-tween the hammer-psaltery (in Italy called *Salterio tedesco*, in Germany, *Hackbrett*, and in England, *Dulcimer*) and the true psaltery. From the latter the line of development led directly to the harpsichord; from the former it led to the pianoforte.

BOOK II

STRINGED INSTRUMENTS WITH FINGER-BOARD

INTRODUCTION.

CLASSIFICATION AND PLAN.

The instruments on which the strings are shortened by stopping fall naturally into two main groups. In one of them the stopping is effected by dividing an *open* string (stretched over an open space) either by means of the fingers (nails or knuckles), a movable bridge, or a fixed keyboard acting from the side or from below. In the other, by using the finger-tips in the normal way to press the strings from above, against a firm surface—the finger-board.

Compared with the second group, the first contains a remarkably small number of instruments, viz.: (1) in antiquity, not more than one—the ancient Greek monochord; (2) two mediæval instruments, known as the tallharp and johicantele, rediscovered in recent times as folk-instruments on the Esthonian islands and in Finland, and attracting a good deal of attention among historians because they dispelled, to a certain extent, the darkness which had hitherto enveloped the development and origin of the bowed instruments; (3) the Icelandic fidla; (4) the mediæval keyboard monochords (organistrum, tangent-fiddle and clavichord).

The second group, on the other hand, embraces the whole of that great and well-known family of musical instruments which, under the name of " fingerboard instruments," branches out—in a multiplicity of forms and methods of handling (by means of bowing or plucking)—into so great a variety of species, that they unquestionably form the greater part of the stringed group of instruments.

The Fundamental Component Parts of the Fingerboard Instruments.

As a guide to the meaning of the terms : upper end, lower end, front, back, right and left, in the pages that follow, these remarks may be of service :

Upper end means that end of the fingerboard instrument which contains the tuning pegs (the head of the instrument).

Lower end is used to designate the opposite end (tail-piece or button).

Front means that side of the instrument on which the strings are supported (belly or table).

Back is used in its dictionary sense.

Right means the side of the instrument on the right of the observer when he views it from the front and in its normal position, with its head uppermost.

Left is the opposite side.

The *body* or *sound-box* may be composed either of back and belly (the back being vaulted, as in the lute or rebec), or of back and belly connected by ribs (the back being slightly moulded as in the violin family, or flat as in the guitars).

In the cavity of the sound box in the bowed fingerboard instruments stands a small stick, the *sound post* or (in France) the "soul," through which the vibrations of the strings are conducted from the belly to the back.

Fig. 150. Miniature in Codex Lat., No. 2599, in the State Library in Munich. (Above, the Myth of Pythagoras and the smithy; below, the Monochord and a Round Lyre with Bow.

In the belly (table or sound-board), *sound holes* are usually cut, through which the sound waves of the air-content of the body find their way out. The sound-holes may be round (the "rose" of the lutes and the guitar), crescent, C shaped (viols), heart shaped, the "flaming sword" (viola d'amore), or f-shaped (the modern violins).

The *neck*. When a neck connects the body with the head it may be either long and narrow (when used with few strings, for each string would then have to produce a large number of notes, e.g., the pandur of antiquity and the colascione of the Middle Ages), or short and broad when used with a larger number of strings (the lute, the sixteenth century "lyra" as a bowed instrument, etc.).

The *finger-board* may be placed either along the belly or table (the Monochord, the Scheitholt and the Langeleg), or along the neck inserted in the upper end of the body (the violin, guitar, lute) from which it often extends some distance down over the table. It may be smooth, the notes being found by ear (the violins) or divided by *frets* indicating the places where the fingers are to be applied for the production of the notes (guitar, lute, langeleg).

The *strings* may be of various materials: silk, horse-hair, gut or metal (steel or brass).

The *tail-piece* is the accessory to which the lower ends of the strings are fastened. It may either be a strip of wood glued to the belly, in which case it also serves as a bridge (on guitars) or a wedge shaped piece of wood, of which the upper or wide end is drilled with holes through which the strings are threaded and held there by knots on the under side, while the lower or narrower end has two holes for the string that holds the tail-piece on the tail-pin which is fixed to the back or ribs. Where a collective tail-piece is not used the strings often proceed right down to the lower end of the body, where each is made fast to the back or the ribs by a stud (the cittern).

The *tuning-pegs*. While in early times the stretching and

tuning of the strings were often effected by means of straps or braids which were attached to the strings and tied round the neck end (as in ancient Egypt), tuning-pegs were adopted later on, being placed together in the *peg-box*. This can be merely a board, a closed box, or a groove cut in the end of the neck. In the first two cases the pegs are inserted either from above or below (lyre, guitar, nyckelharp); in the third they are inserted from the side (the violins, etc.). Above the peg-box the *head* of the instrument terminates in a *scroll* (on the violins, etc.) or in an artistically carved animal or human head (on the rebec, mandora, lyre, cittern, etc.).

Bridge and *saddle* (or *nut*). On their way from the tail-piece to the pegs, the strings on bowed instruments pass over a small piece of thin wood set up on the table, usually with a perforated design, called the *bridge*, and then, just before they reach the peg-box, they cross a narrow strip of hard wood—the *saddle* or *nut*—found on all finger-board instruments. The same names are given to a corresponding projection which, placed at the lower end of the belly, is either crossed by the strings (when they are not fastened to a tail-piece) or by the loop that holds the tail-piece to the tail-pin or button in the lower rib. The strip which, on instruments of the lute and guitar type, serves both as bridge and tail-piece, is often called the "bridge," as is also the "slider" which on the monochords was moved to and fro over a scale under the strings.

ANTIQUITY

Although finger-board instruments can be traced back pictorially to ancient times, they are by no means so well represented as the instruments without finger-board. We may therefore be justified in assuming that, as compared with the lyre and the harp, this class of instruments played a relatively unimportant part in the music of antiquity. Nevertheless, the antique pictures make so important a contribution to the early history of finger-board instruments that we are not justified in ignoring them here. We learn from them that the instrument makers of those days adhered generally to the same principles of construction in the finger-board instruments as are followed to this day. We even find interesting parallels in these pictures with the forms in which the instruments occur in the Middle Ages and at the present time.

A. THE MONOCHORD.

(*Monos*, one, and *Chord*, a String.)

Among the finger-board instruments the monochord, the origin of which is to be sought in classic antiquity, may be looked upon as a norm, for in it theory and practice meet in the strictest sense of the words. On the monochord the theorist shows how the length and pitch of a string coincide in a mathematical sense, and a whole series of practically useful musical instruments have been developed from it.

The normal arrangement of the monochord. A long quadrilateral body (sometimes merely a board), along which is stretched a single string, of which the middle or sounding part is bounded at each end by a fixed bridge. On the front of the box is a scale similar to that found on any thermometer, and between this and the string is a slide or movable bridge which can be shifted by the hand from place to place, thus shortening and stopping the string at any point.

If the slide were placed under the centre of the string, each of the two halves would give the octave above the note of the unstopped string, while together they give a unison. If the slide has on one side of it a third of the string, and on the other side two-thirds, the longer portion will produce a fifth in relation to the unstopped string, while the two parts of the string will give an octave. If the slide has one-fourth on one side of it and three-fourths on the other, the longer portion of the string will give the fourth and the two parts will produce a tweifth, and so on. For all the details connected with the stopping of the monochord string it will be best to consult the special works on the theory of acoustics (e.g., H. Helmholtz, "Lehre v. d. Tonempfindungen"; L. Riemann, "Populäre Darstellungen der Akustik in Beziehung zur Musik"; E. Mach, "Einleitung in die Helmholtz'sche Theorie der Musik").

THE MONOCHORD OF ANTIQUITY.

Pictures. In order to find original reproductions of the ancient monochord, we must turn to the antique treatises on mathematics and scientific music, although we shall usually find them only in diagrammatic form. In his "Harmonica," Claudius Ptolemaeus (second century B.C.) showed two types of monochord, both employed in his period for instructional purposes. One of these, shown in Fig. 151 and called *anti-phonic*, is in every respect the same as the normal monochord already referred to. The name "antiphonic"—anti-sounding—was given to this monochord by Ptolemaeus because it was useful for comparing the two lengths of string on either side of the movable bridge which divided the string. This experiment could not be performed on the other type of monochord illustrated by him and called the *paraphonic* or "comparing monochord." The latter in its general make-up already has the character of a musical instrument (see Fig. 152). A small oval sound-box, in the sound-board of which a round sound hole was cut, is connected, in his instrument, with

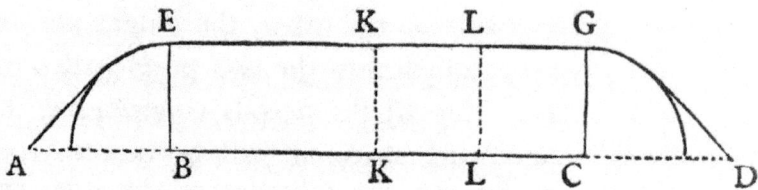

Fig. 151   Ptolemaeus's Antiphonic Monochord.

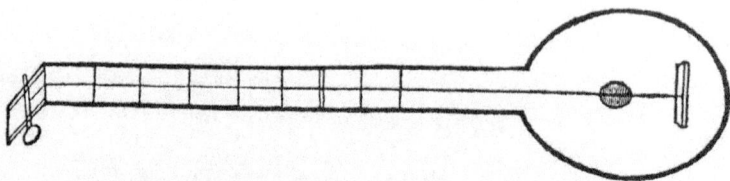

Fig. 152.   Ptolemaeus's Paraphonic Monochord.

a long thin neck, divided by frets and ending in a bent peg box which contains a single peg for tuning the only string on the instrument. At the lower end is a bar (like that on a guitar), glued to the belly.

Here we clearly recognise the lute-type in its simplest form, and should note the oval and undoubtedly vaulted sound box, the circular sound hole (the rose), the neck attached to the body, and the sharply bent peg-box.

Ptolemaeus states that this paraphonic monochord was especially useful in practical musical instruction—for teaching singing—whereas the antiphonic type was used solely for the scientific investigations of the mathematicians.

The remarkable resemblance of the paraphonic monochord to the musical instrument, in the form of which the finger-board family made its debut in the musical records of antiquity (*v. infra*), gives rise to the assumption that it was by moving the finger from fret to fret on a musical instrument that it was originally discovered how the notes made by stopping the strings were in a mathematical sense related to the fundamental note of the open string. In this case the antiphonic monochord would mark the second stage of experimentation, when the object was to find out what was the relation between the two lengths of string that lay on either side of the point at which it was stopped.

It is interesting to note that the first appearance on the scene of this class of instruments already shows us the two methods of stopping described above; the notes on the antiphonic monochord were produced by the pressure of the movable bridge or slide against the open string, while on the paraphonic monochord they were produced in the regular manner by finger pressure against a finger-board below the string.

The traditional inventor of the monochord is said to have been the Greek philosopher, Pythagoras (born on Samos in 582 B.C.); but Julius Pollux seeks its provenance in Arabia. Modern investigators dispute as to whether the credit for the discovery is to be given to Assyria or Egypt, in the latter of which countries Pythagoras actually lived for twenty-two years as a member of the college at Thebes.

B. The Finger-board Instruments on the Ancient Monuments.

It was formerly supposed that the oldest illustration of a finger-board instrument used in musical practice was the Egyptian hieroglyph Nfr (see Fig. 153) which is already found on the pyramid texts in the days of the Old Empire. As the finger-board instrument in Egyptian musical reproductions, however, does not occur until the time of the New Empire (i.e., from about 1580 B.C.) this idea has been abandoned, and the

Fig. 153. The Egyptian Hieroglyph *Nfr*.

Fig. 154. Playing Herdsman on a Terra-cotta Plate from Nippur, *circa* 2500 B.C. (Hilprecht's "Exploration in Bible Lands," page 529.) Now in the Philadelphia Museum.

hieroglyph is construed either as a rudder or as the heart and windpipe (Griffiths, "Hieroglyphs," in the "Archaeological Survey of Egypt," sixth memoir). Thus it is not Egypt but Western Asia that must enjoy the honour of exhibiting the earliest example of this kind of instrument.

(A) IN WESTERN ASIA.

Of all the excavations commenced in 1889 by the North American archaeologists in the vicinity of the Euphrates and the Tigris, the most remarkable was the uncovering of prehistoric Babylon, the seat of the oldest civilisation in the world—that of the Sumerians. The greatest interest attaches to the discoveries made in ancient Nippur which, according to a Talmudic tradition, corresponds to "Calneh in the land of Shinar," one of the four capitals in Nimrod's realm (Genesis x, 10). A number of large clay tablets inscribed with cuneiform references to the time when the country was ruled in the fourth millenium B.C. by Kings Lugal-kigub-nidudu and Sargon I, was found. On a small clay relief from the school attached to the ancient temple of Bel, and dating back to the third millenium, the fingerboard instrument is, as far as we can tell, illustrated for the first time. Surrounded by his flock, a shepherd sits on a stone and plays a stringed instrument which, with its small oval body and long neck, most decidedly recalls Ptolemaeus's paraphonic monochord. On one side of the shepherd is a sheep, on the other a dog which, with open jaws, howls to the music of the instrument. The latter rests horizontally before the body of the player, so that the sound box is supported by his right arm, while the neck, three times as long as the body, is held by the fingers of the left hand, which performs the stopping (see Fig. 154). As the relief only shows the outlines of the instrument, we cannot judge of its details, such as the number of strings, means of tuning, etc.

The next reproductions of a finger-board instrument appear on two Hittite sculptures dating from pre-Phoenician times, i.e., circa 1500 B.C. One of these was found during excavations at Sendschirli in North Syria by German archaeologists. In its prime Sendschirli was a large royal residence, though now but a village. In the double wall surrounding the remnants of the ancient capital are several gates whose pillars, decorated with reliefs, are still preserved; and on one of them we find a relief showing a seated long-bearded man manipulating a stringed instrument (Fig. 155). Here again the sound box is small, and the neck disproportionately long. Whether the two small holes which appear at the lower end of the body are flaws in the stone or were meant to indicate the existence of small sound holes made in a membrane belly (*cf. infra*, Egyptian tomb pictures), I would not venture to say; but their symmetrical placing and their being found in both sculptures at any rate points in that direction. Unlike the

Fig. 155. Gate Relief from Sendschirli (circa 1500 B.C.). Now in the Vorasiatische Museum in Berlin.

Nippur instrument, the Hittite example, which is provided with a sling by which it was carried, is held in an upright position, so that the body rests on the right knee of the performer while the neck passes before his eyes which are evidently fixed on the stopping fingers of the left hand. Above the table of the sound box, the fingers of the right hand twang the strings. In the other Hittite instrument, appearing in a sculpture on the castle ruins of Bos-öjuk, in the northern part of Asia Minor, we discover the following interesting details for the first time: the sides of the body are decidedly incurved so that the instrument bears a striking resemblance to the guitar. The small sound holes, which in the preceding instrument could just be made out, here appear so clearly that on both sides of the strings it is possible to discover no fewer than five; and the frets which appear in a regular series down

Fig. 156. Hittite Sculpture from Bos-öjuk. Now in the Ottoman Museum, Istanbul.

the fingerboard, indicate the existence of a graded scale. The two ends which fall from the head show that two strings were stretched on the instrument, while the ribbon which falls on the right shows that the plectrum with which the strings were plucked, was tied to the instrument (see Fig. 156).

part of Asia Minor, we discover the following interesting details for the first time: the sides of the body are decidedly incurved so that the instrument bears a striking resemblance to the guitar. The small sound holes, which in the preceding instrument could just be made out, here appear so clearly that on both sides of the strings it is possible to discover no fewer than five; and the frets which appear in a regular series down

Fig. 156. Hittite Sculpture from Bos-öjuk. Now in the Ottoman Museum, Istanbul.

the fingerboard, indicate the existence of a graded scale. The two ends which fall from the head show that two strings were stretched on the instrument, while the ribbon which falls on the right shows that the plectrum with which the strings were plucked, was tied to the instrument (see Fig. 156).

In the regular oval form of the Nippur type, the finger-board instrument again appears on two Elamite sculptures unearthed at Susa—reproduced in "Delegation en Perse" ("Memoires," table I, series 1, "Fouilles en Suse," 1898-9) —and in some Assyrian pictures. The best of them is a relief from Khorsabad (Nineveh), circa 1000 B.C. Facing two dancers who are disguised in lions' skins, there is a musician with a stringed instrument provided with a small oval body and a long neck; but the only details which it is possible to make out are two ends of ribbon indicating that the instrument had two strings (see Fig. 157).

Fig. 158. Persian Fingerboard Instrument, *circa* 500 B.C. (Clercq, "Cat. d'Antiquités Assyriens," 1903.)

Fig. 157. Relief from Khorsabad (Engel).

Finally I would mention a little known picture on a seal belonging to the time of the Achamenides (559-330), i.e., belonging to the oldest Persian dynasty, when the Persians as regards their religion, art and civilisation were still in close contact with the Assyrians. In the diminutive picture which is here seen enlarged, a divinity sits on a throne with an oblique lyre in his lap; before him stands a person holding a long-necked instrument with an almost circular body of relatively small size.

B.   IN EGYPT.

While most of the stone pictures from western Asia only give an idea of the outlines of the finger-board instruments, it is possible to see in the painted Egyptian pictures, where this group of instruments is very frequently represented, a multi-

Fig. 159. Finger-board Instrument with vaulted back. From "Mémoires Publiés par les Membres de la Mission archéologique Française du Caire." 1894. V.

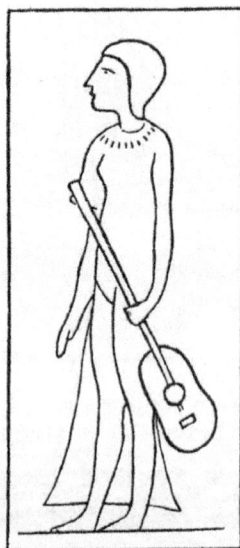

Fig. 160. Guitar-shaped body. From Guimet, "Annales."

tude of details as to their construction and manner of playing. Here again a chief feature is the strikingly small body, and the disproportionately long and thin neck.   Seen from the front, the sound-box in most cases looks like a more or less lengthy oval (see Figs. 162 and 163). Only in two isolated cases do we find the guitar and the pear-shaped instruments (see Figs. 160 and 169).

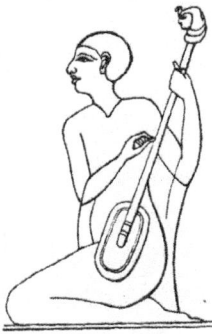

Fig. 161. Neck with carved Sphinx Head. (Wilkinson.)

Fig. 162. Oval Body. After Champollion.

Where—in a single example—the body is seen in profile, it has a vaulted lute-like back (see Fig. 159). Cut in the table we often find the same diminutive sound-holes that are present in the Hittite stone carvings, and which are still used by primitive peoples when the sound-cavity has a membrane belly (see Fig. 163). On the method of fastening the strings, the pictures give very little information. If we confine ourselves to the only preserved fragment of the original Egyptian lute (see Fig. 170), we find that the strings were stretched from one end of a long cylindrical stick to the other, and tied after passing through holes at the lower end of the body, hidden beneath the belly. At the upper end of the neck was

placed the tuning apparatus, consisting of lengths of ribbon
provided with tassels to which the strings were tied for winding round the end of the stick for tuning. From the number
of tassels it is possible to make out the number of the strings
—generally varying from two to three (see Figs. 159, 163,
164, 165 and 168). The number of the tassels is not, how-

Fig. 163. Small Sound-holes in
the Table. (After Wilkinson.)

Fig. 164. Fiddle (?) Tail-piece.

ever, any absolute guarantee of the number of the strings, for
they are sometimes merely used as a decoration and are added
to those belonging to the tuning ribbons. Instances of such
tassel decoration are to be seen in Figs. 166 and 167. Where
the strings cross the table, the pictures in most cases show a
mark which at first glance suggests a guitar or fiddle tail-
piece.

In the Egyptian lute the persistent provision of graduated
marks on the neck is very interesting (see Fig. 168). If it is
possible to trust the accuracy of the artist, we might be able,

by measuring the distances, to draw valuable conclusions as to the nature of the scale-series which would be produced on the instrument when the fingers were placed on these frets. (Such accuracy in the draughtsmanship, however, is greater than we have the right to expect.—Ed.) The regularly ar-

Fig. 165. Musical Scene (Fresco) on the Tomb of Rat-eser-kasemb. (From same source as Fig. 159.)

ranged holes on the ancient Egyptian flutes have in this manner thrown much light on the nature of the diatonic system of ancient Egypt. From the closeness of the markings on the lutes, however, one could with certainty only ascertain the use of a scale containing much smaller intervals than those which are produced on the chromatically divided European fingerboard, but this agrees well enough with the music that still characterises the East. (That our authoress hopes to arrive at any definite acoustic conclusions on the strength of the marking on the necks of the lutes is very surprising, even a little fantastic; not even the careful Egyptian artists can be trusted with sufficient accuracy to make their "frets" serviceable to us. The wind-instruments, with their fixed finger-holes, are a far more trustworthy guide. To suggest that the ancient Egyptians employed microtonal intervals on the strength of the fretting in the pictures is, to say the least, rather misleading.)—(Ed.).

Fig. 166. Bas-relief from Heliopolis (Saite Period). Alexandria Museum. From "Musée egyptienne," Tome II, Maspero, 1904.

The neck of the ancient Egyptian lute, like many medi-æval finger-board instruments, ends in a carved animal's head—that of the sphinx, or a curve suggesting the violin-scroll (see Figs. 161, 162 and 168). When played, the instrument was often slung round the neck of the performer by a ribbon (see Fig. 163).

Fig. 167.   Tassel Decoration.
(Wilkinson.)

Fig. 168.   Cord for Graduating
the Neck (?).   Lepsius, "Aus-
wahl d. wichtigsten Urkunden d.
aeg. Altertums."

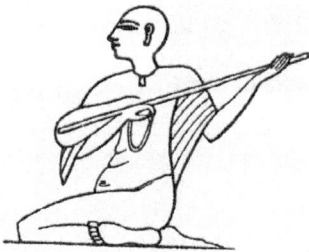

Fig. 169.   Pear-shaped
Body. After Wilkinson.

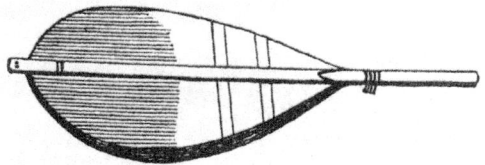

Fig. 170.   Fragment of an Original
Ancient Egyptian finger-board instrument.   (Wilkinson.)

Concerning the mode of playing, the position of the hands is important. Thus the left hand while stopping on the instruments with few strings, often uses the thumb only (see Figs. 159, 162 and 167), in the last of which the middle fingers with stretched forefinger support the neck from below, drawing the thumb from one part of the string to the other. The strings are plucked either with the fingers of the right hand or, more frequently, a plectrum, which is often tied to the instrument with a ribbon (see Figs. 162, 163, 164 and 169). We may be surprised to note that the plectrum does not invariably strike in any definite place, but sometimes plucks the string over the table and sometimes over the neck (see Figs. 161, 163, 165, 167 and 169).

The few examples of original Egyptian finger-board instruments that have been preserved are too defective to provide any trustworth material for study (see Fig. 170). What this fragment shows is, (1) the existence of a vaulted back, and (2) the prolongation of the neck by a thin rod continued along the entire length of the belly and kept in place above by two cross-fillets; it extends beyond the lower edge of the body so far that, by boring two small holes, it is possible to use it for fastening the two strings of the instrument.

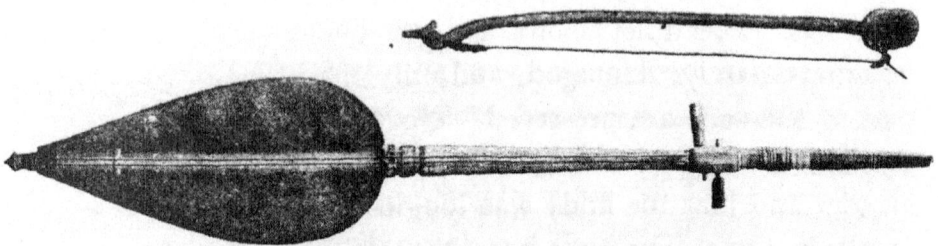

Fig. 171. Gesso from the Celebes. Original belonging to the Author.

Very like this Egyptian type is a stringed instrument (gesso) still used in the Celebes. It is made of a split pear-shaped calabash, across the opening of which there is a closely-fitting framework covered with a membrane. Behind this the rod which continues from the neck to the button is clearly seen. From the button the strings are taken across a low bridge to the long tuning-pegs—one on each side of the head. While the calabash in the gesso is turned so that the pointed end forms the base of the sound-cavity, it is reversed in the Egyptian instrument, where the narrower end joins the neck.

C. IN GREECE.

While antique Greek art affords the best opportunity for studying the lyres and harps, it provides very poor material for the examination of the finger-board instruments, affording only three reproductions in all.

The first is the fragment of a relief unearthed at classic Mantinea in Arcadia (1887) and now in the Centrikon Museum at Athens. It is supposed to have belonged originally to a famous group by Praxiteles, and in this case it must be attributed either to the master himself or to one of his pupils. If this is so, the work of art must be placed in the fourth century B.C. The relief shows a finger-board instrument which is, unfortunately, damaged, and only the body and the upper part of the neck are preserved. Nevertheless, it is possible to determine from these fragments that the neck was long and slender and that the body was longish and hexagonal, though small in size. The type thus has the character of the lute, as the outlines of the body and the presence of a vaulted back prove. Beyond this no details can be made out, for neither the strings nor the tail-piece are reproduced, and the neck ends bluntly with no tuning device. The method of playing is the normal one, the fingers of the left hand being used to stop the strings, while the fingers of the right pluck the strings.

Fig. 172. Fragment of a Relief from Mantinea. 4th cent. B.C. (From "Bulletin de Correspondances Helleniques," XII.)

The other two examples, of the club-shaped type, occur on two terra-cotta statuettes found in Tanagra and Myrina respectively and which are now in the Louvre. To the first of them (Fig. 173) archæologists have given a fourth-century date, while the other (Fig. 174) has been placed in the second century B.C. The two instruments, however, are exactly alike. On the Tanagra statuette the instrument is held horizontally, while on the Myrinan example it is held obliquely with the lower end of the body uppermost and the head down. In the Tanagra instrument we lack the central portion of the neck and all details of its construction; and all that is recognisable is the club-like outline. On the Myrina statuette we see at the broad end of the body a button, which I am sure served to fasten the strings, i.e., as an end-button, while on the head we see the acutely bent peg-box which characterised the mediæval lute and usually indicated the existence of tuning-pegs.

Fig. 173.
Statuette from Tanagra. ("Revue des Etudes Grecques," VIII, 1895.) In the Louvre.

Fig. 174.
Statuette from Myrina (Louvre).

Fig. 175. Phœnician Clay Statuette. (Louvre.)

On the Tanagra statuette the fingers of the right hand are used for plucking the strings; on the one from Myrina we see a bent plectrum.

It is interesting to discover in these two Greek instruments the forerunners of a class of finger-board instruments which from the ninth century onwards made their way from the East to Europe, there to become widely distributed and firmly established. It cannot be decided with certainty where this club-shaped instrument originated. In antiquity it occurs in a few cases outside of classical Greece—in Phœnicia (a clay statuette in the Louvre, Fig. 175), and a terra-cotta figure from Alexandria, now in Stuttgart, Fig. 176—but it is only found more frequently in a collection of Persian silver objects excavated at Irbit, in South Russia, and referred by archæologists to the time of the Sassanideans, i.e., between the fourth and seventh centuries. The prominent part played by this type of instrument in the exceedingly numerous musical scenes bears witness to its having been, at that time, at any rate, as popular in Persia as the lyre was, contemporaneously, in Greece. Strangely enough, one of these Persian pictures borrows its subject from Hellenic art, as it reproduces Cupid riding on a lion. But while the Greek artist placed the Greek national instrument, the lyre, in the hands of the god of love, the Oriental artist preferred to give Cupid the club-shaped instrument which predominated in his country (see Fig. 177).

As a descendant of this type we easily recognise the Arabian rebab, which is still used in North Africa in the Arabian orchestra, and which in the Middle Ages was brought to Spain by the Moors, becoming quickly the model for a European instrument—the rebec—which was so popular in the Middle Ages (see Book III).

Side by side with this narrow type we see, on the Persian works of art, another which is much broader and which is reproduced with features so clear that all the details of its construction are visible. In these two pictures we see clearly that

Fig. 176. Terracotta Figure from Alexandria. (Stuttgart.)

Fig. 177. Cupid riding on a Lion. Persian Silver Plate from Irbit, South Russia. 4th to 7th cent.

Figs. 178 and 179. Persian Finger-board Instruments on Silver Objects from Irbit.

the strings were fixed to a broad guitar tail-piece and that they were tuned by means of long-stemmed tuning-pegs which were inserted in the peg-box from the side. Moreover, the number of strings is four as against three on the narrower instrument, and in the belly wavy sound-holes are seen resembling those which were used in more recent times in the European viola d'amore, and sometimes called "flaming-sword" sound-holes.

Fig. 180. Chinese Pipa.

This broader pear-shaped type recurs in the Chinese Pipa (see Fig. 180) and the Japanese Biwa. It is possible to trace the former back to the fifth century, being reproduced on mural paintings in Chinese Turkestan. It is interesting to observe in this connection that the type in one of the Persian silver pictures is used in conjunction with an ancient east Asiatic wind-instrument, the Chinese Cheng (see Fig. 179), the invention of which is dated by tradition as early as 2500 B.C. In Europe this pear-shaped type reappeared in the mediæval Mandora.

On the Roman monuments it is the lute-type which predominates, but the primitive Asiatic type is no longer the absolute model. The long and slender neck characterising the former is very rare among the Romans. Fig. 181 shows one of the few examples with a long neck, giving the outline only and no details of the instrument. In Fig. 182 the neck is also disproportionately long, but broad at the same time, and here, too, the number of the strings and the meaning of the forked head are alike unknown.

Fig. 181. Figure on the Lid of a Sarcophagus in Rome. Robert, "Die antiken Sarkofag-Reliefs."

Fig. 182. Roman sarcophagus relief. British Museum.

With a short neck and with a body possessing a back as vaulted as that of the late mediæval lutes, the finger-board instrument is, on the other hand, shown on a Roman sarcophagus found at Arles in France (see Fig. 183). The three tuning-pegs inserted in the neck indicate that it was three-stringed. The instrument reproduced in Fig. 184, from another sarcophagus fragment in the Lateran Museum, is of similar form, but the shape is more elegant and the back less vaulted. Since the strings are in this case shown merely as a

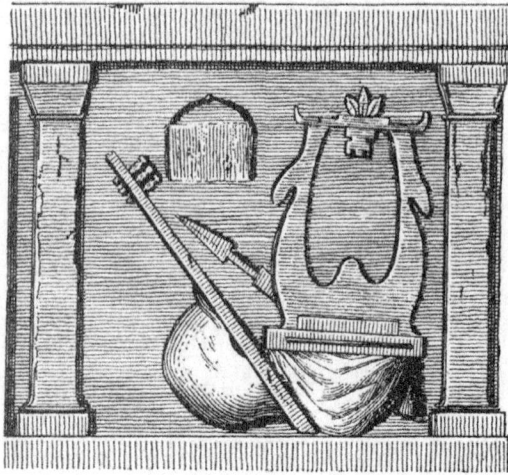

Fig. 183. Lute-like instrument on a Roman sarcophagus at Arles. Millin, "Monuments antiques inédits," Tome II

Fig. 184. Fragment of a sarcophagus. Lateran Museum. "Bulletino della Commissione Archeologica communale di Roma," 1877. Visconti; plate 17.

roll running along the table, and the tuning-pegs are not reproduced, we have no clue to the number of the strings present. With both instruments we see an arrow-headed plectrum.

The lute-type as a sham finger-board instrument. As a curiosity, we find in several Roman sculptures a musical instrument which looks like a lute, but which is manipulated as a lyre, i.e., without stopping the strings. Along the comparatively small oval and evidently bulging sound-box and the broad and rather long neck connected with it, there are

Fig. 185. Sarcophagus relief in Girgenti Cathedral. A reconstruction from a photograph of a design found in "Illustrazione al sarcofago Agrigentino," Palermo, 1822; Politi, "Opere," giving an incorrect idea of the two instruments, in that only one of them is reproduced with a separate sound-box, while the other looks like a broad stringed bar-like box, a mistake which Carl Engel ("Hist. of the Violin Family") makes still worse by transferring it to both instruments. In the original, both instruments are provided with round bodies and are exactly alike.

seven to nine strings proceeding from a block-like square
guitar tail-piece, continuing to the end of the neck, where in
some way or other—the reproductions do not show how—they
are stretched and tuned. On the underside of the tail-piece
the strings are secured by knots from which the loose ends fall
as a fringe. In all the pictures the left hand is used only to
support the body and to keep the instrument in place, while
the right hand plucks the unstopped strings at the neck. The

Fig. 186. Græco-Roman sarco-
phagus relief in the Louvre. C.
Robert, "Die antiken Sarkofag-
Reliefs," Vol. III, Pt. 2.

Fig. 187. Roman picture on a
sarcophagus in the Louvre.
Schlesinger, "Instruments of
the Modern Orchestra."

earliest example of this sham finger-board instrument appears
on a sarcophagus relief in the Cathedral of Girgenti, in Italy
(see Fig. 185). Archæologists have dated this work between
the first and fourth centuries. It illustrates (for the tragedies

of Euripides and Sophocles, "Hippolitos" and "Phædra") Phædra's despair on receiving the tidings of Hippolitos's tragic death. Sympathetically her maidens gather round her. The nurse whispers consoling words, and two girls, one sitting and the other standing, attempt to comfort her by playing instruments of the type described above.

Exact counterparts of the Girgenti instruments occur in two Roman sarcophagus reliefs in the Louvre (see Figs. 186 and 187). In one of them the instrument is played by two persons, whose left hands merely hold the instrument at each end, their right hands plucking the unstopped strings, one of them operating the treble, and the other the bass strings. In Fig. 187, where the lute-form is evidently replaced by the club shape, the neck of the instrument ends in a broad saddle, in which are cut two deep zig-zag furrows. I would not venture to express an opinion as to whether they served for fastening the strings (cf. Book I, on the tuning methods of the lyre), or were added merely as a decoration.

C. The Fingerboard Instrument in Ancient Greek Literature.

Literally translated, the name *Monochord* means, as mentioned before, "an instrument with one string," and therefore the customary connotation of the name is only the Pythagorean monochord used for scientific purposes both in antiquity and in the Middle Ages (*v. sup.*). A passage in Nicomachus, however, indicates that the name was also used in ancient Greece in another, broader, meaning. In his "Enchiridon," chapter 4, he divided the stringed instruments into two main groups, one of which included the instruments in which the tuning of the strings was determined by the tension applied to them, while the other contained those in which the tuning depended upon the length of the strings. In the first category Nicomachus placed the kithara, the lyra, the spadix, and several others, i.e., the lyre instruments. In the other he included, on the one hand, the monochords (those in which the notes were made by shortening the strings, i.e., the finger-board instruments), and on the other, the *trigonon*, in which the notes were produced by strings of unequal length, i.e., the harps (harp and psalterion).

Nicomachus says of the monochords that they were generally called *Pandouras*, but by the Pythagoreans named *Canons*. Pandoura, in other words, was the popular name for the finger-board instrument used by the practical musicians, while Canon was the Pythagorean's specialised name for the scientific monochord and was due to the express application of this instrument as a guide *(canon)* for the working out of the intervals. In literature, therefore, it is under the name of Pandoura that we must seek the musically useful finger-board instruments.

On perusing our written sources of information we learn that the pandouras of Greece were said to have been introduced from a foreign country. Pythagoras attributed them to a people from the Near East, the *Troglodytes*. Pollux localised their invention to Arabia, but allowed the Assyrians to name them. Martian maintained that the pandouras were of Egyptian origin. In Arabia, they preferred to give the pandouras three strings; the Assyrians, on the other hand, had a predilection for the two-stringed variety (the *Bichords*). Both countries to which the pandoura was ascribed, as well as the number of strings mentioned, send one's thoughts to that long-necked, two or three-stringed type so often seen in the ancient pictures, and which, judging by its occurrence on the oldest monuments, presents itself as the germ from which the finger-board instrument in all probability grew.

The word Pandoura in the course of time degenerated into the Oriental Tanbura, which in the East was principally used to indicate the long-necked original type, but which, in the combination *Tanbur Korassan* was also used by the Arabs to designate the pear-shaped instrument. It is therefore probable that in antiquity the pear-shaped type was also one of the instruments called Pandoura.

The name *Skindapsos*, mentioned by Athenæos, has been assumed to have been the name of a finger-board instrument other than the monochord, the canon and the pandoura; but this hypothesis is contradicted by the explanation given by Theopompos of Colophon to the effect that it was a lyre-like instrument made of the branches of a supple willow.

SUMMARY.

With the help of the monuments it is possible to follow the finger-board instrument back to the third millennium B.C., when it was already used by the oldest civilised people in the world, the Sumerians, living in prehistoric Babylon. It is there a poorly-strung, feeble-toned instrument, for a disproportionately long and slender neck is connected with a rather diminutive sound-box. In this form, like an oar with a rounded blade, the finger-board instrument existed for thousands of years among the civilised peoples of Western Asia: the Sumerians, Hittites, Elamites, Assyrians and Persians, and (from the time of the New Empire) also in Egypt.

While the instrument in the west Asiatic sculptures is only seen full face, so that only the surface of the sound-box indicates its form, the Egyptian tomb-pictures also explain its outlines, and give some details of its construction. Thus we discover that the finger-board instrument almost invariably had a vaulted back, frets on the neck for stopping, sound-holes in the belly, a tail-piece for fixing the lower ends of the strings, and means of tuning the latter, in most cases straps tied to the upper end of the string and stretched to the end of the neck. Moreover we see the existence of a saddle or nut, over which the strings passed to the neck. At the same time it appears that the instrument was in most cases carried in a shoulder-strap and plucked alternately with the fingers and a plectrum carried in the right hand, while the fingers of the left hand, or sometimes only the left thumb, consistently took over the stopping of the strings by gliding from place to place on the slender neck.

From Egypt the slender form of the finger-board instrument may be followed to Greece, but there it was joined by another type, i.e., the club-shaped instrument. The assertion of Greek authors that all the finger-board instruments were brought to Greece by strangers, however, indicates that the early occurrence of this type in two Greek works of art was merely accidental. In all probability the club-shaped type, like the long-necked original type, was of west Asiatic origin. A pointer in this direction is given by a number of antique Persian works of art, where the club-shaped type is depicted in a slender and also a broader (pear-shaped) version, and where the slender form, by using a classical Greek motive, was deliberately used as an Oriental substitute for the Greek national instrument—the lyre.

The Greek authors first make known to us the name used in antiquity to indicate the finger-board instrument. They state that they generally—i.e., colloquially—called the finger-board instrument the *Pandoura*. Only when classifying all the stringed instruments was it a question of distinguishing between them and the other kinds of stringed instruments—the lyres and the harps; and they were then given as Monochords, a name which, indiscriminately with *Canon*, was also used as a special designation for the experimental apparatus, the real "one-string," by means of which the mathematicians demonstrated the intervals.

In the Roman sculptures the instruments provided with a distinct neck and sound-box made an attempt at striking out in a new direction; the desire for a greater number of strings there led to the use of a broader neck, which, practically speaking, must be considered as a progressive step, because the fingers of the left hand were thus enabled to produce a longer scale of notes without undue gliding about. It appears almost as if it were the richly-strung lyre that suggested this increase in the number of strings. In several reproductions of a comparatively early date there is proof that at the beginning these broad-necked instruments deserted the principle of the fingerboard instrument by using unstopped strings in order to compete with the main representative of the stringed instrument in classical antiquity—the lyre.

THE FINGER-BOARD INSTRUMENT IN THE
MIDDLE AGES.

INTRODUCTION.

(PLUCKING AND BOWING.)

Round about the year 1000 the mediæval pictures of
Europe announced the introduction of a new mode of playing
the stringed instruments. It had hitherto always been the
fingers or a plectrum that had thrown the strings into vibration; now a bow or a rotating wheel was often used with the
same object.

Whence this new method of playing came, and when it
was first employed, was for a long time a very open question.
While one school maintained that the stringed instruments
played with the bow came from the Near East, another maintained, with evidently the same justification, that they must
have been originated in Europe.

By calling comparative science to his aid and consulting
ethnology, the German musical historian, Curt Sachs ("Die
Streichbogenfrage; Arch. f. Musikwissenschaft," 1918, I)
finally came to the conclusion that bowing did not, as was
hitherto supposed, indicate a later stage than the plucking
method. Even if the monuments did not show any instance
of the use of a bow in antiquity, he found in the fact that the
most primitive stringed instruments in the world, used by the
most primitive peoples of the present day, are consistently
played by bowing, whereas the later types are always mani-

pulated by plucking the strings; a proof that the question of plucking or bowing cannot be answered by chronological or technical evidence, but is a popular psychological problem. The highly cultured Persians in their most flourishing period, knew only of plucking the strings of their instruments (see " The Fingerboard Instruments in Antiquity "). Among the primitive Asiatic peoples, such as the mountain and island dwellers of India, who retained their ancient customs, it was, and is still, the bowing method that took the lead. Not until the Persians eventually came in contact with other nations that were culturally their inferiors, did they become acquainted with the bow. In the same manner the classical peoples of the Mediterranean appeared in history plucking the strings of their instruments, while the primitive Gothic peoples—and chief among them the Germans—introduced themselves as users of the bow. Not until some time in the Middle Ages did the Mediterranean peoples have an opportunity of making the acquaintance of the gigues and fiddles of Nordic, Slav and Arabian origin.

During the interchange of cultural ideas between the nations, which took place in the Middle Ages, the national peculiarities of the instruments were gradually levelled, so that the bowed and plucked types, in many cases, changed their mode of playing and, with the co-operation of the *luthiers*, their nature also. Of the later mediæval plucked instruments, therefore, some appear clearly.as descendants of bowed instruments (e.g., the Spanish Vihuela, Chitarra Battente, and Guitar), just as some of the instruments played with the bow show their origin in instruments that by their nature were destined to be plucked, (1) the mediæval rebec developed from the originally plucked Moorish rebab, and the oldest types of fiddle; and (2) the German Grossgeige, still traceable in the works of Virdung and Agricola.

FINGER-BOARD INSTRUMENTS WITHOUT NECK.

I. The Mediæval Round Lyre as a Bowed Instrument.

A. ON THE MONUMENTS.

Strangely enough, a prominent place among the stringed instruments played with the bow is occupied in the late mediæval pictures by the well-known round lyre, which was originally destined to be plucked (see Book I). The round lyre played with the bow was produced in three shapes which evidently indicate different stages in its development, and here numbered 1, 2 and 3.

(1) In the first stage the instrument resembled the plucked round lyre closely (see Book I), the only difference being that its strings, stretched clear of the frame, were stopped by the pressure of the fingers of the left hand. (2) In the second stage the round lyre showed signs of having been the subject of experiment, and appears on the one hand as a closed sound-box instrument in the form of the *Cythara Teutonica*, and on the other as a *Cythara Teutonica* with a narrowed string-space. Now and then the position of the left hand suggests the existence of a short finger-board-like surface, but this does not become the rule until the oval form of the *Cythara Teutonica* is definitely given up, and in the third stage replaced by the square form of the Anglo-Saxon lyre, thus making room for a

comparatively long finger-board and transforming the round lyre into a decided finger-board instrument, e.g., the Welsh *crwth*, which retained its popularity until comparatively late.

1. THE UNCHANGED ROUND LYRE.

In St. Leopold's prayer-book in the Conventual Library of Klosterneuburg, near Vienna, may be seen a miniature of King David with his four followers: Ethan, Jeduthun, Asaph and Heman. Each of them handles an instrument, and three of these instruments are round lyres which by their form at once suggest the *Cythara Teutonica* (the rounded lower part and the gently incurved sides) and the Nordic Gunnar harp (the slender form, the upward aspiring yoke and the pear-shaped string-opening; see Book I). The three lyres are of different sizes. An instrument of medium size is held by King David who, as the main figure, sits in the centre of the picture and is drawn to a larger scale than the others. His instrument, therefore, is reproduced with special care. On the belly we see two oblong sound-holes running parallel with the outlines of the sound-box, and between them a fixed tail-piece. Unfortunately, the strings, which run from the tail-piece to the yoke, have been omitted. The bow has the shape of the hunting-bow prolonged at one end into a long handle. David's instrument gives no indication of the method of playing, since it is not in action. We are only able to presume the perpendicular position of the lyre on the knee of the performer, so that the sound-box is downwards, and the yoke on top. The fingers of the left hand encompass the yoke, while the right hand, resting on the right knee, holds the bow. In order to understand the mode of playing this bowed-lyre, it will be necessary to observe the other two performers whose instruments are being played. The smaller lyre, the player of which is placed on the left and who, unlike King David, is standing, is reproduced only in outline without any details other than the three strings seen through the string space. On the other hand, the picture shows that the instrument when in use was held like a violin, as the curve of the body rests against the chest of the player, while the curve of the lyre-arm is enclosed by the right hand, which at the same time raises it so that it is opposite his face. The bow, wielded by the right hand, is thus obliged to move up and down in almost perpendicular strokes. That the left hand, besides keeping the instrument in place, stops the strings with the fingers, is probable, but this cannot be decided owing to the defective drawing. Definite proof that this kind of lyre was played by stopping the strings is, however, provided by the third lyre seen in the right-hand corner of the picture. Being the largest instrument in the group, it gives the draughtsman the opportunity of repeating the details shown on David's instrument, namely, the two oblong, symmetrically-placed sound-holes and the tailpiece between them. Like David's lyre, the instrument is drawn without strings. Concerning the manner in which it was played, the picture tells us that, like the smallest lyre, it was held in a perpendicular position so that in performance the base rested on the right knee while the yoke touched the left shoulder. With lowered arm the bow was drawn horizontally backwards and forwards across the strings. The placing of the left hand midway in the open lyre-curve (yoke) certainly indicates that it was used to stop the strings, which were evidently stretched freely across the open space. (It seems to me highly improbable that the strings of this type of instrument were stopped with the fingers as our authoress suggests; there is no indication of a finger-board, and the pressure of a finger on a string in the open space would have produced—at best—an harmonic, or, if the pressure were heavier, a buzz when the string touched the edge of the opening. The strings were doubtlessly tuned to a chord and bowed open.—Ed.).

Almost akin to the Klosterneuburg lyres is the instrument reproduced in Fig. 189 and illustrated in a manuscript in the Court Library at Munich. It is undoubtedly a *Cythara Teutonica* provided with six strings. To the right and left

Fig. 188. The Round Lyre as a bowed instrument. St. Leopold's Prayer-book. 11th cent.

Fig. 189. Round-Lyre and Bow. 13th cent.

of the strings semicircular sound-holes are cut in the table; in the corresponding places in the lyre-curve are seen two faintly indicated oblong patches which look like sound-holes in an inlaid sound-board, but which, I am certain, are only to be considered as a suggestion of the strings passing over an empty space; for by blackening the whole lyre-opening the artist would have made the strings invisible. The bow—contrary to the usual custom of the time—is straight instead of curved, is illustrated above the instrument and shows that the latter was bowed.

2. THE ROUND-LYRE AS THE SUBJECT OF EXPERIMENT.

(a) As a Closed Sound-box Instrument with the Outline of the Cythara Teutonica.

In an eleventh century Anglo-Saxon manuscript at Cambridge, King David is once more shown in a miniature, with his staff of musicians. He is playing the harp, Ethan and Jeduthun play a wind-instrument and a hand-drum respectively, while Asaph and Heman play stringed instruments of a very strange form (see Fig. 190).

Fig. 190. Miniature in an Anglo-Saxon MS. 11th cent. Westwood, "Palæographia Sacra Pictoria," 1885.

The outlines of these two instruments involuntarily make us think of the round-lyre. One of them is being played by plucking, the other by bowing. In the plucked instrument the considerably deeper sound-box seems to have no table, but is surrounded by a broad oval frame with the outline of the *Cythara Teutonica*. Lengthways over this frame three strings are stretched, the lower ends of which pass under a cross-bar which evidently limits the vibrating part of the strings and at the same time serves as a support for the hand which, just above it, plucks the strings with outstretched fingers. The stopping of the strings is effected from the upper end of the frame by the four fingers of the other hand, which stretch across the open strings as far as they can reach. That in this picture, and contrary to rule, it is the left hand which makes the strings sound and the right that stops them, must be considered a liberty taken by the artist in order to establish symmetry between the pair of figures. (Here, again, I think it highly improbable that the strings were stopped; at most the four fingers damped the strings.—Ed.).

Unlike the plucked instrument, the bowed example is provided with a sound-board over which the strings pass. A tail-piece, which serves as a bridge, as in the guitar, is fixed to the belly. Both on account of its small size and poor stringing the instrument reminds us of the smallest of the Klosterneuburg lyres. When played, it was held in the same manner and was bowed with almost perpendicular strokes with a short and slightly curved bow. As in the plucked instrument, the stopping of the strings was effected by the fingers of the left hand placed over the head of the instrument. (It is possible that the fingers were used to raise the pitch of the strings by a semitone rather than for the purpose of regular stopping, though the latter was in this case—by reason of the underlying sound-board—at least feasible.—Ed.).

On a voyage to Ireland in 1927, the Norwegian musical historian, Dr. O. M. Sandvik, discovered the portrait of a wandering musician on a column in an old Irish church. The minstrel is playing a rather large instrument with a bow, and the instrument bears a striking resemblance to Asaph's lyre in the Cambridge manuscript (see Fig. 191). It is true that only the outlines are discernible, for the monument is considerably worn; all the details of its construction are gone; but the round-lyre outline, the manner in which the left hand stops the strings from the upper end of the sound-box, the form of the bow and its position on the strings, are all of them, at any rate, features which are common to the two instruments. Legend tells us that the church was erected in the sixth cen-

Fig. 191. Sculpture on a column in St. Fianan's Church at Waterville, Co. Kerry.

tury which, however, does not preclude the possibility of the column on which the instrument is depicted, having been a later addition. But even if the dating is uncertain, the monument, at all events, illustrates a bowed instrument, the primitive nature of which proves its existence at a period that cannot be placed later than the eleventh century, when the Cambridge manuscript was written.

(b) The Round-lyre with Narrowed Opening.

In this form the instrument is first found in a manuscript (from Limoges in Brittany) which is preserved in the National Library in Paris (see Fig. 192). On the left knee of a seated figure rests an instrument with the outlines of a *Cythara Teu-*

tonica. The bow, which is a true copy of the Klosterneuburg bow, is held in the right hand. That it is placed on the far side of the bridge shows that the player is resting, for the effect of the stopping, of course, is limited to that part of the string which is above the bridge. Lengthways over the oval instrument three strings are stretched, proceeding from the

Fig. 192. Round-Lyre with narrowed opening. 11th cent.

Fig. 193. Similar type on an
English Sculpture. 12th cent.

lower end of the sound-box, crossing a disproportionately high and perfectly flat bridge, and taken to the tuning-pegs which are seen just above the opening, which in this case is quite small. Through one side of this opening the fingers of the left hand are placed to stop the strings. The illustrations give but an indistinct idea of the form of the opening. Some investigators state that it is square, and take it for granted

225

that the stopping is accomplished on free strings. Grillet's rather detailed reproduction which is used here, however, indicates the existence of a finger-board which reduces the open space to two distinct slits, i.e., a short one to the left of the finger-board and a longer one to the right, through which the fingers are placed. (Here there can be little doubt that the strings were actually stopped, for the presence of the bridge, its position, and the existence of a finger-board under the fingers, render it possible.—Ed.).

Later instruments comparable with the Limoges lyre are to be seen on a bas-relief in Worcester Cathedral (twelfth century; see Fig. 193), and on a wood-carving in St. Mary's Church, Shrewsbury (fourteenth century; reproduced in Galpin's "Old English Instruments of Music"). The model in both cases is still the *Cythara Teutonica*, but the instrument is held in an inverted position, so that the sound-box of the lyre rests against the left shoulder of the player, while the upper end is placed between the knees, probably because here the instrument is in use. In the Worcester lyre the violin-like tail-piece and the C-shaped sound-holes are borrowed from the fiddle; on the other hand, we miss the bridge used in the Limoges lyre. The manner in which the left hand approaches the strings, again indicates the existence of a short finger-board. As usual, the bow is curved, and it is applied immediately above the opening at the spot where the sound-box curves inwards on both sides and where, consequently, it is narrowest.

3. THE ANGLO-SAXON SQUARE LYRE BECOMES A FINGER-BOARD INSTRUMENT.

The oval form of the *Cythara Teutonica* was in reality rather unsuitable for use with a finger-board. The openings left when the finger-board was added, and through which the fingers had to find their way to the strings, were so narrow that the hand literally was tied to one spot. From a very early date England had another type of lyre which was far more suitable than the oval *Cythara Teutonica* of the Continent for accommodating a finger-board. This was the old Anglo-Saxon square lyre (see Figs. 81 and 82). In its square opening the finger-board fitted naturally, and it could at the same time be lengthened. By running parallel with the straight arm of the instrument, the finger-board was also in harmony with the rectilinear form of this lyre, and gave unlimited freedom to the hand and fingers. The earliest known example of the square finger-board lyre dates from the thir-

Fig. 194. Square Finger-board Lyre with inlaid finger-board. 13th cent.

teenth century and is found in a manuscript in the British Museum (see Fig. 194), but the artist cared nothing for detail and was content to draw the outlines of the instrument and the lower part of its four strings, which were probably so distributed that only one of them lay along the finger-board. The other three certainly passed through the openings to the right and left of the finger-board.

With a clarity that guarantees the trustworthiness of the artist, the same instrument is reproduced in a fresco in the Chapter House at Westminster Abbey (fourteenth century; see Fig. 195). In this picture a king holds, in his left hand, an instrument which by its form clearly shows its descent from the old Anglo-Saxon square lyre, while in his right hand he holds a curved bow. Three strings lead from a violin tail-piece, attached to the base of the sound-box, to the head of the lyre, where they are fastened and tuned. It must be taken for granted that the strings ran over a finger-board at the opening, for without it they could not have given any tone worth men-tioning, as the fingers of the left hand close right round them. In the sound-board we see two angular C-shaped sound-holes, one on either side of the strings, but no bridge. (It is pos-sible that what the authoress takes to be sound-holes are the draughtsman's attempt at showing the bridge.—Ed.).

Fig. 195. Square Finger-board Lyre. 14th cent.

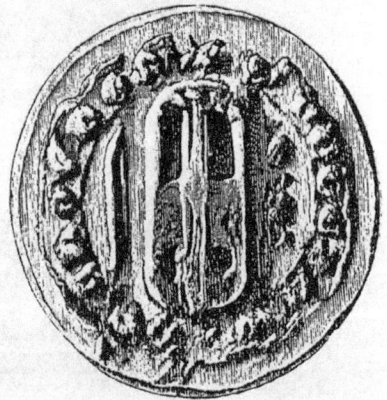

Fig. 196. The Seal of Roger Wade. 14th cent.

Another, and more detailed, reproduction of this square lyre appears on the seal of the Welsh player, Roger Wade, dated 1316. The instrument is unmistakably provided with a neck-like finger-board, a flat bridge and two round sound-holes; finally, we see on the yoke the heads of the tuning-pegs which regulate the tuning of the four strings from the back (see Fig. 196).

As the mediæval pictorial proofs of the bowed lyre end with the example belonging to Roger Wade, and as the instrument already possessed the main features which characterised it when it was rediscovered five hundred years later under the name of *Crwth* in Wales, "as a popular instrument inherited from ancient times," it will be proper now to pass to the popular European instruments that have remained up to the present time as unmistakable descendants of the mediæval bowed lyre. They partially fill up the gaps in the stages of development as shown in the pictures; throwing light on the intermediate forms of which the mediæval lyres gave us no indication; and in Wales showing the final solution of the problem in the emergence of a bowed lyre which is technically far above the ordinary level of the popular instruments.

B. AS A FOLK-INSTRUMENT.

(1) IN THE NORDIC COUNTRIES.

(a) The Tallharpa.

On a voyage made in 1903 by the Finnish musical historian, Otto Andersson, to the Esthonian Islands in order to collect popular melodies among the Swedes living there, he saw both in Nuckö and Wormsoe a strange stringed instrument which was formerly looked upon by the inhabitants as national property and which fifty years ago was still being played by everyone. "He who did not know how to play it," said the inhabitants of Wormsoe at that time, "was not much of a man" (Otto Andersson, "Strakharpan"; in "Etnologiska Studier tillägnade," N. E. Hammarstedt, Stockholm, 1921). The instrument was called the Tallharpa and, according to popular belief, it received that name because it was made of pine (Swedish: *Tall*). Andersson, however, does not accept this explanation and traces the name to *Tagel*, horse-hair, because the strings were originally made of this material; in a shortened form *Tagel* is called *Tall* in compound words. That the instrument is now rare is due, according to Andersson, to a religious revival which took place in Wormsoe at the end of the last century and which "preached music to death so that all the harps were gathered and burnt as the tools of the devil."

Fig. 197. Tallharpa from Nuckö. Photograph.

Fig. 198. Tallharpa-player from Wormsoe (from Andersson).

In Figs. 197 and 198 we see a tallharpa from Nuckö (now in the Nordiska Museum in Stockholm) and a player on that instrument from Wormsoe. As the tallharpa appears in the pictures it recalls the old Anglo-Saxon square lyre. In common with the latter it has the open square space with the pegs inserted into the yoke. On the other hand, new features in the

Esthonian instrument are the reduction of the strings from six to three or four, the use of a violin tail-piece, the presence of two C-shaped sound-holes, and a bridge placed between them, improvements which are clearly enough due to the influence of the modern bowed instruments. Of great interest is the way in which the tallharpa is played. Only one or two of the strings are used for the melody, which is produced by the fingers being inserted from the back and directed sideways against them. The other strings are only used "open," and produce a fixed, continuous, accompanying chord. The bow, which has the curved form of its mediæval ancestor, is com-pelled—by the flat bridge and the straight sides of the instru-ment—to vibrate all the strings simultaneously. Andersson states that the bow was originally made of a bent branch and that the horse-hair was not tight, but could be tightened by the right hand according to necessity, a method still employed by primitive peoples (cf. the Gesso from the Celebes repro-duced in Fig. 171) and is also used with the Uppland Nyckel-harp-bow (see below).

The tone of the tallharpa is described by Andersson as soft and subdued, "like a violin *con sordino*."

Outside of Wormsoe and Nuckö the tallharpa was also used in a somewhat modified form in Dagö. There are ex-amples of it in the Museum at Dorpat, the National Museum in Helsingfors, the Nordiska Museum in Stockholm, and the Musikhistoriska Museum in the same city.

Since the tallharpa in Esthonia is called *rootig kantele*, "Swedish Kantele" or "Swedish Harp," and as the example in the Musikhistoriska Museum was said by the vendor in 1912 to be a popular instrument in Smaaland, Andersson supposes that the instrument was of Swedish origin and was known in Sweden before it went to Esthonia, and in the Esthonian Islands it is especially the Swedes who play it. Andersson takes it for granted that Swedish emigrants at some unknown period took the tallharpa to Esthonia. Concerning the early

colonisation by the Swedes of the Esthonian Islands, see the
"Kongressbericht der I.M.G.," 1909; Otto Andersson, "Alt-
nordische Streichinstrumente."

The possibility that the tallharpa was formerly used in
Norway is suggested by the *Kravik lyre* (shown in Fig. 84),
the external form of which comes very near to that of the tallharpa. It is true that no bow was found with it, and the
number of the strings is six as compared with three or four in
the tallharpa; but the former circumstance may be accidental
and the latter is not necessarily a proof to the contrary, for
among the mediæval bowed lyres there is, at any rate, one
with the same number of strings (see Fig. 189). The Welsh
Crwth, which belongs to the bowed lyres, also had six strings
(see below).

(b) Tallharpa Varieties.

After having discovered the tallharpa in the Esthonian
Islands in 1903, Otto Andersson succeeded in finding other
stringed instruments on Finnish and Swedish soil of nearly
the same design and played in almost the same manner. In
the National Museum at Helsingfors there are thirteen examples of the *Kanteleharpa* which definitely direct one's thoughts
to the tallharpa, except that the open space which in the
former exposed all the strings, is in the latter narrowed to a
broad slit placed in the upper left-hand corner of the sound-
box and leaves only one string for stopping by the fingers inserted from the back. The second and third strings run parallel with it across the sound-box and are therefore accessible
only from the front, where the bow makes them and the
melody-string sound simultaneously (see Figs. 199 to 201).
The most primitive example of such an instrument in the
Museum has only two strings—one melody and one accompanying string which, in their unstopped state, were probably
tuned in fifths.

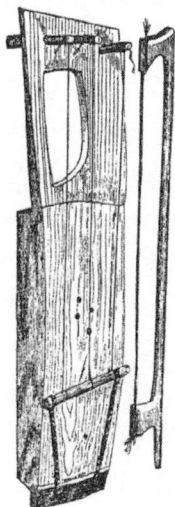

Fig. 199. Primitive three-stringed Kanteleharpe (Retzius).

Fig. 200. Kanteleharpe (Finnish). After Andersson.

Fig. 201. Kanteleharpe (Finnish). Andersson.

Fig. 202. Kanteleharpe from Oestre Karelen (Finnish). *Id.*

In other specimens the sound-box is both longer and broader, and often takes other forms, too. Thus the sides are sometimes incurved, hardly to facilitate the bowing, but rather to support the instrument which, when played, rests on the knee of the performer (see Fig. 201).

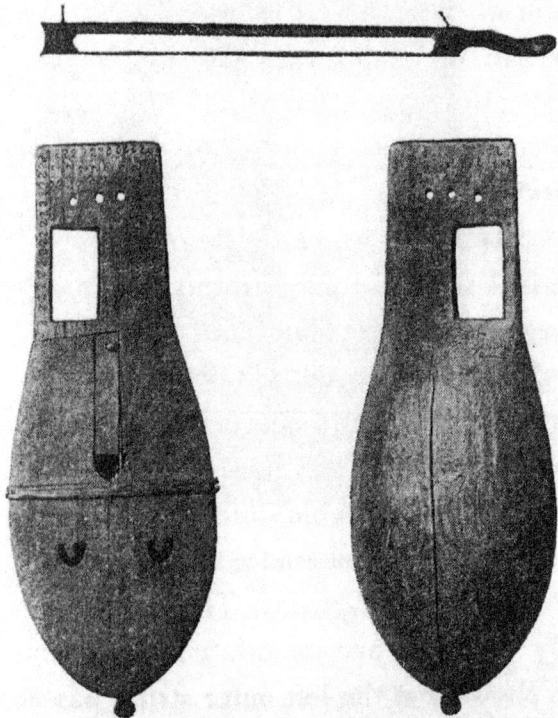

Fig. 203. Luta, a Swedish relative to the
Finnish Kanteleharpe (front and back).

As an isolated type the bowed lyre reproduced in Fig. 202, from Oestre Karelen, very forcibly recalls the Welsh crwth as reproduced for the first time in the thirteenth-century manuscript now in the British Museum (see Fig. 194). Midway in the extensive opening of a regular tallharpa there is, parallel with the sides of the frame, a bar dividing the space into two parts, and the strings—three in all—are so distributed that the middle one runs along the bar, while each of the outer strings passes over one of the side-openings. In the similarly constructed Welsh crwth the bar serves as finger-board; in the Finnish instrument where the stopping, as in the tallharpa, takes place on the left free string, the players explain the design of the instrument by saying that "they have sought to remove all unnecessary wood from the instrument," an explanation with which the investigator cannot rest content. Andersson notices four of these bowed lyres. Two are owned by the National Museum in Helsingfors, one by Andersson himself, and one by Mr. Väisänen, M.A.

An isolated instance of this so-called Kanteleharpe is also found in Dalecarlia in Sweden; but in the Swedish instrument the sound-box has a form which, in its oval contours narrowing at the top and its vaulted back, remind us of the Gunnar harp in the Norwegian wood-carvings and of the mediæval rebec (see Fig. 203). It is this square opening cut into the upper left-hand corner of the sound-board that indicates this instrument as a sister to the Finnish Kanteleharpe. Two C-shaped sound-holes are cut in the table, and at the lower edge of the body is a button-like protuberance (tail-pin) which probably served to hold a violin tail-piece. The three holes in the head were probably bored to accommodate three tuning-pegs, and their position shows that the left outer string passed freely over the oblong opening, while the other two strings, parallel with it, passed longitudinally over the sound-board. The Finnish type must have been known in Norway also. It occurs on a stone monument in the Trondhjem Cathedral, dating from the twelfth century (see Fig. 204). Although the material in which it is cut, made a detailed reproduction of this four-stringed instrument impossible, the position of the left hand clearly indicates the existence of the slot which in the Kanteleharpe enables the melody-string to be stopped by lateral pressure of the knuckles. The position of the bow is also the same as that still maintained on the Finnish instruments. That in a former treatise ("De folkelige Strengeinstrumenter i Nordens

Middelalder" in the annual report of the "Foreningen til norske Fortidsmindesmaerkers Bevaring," 1905) I referred this instrument to an hitherto unknown category of stringed instruments, was due to my ignorance at that time of the existonce of the Finnish Kanteleharpe.

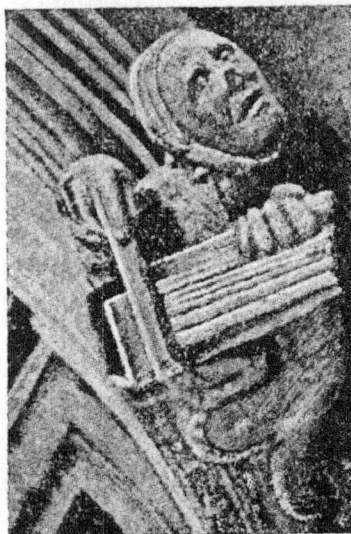

Fig. 204. Stringed instrument in Trondhjem Cathedral. (Photograph.)

2. IN WALES.

A popular bowed instrument recalling the mediæval bowed lyres still existed in Wales at the end of the eighteenth century. It was called the Crwth and was said to be very ancient. There were, however, so few who knew how to play it, that its days seemed to be numbered. It was therefore in the nick of time that Sir John Hawkins and Daines Barrington received an inkling of its existence; and they saved it from oblivion by almost simultaneously illustrating and describing it in the "History of Music" (1776) and "Archæological or Miscellaneous Tracts relating to Antiquity" (1775) respectively.

(a) *The Welsh Crwth* (see Fig. 205). To all appearances this instrument was a direct continuation of the mediæval attempts to provide the round-lyre with a finger-board, with the fiddle as model. The sound-box and lyre-arms make an oblong, 57 centimetres long by 25 broad. The sound-box consists of a hollowed wooden block covered with a table, or it is made of a table and back connected by rather deep ribs. The finger-board lies longitudinally in the centre of the ob-

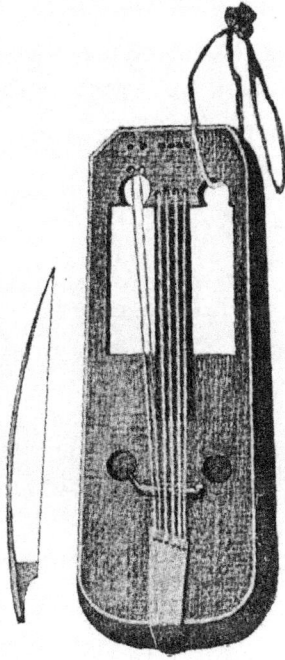

Fig. 205. Welsh Crwth.

long, reaching from the sound-box to the yoke, and approached by the stopping fingers through one of the window-like side-openings. Of the six gut strings with which the crwth is strung, four run over the finger-board and are played by the bow, while the other two lie at the side of the finger-board and are plucked, open, by the thumb. All the strings are attached to a violin tail-piece, the lower end of which is fastened to a tail-pin. In some instruments the tail-piece is cut straight at the top so that its upper edge runs parallel with the lower edge of the sound-box; in others it is cut obliquely so that its upper edge runs in the same direction as the

obliquely-placed bridge. This combination of an oblique
tail-piece and a bridge running parallel with it, is also en-
countered in another popular Nordic instrument of mediæval
origin—the Swedish Nyckelharpa. Like the Welsh crwth,
it hangs by a ribbon from the neck of the player, and is thus
in a horizontal position, so that the bow is moved by the right
hand slantingly near the bridge (see also s.v. "Keyboard
Fiddles"). From the tail-piece the strings are taken, four
over the finger-board and two at the side of it, to the yoke,
where they are drawn through six holes to the T-shaped tuning-pegs inserted from the back and which are turned either
by the fingers or a wrest. In the belly there are two round
sound-holes. The bridge, the top of which it not curved like
that of the modern violin-bridge, but almost flat, is so made
that the bow is nearly always compelled to touch several
strings at once. The feet of the bridge are, moreover, of different lengths: the right, only two centimetres long, rests on
the table just before the right sound-hole; the left, which
measures seven centimetres, passes *through* the left sound-hole
and the sound-box, and rests on the inner side of the back.
It therefore serves the purpose of the sound-post in the modern
violin. This combination of bridge and sound-post is found
again in the modern Greek lyre, a bowed instrument. (The
position of the crwth bridge-foot that passes through the
sound-hole is clearly shown in the example in the Victoria and
Albert Museum and illustrated in Pulver's "Dictionary of
Old English Music."—Ed.).

In the eighteenth century the six strings were tuned thus:

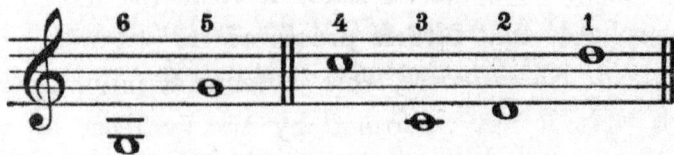

(The octave G for the strings beside the finger-board, and the
rest for the stopped strings.)

There were thus in reality only three different notes and their octaves:

The advantage of this tuning was that the strings could be tuned in pairs of fifths and octaves:

A traveller, W. Bingley, who visited Wales in 1801, and there heard the instrument played by an old peasant of Caernarvon, says that it was tuned in a different manner and nearer to the violin-tuning in so far that the pairs of strings were a fifth apart:

The first tuning given above, however, is doubtlessly the older.

What has been said here of the shape, the arrangement, and the manner of playing the Welsh crwth, makes its descent from the bowed lyre as we know it from the monuments, so highly probable that further proofs of its origin seem almost superfluous. Nevertheless, this conclusion might seem to be too rash were it not confirmed by the evidence afforded by Welsh literature, which illustrates the history of this ancient folk-instrument in the country that has retained it down to the present day.

Literary Evidence relating to the Welsh Crwth.

Etymologically, *Crwth* corresponds to the ancient Irish *Cruit*, which seems originally to have indicated a lyre-type, but which was later also used for the harp (see pp. 124 *ff.*).

The Crwth as a Bardic Instrument. It appears clearly from ancient Welsh sources that poetry and music formed the central features of the bardic art from the earliest times. As early as the seventh century we hear of a bardic gathering at which the king issued important decrees relating to poetry and music. Then mention is made, in 1066, in 1107, in 1135, and 1176, of great bardic festivals attended by bards, poets and singers. Especial splendour attached to the Eisteddfod of 1176, which, after having been announced six months in advance, took place in Aberteifi (Cardigan), and at which two contests were arranged; one between the telyn and crwth players and the pipers, the other between the bards and the poets. As will be generally known, the bards were divided into two main classes: the higher, real, bards who had graduated, and the despised uncrowned *(bôn y glêr)*, who were considered as the weeds among the bards—those whom the devil had enticed to idleness and a dissolute life. While the graduates played seated, the ungraduated had to stand while they played, and their pay was only a penny.

In Welsh literature the crwth was thus, in the eleventh century already, a bardic instrument which existed in two forms: the aristocratic six-stringed crwth, the privileged instrument of the higher bards, and the simpler crwth with three strings, in the handling of which much less art was necessary, and which was therefore left to the lower bards.

There is no description whatever of the three-stringed crwth in the Welsh manuscripts. It is therefore merely hypothetical when Fétis ("Antoine Stradivari," Paris, 1856), Engel ("Researches into the Early History of the Violin Family," London, 1883), and Edward Jones ("Musical and Poetical

Relics of the Welsh Bards," 1799) identify it with the ancient Irish *cruit thritant* and with the *chrotta* mentioned in the poem of Fortunatus; and still more so when Fétis describes it as a guitar-shaped instrument of small size, and Jones presents it as a violin or "rather a rebec."

On the other hand, there is a fifteenth-century poem containing a contemporaneous description of the six-stringed crwth of the crowned bards. The author is the Gaelic bard, Grufydd ap Darydd ap Howel, and the poem in Edward Jones's translation runs thus:

> A fair coffer with a bow, a girdle,
> A finger-board and a bridge; its value is a pound,
> It has a frontlet formed like a wheel,
> With a short-nosed bow across;
> And from its centre it winds in a ring;
> And the bulging of its back is somewhat like an old man.
> And on its breast harmony reigns:
> From the sycamore music will be obtained.
> Six pegs, if we screw them,
> Will tighten all the chords.
> Six strings advantageously are found,
> Which in the hand produce a hundred sounds,
> A string for every finger is distinctly seen,
> And also two strings for the thumb.

The manner of playing the crwth has been hinted at in a single source consisting of two manuscript fragments which are copies of copies of an original written during the reign of Henry VIII by the harper, W. Penlyn, who, in the opinion of Welsh investigators, undoubtedly drew his knowledge from very ancient sources. These fragments were printed in "Myvyrian Archæology," III, pp. 438 and 439 and 627; translated in the "Cambrian Register," Vol. I, p. 387, col. 2, and p. 388, cols. 1, 2. See also Walter, "Das alte Wales." Unfortunately, however, the translation of the fragments found in the "Cambrian Register," one of which deals with the keys and is intended for teaching crwth-playing, while the other contains the principles of handling the instrument, is so bad that nobody has hitherto, as far as I know, been able to make it out. The translator clearly worked without any knowledge of the current musical terms, and therefore made use of words that leave the sense quite uncertain. Only two questions are decided in this clumsy translation—namely, (1) that the crwth of the fifteenth century Celtic bard was a stringed instrument and had been so within the memory of man, and (2) that it was used not only to accompany song but also as an independent solo instrument in the widest sense of the word. One of the fragments contains the expressions *craviad dyblyg*, *craviad unig*, and *hauner craviad*, translated by "double scratching," "single scratching," and "half scratching," which were clearly enough bowing directions. The other describes seventeen different methods of manipulating the instrument, and indicates that considerable technical skill and knowledge were required for playing the Welsh crwth.

C.   SUMMARY.

In comparing the details obtained from our examination of the bowed lyres illustrated in the Middle Ages with the original instruments retained in the service of the folk-music of northern Europe, we are in the first place surprised to find a bowed instrument which in appearance and details corresponds with the plucked lyre-type of the Middle Ages. The particulars given by both sources regarding the treatment of the bowed lyre are in agreement *inter se*, as far as the stopping of the strings, both on the earliest bow-lyre and that of the Middle Ages (Figs. 188 and 189), and on the Esthonian tallharpa (Figs. 157 and 158), is concerned; this was performed by pressure of the fingers against the free strings of the instrument. If it is thus easy to recognise the stage of development to which the normal tallharpa must be referred, it is somewhat more difficult to place its variety, the Finnish kanteleharpe. It is true that a lyre-type with a narrowed string-space also occurs in the mediæval pictures; but the opening there is placed centrally, and the position of the fingers often indicates the existence of a short finger-board; while the opening in the Finnish instrument is placed in the upper left-hand corner of the sound-box, and is so narrow that it only leaves one string free, and is, without the assistance of a finger-board, stopped by the fingers inserted from the back. The kanteleharpe may therefore indicate a hitherto unknown and earlier stage in the development of the mediæval instrument with the narrowed string-opening; and this suggestion to all appearances finds support in a remark in Galpin's "Old English Instruments of Music." By his description our thoughts are sent involuntarily to the Finnish kanteleharpe with its obliquely-placed string-opening of the smallest size, and thus, strikingly enough, this strange instrument originated just in those countries where the bowed-lyre of the Middle Ages was especially made the subject of reforms.

As we have seen, the last stage in the evolution of the bowed-lyre was reached in the thirteenth century, when the old Anglo-Saxon square lyre, instead of the *Cythara Teutonica*, was chosen for the insertion of the long fingerboard borrowed from the fiddle, and through it was applied to the Welsh bardic crwth. That it is also represented in one of the Finnish bowed lyres shows that, like the first type, it was known far beyond the confines of England. The only difference is that the modern Finnish players disregard the true intention of the finger-board and handle the instrument as they are accustomed to handle their other kanteleharpe, i.e., by pressure of the fingers against the open strings placed alongside the finger-board.

Through all these stages in the development of the bowed-lyre the oval and the "square" round-lyre fought for supremacy. The Klosterneuburg lyre is thus oval, the tallharpa square. The Finnish kanteleharp is square, while its Swedish counterpart, the luta, found in the Dalecarlia, is oval. The lyres from Limoges and Worcester are both oval, but with the last English bowed-lyre of the monuments and the Welsh crwth of the fifteenth century the square form was finally adopted as that most suitable for the finger-board lyre.

As the starting-point in the development of the bowed lyre the monuments decidedly point to the countries which were under the influence of Celtic culture. Unquestionably the most important contributions to the elucidation of its history are given by the English monuments. Even the reproductions which appear exceptionally in Austria and in a Munich manuscript may without difficulty be traced to the British Isles and their Celtic inhabitants. It was from England that the Continent received the first missionaries when Christianity was introduced. Priests and monks of Celtic origin long continued to leave their mark upon intellectual life in the German and Frankish monasteries and convent-schools. The reproduction of a Celtic instrument of music in the Klosterneuburg and Munich manuscripts need therefore not surprise us. At the same time it is easy to understand why the bowed lyre in these manuscripts was illustrated in its earliest form. When later on that stage in its development was reached in which the strings ran over the finger-board, the missions which at that time connected Germany and England had long ceased, and others, introducing in part the Oriental stringed instruments, made their way to the Continent. In the British Isles and Brittany, which was also inhabited by Celts, the Celtic instrument was still used; and it is therefore the English woodcarvings and sculptures which enable us to follow the development of the bowed lyre right up to the time when the pictures of the fourteenth century suddenly cease to take notice of them, and compel us to seek the assistance of the folk-instruments so that we may learn its ultimate destiny.

It is exceedingly interesting to recognise the bowed lyre as a popular instrument among the Nordic peoples, who in ancient times were so greatly influenced by Celtic culture, and to find it both in the form in which it began its development (e.g., the Klosterneuburg lyre) and in a stage unknown to the monuments—the Finnish kanteleharpe and the Swedish luta, which looks like a transitional form between the regular unchanged round-lyre and the earliest form of the fingerboard lyre (the Limoges lyre). Like the tallharpa, this transitional type seems to be a survival from the time when Christianity first came to these countries. On its way from West to East, i.e., from England to Denmark and Norway, and thence to Sweden and Finland, Christianity was in this case also a natural means of spreading Celtic culture. Thus the bowed lyre native to the British Isles made its way together with Christianity to the remote parts of Europe, where it was recently rediscovered, and where it retained its life in folk-music for seven centuries.

It was also a love for the traditional that caused the inhabitants of Celtic Wales to cling to a form of the bowed lyre that seems to indicate the final stage in its development—the strange Welsh crwth, the well-known instrument of the Celtic bards, which as an instrument in the service of art was surprisingly well developed.

That the bowed lyre was a national Celtic possession also appears with certainty from Welsh literary sources. These allude to two bardic instruments, both called *crwth;* i.e., a six-stringed instrument belonging to the crowned bard, and a three-stringed form played by the undistinguished *bôn y glêr*.

When we examine the monuments, we find in one case (the Klosterneuburg picture) three different bowed lyres portrayed together and thus belonging to the same period. It is true that only one is reproduced with strings; but the distribution of the instruments among a superior (crowned) performer playing his instrument sitting, and two inferior (bareheaded) musicians who play standing, involuntarily takes our thoughts to the distinction made in Welsh literature between the sitting crowned bard, and the standing ungraduated novice. If the players are bards, the instrument of the sitting player will be an example of the six-stringed bardic crwth of the eleventh century, while the smaller bowed lyre played by the standing performer on the left, which in fact has three strings, must be described as the three-stringed crwth mentioned by the ancient writers. The existence of the third lyre, also played standing, and which is again placed in the hands of a bareheaded player, cannot be proved from the written records, but suggests the possibility of there having existed, together with the aristocratic six-stringed and the despised three-stringed crwth, a third bardic instrument, which perhaps ranked above the three-stringed, but was held in less esteem than the six-stringed instrument. If we consider the Klosterneuburg picture as a collective representation of the Celtic bards' instruments, the one in the centre should be the crwth of the higher bard in its oldest form, and the six-stringed bowed lyre of the Munich manuscript must also be explained in the same way. The three-stringed crwth of the lower bards is perhaps concealed, apart from the Klosterneuburg evidence, in the small three-stringed bowed lyre of the Anglo-Saxon manuscript in Cambridge. The Limoges lyre, on account of its three strings, might be said to have been a later edition of the same, if the player did not expressly designate himself as a distinguished player by his royal crown. Wewertem ("Zwei veraltete Musikinstrumente," in the "Monatshefte für Musikgeschichte," Series 13, 1881) is therefore of opinion that the coronet is not to be looked upon as a royal crown, but rather as the insignia of the French *Roi des Menetriers*, i.e., king of the French minstrels' guild. If so, the dating of the picture is, it is true, somewhat disturbed, for the existence of the French guild cannot be traced farther back than 1295; but the acceptance of the instrument as an example of the one used by inferior bards might be upheld by this explanation. In any case the dating of the Limoges manuscript in the eleventh century is also not absolutely reliable.

To follow the three and six-stringed crwth step by step

through the ages on the basis of the number of strings can only be done with difficulty, for those on the bowed lyres in the pictures vary from three to six. That six was the number of strings used by the Celts at all times on the instrument used by the crowned bard must be looked upon as certain. This is proved by the fourteenth-century picture of the bard Roger Wade's crwth, by the description of the six-stringed bardic crwth in Grufydd ap Darydd's poem of the fifteenth century, and by the six-stringed bard's crwth that was still played in Wales in the eighteenth century. I am inclined to consider the bowed lyres with fewer strings which are illustrated on the monuments, and at a later date still used as folk-instruments, on the one hand, as descendants of the less esteemed three-stringed bardic crwth, and on the other as the result of the fusion of the originally separated types. This fusion sometimes takes place in the case of instruments whose traditions were forgotten in the course of time, and the individual properties of which were therefore no longer respected in all their details. I am disposed to place in the first category the three, four, and five-stringed bowed lyres of the English monuments, and in the other the traditional Esthonian, Finnish, Swedish and Norwegian lyres.

In the six-stringed Norwegian *kravik* lyre the classical number of strings of the higher bardic lyre is thus still held in honour, while the Esthonian tallharpa—the customs of the past having been forgotten and the bowed instruments of modern times being approached—reduced the number of its strings to four or three. Finally, the Swedish luta and the Finnish kanteleharpe with their few strings come nearer to the simpler instruments of the uncrowned bards.

II. The Monastery Monochord and its Descendants.

In the mediæval convent-schools the monochord played the same part as it did in the schools of antiquity. While theorists used it as a means of scientific demonstration, the practical musicians employed it as an aid in the teaching of singing.

It was without doubt the example of the monastery mono-chords that led the practical musicians to the instruments of music related to the monochord which, during the Middle Ages, were principally to be found in the hands of secular

Fig. 206. Guido d'Arezzo and his patron, Theodal, at the Monochord
(late Royal Library, Vienna).

players, and whose music, favouring an organ-point, recurs among their descendants that still live as national folk-possessions in different parts of the world.

Among the mediæval instruments which we recognise with certainty as having been related to the monastery monochord, we find: A. The balk monochords provided with a finger-board, i.e., the Trumscheit and the Scheitholt, from which in time both the Nordic Langeleik, the Icelandic Langspil, the Dutch Humle, and the French Vosges Spinet arose. I have chosen the word "balk" because the names originally attached to this type of monochord expressly referred to its external re-semblance to a balk (German, *Scheit*, Dutch, *Balk*, French, *Bûche*). B. The keyboard monochords without finger-board. i.e., the lyre, the keyboard-fiddle, and the clavichord.

A. THE BALK MONOCHORDS.

i. TRUMSCHEIT (TRUMPET MARINE) AND ITS MEDIÆVAL PROTOTYPES.

When the French poetical works of the Middle Ages enu-merate the instruments used by the jongleurs, they often mention a "monocorde qui n'a qu'une corde." If we ex-amine the mediæval illustrations, we find only two examples of the one-stringed instrument of music. One is a small pear-shaped bowed instrument, which is often reproduced in French sculptures and in German manuscripts from the tenth to the twelfth century. As the manuscripts, however, call it "lyra," and it seems to have been used chiefly for ecclesiastical music, the French poets could scarcely have meant this instrument with their "monocorde." It is far more reasonable to connect the name with the other one-stringed instrument illustrated, for both by its construction and its use it proclaims itself·to be the instrument of the wandering minstrel.

The instrument in question consisted of a long box made of three tapering boards, of which two formed the angular back of the sound-box, while the third served as a belly over which the single string (sometimes, however, two or three) passed. This use of two or three strings, which converted the monochord into a dichord and trichord respectively, does not exclude the possibility of these monochord-shaped instruments having been called "monochords" in the Middle Ages. Another descendant of the theoretical monochord, the clavichord, for a time still kept the name after having severed all connec-

Fig. 207. French plucked Monochord. 12th cent.

Fig. 208. Dichord. 14th cent. Fragment of a mural painting in Beauvais (Grillet).

tion with the mother instrument (v. below, s.v. Clavichord). The string of the true monochord reached from the broad base of the instrument to the tuning-peg inserted in a square plate. In the earliest pictures (twelfth-fourteenth centuries) the string was plucked with the fingers of the right hand, while those of the left hand performed the stopping in the normal manner immediately below the tuning-peg (see Fig. 207). The instrument was to all appearances built of thin material and had no great length. When played, it was placed perpendicularly before the sitting player, so that it ran lengthwise along his right leg. Where the instrument lies across the breast of the mermaid in Fig. 208, the position of the hands indicates that it is not being played. Where the obliquely-cut back-boards meet in a point at the base, the belly ends (as in Fig. 207) and shows the inside of the lower part of the sound-box. In Fig. 208, however, the belly continues to the base of the body, and the strings are supported by a bridge.

From the fifteenth century onwards this wandering minstrel's monochord was consistently illustrated as a bowed instrument, and it occurred in a large and a small form. The sound-box was then often made of four boards instead of three, and in the table there was frequently a round or square soundhole. On this bowed monochord, moreover, there was a novelty in the altered position of the hands, for the left hand came to be applied to the lower end of the string, while the right hand used the bow near the tuning-peg (see Figs. 209 and 210).

From this monochord it was but a short step to the instrument which, under the name of *Trumscheit* or *Tympani schiza*, was illustrated by Virdung in " Musica getutscht " (1511) and by Agricola in " Musica instrumentalis deudsch " (1528, 1529). In Glareanus's " Dodecachordon " (1530) it is minutely described for the first time.

Trumscheit, Trompet Marina, Tympani schiza. Glareanus tells us that the Germans and the Gauls living on the Rhine used an instrument closely related to the theoretical monochord, and which was called the trumscheit or tympani schiza. It was composed of three tapering boards, which gave it the shape of an elongated three-sided pyramid. Extended across one of the faces was a string which was set in vibration, " or rather scraped," by a horse-hair bow rubbed with resin. Sometimes, besides this string, there was another, of only half

Fig. 209. Minstrel's Large
Monochord (Dichord). 15th
cent.

Fig. 210. Small Monochord (fragment
of painting by Hans Memling). 15th
cent.

Fig. 211. Dichord (by Seb.
Brandt: *La nef des fous*, 16th
cent.). Here the stopping of the
strings, by way of exception, is
still performed between the tuning-peg and the bow.

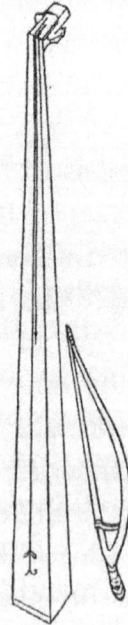

Fig. 212. Trumscheit of the
early 16th cent. (Virdung).

the length of the first, meant to increase the resonance of the long string by giving the octave sympathetically. The players carried the instrument about the streets and rested the pointed end, in which the tuning-peg was inserted, against the chest. The other end, which was hollow and open, and constituted the triangular base of the instrument, they held with the left hand. While the left thumb touched the string lightly at the appropriate places, the right hand carried the bow within the limits set by the thumb. Generally only the fundamental tone, the third, the fourth, the fifth, and the octave, were produced on the instrument. If the points producing the "harmonics" of the strings on the bowed instruments are touched lightly while the bow is carried across the strings, the flute-like so-called flageolet-tones or "harmonics" are heard—i.e., the upper partials of the fundamental note of the string concerned. "The players have difficulty in finding the whole and half tones," says Glareanus, "because they are ignorant of music. They even tried to convince me that they could not even be produced on the instrument. As I wondered greatly at this, I experimented myself on one of their instruments and thereby found that the assertion of the players was due partly to ignorance of music, as they only knew how to divide the strings by means of the 'thick' fingers, and partly to the fact that the buzzing of the longest strings only takes place when the points of division are touched, and not by making whole or half-tones." To produce this buzzing there was a curved bridge, one foot of which, broad and thick, supported the string near the base of the sound-box, while the other foot, which was thin and narrow, rested upon a piece of ivory or other hard material. When the string was touched by the bow, its foot vibrated against the board, so that the tone trembled or quivered. In order to increase this vibration, a thin nail was often inserted in the tip of the loose foot. "I could not help laughing at these people's invention," said Glareanus. The instrument was about five feet long, and each of the three boards measured three and a half inches at the broad end and one and a half at the top.

Prætorius, in his "Syntagma musicum" (1618) adhered to the description of Glareanus; but the Trumscheit he reproduced and explained was seven feet three inches long, and was provided with four strings tuned to C, c, g, c'. Of these only the C-string was used to produce the melody; the other three only responded sympathetically, and the effect was "that at a distance it sounds as if four trumpets were blown at the same time" (see Fig. 213).

The trumpet-tone, which was produced by the combination of the harmonic produced by the thumb and the buzzing created by the bridge, caused the instrument, outside of Germany, and later also in Germany, to be called *Trompet Marina*, and by this name it was known when it came to be described in Mersenne's "Harmonie Universelle."

Mersenne illustrated two trumpets marine, an earlier one which, like Virdung's and Glareanus's Trumscheit, had two strings (a long and a short one) giving the octave of one another, and a later one, which was only provided with a single thick string. In both cases the string was attached to a tail-piece glued to the sound-board immediately below the vibrating bridge, which for the first time was clearly illustrated and enlarged in Mersenne's work (see Fig. 214). We can here see clearly the fixed end of the bridge with its groove into which the string was laid, and the long vibrating end or tail that caused the trumpet tone. Mersenne said that it was exceedingly difficult to place this bridge so that the string vibrated exactly as it should. If it were placed wrongly, the vibrations were either too strong or too weak. "Often," he wrote, "several hours elapse before the proper place for the bridge can be found." As the bow touches the string just below the tuning peg, it was necessary, in order to obtain a grip on this unwieldy instrument, "either to support its broad end against a wall or on the ground." To the right of the string

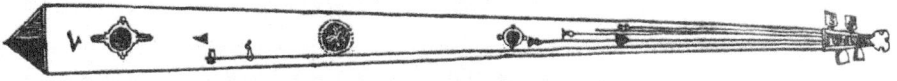

Fig. 213. Trumscheit. Prætorius, 1618.

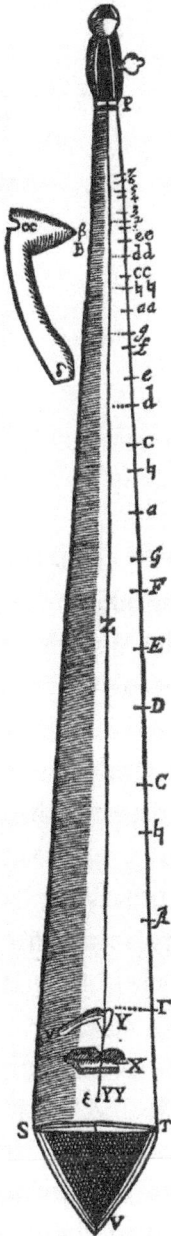

Fig. 214. One-stringed *Trompet Marina* (Mersenne). To the left of the instrument the vibrating bridge is shown, enlarged.

Fig. 215. English Trumpet Marine. XVII Cent.

we see a series of strokes in Mersenne's picture, which indicate the points at which the thumb was to be placed in order to produce the notes of the Guidonian scale from *Gamma*, which is produced by the open string, up to *e′*, whence the scale is continued another octave by using the figures 1-7. The places where the trumpet tone is produced, are marked by Mersenne by a dotted line. They are found at *d* (the twelfth of the note given by the open string), *g*, *b*, and *d′*, and at the figures 2-7, producing the notes *g′*, *a′*, *b′*, *c″*, *d″*, and *e″*. Beyond these places the trumpet tone could also be produced by touching the unstopped string at Γ and by its octave at *G;* "but in general only the trumpet tones from *d* and upwards are used."

Mersenne said that the trumpet marine was so difficult to handle that there were only a few who could play it well; for great dexterity was required to allow the thumb to glide from place to place quickly enough. "However," he wrote, "I do not doubt that he who would devote as much time to this instrument as he would otherwise spend on manipulating a violin or a lute, would be able to learn to play it very well." That the bowing was performed at the upper end of the string was explained by Mersenne by the circumstance that the right hand holding the bow found it easiest to work near the tuning peg, and that the thumb of the left hand rested lighter on the string when placed on the far side of the bow. · The tighter the string, the better was the trumpet tone. The thickness of the string also played an important part in this connection. On the later trumpet marine Mersenne did not show any sound holes; but in the earlier one, he gave a single hole: "not because it is absolutely necessary; for that matter we could even have two or three."

While it is possible, judging from the position of the hands, to come to the more or less certain conclusion that even the minstrel's monochord must have used the harmonic notes from the moment it began to be bowed, it is uncertain when the idea of the vibrating bridge was applied to the instrument for the purpose of transforming the flageolet tone to the trumpet tone. In Virdung's and Agricola's illustrations this bridge is not yet seen; but as Glareanus in his "Dodecachordon" described it in 1530 as a peculiarity of the instrument, it must have been used at that time.

In Germany the Trumscheit does not seem to have been held in great esteem. Virdung and Agricola both described it as "ein unnutz Instrument," because it lacked the frets which would enable the performer to play it "secundum artem"; Glareanus declared that it sounded best at a distance and was ironical about the "ridiculous" attempts of the players to increase the trumpet effect by inserting a thin nail in the tip of the loose foot.

Things were quite different in France. Mersenne sounds quite respectful when he says that he who devoted sufficient time to the instrument could certainly learn to play it well. So much is at any rate certain, that this primitive instrument was later on improved in France by means of a violin neck with a scroll and tuning pegs on each side, a carefully made sound box, and sympathetic strings of metal (see Fig. 215). Thus the *Trompet marina* rose in esteem; it became a musician's instrument and in France for a time even formed a regular part of the royal orchestra. At the performance of Cavalli's opera, "Xerxes," on the occasion of Louis XIV's marriage in 1660, there was a scene with sailors playing the *Trompette marine.* Not until 1780 did the old instrument disappear definitely from the French orchestra, to be replaced by the contrabass viol.

The trumpet marine, however, was retained longest in the German nunneries, where it was still being used in the nineteenth century to replace the real trumpet.

It is not known whence the German name *Trumscheit* or *Trummescheit* was derived. As it was sometimes called *Trumbescheit* (*Trumbe* meaning trumpet) it is possible that this name, like *trompet marina*, pointed to the trumpet-like tone of the instrument; this was also the case with the later German name of *Trompetengeige*. All agree that *trompet marina* as the international name for the instrument (German and Danish *Marine trompet*, Italian *Tromba marina*, English *Trumpet marine*, French *Trompette marine*, Spanish *Trompeta marina*, Portuguese *Trombeta marina*) was due to its trumpet-like tone; but there is no satisfactory explanation for the addition *marina*. Some have ascribed it to the fact that the instrument was especially popular in the English navy; Mersenne was of opinion that it was possibly invented by mariners; but there is really no proof that the trumpet marine was at any time used by seamen or at sea. The addition to the name was possibly due to a confusing of the bowed instrument, trumpet marine, with a wind instrument of the same name which was used on board ship as a signalling instrument. Galpin traces the name to a French trumpeter named Marin or Maurin, and thinks that the instrument may have been named after him, "because it was perhaps he who invented the vibrating bridge." In Germany it is said that Marine-trompet was a corruption of *Marientrompet* (also called *Nonnengeige*), because the instrument, as mentioned above, was chiefly used in nunneries. A *Trompet Mariae* was actually mentioned in 1773 in the inventory of the instruments in the orchestra of the Prince of Anhalt Cöthen. As Daniel Fryklund says ("Studier over Marintrumpeten; Svensk Tidskrift för Musikforskning," I, 1919), it might be a question whether the name *Marinetrompet* is not older than *Marientrompet*, so that *Marientrompet* was a corruption of *Marinetrompet* and not vice versa. The correct answer was evidently given by Curt Sachs ("Handbuch der Musikinstrumentenkunde," 1920) when he said that the *Trompet marin* in Poland was called *Tub maryna*, and that *maryna* in the modern colloquial Polish language means a bass viol. As *Tub* means trumpet, the Polish name thus corresponds to the German *Trompetengeige*.

Its place of origin is equally doubtful. Riemann maintains, though without supplying any evidence in support of his claim, that it was of German origin; others, and primarily Curt Sachs, think on the other hand that it was of Slav provenance, basing their views on the triangular form common to the *Kirghiz* and the Tartar *Tanbours* and the Russian *Balalaika*, and on the almost exclusive use of the trumpet marine for providing flageolet notes, which always were and still are characteristic of the playing of the bowed instruments by the Slav peoples. (I must confess that these reasons do not seem to me to be sufficient.—Ed.)

A degenerate descendant of the trumpet marine is without doubt the one-stringed instrument which in our own day is still

Fig. 216. Bumbas.

used by wandering beggars, and which, during the Great War, was used by the German soldiers in the trenches (see Fig. 216). It consists of a long pole hung with bells and provided with a single string carried across one or two ox bladders attached to the pole. When the string is rubbed with the bow, the string, through its contact with the bladder, produces a rumbling tone. In Germany it is called the *Bumbas*, in England the Bladder and String, in France the *Basse de Flandre*. It is clearly enough this degenerate instrument which Moth described in his Danish dictionary under the heading *Trompet marin*. "Trompet marin," he wrote, "is a musical instrument made of a long piece of wood on which is stretched a coarse string over an inflated bladder which is placed below, and which is played with a bow, making a sound like a drum."

2. THE SCHEITHOLT FAMILY.

a. *In the Middle Ages.*

Scheitholt is the German name for an instrument which in name and appearance recalls the Trumscheit, but which is quite different in its effect and manner of manipulation.

The first account of this instrument comes from Praetorius ("Syntagma musicum," 1618) who described it as a small monochord made of three or four boards, provided at one end

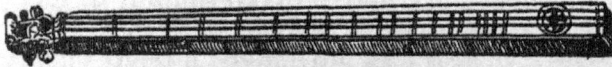

Fig. 217.   Scheitholt (Prætorius).

with a peg box in which are inserted three or four pegs for tuning the brass strings of the instrument. Of these strings three are tuned to the same note, while the fourth (which was added ad libitum) was tuned an octave higher. One of the unison strings was pressed on to the finger-board by a little metal hook halfway (?) down, so that its pitch was raised a fifth. Near the nut the thumb of the right hand made the instrument sound by crossing all the strings, while the left hand made the melody by drawing a little smooth rod backwards and forwards over the foremost string. Brass frets indicated the places where the various notes were to be found.

Although this description originated long after the Middle Ages, it cannot be doubted that the instrument described was of mediaeval origin. Its simple construction, its close relationship to a definite group of mediæval instruments (cf. inf.), and its early distribution over almost all parts of Europe, are proofs of this fact.

In principle the Scheitholt may be called a monochord arranged for practical use. It had but one string, i.e., the melody string, passing over the frets and intended for stopping. The other strings, unstopped, merely served to support the melody since they gave a consistently consonant bass chord (cf. the lyre and the keyboard fiddle).

The manner in which the strings were made to sound by means of the thumb and the production of the melody by means of a rod gliding backwards and forwards were also very primitive features.

It is unknown whence the Scheitholt came. As a popular instrument among some European nations it was said to have originated first in one country, then in another. In the sixteenth century the Italians considered it to be a very old Tuscan instrument (Zarlino); in Germany it was sometimes called "Spanish"; in Holland it was said, at the end of the seventeenth century, to have been Scandinavian; in France it was called a Flemish instrument, but was later given to the Vosges mountain districts as the *Épinette des Vosges*. Curt Sachs suggests the possible descent of the Scheitholt from a West Asiatic instrument, a kind of zither, used by a Turkish tribe—the Katschinzes—and called the *Tschat'han*. It is true that this instrument (reproduced in "Verhandlungen der Berliner Gesellschaft für Anthropologie," 1895, page 618) is reminiscent to all appearances of a Scheitholt or *Langeleg*, as here again seven equally long and similarly tuned strings are stretched over a long square chest, which terminates at both ends in a scroll. In the Turkish instrument, however, we miss the divided finger-board which is the most characteristic feature of the Scheitholt. To produce the different notes the *Tschat'han* used small jacks which were distributed under all the strings and which, when necessary, were moved to different places.

Like a favoured child the Scheitholt received many names during its vagabond life, and in a naive manner these often referred to the properties especially noted by the individual player. As mentioned above, the resemblance of the instrument to a balk produced the name Scheitholt in Germany. The same conception was the basis of the Dutch name *(noord'sche) Balk*, and the French *Bûche (de Flandre)*. The elongated form of the instrument made Icelanders, Norwegians and Danes call it *Langspil, Langharpe* and *Langeleg* respectively. Finally the persistent consonant bass chord gave it the name *Hommel* or *Humle* (from the Dutch *hommeln*, to hum, *cf.* humble bee), which was afterwards used in Holland, Germany *(Spanische Hummel)*, Schleswig-Holstein and Sweden.

b. As a Popular Instrument.

After having lived a roving life as a folk instrument among most of the European nations, the Scheitholt at length settled in the north of Europe as a special Nordic folk instrument. As such it was already described in a literary work which—in addition to Prætorius's "Syntagma"—deigns to mention it. Volume II of "Grondig Onderzoek van de Toonen der Musijk" by the Dutch organist and teacher, Klaus Douwes, of Tynn in Friesland (1699).

The instrument was there expressly designated as the *Noord'sche Balk* and was described as a hollow four-sided instrument, two or three feet long (or somewhat longer or shorter), and with three or four strings which were stretched over a bridge. The melody was produced on the foremost string, below which inlaid copper frets indicated the diatonic succession: *c, d, e, f, g, etc.* The other strings were all tuned to the same note and formed the bass. Some played the instrument with two plectra, with one of which they swept across the strings, while the other was shifted along the foremost string to produce the melody. Others, however, played with a violin bow and glided the thumb of the left hand backwards and forwards to the various frets of the melody string. The first method described coincided in the main with that indicated by Praetorius. The second, on the other hand, suggested new ways of using the Scheitholt by converting it into a bowed instrument and making the thumb of the left hand perform the stopping.

The fact that the instrument was not known in Holland, either before or after, as a bowed instrument, while in Iceland it is now only known as such, and the fact that the Dutch author expressly called the instrument the northern Balk, tempts us to ask whether the playing of the instrument with a bow was not an idea originating in Iceland. To support this hypothesis it is, however, necessary to examine the evidence provided by such of the Icelandic literature as refers to the Icelandic *Langspil* and its past.

The Icelandic Langspil. In Icelandic literature the Scheitholt did not make its appearance until the eighteenth century in Jon Olafson's dictionary, under the name *Langspil*. In 1772, i.e., about ten years later, a Swedish traveller, Uno v. Trojel, stated that in Iceland he found only two instruments of music, the *Langspil* with six brass strings, and the *Fidla* with two horsehair strings; both being played with the bow. The next two pieces of evidence were produced about thirty years later, again by two travellers—the Englishmen, William Jackson Hooker and M. Mackenzie. The accounts they gave of the Langspil were almost identical; the instrument consisted of a narrow pine box about three feet long, which widened at one end to a rounding, affording space for a large round sound hole in the belly. At the other end the instrument ended "like a violin." Along the sound box three metal strings were stretched, of which the two foremost were tuned in unison and the third an octave lower. The foremost of the two unison strings ran over frets and was stopped by the pressure of the left thumb nail; the other strings had the same mission "as the bourdon pipes of the bagpipes." A violin bow made all the

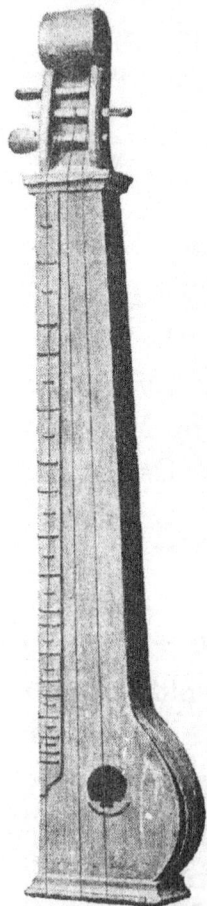

Fig. 219. Playing the Fidla.

Fig. 218. Icelandic Langspil. Photograph.

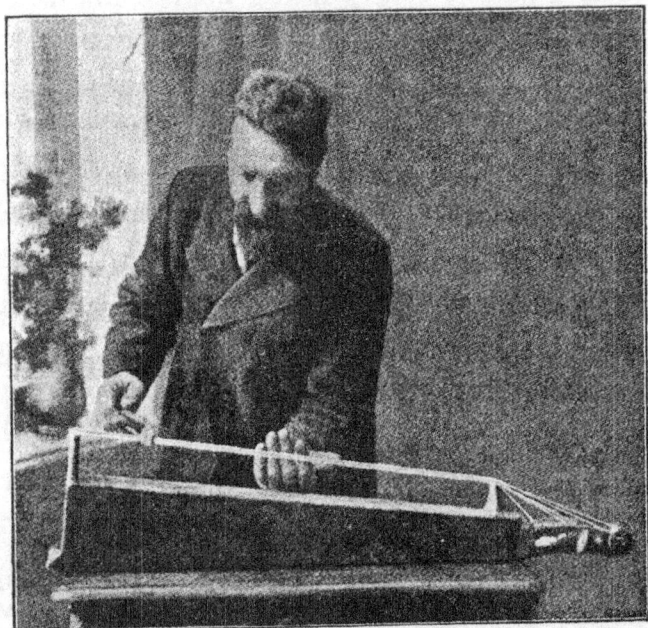

strings sound simultaneously (see Fig. 218). At close range the instrument sounded rather crude, but from an adjacent apartment its tone was rather pleasant.

While Uno v. Trojel and Mackenzie persisted in having the Langspil played with the bow, Hooker wrote, after mentioning the bow : " The player also often used her fingers alone as on a guitar." This statement involuntarily forces the question whether the Langspil in Iceland was always associated with the bow or whether, as in all other places, the strings were originally made to sound either with the fingers or a plectrum.

In the eighteenth century Uno v. Trojel described the Icelandic Langspil as a six stringed bowed instrument, while all later sources state that it had only three strings. With the transformation of a plucked instrument into a bowed instrument there usually followed a reduction in the number of the strings, and the close connection of Iceland with Norway makes it likely that the Langspil, played with the violin bow in Iceland, had a precursor in the Norwegian *Langeleik* played with a plectrum which, in comparison with the German Scheitholt, was a generously strung instrument *(v. inf.)*. This assumption is supported by the statement made by Mackenzie that the Langspil was chiefly used for playing " Danish and Norwegian melodies," and by M. Stephensen's name for the instrument—*Langelejer* ("Island," i, 18, Aarh.). Conversely, Langspil is often used in Norway for Langeleik. A suspicion that the Langspil had previously actually been played " in the Norwegian fashion " in Iceland, is aroused by an old Icelandic verse : " Little Marja played the Langspil well; dexterously she moves her supple fingers "; for in Norway the stopping of the strings was not performed, as in Germany and Holland, with a rod or the stiff thumb which glided from one place to another, but with the flexible fingers of the left hand *(v. inf.)*.

If we may thus with a certain degree of assurance take it for granted that Iceland received her Langspil from Norway, the next question is : How did the Langspil in Iceland come to be played with a bow ? As mentioned above, the Swede, Uno v. Trojel, found in Iceland in 1772, not only the Langspil but also another musical instrument,. viz., the *Fidla*, "which had two horsehair strings and was played with a bow." In his book, "Iceland in the Eighteenth Century," Magnus Stephensen also mentioned this instrument and characterised it as very primitive and "unbearable to listen to." Both described the instrument as an oblong wooden box over which were stretched one or two coarse strings, of twisted horsehair, and played with a still coarser bow. In close accordance with this evidence was the account given of the Fidla in an Icelandic folk-verse and in an old Icelandic riddle:

> I. Horsehair in the strings and hollowed wood;
>   The Fidla had no other wealth.
>
> II. "Who is it we praise?"
>   She bids us sing,
>   And needs ten thralls to serve her;
>   Your hand turned back,
>   Her palate cleft,
>   And she has many hairs.

The "ten thralls" mean the fingers, the hairs the material of which the strings are made; the "palate cleft" probably suggests that the sound-box was open (i.e., without a back); that the back of the hand was turned towards her is explained by the peculiar manner in which the Fidla was played.

A full account of how the instrument was played is to be found in an article, "Islensk Fidla" (in the "Aarbok hins islenska Fornleifafelags," 1919), by Matthias Thordarsson, who obtained all his information from people who had seen or heard the Fidla. Across the oblong sound-box, in most cases open at the back and rather deep, broader at one end than the other, the strings were stretched at such a distance from the sound-board that they could not be stopped by finger-pressure as was generally the case. The left hand, placed at the narrow end of the sound-box, stopped the strings by turning its back towards the instrument while the fingers were turned upwards so that the strings were stopped by the knuckles. In the meantime the right hand drew the bow across the strings (see Fig. 219). In this undoubtedly very ancient Icelandic instrument we thus again find an instance of an instrument which was played by the pressure of the fingers against a " free " string, i.e., without a finger-board (cf. the Tallharpa and the Jonki kantele).

The Fidla and its mode of playing, as they are here described, undeniably give the impression that the instrument was a primitive one, created by making use of the natural materials near at hand, to produce a musical instrument that

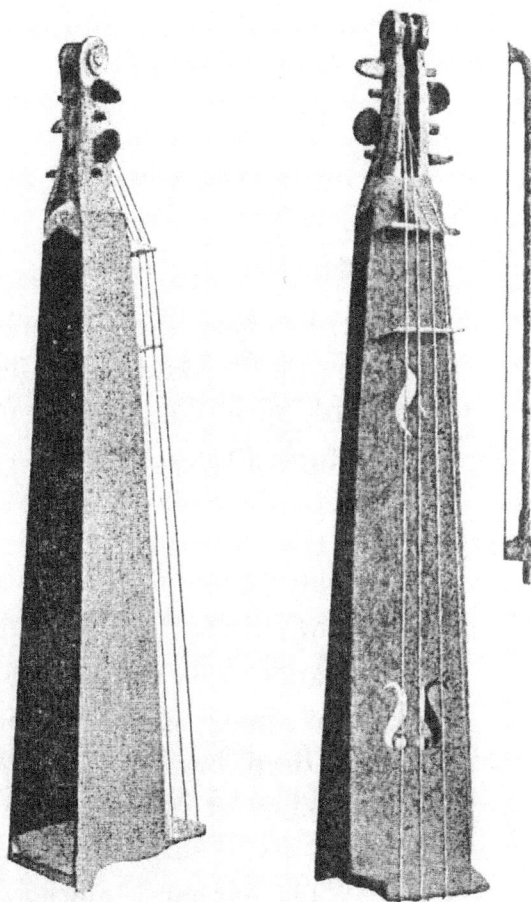

Fig. 220. Icelandic Fidla (Thordarsson).

would not make very exacting demands upon the player. The use of horsehair for the strings, the existence of only one or two strings, and the sound-box without a back (probably originally made by merely hollowing out a thick wooden

267

plank), are all features that seem to bear witness to the antiquity of the Icelandic Fidla (cf. the hair-strung Welsh Telyn of the twelfth century, and the old Finnish horsehair Kantele described in the "Kalevala," with its sound-box made of birch; see Book I). The Esthonian Tallharpa and several other instruments were also originally strung with horsehair. In short, it would appear that the circumstances say much for the Fidla having been known in Iceland long before the Langspil was introduced, and consequently I have no doubt that it was the former which gave the Icelanders the idea of employing the bow on the Langeleik, which had come to them from Norway.

If the Fidla has to be credited with the alteration of the Langspil into a bowed instrument, and thereby reducing the number of its strings from six to three, the Langspil seems in return to have the honour of having effected the improvements which were gradually made in the Fidla while the two instruments were being used side by side in Iceland—improvements which were made known by the modern descriptions and illustrations of this undoubtedly original Icelandic instrument. While referring to Thordarsson's excellent treatise for further details, I shall mention only such improvements as, (1) the increase in the number of the strings from two to four, five, or six, (2) the replacing of the horsehair strings by metal strings, brass or steel (in imitation of the violin, the Fidla was later on also occasionally strung with gut), (3) the occasional addition to the Fidla of a fretted scale and a fixed and movable bridge, (4) the addition of a back to the sound-box, and (5) the violin or Langspil peg-box used on the later Fidlas. In the latest examples the construction on the whole varies considerably, and some of them really come so near to the Langspil that they might just as well be considered as varieties of that instrument. Thordarsson gives the special characterising features of the true original Fidla as having been : the absence of a bridge and fretted scale for aiding in the stopping of the strings (which was a direct consequence of the peculiar manner in which the Fidla was played), the small number of strings, and the backless sound-box.

It is impossible to decide with certainty how old the Fidla described above really is. With the fiddle which is so often mentioned in the Saga literature, together with the Gigue, it has hardly anything in common but the name and the bow It was in all probability identical with the fiddle known every-

Fig. 221. Musical Scene in an Icelandic Farmhouse.

where in Europe from the twelfth or thirteenth century. The history of this saga fiddle will not be dealt with here until the finger-board instruments with neck are examined in Book III.

In Iceland, the popular instrument described above can be traced in literature no further back than to the Icelandic report of the sixteenth century from Skagafjord, in which we are informed of one Björn who played the Fidla so well that he was generally called "Fidlubjörn." He travelled with his instrument from one farm to another, and everywhere in Iceland aroused great enthusiasm. Even the elves, whose love of Fidla-playing is traditional in Iceland, were his patrons and on a certain occasion helped him to find his way home when one night during his wanderings from the south to the north of the island, he lost his way in the fog.

Summary. The Icelandic Langspil seems to have originated in the Norwegian Langeleik. It was without doubt under the influence of the national Fidla that the Langspil was converted into a bowed instrument in Iceland. That the method of its manipulation was not at once changed seems to appear from the account given of the Northern Balk by a Dutch author of 1699, who described it as having been handled both as a plucked and a bowed instrument.

In Iceland the Langspil nevertheless seems to have severed itself quickly from the Norwegian sister-instrument, gradually to blend more and more with the local Fidla, and finally to take its place as Iceland's chosen national folk-instrument.

At the beginning of the nineteenth century the Langspil was referred to as a very rare instrument in Iceland; but in 1855 it lived to see a renaissance, for in that year Ari Saemundsen, in Akureyri (Öfjord), published a "Leidarvisir i Langspil" with 120 hymns set to music. Under the directions given, so many Langspils were made "that the instrument has hardly ever been so common in Iceland as during the first years after the publication of Ari Saemundsen's book (Ol. Davidsen, "Islenzkar Gatur," 1892). Since then, however, the Langspil is said to have become so rare again that it is now almost unknown except by name.

In connection with the Langspil I shall here mention and illustrate a Finnish instrument closely related to it and reproduced in Gustav Retzius's monumental work, "Finska

Kramer," and there called the Kanteleharpe (see Fig. 222).

Over a long balk-like sound-box, two brass strings were stretched, one long and one short. The longer, which ran in front and reached from end to end of the body, had under it fourteen raised wooden frets, which indicated that it was the melody-string. The shorter string, which only covered two-thirds of the sound-box, was, on the other hand, not stopped and was consequently used only in the "free" state—i.e., open, as a bourdon string. The bow, which vibrated both strings at once, was probably used at the right-hand end of the sound-box where the frets ended. The strings were evidently fastened to the two small nails which protrude from the outer edge of the sound-box on the right, and were tuned by the long pegs placed on the left. Where the peg of the shorter string was inserted, the back of the sound-box broadened into a bulge. The bow had the curved form of the Middle Ages. So much, but no more, can be seen from the picture. From the few words which Retzius devoted to the description of this instrument, we learn only that the sound-box was, as a rule, open —i.e., without a back. In stating that the instrument was provided with but one string, Retzius was certainly mistaken, for the two nails at the extreme right of the body certainly indicate the existence of two strings. Nor can one fail to observe that the peg on which the bow hangs, and which is placed at the very spot where the body broadens, is a tuning-peg, i.e., the one belonging to the shorter string. Naturally enough, Retzius, being inexperienced in this special domain, and finding the shorter string missing from the instrument seen in the photograph, overlooked these details. The two pegs which have the same length and shape resemble those of the pianoforte, and were therefore without doubt tuned with a wrest. Whether this Kanteleharpe had any connection whatever with the Icelandic Langspil is rather doubtful. It was probably an independent Finnish attempt at adapting the Scheitholt-type, so well known in the Scandinavian countries, to the bow.

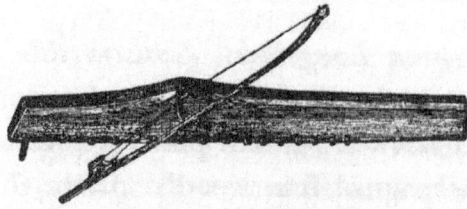

Fig. 222. Finnish Kanteleharpe. Retzius, "Finska Kranier."

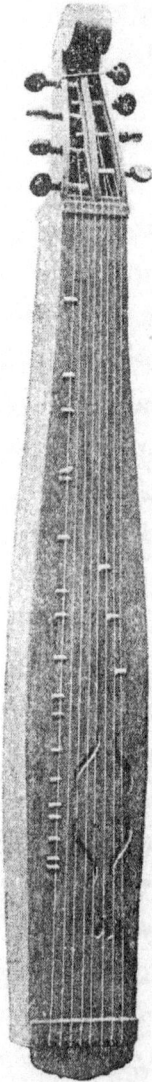

Fig. 224. Plectrum of
the Langeleik (half
natural size).

Fig. 223. Norwegian Langeleik (later Valdres type).

Fig. 225. Norwegian Lan-
geleik with two peg-boxes
(earlier Valdres type). Property of the Author.

The Norwegian Langeleik. Construction (see Figs. 223
and 225). Stretched over the cover of a long and narrow box,
which is either hollowed out of a plank without back (the older
type), or is made up of four wooden plates (back, table and
ribs), there are on the Norwegian Langeleik seven or eight
steel strings which are attached at one end, beyond a nut, to
small iron nails, and at the other end, over a second nut, run
to the tuning-pegs inserted laterally into a violin peg-box.
In the older types the tuning-pegs were often divided between
two peg-boxes, one at each end of the body (see Fig. 225). In
the table, heart-shaped and sometimes even f-shaped sound-
holes are cut. The strings are tuned either to the notes *a*, *a*,
a, *a*, *e'*, *a'*, *e"*; *a*, *a*, *a*, *a*, *e*, *e'*, *e'* ; or *a*, *a*, *a*, *a*, *e'*, *a'*, *c-sharp"*,
e". Means of tuning used in addition to the pegs are (1) for
the highest strings, small bridges or wedges inserted between
the sound-board and the string, and moved about in order to
correct the tuning, and (2) for the foremost string *(ad libitum)*
a so-called "holder" or *Capo Tasto*, the foot of which goes
down into a hole bored into the sound-board, the head being
thereby pressed against the string and raising its pitch by a
fifth (cf. the small metal hook used for the same purpose in
the German Scheitholt).

The frets placed below the melody-string (small wooden
cross-bars glued to the sound-board) give a normal major
scale: *a*, *b*, *c-sharp'*, *d'*, *e'*, *f-sharp'*, *g-sharp'*, *a'*, *b'*, *c-sharp"*,
d", *e"*, *f-sharp"*, *g-sharp"*, *a"*, *b"*, *c-sharp'''*. In earlier times
the frets seem to have been placed so that some of the notes
affected were "unstable," i.e., either slightly too sharp or too
flat. In the "Norske Universitets og Skoleannaler" for 1850
we find the following scale: *a*, *e'*, *f'-sharp* (too flat), *g'* (too
sharp), *a'*, *b'*, *c-sharp"*, *d-sharp"* (too flat), *e"*, *f-sharp"*, *g-
sharp"*, *a"* (too sharp), *b"*, while Lindeman in his unpublished
notes gives this scale: *e*, *f-sharp*, *g-sharp*, *a* (too flat), *b*
c-sharp', *d-sharp'*, *e'* (too sharp), *f-sharp'*, *g-sharp'*, *b-flat'* (too
flat), *b'*, *c-sharp"*, *d-sharp"*, *e"*, *f-sharp"*, *g-sharp"*.

Method of Playing. A long elastic plectrum (of horn or whalebone; see Fig. 224), held in the right hand, makes the instrument sound by gliding backwards and forwards across all the strings while the three middle fingers of the left hand produce the melody by gliding on the foremost string from fret to fret.

Apart from the occasional use of two peg-boxes and the comparatively large number of strings, the Norwegian Langeleik thus comes near, in its construction, to the German Scheitholt. In the method of playing, however, as we have seen, it differs both from the Scheitholt and from the Icelandic Langspil. Peculiar to the Langeleik are the employment of the middle fingers on the melody-string, and the manner in which the plectrum makes the strings sound. The little rod and the stiff thumb, which produced the melody on the German and Icelandic instruments, only made it possible to glide slowly from one note to another; but by using the three middle fingers on the melody-string, the Norwegian Langeleik-player is able to perform quickly and legato, to phrase the melody, and to embellish it with all the small shakes, mordents, etc., that are so characteristic of the national Norwegian instrumental melodies, and called by the Norwegian peasants "flowers." At the same time the Langeleik possesses in the plectrum an excellent means of giving expression to the playing. By allowing it to glide either lightly or heavily across the strings, the player can make it sound subdued or vigorous at will, or even, just as the singer and the violinist can do, gradually make the tone grow in strength and die away. But primarily the plectrum plays the important part of marking the time and rhythm, a fact which is of special significance in Norwegian folk-music, since dance-rhythms run through all their melodies. Each of the Norwegian dances is performed on the Langeleik with its own particular stroke of the plectrum: in the *Halling* (in duple time) the plectrum is incessantly carried backwards and forwards, in the *Springdans*, in triple time, it is brought forwards twice and backwards once, and in the Waltz once forward and twice backwards. Thus the Lange-leik is, from the musical point of view, an unusually advanced instrument, and in this respect is much superior to most other folk-instruments.

Fig. 226. Norwegian Langeleik Player.
1916.

Like all folk-music, that for the Langeleik is kept alive by being passed, by ear, from one player to another. There is no written Langeleik music. One player copies the melodies of another and produces them in the form in which he remembers them. Langeleik-music, like the vocal folk-melodies, has no stable form. The same piece may be played quite differently at one end of a valley than at the other.

The earliest reference that we have to the existence of the

Langeleik as a Norwegian instrument dates from the seventeenth century and was made by Anders Arrebo, who placed the Langspil (as he called it) between the cruits and the hackbretts, and said that "his girls play a ballad on the Langspil" ("Norske Selskabs Skrifter," I, 259).

That the Langeleik (Langhörpu, Langspil) was, in the eighteenth century, still the only instrument played and loved by the Norwegian peasants, is shown in Landstad's "Sagn om Hjartdölerne," where the instrument is mentioned again and again as the invariable source of joy in the Norwegian farmer's home. Nowadays Valdres is the only one of Norway's principal valleys in which the Langeleik still has any considerable number of devotees. In the Halling valley, which about thirty years ago still witnessed frequent competitions, there were only a few players left in 1916 when I visited Norway, and things were still worse in most of the other Norwegian dales. In recent years, however, interest in the old instrument seemed to be reviving again. Through the lectures of the Rector Sandvik of Hamar, and with the assistance of local players, a movement was recently set on foot to replace the Langeleik on its throne in the country, where it was once brought to the highest pitch, and where as a national popular instrument it fulfilled the important mission of creating and preserving the folk-music peculiar to Norway.

There are neither pictures nor descriptions to give us any information on the early employment of the Langeleik in Denmark. In literature there are only a few short passages, dating from the seventeenth century, and these are of interest only in so far as they prove that the Danish farmer for a time also knew and played this once popular instrument in the Scandinavian countries and in Central Europe.

The first of these references comes from the pen of the headmaster of Slagelse Grammar School, Hans Mikkelsen Ravn, who in his handbook on music, "Heptachordum Danicum" (1646), mentions a musical instrument which was still used in his day by the peasants. Its shape was oblong, it was called the *Langeleg*, and it was not unlike a monochord. "Its simple form and device suggest that it had been used for many years, dating perhaps even from pagan days."

The next piece of information comes from the collector of folk-songs, Peder Syv, who in his "Betragtninger over de cimbriske Sprog," makes "two Danish herdsmen" converse in this wise:

> "Good-day, good-day, neighbour mine,
> What dost thou here so early?"
> "Thou askest what so early
> I do? On this, my Langeleg,
> When days are short or even long,
> I'll busily play my modest lay
> On my fate and kindred subjects."

Stephanius (seventeenth century), in his "Notes to Saxo," mentioned the Langeleg as one of the Danish folk-instruments of his period. The last quotation from a Danish source regarding the Langeleg dates from 1760. It is found in a letter from Sheriff Holck, of Aalborg Castle, to Sheriff Wolf Klein in Nykjöbing on Mors, where an escaped prisoner was hiding, and who "previously ran about the country with a Langeleg." Thus, at that time in Denmark, the Langeleg was a vagabond's instrument.

The Humle. A comparatively young representative of the Scheitholt is the Humle, which in the eighteenth century was still to be found on the islands of the North Sea, in the German-speaking part of Schleswig-Holstein, in the Ditmarsch country of North Germany, and in Sweden. By tradition it is to be traced to a Dutch origin. Its form varied. In some cases it still had the narrow outline of the old Scheitholt, in others the lower part of the sound-box swelled on the right-hand side in a broad curve. There were also triangular Humles, formed like a broad clumsy violin, etc.

The Humle differed from the Langeleg in being still more generously strung and in possessing a distinct finger-board.

The pegs, moreover, were often made of iron instead of wood, and they were then inserted from above into a massive peg-plate which either ended in a scroll or in an artistically modelled animal or human head. In the manner of playing, however, the Humle differed fundamentally from the Langeleg (v. inf.).

The Humle in the North Sea Islands and in the Ditmarsch. A German quotation of 1846 ("Die Marschen und Inseln der Herzogthümer Schleswig und Holstein," by J. G. Kohl) will serve in the first place to describe the Humle of the islands. The author writes: "A Frisian woman of seventy-eight who lived on the island of Föhr in North Friesland, still owned an old musical instrument, a kind of zither of antique form, which she placed before her on the table to play me a piece of music. She called this zither a *Hommel*, and said that there were only a few of these instruments left on the island; but that all of them, as far as she knew, had come from Holland. This Hommel had brass strings, of which some were stretched parallel with each other, while others spread fan-like over the instrument. She plucked the former with her fingers, and pulled at them with a quill. At the end of each phrase she rushed the quill across the slanting strings, which sounded and resounded, so that they gave a sort of echo to the music. My old friend told me that these Hommels had formerly been much more common, and that the people had danced to its music; but now they wanted trumpets and violins for dancing. Most of the folk had had a Hommel at home to be able to accompany the Sunday hymn which was sung in every family. This Sunday afternoon hymn, which was now accompanied by a violin instead of a Hommel, has also disappeared from the houses of most families. Now and then you may, however, still hear the voice of some old man or woman singing an afternoon hymn as in the olden times."

The Humle illustrated in Fig. 227, an example from another North Sea island, Sylt, corresponds closely with the description given by the old Frisian woman of the Hommel she played, and which she said was Dutch. It had twelve strings, of which two ran along the finger-board over frets that gave the diatonic scale of f, g, a, b, c', d', e', f', g', a', b', c'', d'', e'', f'', g'', a'', b'', c''', d'''. The other ten strings were arranged in three groups of three, three, and four strings respectively, and were only used for the accompaniment to the melody played on the front string.

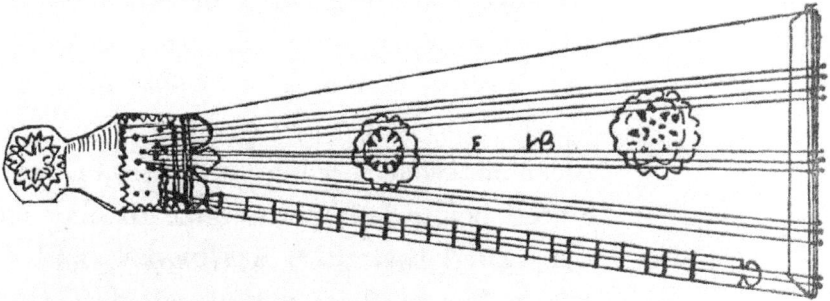

Fig. 227. Humle from Sylt. Formerly in the Kiel Museum, now in Meldorf (Ditmarsch).

The instrument illustrated in Fig. 227, the picture of which was presented to me by Miss H. Boivie in Stockholm (1917), shows none of the frets which I saw in 1885, while the original was in the Kiel Museum when I wrote down the notes it produced with great care. Instead of asking the Museum in Meldorf, whither the original had been taken in the meantime, to send me a photograph, I was content to add the frets *at random* on the drawing given me by Miss Boivie, as the text gave sufficient particulars as to the true nature of the scale-series. The distances between the frets in Fig. 227 are not to be accepted as being acoustically correct.

Another Hommel from Holland, still to be found in Sönderho on Fanö, and differing from the Sylt Humle, has the round broadening of the right side of the body, mentioned above, and is provided with an ordinary violin peg-box and scroll. It has only six strings, of which two are placed on the finger-board and stopped in the usual manner by means of frets, while the other four lie beyond the finger-board and are thus only used open. Mr. P. Brinch, a retired farmer, whose grandmother, Maren Brinch, at one time owned the instrument and played it, said that (like the Nordic balk) it was plucked with two plectra, one of which pressed the two melody-strings on to the frets to produce the tune, while the other made them vibrate, and was now and then swept backwards across the accompanying strings (see Fig. 228). The present owner of the instrument, in order to "decorate" it, painted it over with white oil-colour and has thereby completely damped its

Fig. 228. Mr. P. Brinch with his grandmother's Humle.

resonance. The Flensburg Museum possesses a Humle from the North Sea islands. It was found in 1901 on the island of Amrum, but came originally from the island of Langenes, which, like Amrum, lies just south of Föhr.

The Humles belonging to the Ditmarsch country have in most cases the narrow form of the old Scheitholt-type, with a violin peg-box, but are strung as true Humles—i.e., with more than one melody-string. The Humle was used in the Dit-marsch for a remarkably long time. Mr. Goos, director of the Museum at Meldorf, said that in southern Ditmarsch there was, about sixty years ago, an old man called " Karsten with the Hommel," who still went from place to place and played to the farmers.

In the German-speaking part of Schleswig-Holstein the Humle is said to have been at one time a popular instrument with the peasants. A South-Jutland Hummel, shaped like a large clumsy fiddle, is to be seen in the Musical Historical Museum in Copenhagen. The Humle was, above all, well represented in Vierlanden (near Hamburg), where it was still so common in 1860 that several of the local dealers sold Humle-strings. The young Vierlanders generally made their own Humles: "He is'n sinnigen jungen Kerl," it was often said, "Abends in Schummern fummelt he op de Hummel, un se hort im all gern to, un wat sin Ogen seht, konnt sien Hann maken. De Hummel hat he sik ok makt" ("Heimat," February, 1916).

The Hummel in Denmark. What is known of the Hum-mel in Denmark is nil. In his well-known book, "Det gamle Kongens Köbenhavn," Davidsen exhibits it in a popular place of entertainment: "Not far from a public ball-room," he says, "almost where the Viktoriagade now is, there was a strange place of entertainment. It was an open space used on week-days for sheep and lamb-pens and sometimes also for neat cattle. But on Sunday afternoon there was generally an old woman with a table before her on which was a so-called Humle, a stringed instrument. She played it with great skill. She always sung an old ballad in which the young man is warned against entering holy matrimony, and she was always surrounded by a large crowd of soldiers, country bumpkins,

and lasses, who followed her song with the greatest attention."
As Tang Kristensen includes the ballad, "And if you take a
young one," among his Danish comic songs, it must be supposed that the performer was a Danish countrywoman and that
the Hummel thus also had friends among the Danish peasants.

A small "Danish Humle" in the Musical Historical
Museum in Copenhagen was presented by Mrs. Emilie Hatt,
née Demant-Hansen, whose grandmother, Mrs. Demant, once
owned it and played it on a farm near Odense, where she
lived. Mrs. Hatt, however, only knows that it was plucked
with a plectrum and that it was known in the family as
"grandmother's old hummer." The Humle hardly ever
became a common instrument in Denmark.

————

The Humle in Sweden. It was quite different in Sweden.
The large collection of Humles in Stockholm (Nordiska
Museum) bears witness that the instrument must have been
known all over Sweden and must have been used there for a
longer period than in most other countries. The Museum catalogue mentions specimens from Stockholm, Uppland, Dalecarlia, Östergötland, Norrköping, Smaaland, Blekinge, Gott-
land and Helsingland. As late as 1719 Helsingborg was able
to maintain its own maker of Humles—the *Hummelgubban*,
N. Roth.

The Swedish Humle, like the Dutch, was to be found in
a number of different forms. The sound-box often exhibited
a single or a double bulging (see Figs. 229 and 231). When
the bulge appeared on both sides (see Fig. 230) the result was
very reminiscent of the later Cittern. Now and then we meet
with instruments of the old narrow Scheitholt type in Sweden.

On a journey to Stockholm in 1917 I was fortunate enough
to meet and hear in "Skansen" the last Swedish player on
this instrument, which has otherwise disappeared. His name
was Otto Malmberg, and he was born in Ljungby in Smaa-

land. He had been taught to play the Humle by his maternal grandmother, who had been instructed by her father, and all of them had used the instrument he still played.

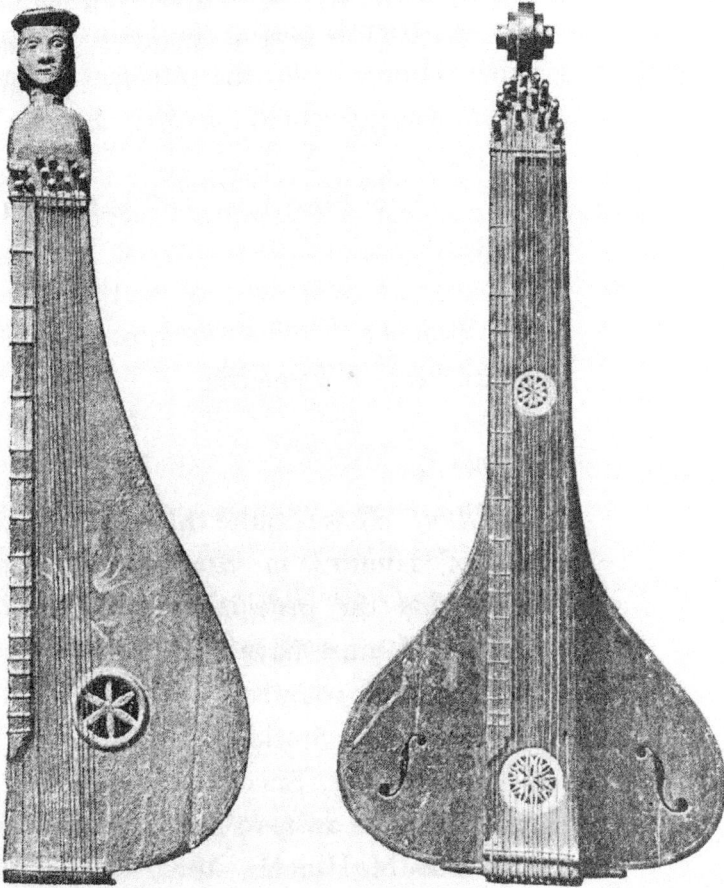

Figs. 229 and 230. Swedish types of the Hummel in the Nordiska Museum. From photographs. ·

Otto Malmberg's Humle had only seven strings, i.e., two melody-strings tuned in unison to B, and five accompanying strings tuned to c', c', c', f, f. The frets on the finger-board gave the scale: c, d, e, f, g, a, *b-flat*, c', d', e' f', g', a', *b-flat'*, c'', d'', and e''. He played it in almost the same manner as the old woman on Föhr, but by personally observing him play, I discovered several details which were not mentioned by the German writer. To stop the double melody-string, Malmberg used two fingers (see Fig. 232); on the first string he produced the melody with the point of the thumb, on the second he made the first two fingers—two frets away—glide along step by step, following the movements of the thumb, and supporting the melody with the third below. Now and then the melody was embellished with a shake, produced by allowing the thumb to glide laterally very rapidly. The other strings were, as usual, only played open to produce the fixed accompanying chord,

Fig. 231. Otto Malmberg and his Humle. Photograph, 1917.

which was used now and again quite unrestricted by rhythmic considerations. To pluck the strings, Malmberg used a coarse plectrum like a slate-pencil, moving it alternately over the melody-string and the accompanying chord. The movement of the right hand was not backwards and forwards as on the Norwegian Langeleik, but always in the same direction (cf. the Fanö Humle).

In Holland where, as we have seen, a large number of the Humles used on the North Sea islands and northern Germany originated, it now exists only in museums, being represented by very few examples that are for the greater part either defective or modernised. The number of pegs inserted in the heads of these Hummels differs from the number of nails that indicate, at the base, the original number of strings on the instru-

Fig. 232. Otto Malmberg Playing.

ment, most Dutch examples possessing no strings at all. Of the two "old Humles" in the Brussels Museum of Instruments, one, coming from a rectory in Ypres, and believed by its former owners to have been two hundred years old, has a chromatically fretted finger-board which proves that it had been modernised. The Humle as a folk-instrument usually gave a diatonic scale in all other examples.

The only trustworthy feature in the Dutch specimens now, is therefore the outline of the sound-box, and in these examples it is just as varied as it was in Germany and Sweden. Sometimes (as in three Humles in the Frisian Museum at Leeuwarden, and in two of the Brussels Humles) the sound-box swells in the lower part into a more or less pronounced bulge (cf. the Fanö Humle and the Swedish specimen shown in Fig. 229); in other cases the sound-box, as in the old Nordic balk, is made of a long hollowed plank and has no back (as in the second of the two old Humles in the Brussels Museum). That in addition to these types, others were made in Holland is proved by the Humles that were carried to the North Sea islands (see, for example, the Humle from Sylt). The number of strings, too, varied very much in the Dutch Hummel, just as it did in the north German and Swedish Humles—from fourteen, twelve, eight, down to four strings.

The Humle at length marked the limit to the popularity of the Scheitholt-type as an organ of the simple folk-music. From it the road leads directly to the eighteenth and nineteenth century "Mountain Zithers" of Bavaria and Austria, and which, as modern instruments, cannot find a place in this work. To complete the instrumental material dealt with in this section, I prefer to give a short description of the French Épinette des Vosges, which externally resembles the original Scheitholt more than any of the instruments described above, but by reason of its double melody-string claims relationship to the Humle.

The French Épinette des Vosges, used in the Vosges mountains from ancient times to the present day, closely resembles the German Scheitholt, consisting as it does of a long oblong body, along the belly of which a number of strings are stretched, i.e., two melody-strings of steel on a diatonically fretted finger-board, and three accompanying strings of brass beside the finger-board. According to Mahillon, the melody-strings were tuned to g', g', and the accompanying strings to g', g', c'. The catalogue of the Musikhistorisk Museum (Copenhagen) gives the tuning of the latter as: C, e, g. The melody-strings were used either in unison by placing a short smooth rod across them, which was moved backwards and forwards by the left hand to the frets on the finger-board, or they were divided between two fingers—the forefinger and middle finger or one of the others—in order to accompany the melody with the third below, or some other interval (cf. Otto Malmberg's treatment of the Swedish Humle). A plectrum made of an elastic goose-quill was used to vibrate the strings.

Summary. Foremost among the musical instruments developed out of the monochord were the balk-monochords: Trumscheit and Scheitholt. Of these the Trumscheit seems to have corresponded in its original form to the fiddler's monochord often mentioned in the mediæval French poems as "le Monocorde." The Trumscheit was a bowed instrument of a peculiar nature, being employed principally to produce "harmonics." When—presumably about the beginning of the sixteenth century—it was provided with a vibrating bridge, its tone resembled that of the trumpet so closely that occasionally (in the German nunneries) it was used to replace the trumpet. Under the name of Trompet Marina the Trumscheit was widely known. It was most popular in France, where in its modified seventeenth-century form it even made its way into the Opera orchestra.

To a greater degree than the Trumscheit, the convent monochord came near to the instrument which in Germany, Norway, Iceland and Holland respectively, was called Scheitholt, Langeleik, Langspil and Nordic Balk, and from which in due course the Humle was derived; for it cannot be explained simply as a monochord provided with an accompanying string, the scale-board of which was transformed into a finger-board supplied with frets on which the melody was produced by finger-pressure or by a little rod taken backwards and forwards. The thumb of the right hand was originally used to produce the melody and the accompaniment simultaneously; at a later date a plectrum or a violin-bow was used.

After having spread all over Europe in the Middle Ages,

the Scheitholt at last settled down as a specifically Nordic instrument. It seems to have made its way from Germany via Denmark to Norway, and thence to Iceland. In the seventeenth century it found its way back to the Continent where, in 1699, it was described in Holland for the first time as the Nordic Balk. In Norway the mode of playing was changed under the influence of the peculiar Norwegian folk-music. Instead of the gliding rod, the Norwegian peasant made use of the flexible middle fingers of the left hand, thus making it possible to perform their richly ornamented national melodies. To produce the vibrations they used a flexible plectrum made of horn or whalebone. In Iceland, on the other hand, they preferred to place the nail of the left thumb on the melody-string, while the strings were stroked by the bow known to them from the Icelandic Fidla. When the Langspil, therefore, under the name of Nordic Balk, at length returned to the Continent, it was described as being played in two ways, as some performers played it in the Icelandic fashion, while others retained the original method of stopping the melody-string with a rod and plucking the strings with a plectrum.

Later on another Scheitholt-type appeared in Holland, i.e., the Humle, most often provided with a more capacious sound-box and a larger number of strings. The melody-string was doubled to play the tune under the action of the fingers or a rod, while a large plectrum or quill brought it and the bass-chord produced by three or four accompanying strings into vibration. Danish and German seamen brought the Humle from Holland to the North Sea islands, Schleswig-Holstein, and the Ditmarsch, but it also made its way to Sweden, where it became very popular and was used well into the nineteenth century. A descendant of the primitive Scheitholt still lives in France under the name of Épinette des Vosges. The Bavarian and Austrian mountain-zithers also point back to the mediæval family of the Scheitholt-type as their ancestors.

B. THE KEYBOARD MONOCHORDS.

1. THE BOWED INSTRUMENTS.

The Lyre and the Tangent-Fiddle.

These are related to the Balk-Monochords, inasmuch as here again a stopped melody-string is connected with a larger or smaller number of unstopped accompanying strings; but the melody-string is not provided with a finger-board against which the strings are pressed, but by a keyboard, the keys of which move small stopping-pegs, pins, or "tangents" against the stretched strings. Peculiar to them are, on the other hand, the use of a keyboard and the consistent vibration of the strings by a piece of mechanism to replace the bow.

a. The "Lyre."

Construction. Across a sound-box shaped like a guitar, a chest, or a lute, one or two melody-strings tuned in unison are stretched and stopped by means of a keyboard, and two or four unstopped accompanying strings which together produce a fixed bass-chord. The keyboard is built in a frame or box attached to the cover. Hidden under the lid lies the mechanism which stops the strings. Along the outer side of the frame the keys (claviers) project, operating the mechanism. A wheel covered with powdered resin and generally protected by a wooden hoop, acts as a bow, and is moved by means of a handle in the base. This wheel touches all the strings at once. The result therefore is again a melody which is persistently accompanied by a pair of bourdons, consisting of the keynote and the fifth above it.

Literary Evidence. The lyre may be followed in literature back to the tenth century when, under the name of Organistrum, it was described in a treatise by Odo de Clugny, "Quo-
modo organistrum constructur," printed in Gerbert's "Scriptores ecclesiastici de musica sacra potissimum" (1784, I, page
303). The length of the instrument is here given as the equiv-
alent of almost one and a half metres, and it is said to have
had eight keys designated by letters "in order to make it possible to be played even by those who were not skilled in
music." The wheel is also mentioned, and it is explained how
the "plectra," i.e., the keys, are to be placed so that they may
stop the strings inside the case.

On the Monuments. In the large size here described the
lyre appeared in the twelfth century when it was illustrated for
the first time being played by two performers, one of whom
turned the wheel while the other manipulated the keys. The

Fig 233. Organistrum. MS. in the Univ. Library of Glasgow.
12th cent.

form of the sound-box was borrowed from the contemporary
fiddle-type, called by Curt Sachs "the figure of eight fiddle"
because its outline recalls the figure 8. The instrument had
three strings and twelve keys projecting from the upper edge
of the fiddle-neck (see Figs. 233 and 234).

Although the inner mechanism of the keyboard is hidden under the lid, we obtain an idea of its nature from the mode of playing the S. Iago Lyre. As will be seen from the picture, the twelve keys which project like round buttons from the upper edge of the neck were provided with shafts, and were operated by being drawn up and pushed back with the fingers. The notes may have been produced by the insertion of a nail at the lower end of each shaft. The shafts, when raised, were

Fig. 234. Organistrum. Church-door of Sant'Iago, Spain. 12th cent.

pressed against the lowest or melody-string, and when pushed back, left it. The players seem to have been performing a descending scale. While one of them diligently turns the wheel, the other, who sits behind the keys, is pushing the sixth key back with his right thumb to release the note it produced, in order to follow it with the note of the fifth handle, which is drawn up. When this should cease to sound, the player will push back the fifth handle and raise the fourth, for which operation the left hand is already preparing; and so on (see Fig. 235 and cf. Fig. 234). This drawing out and pushing back of the keys was also practised at that time on another

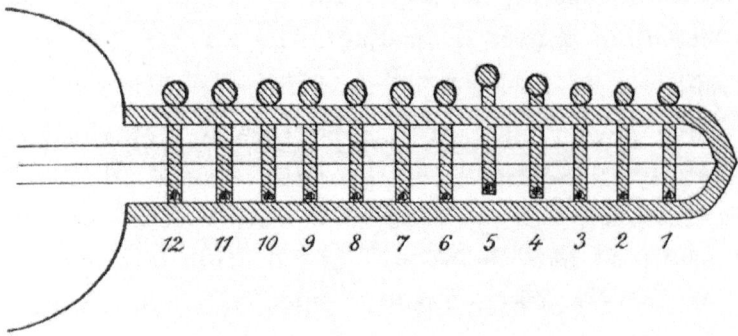

Fig. 235. Suggested construction of the Keyboard Mechanism on the S. Iago Lyre.

Fig. 236. Small Organ, the Keys (Slides) of which are operated by drawing and pushing. 11th cent. Buhle, " Die mittelalterliche Musikinstrumente in den Miniaturen des früheren Mittelalters."

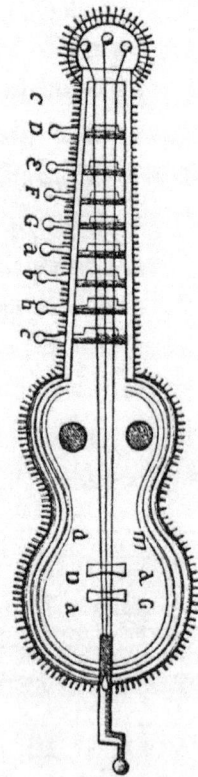

Fig. 237. Organistrum. 13th cent. (Gerbert).

keyboard-instrument, the organ, but on it the keys or " slides' were meant to admit or exclude the air for the pipes (see Fig. 236).

That the S. Iago Lyre cannot be looked upon as the standard key-mechanism of the twelfth and thirteenth centuries is proved by an Organistrum illustrated in Gerbert's "De Cantu et Musica Sacra," taken from a German manuscript of the thirteenth century, since destroyed, not, as was formerly supposed, of the ninth or tenth century (see Buhle's work quoted earlier). Contrary to the usual practice, the inner part of the keyboard is here laid open and reproduced by the draughtsman with a care that fully guarantees his trustworthiness (see Fig. 237). As will be seen, the handles governing the mechanism are in this case, as in that of the S. Iago Lyre, provided with shafts; but here each of them is attached to a broad projection under all the strings (tangents). To be brought into contact with the strings these tangents were turned upward by rotating the handles from left to right, all three strings being stopped at the same time. Tuned to a key-note, the fifth, and the octave, the strings could not, as in other cases, have produced a melody supported by a fixed bass-chord, but a melody accompanied by two other parallel voices, producing a series of parallel fifths and octaves—i.e., an instrumental counterpart of the parallel Organum of the period.

(b-flat. b)

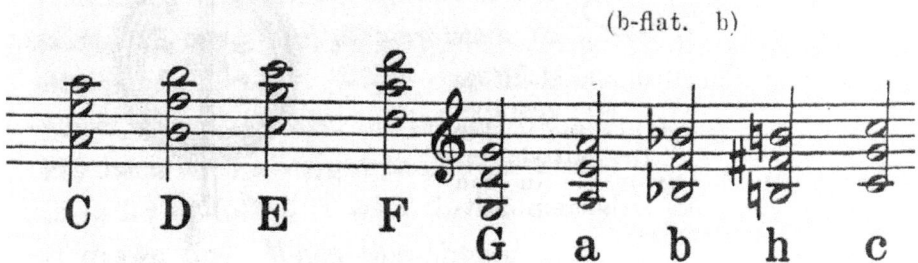

C   D   E   F   G   a   b   h   c

The music peculiar to this type of lyre to a great extent confirms the assumption that the vocal Organum arose from an attempt to imitate the instrumental effect. However, we must not forget that English musical historians especially, hold the opposite theory : that the mechanism in question may have been inserted in order conveniently to support the church-song instrumentally.   In this respect Carl Engel's conjecture is interesting : that the name first attached to the Lyre, i.e., the Organistrum, may have been a combination of *Organum* and *Instrumentum*.

An interestng feature in Gerbert's picture is the lettering placed opposite the keys of this Organistrum, indicating which chords the keys produce.   The chord of the open strings is indicated by the letter C, which precedes the keys.   The letter D, standing opposite the first key, indicates that it operates

the tangent for the chord $\frac{d}{a}$; E, opposite the second key, de-
$\qquad\qquad\qquad\qquad\qquad\quad\ D$

notes that it prcduces the chord $\frac{e}{b}$, and so on (cf. Odo de
$\qquad\qquad\qquad\qquad\qquad\quad\ E$

Clugny's Organistrum).   As indicated by the letters, the scale is absolutely diatonic and comprises an octave.   The use to which this two-man Lyre was put, as suggested by the illustrations, was chiefly to assist in the performance of church-music, and in most cases it was the centre of a large orchestra. It is, moreover, frequently seen in the hands of illustrious persons, especially kings.

With the thirteenth century the two-man Lyre definitely disappears from the pictures, and is replaced by a smaller instrument manipulated by a single person.   From having been a deep-pitched instrument the Lyre was now changed into a treble instrument, and at the same time its appearance was partially changed.   The figure 8 shape, which had already been reduced to the regular guitar-form in Gerbert's Lyre (see Fig. 237), was now neglected and replaced by an oblong box (Fig. 238).

From the upper edge of the neck the keyboard is here moved to the lower side of the sound-chest, and consequently there is a change in the mode of handling the instrument.

While the keys on the S. Iago Lyre were drawn to, and pushed away from, the string, and while on Gerbert's Lyre they were turned into place, it is now by finger-pressure from below that

Fig. 238. Spanish box-shaped Lyres. 13th cent. Juan F. Riano, "Notes on Early Spanish Music."

the key is pressed against the melody-string, falling back by its own weight (see Fig. 239). This is indeed the principle of the S. Iago Lyre carried out in a more convenient manner. Instead of two movements (drawing up and pushing back) the hand here needs only to make one—an upward pressure.

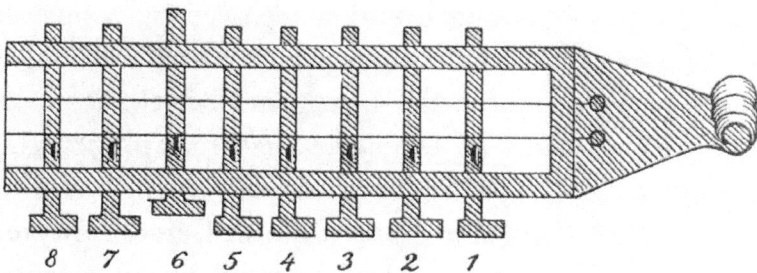

Fig. 239. Keyboard of One-man Lyre (after 13th cent.).

While the two-man Lyre only allowed a slow change of notes, the one-man Lyre was naturally adapted to quicker movements, thereby creating the effect which now became char-

Fig. 240. Lyre. 13th cent. MS. in the Royal Library, Copenhagen (Old Roy. S. 4to, 1606, *fol.* 22 b.).

Fig. 241. Four-stringed Lyre. 16th cent. (Carter, "Specimens of the Ancient Sculptures").

Fig. 242. Lyre. 15th cent. (Carter, as Fig. 241).

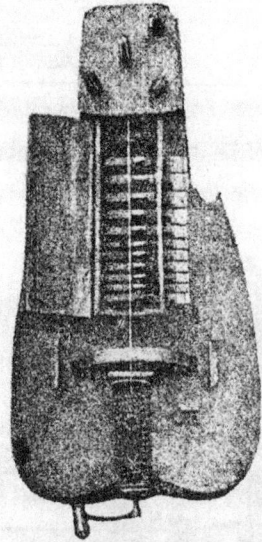

Fig. 243. Four-stringed Lyre with keyboard uncovered, and wheel: one Melody-string and three Bourdons, i.e., one behind the keyboard, two in front of it, and twelve keys producing the Scale: *g′, a′, b′, c″, d″, e″, f-sharp″, g″, a″, b″, c‴, d‴* (Mahillon).

acteristic of the Lyre—rapidly running scales against the background of a fixed bass-chord.

These changes, however, were not effected suddenly by any means. The Lyre seen in Fig. 240 was worked by a person wearing a crown, and had the guitar-shape of the two-man Lyre with its keyboard on top. It also looks as if the keys here, as in Gerbert's Organistrum, were still being turned; finally, the number of strings is as before, with the sole exception that the three single strings are here replaced by double strings. The Lyres illustrated in Figs. 241 and 242 are, on the other hand, box-shaped and have the keyboards underneath. In Fig. 241 the use of four strings is faintly indicated—a notable departure from the three which were consistently used in the older instruments, and which in many cases have persisted to the present day.

From the Seventeenth to the Nineteenth Century. In the seventeenth century the number of strings was raised for a time to four or five (more rarely six; see Figs. 243 and 244).

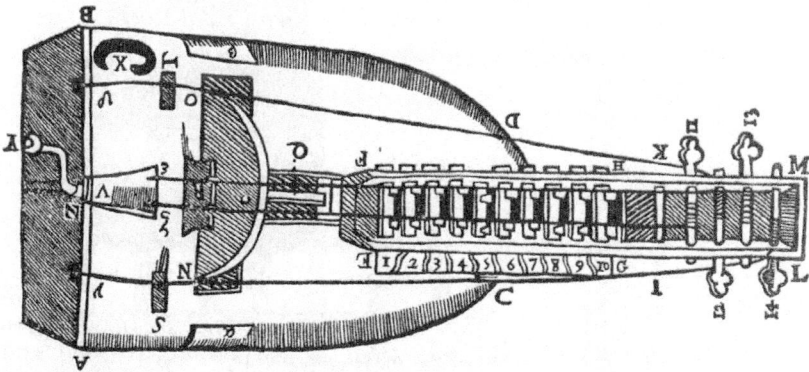

Fig. 244. Four-stringed Lyre. 17th cent. With Keyboard, Wheel, and two Melody-strings, uncovered. Mersenne, "Harmonie Universelle," 1636.

A B C D: Sound-box. E F G H: Keyboard-frame. I and K: Accompanying strings *(les Bourdons)*. 3 and 7: Melody-strings *(les Chanterelles)*. L M: Peg-box. N O P: Wheel. R S T: Bridges. V: Tail-piece. X: Sound-hole. Y: Handle for turning the wheel. 1-10: Ten keys. 11-14: Four pegs.

Each of the keys here has two stopping nails inside the frame, each stopping one of the two melody-strings tuned in unison, and placed closely enough to enable both strings to be stopped at once (see Fig. 245). Mersenne says that the two *bourdons* may be tuned alike (an octave below the two *chanterelles*), or an octave apart.

Fig. 245. Enlarged reproduction of the inner mechanism of the above Lyre with two melody-strings.

The use of six strings did not become at all general until the eighteenth century, when the French players laid down the following arrangement for the strings: within the frame only the two melody-strings *(les Chanterelles)* were placed; outside the frame ran the "Trumpet" *(la Trompette)* and the "Fly" *(la Mouche)*, and opposite to it the small bourdon *(le Petit Bourdon)* and the large bourdon *(le Gros Bourdon)*. The melody-strings were tuned in unison to g', the "fly" was tuned an octave lower to g; the large bourdon, which was only used in G-major, was tuned to G. The "trumpet" was tuned to d' in G-major, to c' in C-major; the small bourdon was tuned to c and was only used in C-major (instead of the large bourdon). The strings not used were made inaudible by removing them from the wheel. The "trumpet" was, as a rule, like the string of the Trumpet Marine, supported on a small movable bridge *(Trompillon)*, the vibrations of which were regulated by means of a peg fastened to the tail-piece.

In the eighteenth century a keyboard was added with a double series of keys (lower and upper claviers), so that chromatic scales could then be performed (see Fig. 246).

As early as the fifteenth century the guitar-shape had come to the fore in place of the box-shape, and the keyboard had been lengthened so that it often stretched from the neck far across the sound-box. Mersenne said in the seventeenth century that the Lyre could have as many as forty-nine keys. In the meantime the sound-box was being made gradually deeper, and the neck shorter. Quite frequently in the eighteenth century the lute was used as a model for the Lyre, and it was given a vaulted back. The Lyre from now on existed in two main forms, both of which are still used in France: as a *Vielle en Guitarre* and a *Vielle en Luth* (see Figs. 246, 248 and 249 respectively).

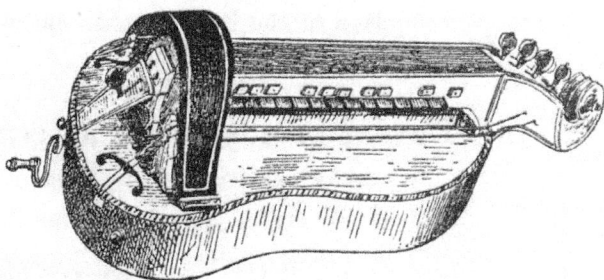

Fig. 246. Vielle en Guitarre (Mahillon).

The Lyre of the Wandering Minstrel. While, as we saw above, the two-man Lyre (Organistrum) belonged chiefly to the Church and to illustrious players, the one-man Lyre was quickly appropriated by wandering players who carried it far and wide, but who as a despised race also helped to bring it into contempt; so much so that in the opinion of the public it was for a long time considered only as the instrument of beggars and the blind. In Germany it was simply called *Lyra Mendicorum* (the beggars' Lyre). In 1618 Prætorius referred to it as "ein Bauern und umlaufender Weibern-Instrument."

In the sixteenth century, during the reign of Henri III,

the Lyre made a slight effort in France to raise its status; but
with the death of this king it was again reduced to a position
held in contempt by "gentlemen." Mersenne, therefore, in

Fit trois pas en arriere, ha que le monde est grand,
La volonte me change D'aller a Montaban .
Mariette grand auec Priuilege du Roy

Fig. 247. Wandering Lyre-player (17th cent.).

his "Harmonie Universelle," endeavoured to defend it: "If
distinguished people," he wrote, "knew how to treat the *Sym-
phony* called *Vielle*, it would not be held nearly so much in
contempt as it is now; but because it is now only played by
the poor, and especially by the blind who earn their living
by it, it is held to be inferior to many other instruments which
do not give nearly so much joy."

The Lyre as an Instrument of the Upper Classes. Mersenne's indirect request to people of distinction, to take up the despised instrument, appears almost as a prophecy in view of the popularity which the Lyre achieved through pure accident during the reign of Louis XIV. Two wandering lyre-players, Janot and la Rose, one day came to Paris and began to play the fashionable dances of French society on their instruments: Menuets, Entrées and Contredanses. Some of the ladies and gentlemen of the royal entourage happened to hear them and exhibited so much enthusiasm at Court on the performance of

Fig. 248. The Lyre as an aristocratic instrument.

the two players that all desired to hear them. Society wished to be taught, and Janot and la Rose readily agreed to act as instructors. Soon all society was infected with a veritable passion to "play the lyre." The *luthiers* became busy making the necessary instruments, and as they lacked material, they were compelled to make use of the instruments that had fallen into disuse. Numbers of lutes and guitars were therefore transformed into lyres, provided with artistically modelled heads and decorated with inlaid work of tortoiseshell, ebony and mother-of-pearl (see Fig. 248). At the same time the Lyre was improved. These improvements had two objects; some provided the instrument with six to twelve sympathetic strings; others made so-called *Vielles organisées*, with small organs built into the Lyre. Composers wrote music for it, and schools were instituted for teaching the now fashionable instrument.

Decline. This fashion quickly came to an end. When Louis XVI ascended the throne, the Lyre had again become

a street-instrument in Paris. From the end of the eighteenth century it was again only in the hands of the *vielleuses* and beggars of the boulevards. During the seventies of the nineteenth century the Lyre definitely disappeared from the streets of Paris, but in many of the French provincial towns it is still seen. It is there played both by itinerant musicians on the highroads and by the well-bred. Clever instrument makers therefore still take a pride in building good instruments, and they are played by many with great skill.

That the Lyre, even in Paris, still has a small circle of admirers is proved by that ensemble of clever French musicians (Grillet, Delsarte, van Waefelghem, and Diémer), who recently, at the instance of Laurent Grillet, allowed it to figure in a quartet of old instruments at an historical concert in Paris. The French musical historian, E. Briqueville, is still a warm admirer of the Lyre, and not only plays it with enthusiasm and has performed on it at historical concerts, but in the "Bulletin de la Société Internationale de Musique" devoted a long article to it ("Notice historique sur la Vielle"), which has been my chief source of information when describing the fortunes of the Lyre in the country where without doubt it lived longest and, during several periods, attracted more attention than anywhere else.

Strangely enough, we know very little concerning the fate of the Lyre outside of France. That it was for a time largely used in Germany appears from the fact that the Italians called it the *Lira Tedesca*, or German Lyre. But the contemptuous manner in which Prætorius mentioned it at the beginning of the seventeenth century proves that it must have disappeared from the scene in Germany at a comparatively early date.

It was illustrated rather frequently in England up to about 1500, when it vanished completely, to reappear for a short time during the eighteenth century as the "Hurdy-Gurdy."

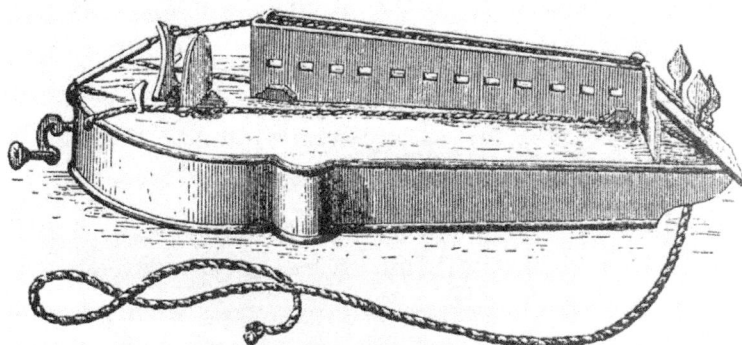

Fig. 250. Swedish Peasant-Lyre with three strings and twelve keys; from Gotland.

Among the Scandinavian countries Sweden retained it longest. In certain parts of that country, such as Smaaland, Helsingland and Gotland, the lyre was still to be found in the eighteenth century. It was superseded by the fiddle and the nyckelharpa. In an old East Gotland ballad we hear of a swain who, to win his love, was obliged to give up the lyre and learn to play the fiddle instead, because the former had fallen into contempt. Nowadays the lyre is remembered only in the nursery jingle by the ordinary Swede:

"Tvaa Strumpor och fyra
Mo'r ha e liten Lira."

Denmark provides us with no more than three literary references dating from the seventeenth and eighteenth centuries: (1) The statement of Hans Mikkelsen Ravn to the effect that "the lyre in his day was still used by the Danish peasants" ("Heptachordum Danicum," 1646); (2) Tycho de Hofman's "Historiske Efterretninger om velfortjente danske Adelsmaend," III, in which we read that Marie Grubbe, after having divorced Palle Dyre (1691), followed Sören Sörensen and "earned her living by playing the lyre, and for many years wandered about with it, until she died in extreme poverty"; and (3) 1719: the note on the title page to the first edition of Peter Paars: "Sung to the melody of 'Arma virumque'; sounds well with all instruments, especially the dulcimer and lyre." The last references to the lyre in Denmark occur in two Danish proverbs. "What use has a sow for a lyre" (said of a person who insists upon interrupting a conversation though he has no idea of what he is talking about); and "Markus is off with the lyre" (said of a person who allows a favourable opportunity to escape).

Outside of Denmark and Sweden the lyre may be found in the Scandinavian countries under the name of Fon and Symfony; in Iceland (where Bishop Jon Astrason, 1484-1550, boasts of owning a fon with a beautiful tone, strings and keys), and in Norway where, in 1619, we hear of a wedding that took place in Hemna (South Troendelag), at which the dance, "according to old Norwegian custom" was accompanied by warriors' songs, while Hvermand played his symfony or his langspil, whichever he could play best ("Nordisk Musikhistorie," I, page 78 f).

Of the names which were used at different periods to designate the lyre, that of organistrum was the earliest (tenth to thirteenth centuries), belonging especially to the two-man lyre. Exceptionally, the name organistrum was still used in the fourteenth century by Johannes de Muris, side by side with symphonia. With the conversion of the lyre into a one-man instrument (thirteenth to sixteenth centuries) came the name symphonia (French, chifonie). The more popular the instrument became the more popular were its names. When it was taken up again in the fiddle-form, the lyre, as mentioned above, received the French romanesque name of vielle, first with the addition *à Roue* (with wheel), and later on, when the fiddle was called viole and violon, without any qualification. In Italy, as we have seen, it was called *lira tedesca* or *lira rustica*. In Germany it was called lyra or leyer, with the prefixes *dreh, rad, bauern,* or *bettler(leier)*, meaning "turning," "wheel," "peasant," or "beggars' (lyre)." In England it was called the crank-lyre or hurdy-gurdy; in Danish, lire; and in Swedish, lira. The names given to this instrument by the Latin authors were, *lira pagana, lira rusticana* and *lira mendicorum*.

b. The Keyboard-Fiddle.

The rotating wheel and the intricate keyboard mechanism of the crank-lyre constituted so complicated a piece of apparatus that it encouraged the invention of instruments easier and cheaper to make. The first instance of such a simplified lyre was illustrated as early as the twelfth century in a German manuscript: "Hortus deliciarum," by Herrad v. Landsperg. In the company of several other instruments we there see an organistrum without a keyboard, the stopping being effected normally by pressing the strings on to the fingerboard with the fingers (see Fig. 251, the instrument on the left of the harpist). Now and then we find the same model in mediaeval pictures of smaller lyres, the last being in Praetorius's "Syntagma musicum" of 1618, where a lyre without a keyboard is given as an example of "allerlei Bauernleiern," and shown side by side with an ordinary lyre (see Fig. 252). Another variety of the lyre can be followed right into modern times. In this instrument the keyboard was retained, but the wheel was replaced by a violin bow, the keyboard, or tangent, fiddle, or, in Danish, *nöglefejlen*.

The Key-board-Fiddle on the Monuments. We meet this

Fig. 251. Organistrum, Cithara (Harp) and Lyra, in Herrad v. Lands-perg's "Hortus deliciarum"; Strassbourg Libr. MS. 12th cent.

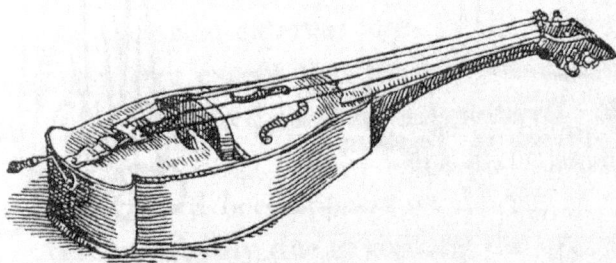

Fig. 252. "Bauern-Leier" without Keyboard. Prætorius.

instrument for the first time on a fifteenth century fresco in Tegelsmora Church in Uppland, Sweden (see Fig. 253). It appears as an oval four-stringed fiddle or lute, though the picture does not show whether it had a flat or vaulted back. Two oblong sound-holes were cut in the table, and on the underside of the neck, as the instrument was held horizontally, was a keyboard with seven keys. The other details, such as the bridge, the tuning pegs, the inner mechanism of the keyboard, etc., do not emerge clearly from the picture. The curve of the bow-stick is very pronounced and almost resembles a hunting bow. When played, the instrument was held in a horizontal position across the player's chest, the bow being

Fig. 253. Swedish Keyboard-Fiddle. Fresco in Tegelsmora Church. 15th cent.

Fig. 254. Swedish Keyboard-Fiddle on a fresco in Hävero Church. *Ca.* 1500.

moved up and down across the strings in the neighbourhood of the sound-holes. A Danish example of the nöglefejle appears on a fresco in Vinderslev Church, dating from the beginning of the sixteenth century (circa 1520).

Our next illustration of the keyboard-fiddle comes from another Uppland fresco (circa 1500) and is to be seen in Hävero Church. Here we are given more details (see Fig. 254).

The sound-box has incurved sides, the four strings are fastened to a violin tail-piece and supported by an unusually high bridge. The pegs are inserted from the back, into an extension of the neck. The inner mechanism of the keyboard is, as usual, hidden under the lid, but along the lower edge of the neck we can count twelve keys which become gradually longer as they approach the body. At the indentation of the sides, where the bow passes, there are two C-shaped sound-holes, one on each side. The bow-stick is provided with a handle, on the flat front of which the hair of the bow is fastened.

In the Scandinavian countries the keyboard-fiddle, outside of Sweden and Denmark, is also found in Norway. An original Norwegian lokkeleje (keyboard-fiddle) from Vefsens in Southern Helgeland, shows that it was also used there (see Prof. K. P. Leffler, "Om Nyckelharpaspelet pa Skansen," page 27).

Germany provides two illustrations, both from printed works. One is from Agricola's "Musica instrumentalis deudsch" (1529) and the other from Praetorius's "Syntagma musicum" (1618). In both works the instrument is called a schlüssel-fidel (key-fiddle). In "Musica instrumentalis deudsch" it has the same external form as the contemporaneous German *grossgeige* except that the tail-piece is not glued to the belly, but is fastened in some other way to the lower edge of the body (see Fig. 255). Contrary to custom, the roughly drawn keyboard here appears on the left of the neck, the reversing being probably due to copying the original on to the block without making the necessary lateral change. The inner mechanism is once again hidden from view. The instrument had six strings (probably arranged in three pairs). The bow resembles that shown at Häverö.

The example in "Syntagma musicum" has a body between the oval lyre and the "figure-of-eight" in shape, but otherwise it resembles the modern Swedish nyckelharpa in several respects. Worthy of special notice are the strange violin tail-piece lengthened by a long slip of wood, the obliquely-placed bridge, and the unusually long pegs inserted from the back. On the keyboard we see fourteen keys. The key mechanism is uncovered, but is drawn so indistinctly that its construction cannot be studied. The instrument has one melody string and three bourdons or accompaniment strings, all placed within the key-frame and using the same bridge. Two inverted heart shaped sound-holes appear in the lower part of the body. The bow has the ordinary curved shape (see Fig. 256).

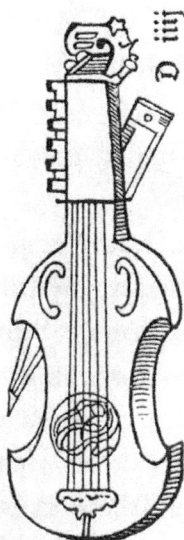

Fig. 255. German Schlüsselfidel (Agricola, 1529).

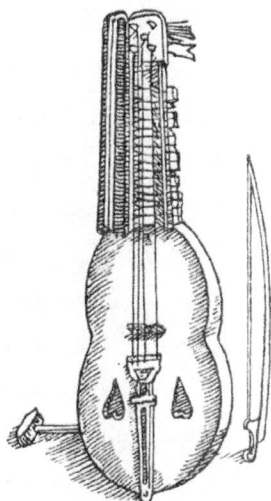

Fig. 256. German Keyboard-Fiddle (Prætorius, 1618).

As a Swedish Folk-Instrument. The body, here made of a hollowed fir plank, resembles a flat, elongated, and very narrow shouldered violin body, with comparatively short central indentations in the sides, and a flat back. The sound-holes are cut in the lower part of the body, however, and are not /-shaped but oval. The neck is relatively short and broad and does not end in a scroll but in a thick plate serving to hold the numerous pegs inserted from the back. The long pegs tune the main gut strings, while the shorter ones tune the thin metal sympathetic strings. The wooden frame containing the keyboard rests on the neck and extends for some distance over the body, taking, in the main, the keyboard of the lyre as a model. The keys in the Swedish nycklerne which are provided with long nail-like stems protruding from the frame, extend to just within the frame where they operate small wooden slips

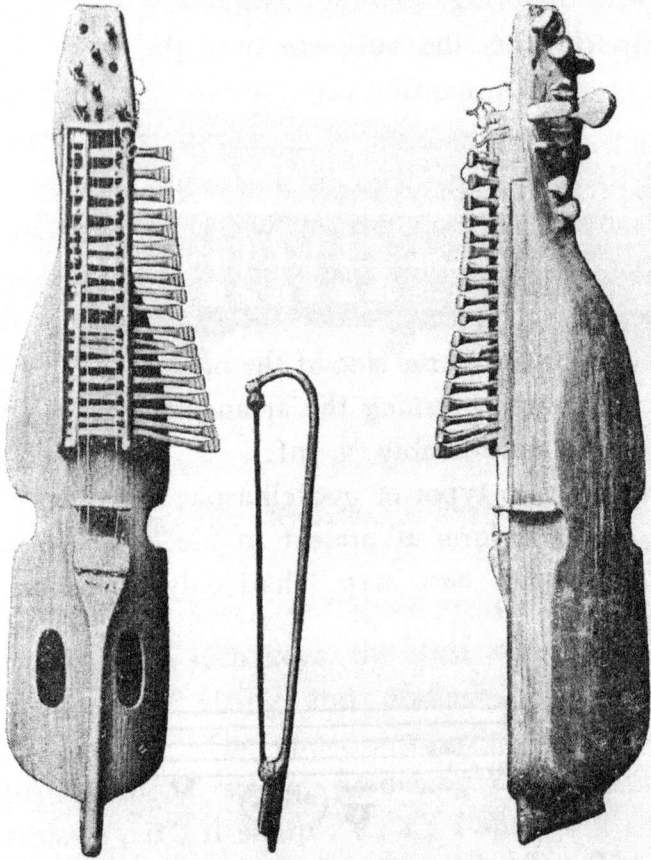

Fig. 257. Uppland Nyckelharpa. Front and back.

which, by the pressure of the fingers from below are brought against the melody string and produce the required notes. In the meantime the other strings only sound faintly by sympathetic vibration and produce the ordinary persistent bass harmony; for the flat bridge forces the bow to touch all the strings at once, just as the wheel of the lyre did. The tailpiece resembles that of the violin, but is prolonged in a rod-like projection below, which enabled it to be used as an attachment for a shoulder strap by which it was carried. After leaving the tail-piece the strings pass over a high, obliquely-placed and perfectly flat bridge. The oblique position of the bridge is a natural consequence of the horizontal placing of the instrument, which compels the bow to stroke the strings obliquely, i.e., parallel with the bridge (see Fig. 259). The four or five main strings stretch from the tail-piece over the bridge, and are fastened to their respective pegs above the nyckler. The sympathetic strings, which vary in number, serve only to reinforce the notes produced by the main strings and are divided into two groups, one of which is carried over the bridge, but in cuts so deep that it is not touched by the bow, while the other is placed under the main strings and runs partly below, partly at the side of the bridge.

The principle governing the arrangement and number of the keys varies considerably (v. inf.).

There are two types of nyckelharpa : an older one, now obsolete, and the form at present in use. The older type, called the " double bass harp," had only three main strings tuned thus :

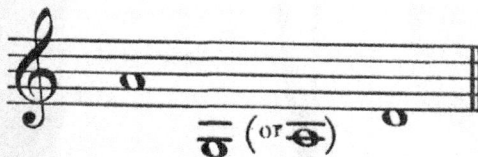

Of these the a' string (which was of silk and hence called the " silk ") served as the melody string and was operated by the keys arranged in a single row. The two others, which were of gut and were called *brummen* and *basen* respectively, produced the *bourdon*. There are not, and never were, any fixed rules as to the number or tuning of the sympathetic metal strings. Some hundred years ago this older type underwent a change. The number of the main strings was increased to four (or five), and the keyboard was altered. The four main strings in this new silfverbasharpa are tuned thus: the melody strings to a' and c', and the bourdons to G and C. The first, second and third strings are of gut, the fourth (the so-called *grofva C string* or *basen*) is spun with silver wire. In the variable arrangement of the keys in the silfverbasharpa, I prefer to keep to the system used by Jonas Skoglund ("Skansen"). He arranged the finger-keys in two rows: the upper, "long

Fig. 258. Nyckelharpa Keyboard.

stemmed," and the lower, or "short stemmed." In the lower row which has five such keys, the slips inserted in the stems act against the c' string and produce the notes, e', f', f sharp', g' and a'. The upper row which contains nineteen keys operates the a' string, producing the notes, a sharp', b', c", c sharp", d", d sharp", e", f", f sharp", g", g sharp", a", a sharp", b", c"', d", e", f"' and g"'. The note d', which is wanting in both scales, is produced by providing the second of the upper keys with an extra slip farther along the stem, acting on the c' string and producing the d' while at the same time the first key on the a' string produces the b" (see Fig. 258).

The nyckelharpa is played just above the bridge with a short curved bow (see Fig. 257), the slack hair of which is tightened by placing the thumb between the hair and the stick, a method still used by the string performers in the Near East (see the bow in Fig. 171, with the bowed instrument from the Celebes; *v.* also the nyckelharpa bow in Bk. III, page 313).

It might be supposed that the manipulation of the nyckel-harpa, both on account of its position when played and because of the irregularly arranged lower and upper keys,

Fig. 259. Uppland Nyckelharpa-player.

must be a difficult matter; but it does not seem to cause the Uppland players much trouble. On the contrary, their fingers run up and down the complicated keyboard with incredible ease. The passages flow from their fingers like pearls on a string, being often ornamented with mordents. The rattling of the keys and the continuous humming of the persistent bass are confusing to the listener who is not accustomed to them, for the drone bass does not pretend to harmonise with the

melody.   Whether C major, G major or F major be played,
the bass chord G$_c^C$ is always heard.   The player seldom goes
beyond C major, G major and 'F major.   He rarely makes use
of any minor key, for most of the nyckelharpa melodies are
played in the major.   The digital mechanism robs the nyckelharpa player of many of the effects at the disposal of the
violinist.   Thus he is unable to glide from one position to
another or from one string to continue a passage on the next.
He is also prevented from using *pizzicato* or harmonics.   Even
the *legato*, which is at his disposal, he can only use exceptionally.   He seldom plays more than two or three notes in one
bow stroke and the bow, therefore, has almost as much to do
as the fingers, moving with feverish haste over the strings.

Where and when the keyboard or tangent fiddle
originated is doubtful.   There are, as mentioned above, early
pictures of it in the Scandinavian countries and in Germany;
but nowhere else.   It is first found in Sweden, and Sweden is
moreover the only country in which it is still used.   The fact
that in Sweden the keyboard fiddle has always been especially
associated with Uppland, has given rise to the well known
tradition that the French Walloons were the first to introduce
it into Sweden when they were called thither in the seventeenth century to work in the iron foundries of Dannemora; a
belief which is decisively overturned by the fact that the
instrument is to be found on Swedish church paintings two
hundred years before the immigration of the Walloons.

It would, on the other hand, be rash to conclude from
these facts that the keyboard-fiddle was invented in Sweden.
The spread of the lyre over almost all of the European
countries, in reality makes the creation of the keyboard-fiddle
possible in any of the countries where the lyre was used in the

Middle Ages. To remove the wheel and use a bow instead, was really just as natural an idea as to remove the keyboard in order to allow the fingers to touch the strings directly *(v. sup.)*. That the keyboard-fiddle was only illustrated in German and Scandinavian pictures, may therefore be quite accidental. Some of the other instruments which by their nature, like the lyre variations mentioned above, attracted the lower class of musicians, may very well have escaped the attention of investigators, because local painters and authors may not have found it worth their while to depict or describe them. Even the lyre which was once so well known, had to suffer in the sixteenth and seventeenth centuries at the hands of Virdung and Praetorius who contented themselves with illustrating it in their works on instruments, but did not describe it, "because it was now only played by peasants and wandering women" *(v. sup.)*.

Other circumstances may also have contributed towards the existence of lyre varieties for a long time. The lyre without a keyboard thus had no special name, but had to share that of the regular lyre. As we saw earlier, a German manuscript of the twelfth century gives it without further ceremony as an ordinary lyre—organistrum (see Fig. 251), while Praetorius reproduces it as well as the lyre in the seventeenth century as instances of "allerlei Bauernleiern." As to the keyboard-fiddle, we have not, it is true, any proof of its having been at any time the name of the mother instrument. When it is mentioned for the first time in literature (in Germany and Sweden), it is called schlüsselfidel and nyckel-harpa or nyckelgige respectively, and thus has its own name which keeps it distinct from the lyre. There are, however, in literature, elements which lead us to suspect that formerly no distinction was made in every case between it and the lyre. When Hans Mikkelsen Ravn, in his "Heptachordum Danicum," mentions the instruments which were still being used by the Danish peasants of his time, he alludes to one of them as the Lyre or Nöglefejle, thus clearly showing that he considered the two names synonymous. Where the names Fon and Symphonia are used in the sixteenth century and the seventeenth respectively, in Iceland and Norway, as the names of an instrument with a beautiful tone, possessing both keys and strings, they may just as well —as they were by Otto Andersson in "The Bowed Harp"— be connected with the Nöglefejle or the Nyckelharpa as with the Lyre. The later French name for the Lyre, i.e., the *Vielle*, belonged originally, as will be known, to the bowed fiddle and was therefore really better adapted to the keyboard-fiddle than to the Lyre manipulated with a wheel. If France, when adopting this name, owned a keyboard-fiddle, it is just as probable that, like the lyre without a keyboard, it bore the name of the mother-instrument and was thus called the *Vielle*.

Our information as to the fate of the keyboard-fiddle in the countries where its existence is proved, i.e., Germany and Scandinavia, is defective. Where Germany is concerned, there are only the reproductions of Agricola and Prætorius, but no comments. As to Denmark, we have but the assertion of Hans Mikkelsen Ravn that the Lyre or Nöglefejle was still used by Danish peasants in the seventeenth century, and the somewhat later allusion of Peder Syv to 'bagpipers and Nöglefejlere as instances of the inartistic musicians of his time. Sweden, therefore, as the only preserver of the keyboard-fiddle, is our only source of information, and the particulars found there, apart from the Uppland church-paintings of *ca.* 1500, apply only to the last representative of this instrument: the Uppland Nyckelharpa.

Under the name of Nyckelgiga or Nyckelharpa the keyboard-fiddle is said by Norlind to have been popular with the Swedes as early as the seventeenth century, and in the eighteenth century it was an especial favourite at wedding-feasts to accompany the dances in Uppland, Södermanland, and Östergötland, as well as in Helsingland and the Dalecarlia. "When the wedding guests go to church," writes Leffler, "and when the dishes are carried to the banquet, the pleasant tones of the Nyckelharpa increase the air of festivity; but first of all it has, sometimes with the clarinet, sometimes with the viol, often also alone, invited the young men and women to play and dance, giving them the best of its old treasures of valses and Polish melodies" ("Om Nyckelharpospelet paa Skansen," in "Bidrag till vår Odlings Häfder," published by A. Hazelius).

Those who wish to hear the Nyckelharpa at the present day must go to Uppland, the only district in which it still exists. There are still a few capable players, among them several prize-winners in the competitions which are held now and then in Swedish towns, to preserve the Swedish folk-music. The best opportunity of making the acquaintance of the Nyckelharpa, however, is offered to travellers at the "Skansen" in Stockholm Djurgaard, where a Nyckelharpa-player, regularly employed on summer Sundays (often with the assistance of one or two viol-players) accompanies the national dances performed in the picturesque national costumes.

II. THE CLAVICHORD.

Like the bowed round-lyre, the Icelandic Fidla, and the Lyre (Organistrum), the Clavichord belonged to Group I of the instruments with stopped strings, and was in so far a descendant of the Lyre that its open strings were stopped by means of a keyboard. But in the Clavichord it was not by a rotating wheel that the strings were made to vibrate. The stopping-pins themselves made the strings sound by striking them lightly while stopping them. What is primarily of interest in the Clavichord, however, is its coming into existence as a result of the attempt to give the theoretical monochord with the movable bridge, a more practical design. The first attempt in this direction was made shortly after Guido's day, and consisted in placing a four-lined scale under the monochord string to indicate the pitch of the eight Church-modes. Each of the lines was used to produce two modes, one Authentic and one Plagal. If the slider was moved according to the scale of the first line, the diatonic sequence A to d was produced, i.e., the notes required to form the first Plagal mode, A to a, and the first Authentic one, D to d. The degrees of the second line served to produce the sequence B to e, and enabled the player to produce the second Plagal mode, B to b, and the second Authentic series, E to e. On the third line the sequence, C-f, and on the fourth, D-g, i.e., the materials for the third and fourth Plagals and the third and fourth Authentic modes respectively: C to c, F to f, and G to g. Aribo Scholasticus, towards the end of the eleventh century, stated that this device gained much favour, so that in his day there were few monochords which were not made in this manner.

The next reform consisted in stretching a string over each of these four lines. Thus the four-stringed monochord came into existence which Johannes de Muris ("Musica speculativa," 1323) recommended in preference to the one-stringed instrument, because by its means it was possible to produce harmonies. But if this increase in the number of the strings meant progress in one way, it increased the difficulty of manipulating the monochord in another; instead of one slider there were now four (one below each of the four strings).

The Theoretical Keyboard Monochord. The next step, therefore, had to be the invention of a practical means of stopping the strings to replace the sliders. The means had been in existence for a long time in the keyboard of the Lyre. When the keys of that instrument were touched, a small pin or "tangent," inserted in its extremity, was, as we have already seen, pressed against the string, which was thus struck and stopped at the same time. An attempt was now made to apply a corresponding keyboard to the monochord strings, the notes of which would thus be prepared beforehand instead of having to be found and fixed by means of the awkward sliders. In this manner a playable instrument was developed out of the monochord and, deserting the theorists, it was quickly adopted by the practical musicians as the earliest form of the pianoforte.

The use of the keyboard monochord by theorists can only be proved by an isolated example, an instrument which Van der Straeten illustrated in " La Musique aux Pays-Bas," I (see Fig. 260), showing a theoretical keyboard monochord with eight strings and the corresponding eight keys. Behind, or rather below, the strings are seen, immediately above the keyboard, the eight wooden or brass tangents destined to be pressed against the strings by the action of the keys, in order to effect the sounding and stopping of the strings.

The Clavichord.

The earliest pictorial representation of a keyboard mono-chord (Clavichord) intended for use as a practical musical instrument, appears on an English carving in St. Mary's Church, Shrewsbury (fifteenth century; see Fig. 261), where a female figure plays a small clavichord with three double strings and nine keys. Each of the three pairs of strings is consequently touched by three keys. On this instrument it was thus only possible to play melodies of not more than nine notes in compass, and because the notes produced on any one string could not be used together, only a limited number of harmonies could be produced.

Much more richly strung was the clavichord shown in a German manuscript of the same period : " Das Weimarer Wunderbuch " (about 1440; see Fig. 262), but the rather sketchy drawing makes it impossible to ascertain how the twenty-four

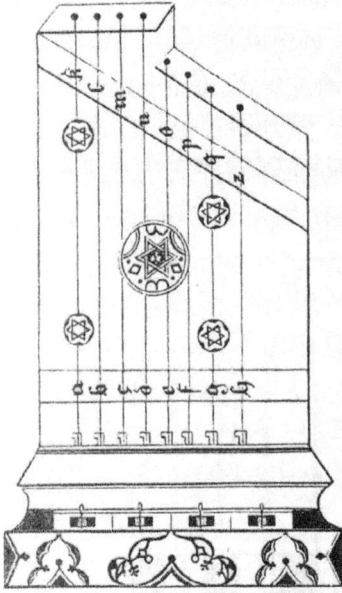

Fig. 260. Theoretical Keyboard-Monochord. (After Van der Straeten.)

Fig. 261. The Earliest Clavichord. 15th cent. (Galpin, " Old English Instruments ").

Fig. 262. German Clavichord. *Ca.* 1440.

keys were distributed over the eleven strings. In the middle of the sound-board, below the strings, is a large round sound-hole. The arrangement of the keyboard is peculiar, for each pair of lower keys is separated by an upper key (see Fig. 263). As the example is the only one in existence, it is quite possible that the regular arrangement of the upper keys is only the result of an error in drawing.

A keyboard containing only two upper keys (for the B-flat in the two higher octaves) appeared for the first time in the fourteenth century on a hand organ. This illustration may be correct, for Sebastian Virdung (1511) reproduced it in his "Musica Getutscht" as a curiosity of the past, and compared

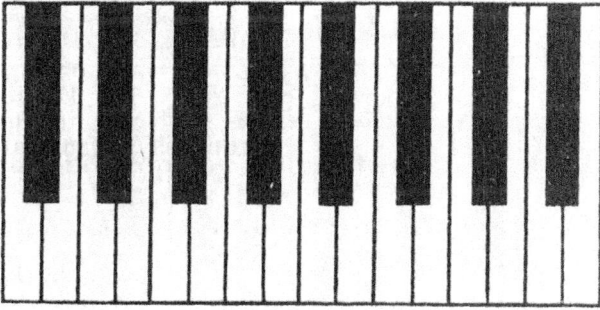

Fig. 263. Keyboard of the Clavichord shown in Fig. 262.

it with the keyboard of his own day, which agrees in every respect with that of modern times, in which the arrangement of the upper keys in alternate groups of two and three makes it easy to discover the position of the notes. (See Figs. 264 and 265.)

In Virdung's work the Clavichord is described so minutely that we are not left in the dark on the details of its construction at that period. In appearance the Clavichord resembled an oblong box without legs (see Fig. 268). The number of the strings might vary. On this point Virdung says: "I cannot name a definite number which it should have, so many or so many, and no fewer or more; but since the instrument comes from the monochord, I think one may put on as many strings as one wishes." The strings were all of the same length and tuned in unison. They were generally arranged in groups of three. Virdung says: "One generally has three strings to a group *(Kor)*, so that should one of them chance to snap, as happens, he should not therefore have to stop playing." The strings for the lower notes were of brass, the higher ones of

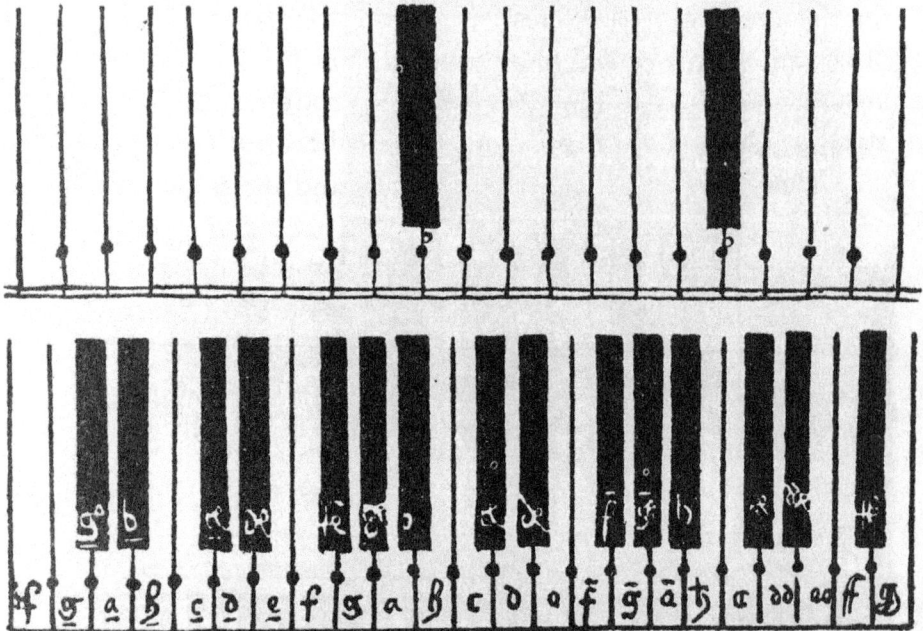

Figs. 264 and 265. Keyboards in "Musica Getutscht" (1511).

steel. Virdung explains: "As brass sounds coarse by nature and steel clear, so one strings the lower groups with brass, and the upper ones with steel strings."

In connection with the strings was a keyboard arranged like that of the Lyre, in which the tangents (the stopping-pins) simultaneously stopped and sounded the strings. In the Lyre the sound produced by the pins contacting the strings was drowned by the singing tone drawn forth by the rotating wheel. In the Clavichord the tone produced by the tangent was not covered by the use of any other sound-producer. Its tone was therefore weak and of short duration, especially since the tangent, after touching the string, continued to press against it until the next note was played. Another consequence of this was that the two parts of the string, one on each side of the point of contact, were both made to sound by touching the keys. In order to prevent the dissonances thus produced, the left-hand portion of the string was damped by interlacing it with narrow strips of cloth. Since, according to Virdung, three keys had, as a rule, to share one string, the number of harmonies which might be produced on the Clavichord was very limited; for the different notes produced on the same string could not, as already mentioned, be used together.

The tuning of all the strings to one and the same note had

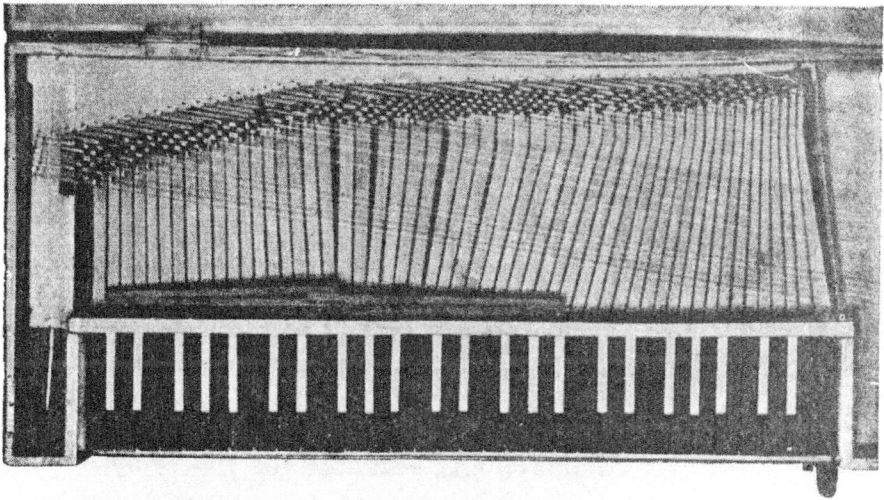

Fig. 266. Clavichord Keyboard. Photograph.

the result of shifting the point of contact between the tangent and the string to one side or other of the key-shaft. The rods, near the ends of which the tangents were fixed, had therefore often to be bent to various degrees (see Figs. 266 and 267).

Virdung's keyboard was, as mentioned above, already provided with the same upper keys as the modern keyboard, so that it was possible to play the complete chromatic series on

Fig. 267. Clavichord Keys. (a) White Upper Key; (b) Black Lower Key; (c) Metal Tangent.

Fig. 268. Clavichord. 17th cent. (Paul de Wit.)

it: *c*, *c-sharp*, *d*, *d-sharp*, *e*, *f*, *f-sharp*, etc. This already fulfilled all the requirements of an instrument destined to produce artistic music. It was so far a willing instrument in the hands of the musician that it was easy to play, and it was also possible to produce effects of light and shade in the music played on it. By modifying the pressure of the fingers the performer on the Clavichord was able to make the tone loud or soft, or even tremble in imitation of the violin-tone.

The Clavichord frankly admitted its descent from the monochord up to the eighteenth century in so far as two or three tangents still touched and stopped the same string over a great part of the keyboard. Not until 1725 did the German maker, Daniel Faber, of Crailsheim, invent a Clavichord on which the number of keys and strings corresponded and on which, consequently, all harmonies could be produced. To distinguish the earlier "fretted" (*gebundenes*) Clavichord from its more up-to-date successor, the latter was called *bundfrei* ("unfretted") in Germany. It could not, however, quite supersede the fretted Clavichord, for both models existed side by side until, during the course of the eighteenth century, they were both superseded by the "hammer-pianoforte."

Names of the Clavichord. The name Clavichord (i.e., a monochord with keyboard) is met with for the first time in a list of instruments in the old German "Minneregeln," by Eberhardus Cersne von Minden (1404; MS. in the Court Library, Vienna):

> Noch cymbel mid geclange,
> Noch harffe edir flegil,
> Noch schachtbrett monocordium,
> Noch stegereyff, noch begil,
> Noch rotte, *clavicordium*,
> Noch medicinale,

Noch portatiff, psalterium,
Noch figel sam canale,
Noch lûte clavicymbolum,
Noch dan quinterna, gyge, videle, lyra, rubeba,
Noch phife, flöyte, noch schalmey,
Noch allir leye horner lûde.

The instrument is also mentioned under the same name in England. In Caxton's translation of Geoffry de la Tours's "Romance" (1483) we hear of a young musician who appears at a castle on a festal day; he bows to the ladies and gentlemen, and after having done so, Sir Geoffry calls him to his side and asks him where are his Vielle and Clavichord, so that he may show what he can do (Galpin, "Old English Instruments").

In the Romance countries it is a fact that far into the sixteenth century the Clavichord was still called *Manicordo* (in Italy), *Manicordio* (in Spain), *Manicorde* (in France), a name which may be translated by "the string played by hand," but which is without doubt only another form of *Monocordo*, intended to keep the keyboard-monochord distinct from the other descendants of the Monochord.

The Clavichord was still in use about a hundred years after the invention of the pianoforte, and was still warmly admired by Carl Philip Em. Bach and Haydn. The former declared in his "Versuch über die Wahre Art das Klavier zu spielen" that a pianist can only truly show what he can do, on the Clavichord. The last Clavichords were made as late as 1812.

The Clavicembalo, used side by side with the Clavichord, originated, as mentioned in Book I (p. 164), from the Psalterium, and therefore does not belong to this group. Unlike the Clavichord, its development led it away from the mother-instrument so quickly, that the main part of its history as an independent instrument falls outside of the Middle Ages. It is therefore only as a former competitor of the Clavichord, and as the second extinct precursor of the pianoforte, that it is dealt with here in a supplementary section in Book III.

Summary.

A peculiarity of the keyboard-monochords was the application of mechanism which either (as in the Lyre and the Keyboard-Fiddle) only served to stop one or two melody-strings, or (as in the Clavichord) affected a greater number of strings.

The oldest Keyboard-Monochord was the Lyre (Organistrum), which, in combination with a keyboard, used a rotating wheel to touch all the strings; i.e., both the melody-string and the accompanying strings not affected by the keyboard.

In its earliest form (from the tenth century to the thirteenth) the Lyre was so large that two persons were required to handle it, one of whom manipulated the keyboard, while the other turned the wheel by means of a crank. In this type of Lyre the keys were always placed on the side turned upward, and played either by drawing them up and pushing them back, or by turning them into place. Later on (after 1300) this type of Lyre was superseded by a smaller one; a one-man Lyre in which the keyboard was placed, as a rule, on that side of the instrument which was turned downwards, where the keys were manipulated by finger-pressure. A small nail or peg, which was inserted into the stem of the key inside the keyboard-frame, was pressed against the melody-string which was thereby stopped; it then fell back by its own weight. While the Lyre only had three strings from the beginning—i.e., one melody-string and two bourdons—the number of strings was increased in the eighteenth century to six—two melody-strings and four bourdons. At the same time the keyboard was extended to comprise a double row of keys, lower and upper.

At the outset the Lyre had the curved form of the Fiddle;

later on it assumed, temporarily, a box-shape; but it soon returned to the fiddle-form, to which was added the lute-form in the eighteenth century.

As a two-man instrument the Lyre was a very distinguished member of the orchestra, especially used in the churches; as a one-man instrument it soon became the property of the vagabond. It subsequently worked its way upwards during different periods—for the last time in the eighteenth century, when for a time it was fashionable in Paris, and attracted the attention of instrument-makers and composers, though its popularity in aristocratic society was of short duration. At the end of the century the Lyre was, even in Paris. already reduced to being the sheet-anchor of the poor and the blind.

Outside of France the Lyre was popular in the Middle Ages in Germany, Italy, Spain and England. As a folk-instrument it still existed in Germany, Denmark and Norway in the seventeenth century, and (up to the eighteenth century) in Sweden.

In its original large size the Lyre was called the Organistrum. When it was later on made in a smaller size, and in several other respects changed its character, it was called the Symphonie (in France, Chifonie), and later, the Vielle. In seventeenth-century Germany it was called the Bauern or Bettlerleier; in Denmark and Sweden it was known as the Lire and the Lira respectively.

An immediate descendant of the Lyre was the Keyboard-Fiddle which, like its ancestor, was provided with a keyboard; it had no wheel, but was played with the bow.

The Keyboard-Fiddle, which still exists in Sweden (Uppland) under the name of Nyckelharpa, is found only in one Danish, two Swedish, and two German reproductions, dating from a period as late as the fifteenth, sixteenth and seventeenth centuries respectively. Where and when the Keyboard-Fiddle came into existence is unknown, but several facts speak in favour of its having made its first appearance as one of the attempts which were already made in the Middle Ages to find a simpler substitute for the complicated Lyre, an assumption which, however, cannot be supported by any positive proof. In Germany the keyboard-fiddle was called the Schlüssel-fidel in the sixteenth and seventeenth centuries; in Denmark, where in all probability it was only used in the seventeenth century, it was called the Nöglefejle, in Sweden Nyckelharpa or Nyckelgige. In Sweden it was still used in the eighteenth-nineteenth centuries to accompany dancing, and in this employment it may still be heard when Swedish national dances are being performed at "Skansen," in Stockholm's Djurgaard.

As the third of the Keyboard-Monochords we finally encounter the Clavichord which, more than any other instrument, has to thank the monochord for its existence. For it was developed while attempts were being made to create out of the monochord a musical instrument by providing it with a keyboard on the one hand, and by increasing the number of its strings on the other. In fashioning the keyboard the Lyre was taken as a model by making the keys like rods, one end of which served to take the pressure of the fingers, while the other stopped the string by means of a brass tangent inserted into it. While the keys of the lyre were taken laterally to the strings, the Clavichord-tangents struck them from underneath, for the key of the clavichord was made and used as a lever. When the finger pressed the front of the key, the other end was swung up against the string, which was thus stopped and vibrated simultaneously. As several of the keys in the older Clavichord acted on the same string, no great number of harmonies could be produced on the instrument. The stopping-principle at the same time influenced the sounding capacity, for only a part of each string was set in vibration. The left-hand portion of the string was damped by being packed with cloth in order to avoid the sounding of dissonances.

The Clavichord was thus an instrument with a feeble tone but capable of very artistic effects when played with taste, for the tone could be modified at will by the employment of a touch of varying weight. *Forte, piano, crescendo* and *diminuendo* were thus possible on the Clavichord. The instrument was developed to this state as early as the date at which Virdung described it for the first time in 1511, and so it remained until the eighteenth century, when the difference between the number of keys and strings, which had hitherto hampered its efficiency to so great a degree, was removed. When at length each key of the Clavichord was made to operate its own string, and thus permitted all harmonies to be used, it did away with the most serious of the shortcomings which, in the early days, had been inherent in the instrument, and which so unpleasantly recalled the memory of its origin in the mediæval Monochord.

BOOK III

FINGER-BOARD INSTRUMENTS WITH NECK

BOOK III

FINGER-BOARD INSTRUMENTS WITH NECK

INTRODUCTION.

CLASSIFICATION.

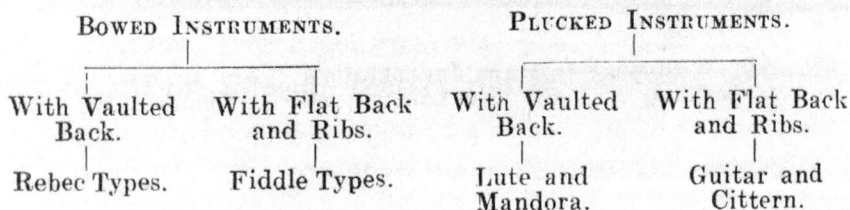

As it was especially with the class of finger-board instruments dealt with here that experiments were made during the Middle Ages in the different methods of playing, and as it was thus at length discovered which peculiarities served each of the two modes of playing best, it will first be necessary to classify this category of finger-board instruments according to the manner in which they were manipulated, and then to follow our earlier plan of grouping them in accordance with their form.

CLASSIFICATION.

BOWED INSTRUMENTS.		PLUCKED INSTRUMENTS.	
With Vaulted Back.	With Flat Back and Ribs.	With Vaulted Back.	With Flat Back and Ribs.
Rebec Types.	Fiddle Types.	Lute and Mandora.	Guitar and Cittern.

Fig. 269. Title-page to Hans Judenkunig's "Ain schone . . . under-
weisung . . . auf der Lautten, etc." Vienna, 1523.

In the middle ages the bow was first made in the manner still employed by primitive peoples; for it was made of an elastic stick, kept bent by means of tightened horsehair attached to the ends, drawing it taut until it resembled a long-bow. For this purpose a hole was in most cases bored at each end of the stick, in which the two ends of the horsehair were fastened (see Fig. 313). Sometimes the hair was fixed at one end in a furrow cut into the stick, and at the other end wound a few times round the stick and then tied into a knot. Occasionally the stick was straight and then, in its most primitive form, had a round perforated projection at each end for fastening the bow-hair—the first suggestion of nut and head (see Fig. 270).

Fig 270. Tallharpe Bow. O. Andersson, "The Bowed Harp."

The next stage is indicated by one end of the bow being reduced to a more or less marked handle or shaft (see Figs. 188 and 192). It was not yet possible to tighten the hair. With the right hand the bow-hair was pressed towards the stick in order to tighten it while playing (see Figs. 277 and 292, etc.). In addition, the method still used by the Uppland Nyckelharpers and by primitive peoples was employed: to press the hair outwards with the thumb or the whole hand (see Fig. 271). There was evidently no rule as to the degree of curvature or the length of the bow, for curved and straight, short and long bows were used indiscriminately for large and small instruments (see Figs. 292, 304, 314, 333, etc.).

Not until the fifteenth century did the instrument-makers begin to reform the construction of the bow by first directing their attention to its two extremities: the nut and the head.

In the middle of the seventeenth century the nut was completed, but was then still connected with the stick. At the end of the century a fillet with metal teeth was placed behind the stick, which made it possible to change the position of the nut and thus to regulate the degree of tension in the hair. As this device proved unpractical, it was replaced in the year 1700 by the modern screw. Both Corelli and Tartini experimented for the further improvement of the bow, especially as

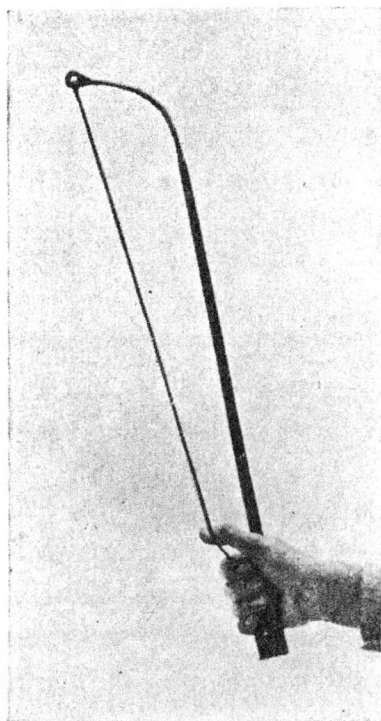

Fig. 271. Nyckelharpa Bow.

regards the head; and in 1780 François Tourte, of Paris, gave the violin-bow the form and construction now familiar. Further to illustrate the history of the bow, reference may be made to Saint-George, "The Violin Bow" (New York, 1896), and to the article, "Der Geigenbogen, seine Entwicklung und seine Meister," in the "Zeitschrift für Instrumentenbau," 1902, XII.

I. THE BOWED INSTRUMENTS.

The bowed instruments provided with a neck are divided, as will appear from the above classification, into two main groups : one comprises the Rebec types with vaulted backs, in which the neck only arises through a gradual contraction of the body, so that the line of demarcation between the sound-box and the neck cannot be determined. The other group contains the Fiddle types with flat backs and generally provided with ribs, in which the body and the neck are clearly to be distinguished from one another.

A. WITH VAULTED BACK.

THE PRECURSORS OF THE EUROPEAN REBEC TYPE.

(A) THE ARABIAN REBAB

(In its native country).

As an instrument played with the plectrum, this type has already been noticed on the ancient Greek, Phœnician and Persian sculptures (see Figs. 173, 175 and 177). As a bowed instrument it still plays a prominent part under the name of Rebab in the Arabian orchestras of Algiers, Tunis and Morocco.

The modern Arabian Rebab (see Fig. 273) consists of a slender wedge-shaped body provided with a vaulted back and made by hollowing a wooden block. Over the cavity at the broad end of the sound-box is placed a skin membrane which serves as belly, while at the narrow end a thin copper plate with three or four decorative sound-holes is used as a finger-board. The two gut strings, tuned to f and c', are fastened to a tail-pin inserted into the vaulted back of the sound-box at the broader end of the belly, pass thence across a low bridge to a peg-holder turned abruptly back, and led to the long pegs inserted from the side. The bow is curved like the hunting-bow. The round sound-holes and the abruptly turned head indicate the original use of the Arabian Rebab as a plucked instrument (cf. the ancient pictures).

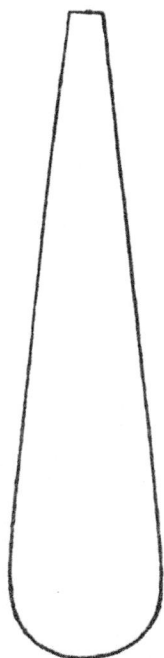

Fig. 273. Modern Arabian Rebab.
Engel. " Musical Instruments in the South Kensington Museum."

Fig. 272. Outline of the Arabian Rebab.

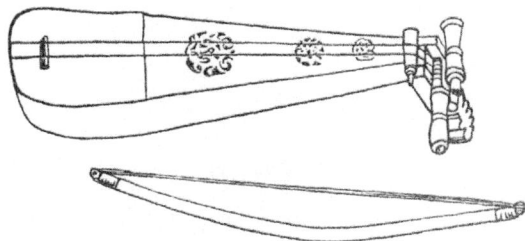

How early the instrument was connected with the bow is not known. The Rebab cannot be traced farther back in Arabia than to the tenth century, when the philosopher, Al Farabi, described the instrument so named as a finger-board instrument with one or two strings; but as he mentions the

Rebab together with the plucked Tanbours—Tanbour Koros-san and Tanbour de Bagdad—and does not mention that, unlike the latter, it was played with the bow, it may be assumed that the Arabians of his time still used to pluck their Rebabs with the fingers or with a plectrum.

AS A MEDIÆVAL EUROPEAN BOWED INSTRUMENT
(XI TO XIV CENT.).

In Spain. Although the Oriental Rebab undoubtedly came to Spain with the Moors in the eighth century, it will be necessary to go as far as the thirteenth century before finding positive proofs of its existence. In literature we find a *Rabé*

Fig. 274. Moorish Rebab. 13th cent. Juan F. Riano, "Notes on Early Spanish Music." Facsimiles of pictures in "Cantingas de Santa Maria."

Morisco (Moorish Rebab) mentioned in a poem by Juan Ruiz (fourteenth century), and we can only guess that this was the bowed instrument which was drawn in the thirteenth century in the famous Spanish manuscript, "Cantingas de Santa Maria" (see Fig. 274), resembling at the same time the modern Arabian Rebab and its ancestor on the old Persian silver reliefs (see Fig. 177). Just as in the case of the Persian original type, the strings were here fastened to a guitar tail-piece, so that there can be no question of tail-pin or bridge, and the head was bent abruptly back from the neck. As a peculiar feature we see, on the other hand, in this bowed Moorish Rebab, the division of the sound-board into three distinctly marked parts, of which the upper one is used for placing the fingers of the left hand, the middle one for the sound-holes, while the lower one finally allows room for the bowing. Like the modern Rebab of Arabia, the instrument was held like a 'cello, with the neck upwards. The size of this Moorish instrument approached that of the modern violin.

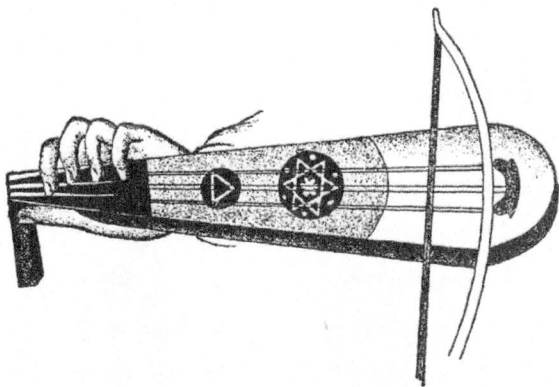

Fig. 275. A larger model of the same. From a painted relic-shrine in the Royal Academy of Hist., Madrid. 14th cent. Riano, "Early Spanish Music."

According to the Spanish pictures at our disposal, the Arabian Rebab was thus, in the thirteenth and fourteenth centuries, a bowed instrument. How long it had been so, is unfortunately not shown by the few Spanish illustrations, but it is probable that its connection with the bow had by that time already persisted through several centuries. Outside of Spain the bowed Rebab may be followed in the pictures with certainty as far back as the eleventh century.

Outside of Spain. In a form somewhat broader than the Rabé Morisco shown in Figs. 274 and 275, the oriental Rebab is thus found in two wedge-shaped bowed instruments, reproduced in a manuscript in the University Library of Leipzig

(eleventh century) and on a Danish stone picture outside Gamtofte Church (Fünen: twelfth century; see Figs. 276, 277 and
278). In these two instruments, the first of which is played
above-arm, while the other rests in oriental fashion against the
knee, we see a distinct attempt at adapting the construction to
facilitate the bowing. The backward turned head of the oriental Rebab is replaced in both cases by a round head, which
in Fig. 276 takes the form of a button, but in Fig. 278 is
flat like a disc, on which two small rings are to be seen—the
ends of the tuning-pegs inserted from the back. The large

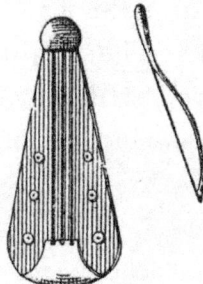

Fig. 277.

Fig. 276.   Fig. 278.

Fig. 276. Bowed Instrument. MS. in Leipzig University. 11th cent.
Hefner Alteneck, "Trachten des christlichen Mittelalters." Fig. 277.
Enlarged copy of the instrument in H. Abele's "Die Violine, ihre
Geschichte und ihr Bau." Fig. 278. The same instrument on a stone
picture on Gamtofte Church, Fünen. 12th cent. Drawn from original.

round sound-holes are, moreover, replaced by six small sound-
rosettes in Fig. 276, three on each side of the strings. In the
knee-rebab, on the other hand, no sound-hole is seen, perhaps
because it has been effaced by the hand of time, having possibly been only faintly indicated on the hard material. As to
the fastening of the strings, the reproductions only give vague
particulars. The tail-piece seen in Fig. 277 cannot be taken

as authentic, as it is an attempt made by Abele at surmounting the difficulties—in reality, insurmountable—provided by the original drawing. The instrument shown in Fig. 278 does not make us much wiser either regarding the mode of fastening the strings. What is seen here is a clearly defined tail-pin and the lower end of the strings drawn upwards towards the pegs. The short line at the foot, which connects the remnants of the strings, may look at a rapid glance like the remains of a fillet glued to the belly to which the strings were attached (i.e., a guitar tail-piece). But a closer examination shows that this possibility must be ignored on account of the existence of the tail-pin. This indicates that the strings were either tied immediately to the tail-pin or were attached to a violin tail-piece looped on to the tail-pin. In this case the line must be regarded as the upper edge of such a tail-piece, which in all other details has been effaced. The arm-instrument has three, the knee-instrument only two, strings. The bow takes the form of the short curved type, which in one case (Fig. 276) is provided with a handle.

(B) THE PEAR-SHAPED "LIRA" OR "LYRA" OF THE MIDDLE AGES (XI-XII CENTURIES).

In his "De Cantu et Musica Sacra," Gerbert reproduced from a manuscript at St. Blasius in the Black Forest (twelfth century) a bowed instrument shaped like half a slender pear cut lengthwise (see Fig. 280). The rather thin neck, therefore, as in the oriental Rebab, only arises through a gradual narrowing of the bulged sound-box, and is thus not definitely separated from the latter. In the table are placed two half-moon sound-holes opposite to one another, and between them is a bridge carrying the single string of the instrument over the belly. The lower end of the string is fastened to a tail-piece tied to the tail-pin, the other end being carried to a tuning-peg

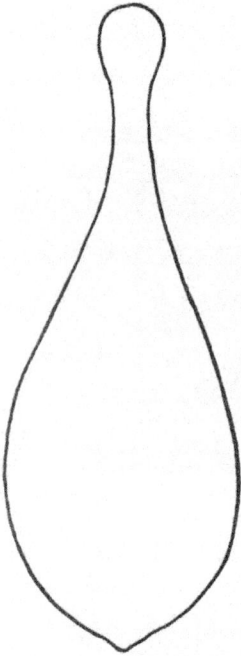

Fig. 279. Outline of the Mediæval *Lira*.

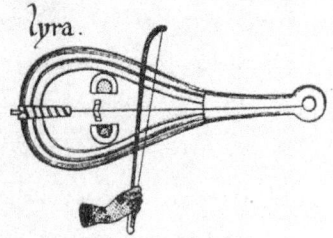

Fig. 280. "Lyra" in a German
MS. 12th cent. (Gerbert).

Fig. 281. "Lira" (on the right) in "Hortus Deliciarum." 12th
cent. MS.

Fig. 284. Three-stringed Lyra in Chartres Cathedral. 12th cent. Photograph by Girandon, Paris.

Fig. 282. Four-stringed Lyra in an Anglo-Saxon MS. (Cotton Tib. C. VI, British Museum. 11th cent. Schlesinger, "Precursors of the Violin Family.")

Fig. 283. Lyres with double strings. MS. in the Bodleian Library, Oxford. 11th cent. Galpin, "Old English Instruments of Music."

which is inserted from the back into the disc-like peg-holder in which the neck ends. A hand conducts the bow across the strings. The name "lyra" is seen beside the instrument. The same one-stringed instrument is reproduced without the bow in an Alsatian manuscript which was written in the twelfth century by the abbess, Herrad v. Landsperg. The instrument is there called "lira" (see Fig. 281). The Alsatian manuscript was the "Hortus Deliciarum" which was burned during the Franco-German war in 1871, but a copy is preserved in the Strassburg Library.

Fig. 285. Bowed and plucked Lyres on a church-door of S. Maria in Oloron. After Kingsley Porter.

Instruments of the same shape and construction are reproduced in great numbers in the sculptures which decorate the Roman churches built in France, Spain and England during the twelfth and thirteenth centuries. The one string is replaced by from two to five, and the peg-holder is just as often diamond-shaped as round. Sometimes (see Fig. 284) it looks rather like a box than a disc (cf. below, in Fig. 389, the open heart-shaped peg-box of the fifteenth and sixteenth centuries).

In several of these "Lyres" the primitive tail-piece is very strange. In most cases it consists only of a strap or ring hanging from the tail-pin and serving to fasten the string (see Figs. 285, 289, 291). The same method was no doubt em-

Fig. 288. Spanish Lyre. Bowed.

Fig. 287. Southern French Lyre without bow.

Fig. 286. Southern French Lyre without bow.

Figs. 286-8. Sculptures in the Archæological Museum of Montpellier. 11th to 12th centuries. After Kingsley Porter.

ployed in Gerbert's Lyre, but the strap is there hidden under a cover decorated with beautiful ornamentation (see Fig. 280).

An application of the same device can be noted in Fig. 283 in two "lyres," the two strings of which are transformed into double strings by each pair being drawn through a sort of bead. In order to keep them in place, a thread or ribbon is evidently used, coming from one side of a broad tail-pin, passing through both beads, and wound round the tail-pin.

Fig. 289. Part of the church-door at Moissac (Tarn-et-Garonne). 12th cent. (Grillet.)

The fact that the Lyre is shown without a bow both by Herrad v. Landsperg and in the Oxford manuscript, and that on the sculptures in Moissac, Oleron, etc., it is played, sometimes with a bow, and sometimes by plucking the strings with the fingers, proves that it was still in reality at the parting of the ways between the plucked and the bowed methods of playing. Hence there seems to be some justification for those modern investigators of the Lyre who see in it one of the parent instruments of the mediæval bowed rebec, and at the same time, the starting-point of the plucked Cittern (v. inf.) which slowly developed by innumerable experiments during the course of the Middle Ages, but which was not fully developed until the sixteenth century.

A three-stringed bowed instrument closely resembling the mediæval West European "Lyre," and strangely enough also bearing this name, is still used in Greece. The likeness which actually exists between this modern Greek Lyra and the medi-æval type forces us to assume that these two instruments must in some way or other be connected with one another, and Curt Sachs came to the conclusion that both instruments may pro-

Fig. 290. Part of the Moissac bowed "Lyra." Phot. Giraudon.

Fig. 291. Copy of one of the Moissac "Lyras." Mahillon, "Cat. desc. et anal. du Musee Instrumental du Conservatoire de Musique de Bruxelles."

bably be traced to a Byzantine ancestor which, in consequence of the intercourse between Byzantium and the West European countries during a certain period of the Middle Ages, was taken to the west of Europe with many other Byzantine instruments and there incorporated into the European collection.

The life of the "Lyra" as a popular European instrument was, as will appear from what follows, not long; but in Eastern Europe it is retained in the modern Greek form of a bowed instrument as seen in Fig. 292. This latter, as mentioned above, besides being its namesake, was in all probability also its descendant.

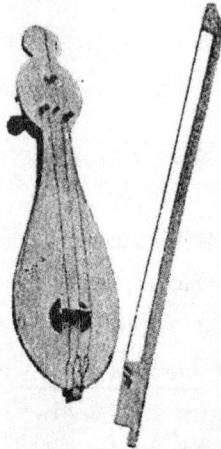

Fig. 292. Modern Greek "Lyra" (Galpin).

THE EUROPEAN REBEC.

(XIII-XVIIIth Centuries.)

I. PICTORIAL EVIDENCE.

During the course of the thirteenth and fourteenth centuries both the Lyra and the Rebab gradually disappeared completely from the mediæval pictures, and in their place another pear-shaped type took the lead. By amalgamating the characteristics of the Rebab and the Lyra the European Rebec-type was developed in the thirteenth century. This had the pear-shape of the Lyra, but through its name, and partly also through other features, it points back to the oriental Rebab. From its two precursors the Rebec inherited its preference for the bow; and the bow itself became so quickly and to such a degree the favourite adjunct, that it grew rapidly to be the natural assistant of the fiddle in the diligent efforts of the succeeding era to find a means of improving and completing the bowed instrument. As to the short career of the Rebec-type as a plectrum instrument, see below, under *Mandora*.

The new Rebec was faced with a long struggle and underwent numerous stages of development before it was adapted to serve as a musician's instrument. Its construction, as may be seen from the reproductions, was for a long time so changeable and accidental that it gives rather the impression of being the result of the groping endeavours of the amateur than that of being the conscious aim of the professional towards a definite object. Not until the fifteenth century did it become individualised and receive a permanent physiognomy.

The Rebec-type was evidently still in an early stage of its development when it was reproduced on a sculpture in the Sant 'Iago Cathedral, and in the Spanish manuscript, "Cantingas de Santa Maria" (see Figs. 293 and 294). In the Sant 'Iago instrument the characteristic properties of the Lyra still predominate: the slender pear-outline, the fastening of the strings to a violin tail-piece, the perpendicular placing of the tuning-pegs in a diamond-shaped peg-holder, and the distinct separation of the fingerboard from the belly (cf. the Lyra depicted by Gerbert, Fig. ?80). The number of the strings is three, and the instrument is held over-arm, i.e., like a violin. The oval sound-hole placed in the middle of the sound-board is, properly speaking, the only feature that points to the oriental Rebab.

The instrument illustrated in Fig. 294, on the other hand, comes, to judge by its construction, rather nearer to the oriental Rebab, as it boasts of only two strings proceeding from a guitar tail-piece and taken to a peg-holder or head, turned abruptly backward, with the tuning-pegs placed at the sides.

Fig. 294. Rebec in the MS., "Cantingas de Santa Maria." Riano, "Early Spanish Music."

Fig. 293. Statue in Santiago Cathedral, circa 1115. Photograph by Ruiz Vernacci.

Finally, it has also inherited from the Rebab the sound-board divided into three parts, and the position in which it was held when played, i.e., like a bass-viol. Only through the slender pear-like shape of the body is this Rebec connected with the

Lyra. When looking more closely, however, we discover that the adoption of this shape necessitated certain alterations in the features inherited from its oriental ancestor. Thus the peg-box in keeping with the lightly-built neck is remarkably slender, and of the divided table the upper part used as finger-board is, just as in Fig. 293, prolonged so that it extends half-way down the strings. Compared with this the relatively short fingerboard of the Moorish Rebab is worth noting. In consequence of this, the central portion taken up by the sound-holes is shortened and the sound-holes therefore reduced in size.

Fig. 295. Rebec with Mandora peg-box. 15th cent. Grillet, "Les Ancêtres du Violon."

As the Rebec-type from Spain gradually made its way to the other European countries, the oriental manner of holding it was soon completely given up, and the practice of using it as an arm-violin was preferred. The inconvenience of the tuning apparatus hitherto used was soon discovered, and with the plucked Mandora as model (v. inf.), a sickle-shaped peg-box was introduced in which the pegs were inserted, in oriental fashion, from the side. This new feature was then surmounted by an artistically carved animal or human head (see Fig. 295).

Fig. 296. Rebec. 15th cent. Danse Macabre in a French MS., Nat. Libr., Paris. Grillet.

The method of fastening the strings remained for some time subject to fluctuation. While some examples retained the guitar tail-piece of the rebab (see Fig. 297), others were given

Fig. 297. Rebec with guitar tail-piece. 15th cent. (Grillet.)

a regular violin tail-piece and bridge. The tail-piece was either, as in the modern violin, fixed by means of a short gut-string drawn tightly round the tail-pin (see Fig. 298), or was suspended by a long fastening (see Fig. 295). Now and then the tail-piece was entirely absent, and the strings were fastened to small pins inserted at the base of the vaulted back (see Fig. 299). The use of a violin tail-piece was not made permanent until the sixteenth century.

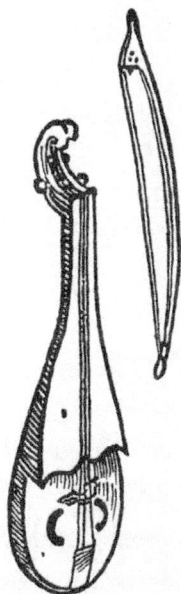

Fig. 298. Rebec with violin tail-piece, independent finger-board, and C sound holes. 16th cent. Virdung, "Musica Getutscht."

Fig. 299. Rebec with strings fastened to the base of the sound-board. 15th cent. Violet le Duc, "Dictionnaire raisonné d'Ameublement."

The Rebec-type hesitated longest before abandoning the divided table and the round sound-holes of the Rebab. The table was, at an early date it is true, changed so that its two upper sections (the finger-board and the central part provided with the sound-holes, which was originally on the same level as the belly) were raised one step above it (see Fig. 300).

As this raised part was in time used throughout its length as a finger-board, and the rose (for at that time only one rose was left) was moved down to the belly and off the finger-board, the trisection was thereby definitely removed, and the instrument was from now onward constructed like a modern violin, in which the finger-board attached to the neck as an independent part overhangs the belly (see Figs. 301 and 302).

Together with the roses inherited from the Rebab, we often find, in this younger development, the symmetrical C-holes transferred from the Lyra. The roses were always cut under the strings, while the C-holes came on either side of the bridge (see Fig. 295). Not until about 1600 did the round soundhole definitely vanish, leaving the C-holes which were displaced by the f holes in the eighteenth century (see Figs. 298, 299 and 302).

Fig. 300. Rebec with raised finger-board. 15th cent. (Grillet.)

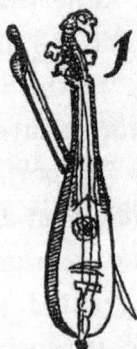

Fig. 301. Rebec with independent finger-board, violin tail-piece, tail-pin, bridge, rose, and a peg-box decorated with a carved animal's head. (Praetorius, " Syntagma.") 17th cent.

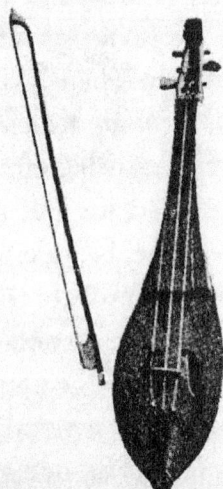

Fig. 302. Rebec in its final form with f-holes and scroll. (Galpin.)

2. LITERARY EVIDENCE. A. NOMENCLATURE.

The names especially applied to the pear-shaped bowed instruments from the thirteenth to the sixteenth century were Rebec, Rubebe, and (eventually) Gigue.

(1) The first two names may in all their forms (Rebec, Rubebe in France; Rebec, Rybybe in England; Ribeca, Ribeba in Italy) be traced to the Arabic *Rebab* or *Rabab*.

The facts that the thirteenth-century French poet, Aymeric de Peyrac, mentions "the loud female voice" of the Rebec, and that the contemporaneous French Dominican, Jerome of Moravia, tuned the two strings of the Rubebe to *c* and *g* (in the small octave), thereby characterising the instrument thus named as of deep pitch, have caused some historians to identify these two names with two instruments. This assumption, however, is countered in the observation made by others that in the numerous lists of instruments given in mediæval literature, the rebec is never mentioned where the rubebe is named; this is believed to prove that the two names were used indiscriminately to indicate the same instrument. Curt Sachs, therefore, endeavours to explain the low pitch mentioned by Jerome of Moravia by referring to the inaccuracy of many mediæval authors when giving the octave pitch. In the diminutives *Ribecchino, Rubecchino* (Italian), *Ribible, Rubible, Little Rebec* (English), etc., there are in any case enough special names provided for the soprano instrument of smaller size. It may therefore be taken for granted that Rebec and Rubebe were used to indicate the type, irrespective of size and pitch.

In the second half of the fifteenth century the name Rubebe disappeared completely, and from that date onward *Rebec* became the general name for the pear-shaped bowed instrument.

(2) The names which tradition has connected with the instruments of the pear-shaped violin-type, also include *Gige, Gigue, Geige*, etc., but absolute certainty that this connection already existed in the Middle Ages is proved only (1) during a short period in France (before *ca.* 1550) and, (2) in an isolated and late case in Germany, i.e., Virdung's and Agricola's definition of the Rebec as a *Kleingeige* (sixteenth century). Reference to *Gige* and *Geige* is made in a later section dealing with the Gigue and the Fiddle in mediæval literature.

B. TUNING.

The earliest information on the tuning of the pear-shaped bowed instruments comes from Jerome of Moravia, who, in his "Speculum musicæ" (1250), gives the tuning of the two strings of the Rubebe as:

permitting the instrument to produce the series:

The strings of the three-stringed Rebec were also tuned in fifths. We thus find Agricola, at the beginning of the sixteenth century, tuning the three-stringed treble *Kleingeige* to the notes, *g*, *d'*, *a'*; the alto and tenor *Geigen* to *c*, *g*, *d'*; and the bass *Geige* to *F*, *c*, *g* (see also the supplementary section on the "Bowed Instruments of the Renaissance").

C. AS THE MEDIÆVAL MINSTREL'S INSTRUMENT.

Both the construction of the Rebec and the small number of its strings rendered it unsuitable for the production of artistic music. It does not seem to have been held in such high esteem during the Middle Ages as were the other contemporary bowed instruments. We may judge from the following quotations ("Lettres de Remission," 1391, 1395, and 1458 respectively) that it was used chiefly to accompany the dance:

"Un nommé Isembart jouait d'une rubebe, et en jouant, un nommé Le Bastard se print à danser."

"Roussel et Gaygnot prinrent à jouer, l'un d'une flûte, l'autre d'une rubebe, et ainsi que les alcuns dansoient."

"Avec lequels compaignons estoit un nommé François Goutaud, qui sonnait d'une rubebe et allèrent danser."
It was therefore mainly favoured by the lower-class musicians who played for rural popular entertainment. It is also striking that the Rebec is consistently omitted from the lists of instruments which the clever jongleur advertises to show his musical prowess.

D. THE FATE OF THE REBEC AFTER THE INTRODUCTION OF THE MODERN VIOLIN.

When the modern violin took first place as an artistic instrument at the end of the sixteenth century, and the demands made upon the musicians increased, the simple Rebec no longer sufficed. During its slow and uneven development it did not benefit by the improvements which the instrument-makers had in the meantime effected in the Fiddle, and after having won for itself a temporary place in the royal orchestras of France and England, it soon fell into the hands of the lowest class of players. Even outside of musical circles it was now made the butt of ridicule and contempt. Thus in Gargantua's lament at the death of his wife Radebec, Rabelais says:

> "Now she is dead, the noble Radebec,
> Who had a face like a Rebec."

This alludes to the head, often grotesquely carved, which at that period generally crowned the peg-box of the instrument (see Fig. 295). In a well-known play by Adrien de Montluc a young girl derides her intended husband in the words, "He is weak and pale as a soaked prune . . . he is dry like a Rebec and flatter than a house-bug."

In Paris a decree prohibiting the use of the Rebec in all places except inns and "obscure places" was issued at the instance of the higher class musicians in 1628.

The last attempt on the part of the mediæval Rebec to sur-

vive was in the dancing-master's fiddle, described by Prætorius in the seventeenth century as a "gar kleines Geiglein,"
and known in France, on account of its small size, as the
"Pochette," because it could be put into the pocket of the

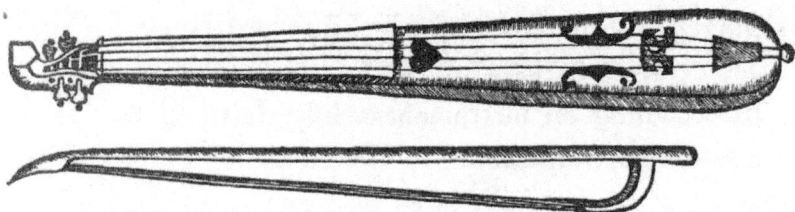

Fig. 303.   French Pochette.   Mersenne, 1636.

dancing-master.   It came into existence at the same time as
the French *Maître de Danse* who needed an instrument that
was easy to carry and produced no more sound than would
enable the pupils to catch the melody and the rhythm.   The

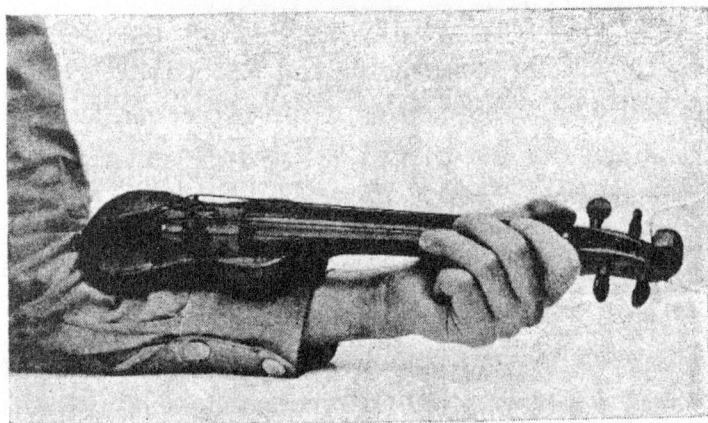

Fig. 304.   Poche of guitar-shape.   Author's property.   1700.

dancing-master's fiddle was made in different shapes : (1) as
a slender club-like Rebec (see Fig. 303) which in certain cases
was made so narrow that it found room in a stick (Stick-
violin); (2) as a violin with either the softly rounded sides of
the guitar (see Fig. 304), or the sharp-cut sound-box of the
normal violin.

SUMMARY.

The Rebec-type was in all probability evolved out of an amalgamation of the Arabian club-shaped Rebab and the east European pear-shaped Lyra which, in the mediæval pictures was played alternatively by plucking and bowing, the Rebab at least being born as a plucked instrument.

In becoming an instrument solely destined for bowing, it was a matter of importance to the Rebec to retain such of the properties of its forerunners as best advanced this object; but the difficulties in making the proper choice at the beginning tempted its naïve producers to make a bewildering array of experimental forms which prolonged the period of development of the instrument. While one preferred to allow the strings to proceed from a guitar tail-piece, another attached them to a violin tail-piece; a third fastened them by means of studs to the bottom of the sound-box over the edge of the belly. Nor was there any unanimity in the shape of the sound-holes, and in consequence the Rebec-type was found to give up half-way, while clever violin-makers in the meantime tried to adapt the flat-backed fiddle-type in order to attack the object directly in the light of experience gained. The rebec-type therefore ended its career as the humble instrument of the minstrels and dancing-masters.

B. Instruments with Flat Back, Ribs, and Distinct Neck.

THE FIDDLE TYPES.

INTRODUCTION.

While the neck in the Rebec-type and in its predecessors (Rebab and Lyra) came into existence by a gradual narrowing of the body, and while the latter in the Rebab and the Lyra consisted of only two parts (table and back), the neck and body of the fiddle-type were distinct and separate parts, and the sound-box was generally made up of three elements: two similarly shaped resonance plates connected by ribs. The outline of the body in the Fiddle-type varied considerably. In the earlier Middle Ages it was predominantly oval, round, or square with rounded corners. At a later date its sides were incurved to facilitate the bowing, and thus the waved outline of the Guitar was reached. From this point it was but a short journey to the modern Violin-type.

Although the stages in the development of the Fiddle-type are thus quickly enumerated, the manifold reforms which it underwent in the course of time indicate that it was in reality the result of prolonged experimentation. Not even the final features characteristic of the Fiddle-type, i.e., the flat back, the sound-box in three distinct parts, and the clear separation of neck and body, can be considered as the original properties of the type. In the oldest Fiddles the body and neck were in all probability still made in one piece, and the sound-box

—as is still the case in the Swedish Nyckelharpa—consisted of a roughly-cut angular cavity with a flat, or at any rate, very slightly moulded back, over which a thin wooden plate was placed. Later on the idea presented itself of making the back angular with the sides by means of perpendicular ribs, and thus the way was prepared for the construction that characterises the Fiddle-type in its final form. This came about through the attempts to make the instrument lighter and more resonant, by glueing the several parts together (cf. Curt Sachs, "Handbuch der Instrumentenkunde," p. 173).

Originally the fiddle was not clearly or invariably connected with the bow. The oldest types, like the Rebab, were still played with the fingers or the bow, *ad libitum*.

(1) ON THE MONUMENTS. THE OLDEST TYPES OF FIDDLE AND THE DEBUT OF THE CLASS AS BOWED INSTRUMENTS (IX C.).

Curt Sachs is of the opinion that the instrument illustrated in Fig. 305 is the earliest instance of a bowed Fiddle, for the Utrecht Psalter from which the picture was taken dates from the ninth century. King David is seen coming from the Tabernacle carrying a harp, a fiddle, and a long pole which Curt Sachs ("Handbuch," p. 170) looks upon as a *bow*, but which Kathleen Schlesinger ("The Precursors of the Violin Family," p. 131) thinks is a sword. Both suggestions are to some extent justifiable, for the placing of the pole across the strings of the Fiddle permits it to be regarded as a bow, while its striking length and breadth, as well as its shape, makes it look uncommonly like a sword.

If Curt Sachs is right in interpreting the pole as a bow, and if Kathleen Schlesinger is right in seeing it as a sword, the artist must have had a purpose when he introduced the two notions into one picture. It is possible that by giving King

David two stringed instruments and a sword to carry, he desired to characterise the Psalmist as musician and warrior;
and the impossibility of placing a bow in the hand of the king
as well as a sword may have given his mediæval mind the idea

Fig. 305.   Illustration from the Utrecht Psalter.   (Ps. CVII: " Exsurge
psalterium et cythara.")

of using the sword to represent the bow.   That the old man is
King David appears to be certain from the subject of the picture, i.e., the threefold glorification of the holy creator of the
Psalms.   At the foot we thus see the king as a young man,
when in "David's City" he directs the choir of singers; at
the top he is represented as an old man, carrying his emblems
(the musical instruments and the sword) and leaving the Tabernacle.   At the upper left-hand corner of the picture he is
finally seen after his death as the radiant centre of a sun, the
beams of which illumine the sanctuary.   In the manuscript the
instrument is reproduced several times, but only in this case is
it treated as a bowed instrument.   In most cases it is merely

exhibited (see Fig. 307). In one picture it is plucked with the fingers, in another the finger-board is provided with frets.

Fig. 306. King David
(enlarged scale.)

Fig. 307. The same instrument
as in Fig. 306, without bow.
(K. Schlesinger.)

In all the reproductions the instrument has the same appearance and resembles a spade, the shaft (neck) of which is double the length of the blade (the body). Sound-box and neck, moreover, give the impression of being made in one piece. At the base of the table is seen a projection like a tail-piece. Neither bridge nor sound-holes can be made out. Where the instrument is reproduced without a bow, the table is solid; where it is being bowed, the bow covers the place where the holes may have been cut. At the end of the neck the tuning mechanism will be found, which in the bowed instruments takes the form of a rounded head provided with three pegs; in another example (see Fig. 307) it resembles a trefoil, each of the leaves being perforated (for the pegs; Ed.). At all events it is certain that the instrument had three strings, though the method of placing the pegs is not clear. In the first case they look as if they were inserted from the top and sides of the head; in the other, from the back of the head.

In mediæval Spain, serving as the door through which many oriental musical instruments entered Europe (among them the Rebab, the Lute, and the Mandora), we see in a mural painting of the twelfth century an instrument (see Fig. 308) which in appearance comes very near to the Utrecht Fiddle. It is reproduced four times in the picture and, like the Utrecht example, is spade-shaped. It is provided with a distinct tail-

Fig. 308. Spanish spatulate Fiddle (not later than the beginning of 12th cent.). A. L. Meyer, "Geschichte der spanischen Malerei."

pin and its rather long neck is quite separate from the body. At the same time it shows several of the details lacking in the picture in the Utrecht Psalter, among others a triangular tail-piece, something like that attached to the violin, two half-moon sound-holes, and frets that are continued from the neck across the belly as far as the sound-holes. In two cases it has three strings, in the other two it has four. A peculiarity of one of the four-stringed instruments (see Fig. 308) is that the frets are placed midway between the strings which are arranged in two pairs, at a place where they are quite meaningless. A comparison of this instrument with the oval Spanish Fiddle of the same period—reproduced below in Figs. 311-13—perhaps gives us the solution to the riddle, for in Fig. 313 we see a single melody-string, stopped by the fingers, between two pairs of bourdons. In all probability a fifth string was once present in the original of Fig. 308, running over the frets, but either forgotten by the painter or effaced by time. In the oval fiddle-type, also, the number of the strings—three and five—is found in a finger-plucked and a bowed instrument respectively. The five-stringed example of these spade-shaped instruments was perhaps, as in the case of the Utrecht fiddle, a bowed instrument, while the three-stringed one was plucked. The omission of the bow may have been caused, as is often the case in mediæval pictures, by the circumstance that the right hand is carrying another object which sometimes takes the form of a large onion, but which is here a goblet or an hour-glass (corresponding examples are to be seen in Figs. 285, 286, 319 and 325).

By reason of the body-outline, the bowed instrument reproduced in Fig. 309, from a Danish fresco in Soendbjerg church (near Thisted), is also reminiscent of the Utrecht fiddle. I shall, however, make no secret of the fact that the picture, as stated by the officials of the National Museum, dates from a time so late (about 1575) that it may quite well be an imaginary creation by the artist or a conscious imitation of some mediæval or possibly oriental instrument. It is therefore only in the sense of its being a Danish monument that the mysterious instrument is noticed here. The spatulate body ending in a point, is in this case rather short and continues without a break in a comparatively long and broad neck. In the original, four or five strings are dimly seen protruding from a strikingly broad violin tail-piece and running up to a peg-disc placed at the end of the neck, in which the pegs, completely obliterated, should—according to rule—have been inserted from the back. A very short bow is used, and the painter, undoubtedly through ignorance, has placed it immediately below the curves over which it should normally have passed. The incurvations cause us to look upon the instrument as a modern improvement on the spade-shape (*v. inf.*, the Guitar-Fiddle).

Fig. 309. Spade-shaped Fiddle on a Danish fresco, Soendbjerg Church.

Fig. 310. Fiddle from Turkestan in the Daschkow Museum, Moscow. (Curt Sachs.)

It is probable that the spade-shaped fiddle originated in the East. This is suggested both by its occurrence on a Spanish painting and by the points of resemblance between it and the fiddle from Turkestan discovered by Curt Sachs in the Daschkow Museum in Moscow (see Fig. 310).

THE OVAL FIDDLE-TYPE.

(As a Plucked and Bowed Instrument).

(XI-XV Centuries).

Far more widespread in mediæval Europe than the spade-shaped Fiddle-type was the above-mentioned oval type which made its appearance in Spanish pictures from the eleventh century onwards. Here also two modes of playing contended with each other. In its earliest form this Fiddle was thus still a plucked instrument with three strings. A long and slender

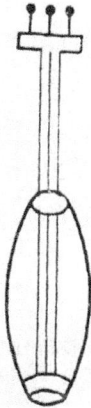

Fig. 311. Spanish Oval Fiddle. (*Add.* 11695, Brit. Mus., circa 1109). Drawn from the original.

Fig. 312. The same instrument. From "Cantingas de S. Maria." Riano, "Early Spanish Music." 11th cent.

neck here continues a large almond-shaped body. A broad ring encircling the base of the sound-box serves to fasten the strings which, without passing over a bridge, go to a corresponding ring at the top of the oval. Beyond the body the two outer strings disappear, but in some mysterious manner reach their respective pegs in the straight peg-board placed across the end of the neck. The centre string continues on the other side of the ring, is carried along the neck, and ends at the middle peg. The instrument is held in the oriental

Fig. 313. The same instrument as is shown in Fig. 311, but played with a bow. MS. in Brit. Mus., from a convent in Silos, Old Castile 12th cent.

fashion, with the neck pointing upwards. The left hand, which grasps the neck, attends to the stopping of the strings; the right hand plucks them just below the upper ring. In several places in the British Museum manuscript the instrument is played by eight or ten performers simultaneously, and it appears that their left hands are placed at various points along the neck. The fingers, while stopping the strings, must thus have glided from one place to another, a practice which reminds us of the manner in which the old Egyptian Nefer was played. The strange arrangement of the strings is to be explained by supposing that the middle string was stopped by the fingers of the left hand to produce the melody, while the outer strings provided a persistent bass-chord when the right hand brought all of them to vibrate together.

Exactly the same principle was employed in the bowed instrument seen in Fig. 313. It has five strings instead of three, but here also the melody is produced on the centre string only, while the accompaniment comes from the two pairs of bourdons which join the melody-string over the body and are brought into vibration by the grotesque bow illustrated. The music played accompanies a burlesque dance performed by the fiddler and another musician who plays a kind of bag-pipe in the shape of a peacock. He fills the bag (the body of the peacock) with air through the beak of the bird, and then with the right hand, which grasps the neck, he squeezes the air out again. Possibly it comes through the legs which may have acted as pipes, supplying a bass to complete the harmony of the fiddle-bourdons. (The authoress is, I think, asking too much of us when she requires us to accept this bird as a musical instrument. Ed.).

The use of bourdons in this Spanish Fiddle was also repeated, as we have seen, in the wheel-lyre of the tenth century, and was continued, as we shall see later, throughout the Middle Ages. It made its final appearance in an immediate precursor of the modern violin, the Lyra da Braccio, which did not disappear until the seventeenth century (see the Supplementary Section: "The Bowed Instruments of the Renaissance").

The contemporaneous employment of the two methods of playing the same instruments considerably disturbed the development of the finger-board instruments with neck, for they both actually counteracted each other. The experience gained, however, bore fruit during the course of the eleventh and twelfth centuries in a gradually increasing and more conscious endeavour to provide each mode of playing with its own instruments. Of the vaulted finger-board instruments, the Rebec-type became definitely at that period a bowed instrument. Of those with a flat back, it was the oval fiddle-type that took the lead; and after long competition with its vaulted competitor it at length succeeded, in a modified form, in gaining the victory.

Just as the vaulted Rebec had to undergo a long struggle before it could emancipate itself from the features inherited from its plucked ancestor (the oriental Rebab), the oval fiddle had also to submit to numerous and fundamental reforms before it was absolutely fit for bowing. Following the example of the vaulted Rebec, it first sought assistance from the Lyra by adopting a tail-piece connected to a tail-pin, and by providing itself with its C-shaped sound-holes. At the same time its pegs were placed in a diamond-shaped or round peg-board or box, and in some instances acquired a bridge. All these reforms were already carried out in the five-stringed fiddle seen in Fig. 314, where the instrument, in spite of its strikingly large size, was held like a violin.

The oval fiddle followed no fixed rule in regard to the length of its neck. While the Spaniards, in their earliest attempts with this type, were attracted by the long neck, because they produced the melody by gliding the left hand from place to place on a single string (see Figs. 312 and 313), it was later preferred to distribute the stopping of the strings over several strings, and a shorter and broader neck was found to be more convenient and serviceable.

In some cases the neck was so short that the fingers could hardly find room on it and were thus compelled partially to encroach upon the table (Fig. 316).

It was, however, evidently some time before this reform could be carried out completely. On the fiddles reproduced in Figs. 314 and 318 the neck is rather long although the left hand consistently keeps near the head.

Fig. 315. Four-stringed short-necked Oval Fiddle with bow. MS. *Sloane* 3983, Brit. Mus. 14th cent.

Fig. 314. Oval Fiddle on the door of the Abbey of St. Denis. 12th cent. (Grillet.)

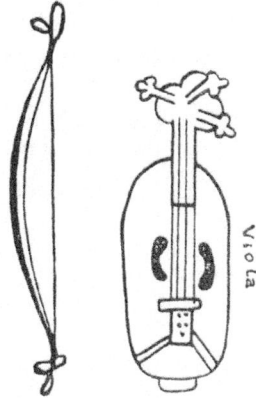

Fig. 316. Three-stringed short-necked Oval Fiddle in a MS. in Thott's Collection, 108, 8vo, Royal Library, Copenhagen. 13th cent.

As the number of strings on the oval fiddle regularly increased to five during the thirteenth century, the deepest string was sometimes removed from the finger-board and carried in an oblique direction from the tail-piece to a peg placed by

Fig. 317. Spanish four-stringed
Oval Fiddle with short neck and
bridge, but without tail-piece.
Riano. 13th cent.

Fig. 318. Three-stringed Spanish Fiddles with long neck.
Riano. 13th cent.

Fig. 320. Oval Fiddle
with bourdon. Early
example. 13th cent.
Copied from *Add*.
28681, Brit. Mus.

Fig. 319. Three-stringed Spanish oval
fiddle with short neck. Cathedral of
Sant 'Iago. 12th cent. Photograph
by Ruiz Vernacci.

itself to the left of the neck or peg-box (see Figs. 320 and 321).

A bourdon was thus regained; but it was not, as in the Spanish oval fiddle of the eleventh and twelfth centuries, abso-lutely inseparable from the melody-string as a fixed organ-

Fig. 321. Italian oval five-stringed Fiddle with bourdon. Painting by Taddeo di Bartolo. 14th cent.

point, but was in all probability only used *ad libitum* where it was quite natural and necessary for the purpose of the har-mony. This extra string was not touched by the bow, but was plucked with the left thumb (Jerome de Moravia, " Speculum musicæ," thirteenth century; cf. also the Welsh crwth, and see below, " On the Tuning of the Five-stringed Fiddle ").

Concerning the form of the back of the sound-box, the pictures give very uncertain details, for the instruments are as a rule reproduced *en face*. As long as the belly appears to be a regular oval, it is impossible to decide with certainty whether it covers a flat back or whether the latter is vaulted. The oval antique Egyptian nefer, which in appearance resembled the Spanish oval fiddle of the eleventh century was, as shown in an isolated picture in profile (Fig. 159), provided with a vaulted back, whereas the profile of the mediæval oval fiddle shown in Fig. 322, exhibits with certainty the presence of a flat back.

The oval fiddle was ill-adapted for the performance of solo music, for the shape of the body forced the bow to touch several strings at once. It is for this reason that we often see

Fig. 322. Oval fiddle with flat back and ribs. Sculpture on La Maison de Musique, Rheims. 13th cent. Photograph by Giraudon.

the players in the pictures seeking to evade the difficulty by using the bow near the neck (see Figs. 314 and 334). It does not therefore seem to be accidental that the oval fiddle in the twelfth century pictures was already accompanied by another in which the oval was incurved at the sides, thus permitting the bow to touch the strings one by one at will.

THE GUITAR-FIDDLE

(As a Bowed Instrument).

When, where, and for what purpose this type of fiddle was originally invented, has hitherto been an unsolved riddle. Strictly speaking, it was not a mediæval invention, for scattered examples of guitar-shaped finger-board instruments have already been seen on the West Asiatic and Egyptian monuments of antiquity (see Figs. 156 and 161). Since the bow was not known in those ancient days, it could not have been this accessory which originally advanced this type of fiddle. There must have been other and hitherto undiscovered æsthetic or practical reasons which furthered its development.

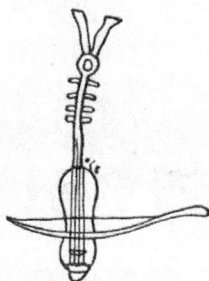

Fig. 323. Byzantine guitar-fiddle. 11th cent. With tail-pin, tail-piece, bridge, four strings, incurved sides, and double-ended pegs.

After having appeared in a few isolated cases, the guitar-type disappeared from the view of the historian, until in the year 1066 it suddenly found a place again in a single manuscript (Brit. Mus. Add. 19352) illustrated by a Byzantine artist (see Fig. 323). If the date be correct, it would appear that the West Asiatic guitar-shape was known in the eastern countries as late as the eleventh century, and that it was there for the first time connected with the bow. The case is peculiar, because it contradicts the hitherto accepted belief that the guitar-fiddle was invented as a bowed type in Western Europe —a type which only fifty years later appeared on European monuments and thence onward was reproduced so often that it gave the impression of having been a violin-type used in these countries for many years.

We thus have the option of choosing between the following two possibilities : either that the application of the violin-bow to a guitar-shaped finger-board instrument must have been an invention brought to Europe from the East, and which assisted the European fiddle-makers appreciably in their increasing attempts to adapt the oval fiddle for bow-use, or that the guitar-fiddle was an independent European experiment which accidentally led to the re-introduction of an ancient type of instrument hitherto unknown in Europe. The discovery of this supposed "improvement" on the oval fiddle was in reality very near, for a bowed instrument with incurved sides already existed at that time in another European bowed-type, i.e., the Central European bowed-lyre originating in the German round-lyre : *Cythara Teutonica* (examples in the Limoges and Klosterneuburg manuscripts of the eleventh century), in which the bow was decidedly conducted across the strings at the point where the sound-box curved inwards at both sides (Figs. 188 and 193). How and when the European bowed guitar-fiddle came into existence and whence it came, must therefore be left an open question for the present, until the mystery surrounding it may be solved by fresh discoveries.

The Guitar-Fiddle appeared originally in the pictures from the twelfth to the fourteenth century, in three main forms (see Fig. 324). In one of these forms a pair of short curves at the crossing of the "figure-of-eight" separated the upper from the lower half of the body (see *a*). In the second the curves were replaced by short straight parallel lines (see *b*). In the third form the incurvity was evenly rounded as in the modern guitar (see *c*).

Apart from the outline, all three types exhibited, in general, the same method of construction (see Figs. 325 and 326).

To fasten the three strings a rather long violin tail-piece was used, at one end of which three holes were bored through which the ends of the strings were threaded and fastened; at the other end there were two holes for the reception of the loop of string with which the tail-piece was attached to the tail-pin. Just beyond the tail-piece the strings passed over a bridge

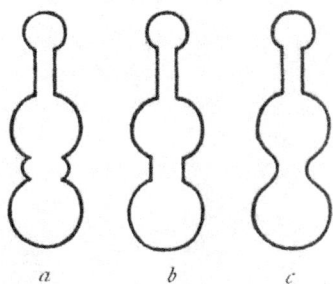

Fig. 324. Guitar-Fiddle types.

which, as a rule, was rather high. The peg-board to which the strings were carried for tuning, was sometimes diamond-shaped, sometimes round, and into it the pegs were inserted from the back. In the table, sound-holes of two different types were cut: (1) two large C-shaped holes which were placed opposite to each other, sometimes in the upper part, sometimes in the lower part, and occasionally in the centre of the body; (2) three or four perforations, arranged in a triangle or square respectively, were generally to be found in the part not occupied by the C-holes. The back, according to the sculptured reproductions, seems, as a rule, to have been vaulted. That the guitar-shaped instrument sometimes exhibited two circular sound-holes, one in the upper half and one in the lower half of the body, will be seen from Figs. 328 and 330.

Figs. 325-328 all belong to the first type, called the "octave" fiddle by Curt Sachs, because its outline is reminiscent of the figure 8. This was the type used in the twelfth century for the wheel-lyre, called the Organistrum, manipulated by two players (see Figs. 233 and 234). In the fourteenth century it was also used as a plucked instrument, but had four or five strings instead of the three of the bowed Guitar-Fiddle

Fig. 325. French Guitar-Fiddle.
12th cent. Chartres Cathedral.
Photograph, Giraudon.

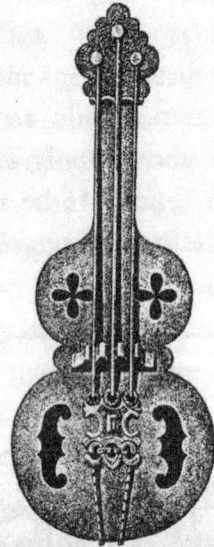

Fig. 327. English Guitar-Fiddle.
MS. University Libr., Glasgow.
12th cent. (Galpin).

Fig. 326. The same enlarged.
From Willemin, "Monuments
françaises inédits."

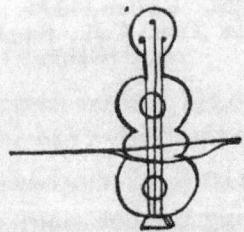

Fig. 328. English Guitar-
Fiddle (Knee-Violin) with unusually short neck and two
round sound-holes. MS. Brit.
Mus., Arundel 157. 13th
cent. (Schlesinger).

(cf. *inf.*, *s.v.* Guitar). There are also some instances of the second type dating from the twelfth century (see, *inter alia*, Fig. 329).

The reproductions most frequently to be met with on the mediæval monuments are of the third, truly guitar-shaped, type. An uncommonly carefully drawn early example of this true guitar-type is to be seen in a British Museum manuscript of the twelfth century (see Fig. 331). Especially noteworthy

Fig. 329. Guitar-Fiddle. Type II. MS. in Trin. Coll., Cambs. 12th cent. (Galpin).

Fig. 330. Guitar-Fiddle (Knee-Violin). Type III, with two circular and two waved soundholes. MS. Old Royal Coll., 4to, 1606. Copenhagen. 13th cent.

here are the bridge provided with feet, and the two knobs, one at each end of the bow-stick, and possibly some device for tightening the bow-hair.

This type predominates as the arm-fiddle during the period of the Crusades and in all the countries where artistic song was popular—i.e., in Spain, France, Italy and England —especially with the jongleurs employed by the troubadours, and in Germany with the Minnesingers. A rich field for the study of the thirteenth and fourteenth century fiddles is primarily offered in the German Minnesinger manuscripts which are so copiously illustrated.

The Minnesinger fiddle (see Figs. 332, 334), however, differed in several respects from the guitar-fiddles of the Romance countries. Here the neck was in most cases rather short, and the curves of the sound-box but slightly indicated. The string holding the tail-piece to the tail-pin was often surprisingly long, and since the tail-piece was also rather lengthy, the bridge had to be moved so far forward, in the direction of the neck, that it was placed well beyond the two large oval sound-holes placed on either side of the tail-piece. In consequence of this, the bow was compelled to cross the strings near the neck, and the instrument therefore came to be held horizontally across the chest of the player. To the tail-piece of this type of fiddle not three, but four, strings were attached, tuned in the ordinary manner by means of pegs inserted into the peg-board or box from the back.

Although we have met with examples of oval fiddles and guitar fiddles as late as the fifteenth century, these types began to assume, little by little, features that characterised the modern and more universal viol-type before the end of that century; and with the advent of the newer form, all the mediaeval bowed types slowly decayed everywhere.

Mediaeval Tuning of the Five-stringed Fiddle.

The particulars given by the thirteenth century Dominican, Jerome of Moravia ("Speculum musicae," in Coussemaker, "Scriptores," I, 1864), regarding the tuning of the five-stringed fiddle, are of great interest and give much information on the manner of playing that instrument. He states that it might be tuned in three different ways:

(1)

1 2 3 4 5

Bourdon

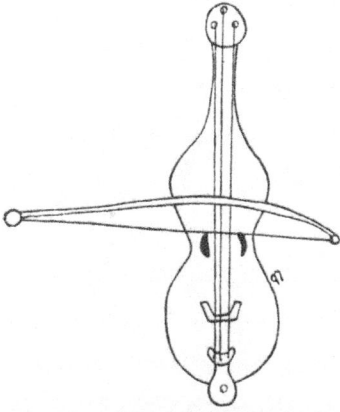

Fig. 331. Guitar-Fiddle. MS.
Harl. 2804. Brit. Mus. 12th
cent

Fig. 332. Minnesinger-Fiddle.
Erfurt Cathedral. Photograph.

Fig. 333. The same from
the Manesische MS. 13th
cent.

Fig. 334. Minnesinger-Fiddle on a Danish fresco,
Oerslev, near Skelskoer, ca. 1400. Guitar tail-
piece and large rose.

Fig. 335. Three-stringed Guitar-Fiddle on a Danish fresco in Noeddebo Church. 15th cent. Type III. Photograph.

Fig. 336. French Guitar-Fiddle with four strings, central rose, and backward turned head. Psalter in the Arsenal Libr., Paris. 15th cent. (Grillet).

Fig. 337. Fiddle on a Swedish fresco in Herkeberga Church. 15th cent. Hildebrand, "Antikvarisk Tidsskrift for Sverige."

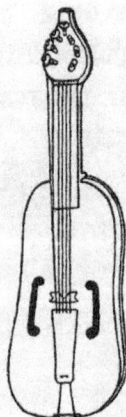

Fig. 338. Fiddle with slightly incurved sides, two curved sound-holes, five strings (one being a bourdon), heart-shaped peg-box. *Ca.* 1500. (Curt Sachs.)

i.e., the first string, beyond the finger-board and thus used only unstopped, as a bourdon. By placing the fingers of the left hand on the other strings, it was possible, on an instrument tuned in this manner, to produce the scale:

If the second string was not stopped, a double bourdon G and a scale from *g* to *g'* became possible.

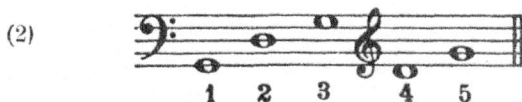

In this tuning, in which all the strings are taken over the finger-board, the scale could be taken without a break from *G* to *d"*:

According to Jerome of Moravia this was the tuning preferred by amateurs and minstrels, "who, in order to play their 'irregular' melodies, must necessarily have the whole series of notes at their disposal."

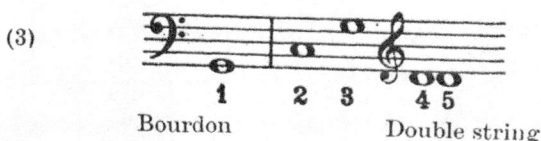

Here the *G* was a bourdon and the scale consequently ran only from *c* to a':

Basing his conclusions on Jerome's statements regarding

the tuning of the fiddle, Curt Sachs decides that it was those who were less clever in the art, i.e., laymen and wandering fiddlers, who invented the guitar-fiddle as being better suited for unaccompanied solos, while the musicians who liked to use double-stopping, preferred the oval fiddle which was provided with a bourdon. Only by assuming this simultaneous use of both types of fiddles was it possible for Sachs to explain why the fiddle without incurved sides still persisted in the fifteenth century, while the three-stringed fiddle was already provided with incurved sides in the twelfth century.

Summary.

As the oval fiddle, to which the modern violin may thus be directly traced, competed in the Middle Ages with the rebec type, it kept pace for a time with its competitor, but later on preferred to take a new path by shortening the rather long neck it originally possessed, by having its body constructed of several parts, etc.

The oval fiddle, not being suitable for the performance of solo melodies, quickly found a new rival in the guitar-fiddle which was in all probability introduced by minstrels, as an instrument which, by reason of its incurved sides, was far better adapted to the performance of such melodies. For a time the two types flourished side by side, for the oval fiddle remained the favourite instrument of the professional musicians for some time, especially when playing their more artistic music, often provided with double stopping and chords. The Italian *luthiers* of the sixteenth century finally decided the question by creating, from the guitar-fiddle, the modern violin which eventually took the bowed instrument to the zenith of its development, to a point at which it has since remained (see supplementary section, "The Bowed Instruments of the Renaissance"). If the bowed instruments with flat backs have been consistently called "fiddles" in the above account, it was because this word is understood at present as the obsolete name for the violin. The latter, being the culminating point in the development of this type of bowed instruments, was therefore given this name when classifying the flat backed instruments as distinct from the vaulted types. It is, however, by no means claimed that this was true in the Middle Ages, for the two violin names—*fiddle* and *gigue*—were used by mediaeval authors with such carelessness that it is really often impossible, in the light of their information, to decide which of the bowed instruments was meant. Only one thing is clear: that the present custom of indiscriminately using the two names for the same instrument, was not invariably followed in the Middle Ages, for the frequent expression "gigue and fiddle" certainly indicates that the names must in some cases have belonged to different types.

THE NAMES "GIGUE" AND "FIDDLE" ILLUSTRATED IN MEDIAEVAL LITERATURE.

(Origin of the Names.)

The name *gigue* (old northern, *gigja*; mediæval northern, *ghighe;* mediaeval German, *gige;* old French, *gigue*, etc.), may be explained in two ways. The first places the source of the name in France and interprets it as a special nickname for the vaulted rebec, because its appearance suggested a leg of mutton—the French *gigot*. The other etymology derives the name from a Nordic or Germanic source, as a development from the verb *geige, geigen*, i.e., to move backwards and forwards, as an allusion to the movements of the bow.

The first of these two derivations—that the word *gigue* was coined in France and there introduced as the nickname for the vaulted instrument—is repudiated by Daniel Fryklund ("Etymologische Studien über Geige, Gigue, Jig," in "Studier i modern Sprakvetenskap," Upsala, 1917), who shows that *gigot*, meaning a leg of mutton, did not appear in French speech before the fifteenth century; while *gigue*, meaning a musical instrument, was mentioned as early as 1230 in the dictionary of John de Garlandia ("Guigue est instrumentum musicum et dicitur gallice gigue"). The accidental resemblance of the vaulted rebec to a leg of mutton cannot therefore have been the original reason for the French calling it *gigue*. It may thus be taken for granted that *gigue* was the French version of the northern and German *gige*, which as stated above described the fiddle of that name as a bowed instrument but gave no other explanation of its nature. The French use of *gigue* as a nickname for the vaulted rebec can only be dated back to the time when this instrument had been degraded to the position of the minstrel's instrument and the people were consequently inclined to ridicule it by comparing it with an object of similar appearance, accidentally possessing a similar name.

On the origin of the name *fiddle* also—old northern, *fiðla*, old German, *fidula*, mediaeval German, *videl*; Anglo-Saxon, *fiðele;* French, *viole* or *vièle*, etc.—opinions are divided, German etymologists tracing the word to the Latin *fides* and *fidicula* (i.e., a string and a stringed instrument respectively), while French experts trace *viole* (*viula*, from Latin *vivula*) and *vièle*, related to *fidula*, back to Latin *vivus* (living, alive). The resemblance existing between the Roman and German forms of the name makes it, however, probable, in the opinion of Fryklund, that the French and the German words had a common origin, i.e., possibly the Latin word *vitulus* from *vitulor*, to rejoice or sing a hymn of thanksgiving, or *vitula*, the goddess of victory. According to this derivation the fidla should have been an instrument which through its jubilantly merry sound aroused merriment (cf., the Anglo-Saxon designation of the harp as the "joy-wood." See Book I). The existing explanations of the word *fiddle* do not, in any case, definitely settle the question as to which instrument the name originally belonged. (See also my lecture before the Musical Association on "The Gigue," which was printed in "The Proceedings of the Musical Association," Session 40, 1913-1914.—ED.)

Gigue and Fiddle in the Northern Literature. (a) In Saga.

Gigue. In the saga literature the name *gigja* is to be found for the first time in Nial's saga where, admittedly, it is not the name of a musical instrument but the nickname of an Icelandic chieftain. We do not know the reason for this nickname, but in the northern languages there is actually only one meaning to be applied to the noun *gigja*, and that is "a musical instrument."

As the name of a musical instrument, on the other hand, *gigja* is given in Sverre's saga, which, according to Axel Olrik, described contemporary events of about 1180. In this saga we are told of the skald Maane who, on his return from the Holy Land, visited the Norwegian king Magnus Erlandsen, just as the latter and his men were whiling away the time by watching two mountebanks who were exhibiting the tricks of two dogs jumping over sticks. The king observed that the players regarded Maane with disfavour and asked him to improvise a verse. Instead of this Maane immediately composed two. The first was: "The cunning fellow goes about with a gigue and a whistle—a foolish form of merriment, buffoonery incarnate. He makes a red bitch jump over a stick. Throw them out, this riff-raff; you should not notice them, for it is arrant rubbish." The second verse ran as follows: "The gigue sings, while the mummers wander. Now they take their whistles; see how the fellow looks askance as he blows; see his open mouth and puffed-up cheeks." This occasioned much laughter, and the men gathered round the players repeating the verse and joining again and again in the chorus: "His open mouth and puffed-up cheeks." The players realised that they had stirred up a wasp's nest and endeavoured to escape as quickly as possible. It does not appear from this narrative whether the gigue was plucked or bowed, but the expression, "the gigue sings," at any rate suggests a bowed instrument. As such the gigue occurs with certainty for the first time in Didrik's saga (thirteenth century), in which we hear of the player Ysung who visits King Ossantrix. The king received him well and asked him what he could do. "We play nothing in Vilkinaland," answered Ysung, "which I cannot play better than the others; I know how to sing, to play the harp, and to stroke ('draw,' *stryge*, *drage*) the fiddle and gigue and all kinds of stringed instruments." From this it will be seen that both gigue and fiddle, in the thirteenth century at least, were bowed in the northern countries, and the juxtaposition of "fiddle and gigue" furthermore proves that the two names, in the days of the Norse sagas belonged to different types.

Fidla. The expression, "fidlu-slattr" (stroke of the fiddle) in an old Norwegian book of homilies dating from the end of the twelfth century ("Cod." AM. 4199, v. 53, published by C. K. Unger, Christiania, Oslo, 1862) and the term "touch fidla" in the Knytlinga saga of 1260, suggest that the fiddle in the northern countries was originally "touched" with the fingers or a plectrum; but the accuracy of this theory is not to be proved, for Prof. Otto Andersson maintains that "touch" *(slaa)* in these countries also had the meaning of "to stroke," just as "plectrum" is now and then defined as a violin bow *(strake)* by earlier Finnish writers (see Otto Andersson, "The Bowed Harp," pages 46 and 166). "While Sigurd Mund was in Bergen," says the saga, "there were in this town two fiddlers, one of whom was called Jarlmand. One day this Jarlmand stole a kid from a peasant, and in addition broke the fast by eating it on a Friday. The king therefore had him arrested and sentenced him to be thrashed. When the punishment was to be inflicted, the skald Ejnar Skulason came and pitied Jarlmand who was to undergo such treatment " . . . " It depends upon you," said the king; "make a poem. He shall be thrashed only as long as you take composing it." Jarlmand had only received five lashes when the poem was finished. It reads: " The wicked Jarlmand who touches the fidla took a kid from a peasant (he was hungry for meat, poor man); the garrulous rascal lies fettered at the cart-tail, while the birch sings the fiddler a long and hard hymn." As we said above, the fiddle occurs for the first time in the saga literature as a bowed instrument in Didrik's saga (thirteenth century), together with the gigue.

b. In the Nordic Folk-song.

In the mediaeval folk-ballads of the northern countries the gigue is not mentioned at all. The bowed instrument is here called "fidel," "fedel" and "fiol" by turn, and in a single Swedish ballad is referred to as "harpa." The first appearance of the bowed instrument in the folk-ballads was made in "The Speaking Stringed Instrument" ("Old Danish Folk Ballads," II, 95). On their way to a wedding, two fiddlers found the body of a woman near the seashore, and of the different parts they made a musical instrument. At the wedding banquet the spirit of the dead girl revealed through the instrument that the bride was her sister and had murdered her, and that the bridegroom was her own affianced husband. The ballad is to be found in English, Danish, Norwegian, Swedish, Färoese and Icelandic variants, but according to Svend Grundtvig, it came originally from England. As the instrument of the fiddlers is given in the English ballad as fiddle, viol or harp, the Danish ballads have *fiol*, the Norwegian and Färoese *harpe*, and the Swedish alternately *viol* and *harpa*. The names "fiddle," "viol" and "fiol," referred to a bowed instrument, not only by reason of their ordinary meaning, but also on account of the contents of the poems, e.g., in Danish variant "E":

> "They cut off her gold-yellow hair,
> They placed it on their bows."

and in variant "A":

> "And they stroked the first (string);
> 'Our young bride drowned her sister';
> And they stroked the second;
> 'Our young bride must be afraid';
> And they stroked the third,
> 'Our young bride will certainly weep.'"

The variants giving it as "harp" do not agree so completely. Some writers describe it as a plucked instrument (i.e., possibly as a harp or langeleg) as (1) the English variant "E" speaks of "a harper fine, that harped to the king"; (2) all three Norwegian variants, which make of the body of the maid the "harp-stick" (sound-box), of her fingers the tuning pegs, and of the hair the harp strings; (3) "B" and "C" of the Färoe variants use the fair arm of the girl as the "harpusk-jarm" or a limb with which the harp is played (i.e., a plectrum). In the Swedish variant "D" the harp on the other hand is explained as a bowed instrument:

> "Ock kroppan gjorde de en harpa utaf,
> Ock benane gjorde de strakor utaf,
> Ock haaret snodde de strängar utaf,
> Ock fingrorna gjorde de skrufvor utaf."

In the Danish "Didrik's and Nibelungensviser" ("Old Danish Folk Ballads," I, 5, 7, 81) we also meet with the *fidel* clearly described as a bowed instrument played with a fiddle bow. Here we find the fiddle in the hands of an aristocratic performer, the noble knight and hero, Folkvar Spillemand, a person who, as will be well enough known, is also the chief character in the German "Nibelungenlied":

> "To our country have come
> Three men of high valour;
> They are clad in steel,
> Their horses come prancing;
> One of them carries

> A hawk on his shield;
> The second, a fiddle,
> A duke's son so brave."
>
> ("Grimhild's Revenge.")

> "In the ninth shield shine
> A fiddle and a bow,
> Borne by Folkvar Spillemand,
> Whose two hands are weary."
>
> ("King Didrik and his Warriors.")

In the first of these two examples, "fiddle" is given as "fiddle-bow" in another version; in a variant of the second, we read:

> "Carried by Markurd Spillemand,
> Who craves to drink and not to sleep,"

in place of the last two lines given above.

The Jutland humorous song of Nils Bosen ("Tang Kristensen," II, 94), who sells his only cow and buys a fiddle, belongs to a later period. He wends his way with his fiddle on his back to a christening, and there asks for his pay in advance; but instead of money he receives a thrashing and has to return home with nothing but his fiddle bag.

c. In the later Northern Popular Legends.

The sources of later date provide us with further details to illustrate the gigue and the fiddle. In 1342 the Latin source of the Danish rhymed chronicle tells of the fiddler who, on his return from Rome, visited Erik Ejegod and was called *cithar-oedus vel fiellator*, "the harper or fiddler." In one of Peter Syv's Danish proverbs the fiddling musician is also described as a "harper": "A bad harper always scrapes on an old string." In Tidemand's "Book of Family Sermons" (1564), the fiddle is mentioned together with the pipe as accompanying instruments for the dance: "They fiddle and pipe to this dance."

As time went on, the gigue was mentioned less frequently in the northern countries. In the seventeenth century both the

gigue and the fiddle were still alluded to in the Bible transla-
tions, but they were not mentioned together as before, i.e., as
referring to two distinct things; *gigue* and *fiddle* came to be
accepted as different names for the same instrument. Only in
a few exceptional cases were remnants of the old usage still to
be found. Thus Hans Mikkelsen Ravn in the "Heptachordum
Danicum" of 1646, still spoke of "the kind of violins which we
call gigues," and in the dictionary of the Society of Sciences,
based on ancient Danish word lists, *gigue* was defined as an
instrument "which fairly resembles a *fiddle* or a *violin*."
Moth, on the other hand, in his manuscript dictionary (dating
from the beginning of the eighteenth century), explained the
gigue as a fiddle. "Gige, gie," he wrote, "is an instrument
with strings, to be played with a bow, a violin, now called
fejle . . . 'Gigemand: an incapable *fejle* player.'"

Some of the conclusions which may be drawn from the
northern proverbs are rather interesting. In that literature the
gigue was described as the ancient instrument: "When an old
gigue gets new strings, it will sound again." As a player's
instrument it is still preserved in the proverb: "When the
player laughs, the gigue plays well." In the proverb: "Let
the gigue grieve" or "let the fiddle grieve," *gigue* and *fiddle*
are used synonymously.

The fiddle-bow was often mentioned, as in the proverbs,
"Juggling without a grin is like a fiddle without a bow," and
"He who fiddles the truth, will be struck on the head with
the bow." With the clumsy nature of the old fiddle-bow in
mind, two proverbs are of interest: "A bad harper always
scrapes on an old string" has already been mentioned. The
other, "Crooked as a fiddle-bow," described the old-fashioned
bow as a very curved instrument which, indeed, also appears
from the very word "bow." "A *fejle* bow," wrote Moth, "is
a curved stick with long horsehair attached to both ends, and
which is supported at the lower end by the *fejle* bow-bridge."

At the present day "Fidel" is only retained in popular

language in the north, whereas "Gigue" has fallen entirely out of use. Among the higher classes "Fidel" is now only used in a contemptuous sense, such as *bierfiedler*—according to Molbech : "a bad player or violinist who must rest content with seeking his livelihood in beer-houses and inns."

Gigue and Fiddle in German Literature.

Gige, Geige. When the name Gige occurred for the first time in German literature in the twelfth century, it was, as in the northern literature, kept distinct from *Fiddle*. In a verse describing the reception of a distinguished man, we read :

> "Mit *Vigelen* jauch mit *Gigen*,
> Mit Rotten jauch mit Liren,
> Mit hüpfen jauch mit springen,
> Mit Tantzen jauch mit singen,
> Chômen si in entgegen."

("Judith." Diemers, "Deutsche Gedichte des 11. und 12. Jahrh.," Vienna, 1849.)

Another source, quoted by Curt Sachs from "Busant" (GA, I 348) of the same century, contributes :

> "Dô hiez er in bereiten
> Mit sidinen seiten
> Ein Videlen . . . .
> Alsus di *geige* wart bereit."

("Then he asked him to make a fiddle with silken strings . . . . and the Gigue was ready.") Accordingly Folker's instrument in the German "Nibelungenlied" (XII-XIII c.) is just as often called *Fidel* as *Gige*, and we find such expressions as *gigen uf Videlen*. Still more lightly did the Germans treat the name *Gige* after the Middle Ages, when, as will be generally known, it became the generic name for all bowed instruments—vaulted as well as those with a flat back. In this wide application the word was already used in 1511 and 1528 in Virdung's "Musica getutscht" and in Agricola's "Musica instrumentalis" respectively, in which the vaulted bowed instrument was called the *Kleingeige*, and the flat-

393

backed examples *kleine Geige* and *grosse Geige*, according to size.

At the time of Prætorius, *Geige* was in principle only used for the smaller kinds of fiddles or violins, i.e., the arm-viols. "The larger ones," he said, "are now called *Viole da Gamba* or *Violes* by the State-musicians of the towns" (Prætorius, "Syntagma," New Ed., p. 52).

Fiedel. The name *Fidula* was mentioned for the first time in Germany in the ninth century, in Ottfried's "De Musica cœleste" (V, 23, 395): "Sih thas oul al ruarit, thaz organa fuarit: Lıra, joh fidula, jo managfaltu suegala" ("There all those move about who play instruments, etc."). But the manuscript does not describe the nature of this *Fidula*.

The fiddle-bow was mentioned for the first tıme in a German literary source in the Magdeburg Chronicle (125, 10): "In dussem Jare geschah eın Wundertecken by Stendal in dem Dorppe gehrten Ossemer. Dar sat de Parner des Midweckens in den Pıngxten und veddelte synen Buren to dem Danse, da quam ein Donnerschlag unde schloch dem Parner synen Arm aff mit dem Veddelbogen unde XXIV Lüde tod up dem Tynn" ("In that year a miracle was performed near Stendal in the village of Ossemer. There the priest sat at Whitsuntide on Wednesday, fiddling his peasants to the dance; then came a thunderbolt and tore off the priest's arm with the fiddle-bow and killed XXIV people at the time").

In the German "Nibelungenlied," the "Fidel" *(Gige)* and the fiddle-bow are mentioned several times:

> "Volker der vil küene zoch näher ûf den banc,
> Einen Videlbogen stark, michel unde lanc."

("Volker, the brave, placed a fiddle-bow, strong, large and long, on the seat beside him.")

> "Volker sîn geselle, von dem tische spranc,
> Sîn Videlbogen im lûte an sine hende erclanc,
> Do videlte ungefüge der künege spileman."

("Volker, his companion, sprang to his feet; his fiddle-bow

sounded in his hand; he fiddled wildly, the brave minstrel.")
It is stated at another place that the well-known Minnesinger,
Tannhäuser, fiddled "until the strings burst and the bow was
torn asunder." In the "Nibelungenlied" Volker was described
as a nobleman who could command many good men of Bur-
gundy; because he could play the fiddle, he was called "the
Fiddler." Another high-born performer was Reinmar "der
Viedeler" who, like Volker, carried a fiddle on his shield
(arms). Of Walter von der Vogelweide it was said "that he
sings a song to the fiddle and plays for the dance." Tristan
also boasted of his having learned to play the fiddle; and of
the beautiful Agnes, the beloved of Wenzel II, King of
Bohemia, it was said that she knew how to fiddle and to sing.

At the same time German literature also shows us that the
fiddle was to be found in the hands of professionals. When
Etzel, king of the Huns, sent a message to the king of Bur-
gundy, he chose for his messengers two fiddlers, Werbel and
Svemmel. Hagen, one of the wildest warriors of the Bur-
gundians, later discovered the fiddler Werbel at table, and
with his sword cut off the musician's hand: "O Hagen,"
cried Werbel, "what have I done to you, and how am I to
make the notes sound, now that I have lost my hand?"
("Nibelungenlied"). The oft-quoted account of the music
made by Volker on his fiddle, as given in the "Nibelungenlied," is very interesting. When on guard outside the house
in which his warriors rest in the enemy's country before battle,
we read how he placed his shield against the wall and grasped
his fiddle "to serve" his friends:

> "Unter die Thür des Hauses setzt er sich auf den Stein;
> Ein kühn'rer Fiedelspieler möchte nimmer sein.
> Da ihm der Saiten Töne erscholl mit süssem Schall,
> Die stolzgesinnten Freunden Volkern dankten sie all.
> Da klangen seine Saiten, dass rings erscholl das Haus;
> Er war an Kraft und an Geschick herrlich überaus.
> Süsser stets und sanfter zu geigen hub er an; er wehte
> Da zur Ruhe gar manchen sorgenden Mann."

When Volker with his fiddle visited Bechlar's queen Gotelinde, he courteously took up his position before her and fiddled "sweet melody, to which he sang a song."

When, thanks to the Italian violin-makers, the bowed instruments reached a higher stage of development in the sixteenth and seventeenth centuries, the name "Fidel" became unfashionable along with the obsolete fiddle-types; and in Germany, as in the northern countries, lyra and viola became the common names of the bowed instruments used for the production of artistic music. Only on the popular tongue was "fidel" still retained as the name of the simpler village instruments and of the *schlüsselgeige* related to the violin.

Gigue and Fiddle in French Literature.

In mediaeval France gigue and vièle in most cases occur together; that is, as the names of different instruments.

> "*Gigue*, ne harpe ne *vièle*,
> Ne vaucissent une cenèle."
> ("Lai de l'Oiselet.")

> "Madame Musique de clochetes
> Et li clerc plain de chançonetes
> Portoient *gigues* et *vièles*,
> Salterions et fleutèles."
> ("La Bataille des Sept Arts.")

> "Estives, harpes et sautiers
> *Vièles, gygues* et rotes,
> Qui chantoient diverses notes."
> ("Roman de la Poire.")

> "On le voit esbanoier
> En estruments oir, soner
> Psaltère, harpes et *vièles*
> Et *giges* et chifonies bèles."
> ("Le Lucidaire.")

> "L'us mena harpa, l'autre *viula*
> L'us flautella, l'autre siula
> L'us mena *giga*, l'autre rota,
> L'us diz los mots, et l'autr'els nota."
> (Giraud de Cabrera.)

Even if, as mentioned above, we have to abandon the idea that it was its resemblance to a leg of mutton that originally named the vaulted bowed instrument "gigue" in France, it by no means removes the possibility that the musical instrument which John de Garlandia described as a "gigue" in 1230, may have been a rebec. We are confronted with the circumstances that the rebec and the gigue are never mentioned together in the French lists of instruments, and that if the rebec is mentioned, the gigue is not, and vice versa; and secondly the instrumental name "gigue" gradually died out during the course of the sixteenth century from French literature, and was replaced by the universal rebec.

The gigue which in mediaeval France was so popular that it was seldom absent from the lists of jongleurs' instruments, was considered there and then primarily as a "merry" instrument. When the troubadour, Giraud de Calençon, gave his jongleur a little good advice, he ended by admonishing him to tune his gigue well, "so that it may enliven the melody of the psaltery." In all probability this gigue was therefore a treble instrument, i.e., a rebec of small size (a ribecchino; *v. sup.*). Frenchmen preferred the gigue for accompanying the dance, and it was therefore quite reasonable that from the moment the name disappeared in France as that of an instrument, it should reappear, or rather live on, as the name of a dance: the lively and sprightly "gigue."

The French *vièle* and *viole*, like the German *geige*, belonged invariably to a bowed instrument, just as the German verb *geigen* and the French *viuler* meant "to stroke with a bow."

> "J'alai o li el praelet
> O tote la *vièle et l'archet*
> Si li ai chanté le muset."
>
> ("Colin Muset.")
>
> "Li uns tiennent une *vièle, l'arçon* fu de saphir."

Like the German "fidel," the French *vièle* was played both by professionals and by distinguished amateurs. The jongleur Cabra was reprimanded by his master, the troubadour Giraud de Calençon, because he could not play the vièle:

> " Mal saps viular
> Mal t'enseignet
> Cel que t'montret
> Los detz à menar ni l'arçon."

Among others, the troubadour Perdigos was known as a distinguished performer on the vièle, being celebrated as a fiddler, a poet and a singer:

> " Perdigos fo joglar et sap tro ben violar e trobar e cantar."

Other French vièle players in high esteem were Colin Muset and Adenès le Roi, troubadour and minstrel to Duke Henry III of Brabant. In a miniature in the latter's romance, "Cleomadès," the author is shown kneeling before Queen Marie of France, with a vièle in his hand and a golden crown upon his head.

Like the German fidel the French vièle was often used to accompany song. In a miniature contained in a romance by Girard de Nevers, the beautiful Josiane is seen dressed as a jongleuse, singing and accompanying her song on a vièle, in order thus to make herself known to her friend Bervis.

The vièle was also frequently employed to accompany the dance:

> " Ce fut en mai
> Au dous tems gai
> Que la saison est belle;
> Main me levai
> Joer m'alai
> Lez une fontenelle;
> En un vergier
> Clos d'eiglentier
> Oï une Vièle
> Là vie dansier
> Un chevalier
> Et une demoiselle."
>
> (" Moniot de Paris.")

The so-called " Chansons de geste " were accompanied by both harp and vièle, and the deeds of Charlemagne were sung in the streets to the accompaniment of the vièle. Constantine l'Africain recommended sick persons to play the vièle as a cure.

The melodies of the vièle were embellished by the harmonies the instrument could produce:

> " Harpes sonnent et vièles
> Qui font les mélodies bèles."
>
> ("Roman du Renard.")

The vièle, in addition, was employed in the performance of the two-part "Conductus":

> " Cil jugleor viellent lais
> Et sons et notes et *conduis*."
>
> (" Roman de la Violette.")

The vièle was also known as the *viole*, and from the fifteenth century onwards, viole was the common name even in France for the flat-backed fiddle, while vièle and *vielle* were from that moment transferred to the wheel-lyre which had hitherto been called *chifonie* (see Book II).

Both Jerome of Moravia and Salomon state that the vièle regularly had five strings (see pages 385, 388, on the tunings for the five-stringed fiddle).

As in the examples given in the Minnesinger manuscripts the fidel was often reproduced with its name attached, so was there a fourteenth century literary reference to the viole in France, with the instrument duly named (see Fig. 315).

Summary.

The name *gigue*, used for the first time in Nial's saga of the tenth century, is either of Nordic or German origin, as it is found in the languages of these races, and in both has the same meaning—that of a bowed instrument.

The name *fidula*, used for the first time in Ottfried's "Musica coeleste" of the ninth century, is Latin and has been traced by German etymologists to *fides*, strings, thus giving the word only the generic meaning of a stringed instrument.

The expression "gigue *and* fiddle" in the northern saga literature and in some of the older mediaeval German and French works justifies the assumption that these two names, which are now used indiscriminately to designate a violin, must have belonged originally to different types of instruments.

Historians are not yet in agreement on the question of a possible difference between these two types. Some suppose that one type was in possession of a fingerboard, while the other had to do without it, because the players placed the stopping fingers directly against the free strings, an example being the tallharpa discovered by Otto Andersson, others being the mediaeval bowed round lyre, and the Icelandic fidla. Others suppose that one of the two instruments was the wheel-lyre and the other a bowed instrument, because the expression used in the sagas—"to draw" on the gigue and fiddle, may apply just as well to a wheel as to a bow.

The fact that the gigue and the fiddle were played with the bow in the northern countries at the same time as abroad (i.e., in the twelfth and thirteenth centuries), and the fact that both instruments were placed by the writers of the sagas in the hands of wandering fiddlers, i.e., foreigners, makes it natural, in the opinion of the author, to regard the northern gigue and fiddle as imported instruments, and to direct the attention to the other two types of bowed instruments popular in the rest of Europe, i.e., the vaulted rebec and the flat-backed fiddle.

The names gigue and gige were used, outside of the northern countries, in France (from about 1250 to about 1550), where it was used for a time as the nickname for the vaulted type, and in Germany, where it was still used in the sixteenth century as the special name for the last German representative of the rebec type, the vaulted *kleingeige.*

The name fidel, on the other hand, was applied in the German Minnesinger manuscripts expressly to the flat-backed Minnesinger fiddle and in a French manuscript of the fourteenth century it was changed to viole and used to indicate the flat-backed fiddle.

The hypothesis that the gigue and fiddle were two distinct types can, however, be sustained with certainty only in respect of a short period during the Middle Ages. As *gigue* in the northern and the German languages meant in itself a bowed instrument, and on the whole seems to have been the oldest designation for such an instrument, it was at any rate natural to Scandinavians and Germans to use this name indiscriminately for all bowed instruments. As early as the German " Nibelungenlied," geige and fidel were used without distinction for the Minnesinger fiddle, and this custom has persisted in Germany to the present day, for the *geige* is still the popular national name for the violin there—i.e., the Fidel developed into an artistic instrument. In the seventeenth century already the name fiddle was considered as obsolete in Germany. Prætorius in 1618 was satisfied to describe the *Grossgeige* as an "alte Fidel."

While Germany retained the name Geige longest, that of Gigue seems to have suffered the same fate in the northern countries as the vaulted type of instruments; for as the latter gradually fell into disuse, the name slowly disappeared in favour of *Fidel* or *Fejle*. In the northern folk-ballad " Gigue " had already completely disappeared, and the bowed instrument there was always called the Fidel.

II. THE PLUCKED FINGER-BOARD INSTRUMENTS.

A. WITH VAULTED BACK.

(1) THE LUTE.

(Its Characteristics and Origin.)

The characteristics of the European Lute in its fully-developed (classic) form were:

(1) Clear distinction between body and neck.

(2) Vaulted back made of from nine to thirty-three ribs.

(3) A single large circular rose in the centre of the table.

(4) Eleven gut strings divided into five pairs of unison-strings and one single string. (A pair or group of unison strings was called a "course" or "rank" in England. *Ed.*)

(5) A guitar tail-piece.

(6) Abruptly backward turned head with pegs placed laterally.

(7) Seven or eight frets across the finger-board (and round the neck).

The birthplace of the Lute was in the Near East or, more exactly, in Persia. Its ancestor is believed to have been an instrument frequently reproduced in the Sassanid reliefs of the seventh century (cf. Figs. 178 and 179), which already had the most essential features characteristic of the European Lute —i.e., the vaulted back, the guitar tail-piece, and the abruptly backward turned head with lateral pegs. On the other hand, the frets were wanting in the Persian Lute, and the single large central rose was represented by no more than a narrow wavy cut beside the four, six, eight, or nine strings. In outline also, the old Persian Lute deviated from its classic descendant in so far that the neck and body merged gradually into one another.

From the Persians the Lute descended to the Arabs, who still use it; and it was obviously the Arabs who brought this instrument, by them described as Al'ûd ("the tree"), to Europe in the Middle Ages. As the instrument did not appear on European monuments before the thirteenth century, and was not mentioned in European literature before the fourteenth century, it could hardly have been among the instruments which the Arabs brought with them when they invaded South Italy and Spain for the first time. It was undoubtedly the Crusades and the lively commercial intercourse of Venice with the East, that brought the Lute to Europe at about 1250, via Spain and Italy. Once introduced, it quickly became known far and wide.

Fig. 339. The Lute in its classic form. Photograph from a painting by Bachiacca. 16th cent.

The Lute on European Monuments.

Only a few Spanish illustrations of the Lute, dating from the thirteenth century, afford us the opportunity of examining the appearance and construction of the instrument when it first came to Europe. For our present purpose the modern North African Lute cannot be taken into consideration, because it may be proved that it is a descendant of the classic European Lute and could therefore not have been the model for the latter. The little information given by Arabian authors on the oriental Lute of ancient days leaves us in complete ignorance as to its outward form and details.

The Lute made its first appearance in European documents in the Spanish manuscript, "Cantingas de Santa Maria," which has already been a valuable source of information on the mediæval bowed instruments. Three thirteenth-century Lutes are here reproduced—two of small dimensions and one larger. All of them still resemble the Persian Lute of the seventh century, for the body still has the pear-shaped

Fig. 340. Spanish Lutes of the 13th century (Riano).

cutline and the strings are attached to a guitar tail-piece. Here again we find the backward turned head and the wavy sound-holes. But both neck and head are somewhat longer, and besides the above-mentioned symmetrical serpentine sound-holes there are several larger circular roses (cf. the Rebab and the Spanish Harp-psalteries reproduced in Book I). On the largest Lute the lines crossing the neck, and which look like scattered frets marking the division of the strings, are new. It is impossible to make out the stringing of these early European Lutes, for the number of strings and pegs in none of the three instruments (in consequence of the draughtsman's carelessness) agrees. In one of the smaller Lutes there are eight pegs and ten strings; in the large Lute nine pegs. The other small Lute, which is provided with nine strings, on the other hand, has eleven pegs—thus more pegs than strings.

European Modifications in the Form, Construction, and Stringing of the Lute.

It was not until the fourteenth century that those reforms were made in Europe that were quickly to make the Lute celebrated as the "Queen of European Instruments." The beginning was made by a re-shaping of the sound-cavity, the pear-shape being replaced in the course of that century by the classic Lute-form, in which the neck and body were clearly defined from each other. At the same time the body was made deeper and the neck shorter. The large central rose, characteristic of the classic Lute-type, began to appear, often, it is true, surrounded by a larger or smaller number of different secondary roses, as in Fig. 341.

The frets placed on the neck to give a chromatic scale, did not appear in the illustrations until the beginning of the fifteenth century—i.e., shortly before the *luthiers* finally removed the secondary roses and gave up the pear-shape in favour of the classic European lute-form (see Fig. 339). The classic lute-type was thus reached, and the interest of the lute-makers from now on was centred round the number of the strings and the placing of the frets.

While the number of the strings in the fourteenth century was still remarkably large on the Spanish Lutes (see Figs. 340 and 341), the German and Italian Lutes of the fourteenth and fifteenth centuries appear with a comparatively small number of strings, for in these countries, from the very beginning, we see no more than six, seven, or eight strings, some of them appearing in pairs and some singly. Not until the second half of the fifteenth century did the Lute receive its normal nine or ten strings, arranged in five pairs, and at the end of the century the number of strings grew to eleven, arranged in five pairs and one single string (see Figs. 339 and 348).

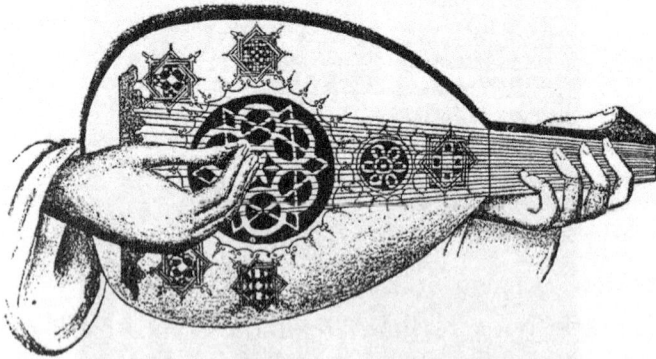

Fig. 341. Spanish Lute of the 14th cent. (Riano). Short neck without frets. Six secondary roses. 18 strings.

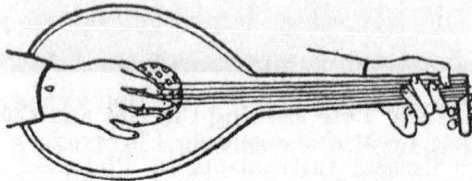

Fig. 342. Italian Lute with pear-shaped outline, 1466 (Curt Sachs).

We may suppose that the tuning of the four-stringed Lute agreed with that of the four-stringed German *Geige* and the Spanish Guitar of the sixteenth century, i.e., that it was tuned to the intervals of a Fourth, a Third, and a Fourth; the five-stringed to a Fourth, a Third, and two Fourths; and the six-stringed to two Fourths, a Third, and two Fourths. The pitch was from the very outset only relative; the highest string was first tuned "as high as possible" or "as high as it will stand," and to this all the other strings were tuned in the intervals named. During the course of the sixteenth century, however, the Lute was employed more and more in the orchestras, and was thus compelled to adopt the pitch and tuning of the other instruments. Its normal tuning then alternated between *G, c, f, a, d', g',* and *A, d, g, b, e', a'*.

Fig. 343. Back view of Lute showing the ribs and the frets tied round the neck. Painting by Michelangelo da Corravaggio. M. Sauerlandt, "Musical Instruments in Pictures."

The Italians named the six strings of the Lute, the *Contrabasso, Bordone, Tenore, Mezzano, Sottana, Canto.* The Germans referred to them as, *Grossprummer, Mittelprummer, Kleinprummer, Gross Gesangsaite, Klein Gesangsaite, Quint Saite.* The last (i.e., the "fifth" string) as the name of the highest string of the six-stringed Lute, dates from the time when the instrument had only five strings; for in Germany they were numbered from below and the deepest in pitch was described as the first, the highest as the fifth. The Italians numbered inversely, calling the highest string the first and the deepest the fifth. (In sixteenth and seventeenth century England the highest Lute-string was called the *Catling.—Ed.*) Of the six strings on the instrument, five were double. The three lowest were tuned in octaves, the others in unison. The sixth was a single string.

In the earliest days we see no more than four frets on the neck of the Lute; from the middle of the fifteenth century a fifth generally appeared; from about 1500 six or seven were used in Germany, eight (and later twelve) in Italy. In France the seventeenth century Lute had, according to Mersenne ("Harmonie Universelle"), nine frets. The frets were lengths of gut tied round the neck (see Fig. 343) and were spaced chromatically. If, for example, the open string was tuned to *C*, pressure before the first fret would give *C*-sharp, before the second fret *d*, before the third *d*-sharp or *e*-flat, and so on.

In the first half of the sixteenth century the Lute had normally eleven strings and seven frets. In 1511 Virdung wrote: " Some play on nine strings; they have only five groups of strings or pairs *(Köre)*. Some play on eleven strings; they have six *Köre*. Some play on thirteen or fourteen, and they have 7 pairs. I think nine strings too few; all Lutes have not thirteen or fourteen; but Lutes with eleven strings are to be found literally everywhere." From that time onwards we note, in the pictures, a gradual increase in the number of the strings to fifteen, sixteen, and even twenty, twenty-two, and twenty-four. That the tuning of these strings was an arduous task need not be surprising: "When a lutenist is eighty years old," wrote Mattheson, "he has certainly spent sixty years of his life in tuning his instrument," and Peder Syv goes still further when he says: "He who wishes to play the Lute for a year must tune it for four years." This increase in the number of the strings took place by gradually adding one string after another on the bass side of the instrument. The first three of these additional strings, which for practical reasons will here be described as the seventh, eighth, and ninth strings, were tuned, according to Prætorius, *ad libitum*. If the Lute had seven strings, the seventh was tuned either a Second or a Fifth deeper than the lowest of the main strings on the finger-board; if it had eight strings, the seventh was tuned a Fifth lower. In the nine-stringed Lute the three additional strings were tuned a Second, a Fourth, and a Fifth below the deepest of the main strings. If ten or more strings were used, the additional strings were tuned in Seconds below the lowest of the main strings, i.e., if it was tuned to *G : F, E, D, C, B, A, G, F; if tuned to A : G, F, E, D, C, B, A, G.*

In conformity with the custom influencing all the instruments of that era, the Lute was made in all sizes, from the small octave Lute through the range of the small treble Lute, the treble, the alto, the tenor, the bass, and thus to the large octave Lute.

From the seventeenth century many lutenists gave up the old mode of tuning the instrument—a method which Mersenne in 1636 already described as *le vieil ton*, "which, however, is still used at concerts and in Italy, and is the basis of all tunings." The French lute-masters of the seventeenth and eighteenth centuries in particular varied the tuning so much that the accordance used was given before each piece of music.

Of later lute-tunings Curt Sachs mentions the following in his "Reallexicon": *G, c, f, a-flat, c', e'-flat; G, c, f, a, c', f'; A, d, f-sharp, a, c'-sharp, e'; A, d, f, a, d', f'*. The tuning *B-flat, d, f, b-flat, d', f'*, was also much used.

The Bass Lutes (Archlutes).

The increasing number of bass strings added to the Lute led, as early as the sixteenth century, to the invention of the so-called bass-lutes which were provided with two peg-boxes, one above the other. The ordinary head which ended the neck, served to hold the pegs belonging to the strings on the finger-board, while the second, more remote, held the pegs which tuned the bass-strings placed at the side of the finger-board and which were only used unstopped. If the two peg-boxes were separated by a short intermediate neck, the instrument was called a Theorbo (Italian, *Tiorbo*); if separated by a long extension of the neck, it was called a Chitarrone (see Figs. 344 and 345).

Fig. 344. Theorbo (Galpin).

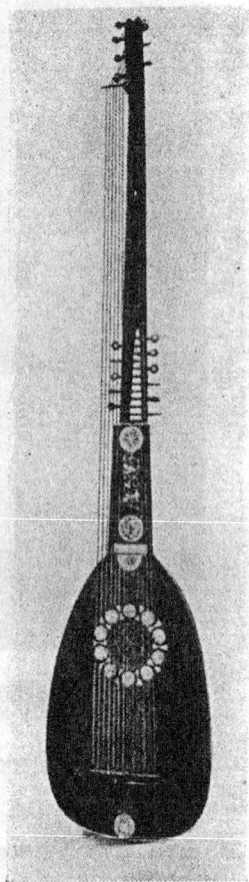

Fig. 345. Chitarrone (Galpin).

In the Theorbo all the strings were originally single, in the Chitarrone, the body of which was generally somewhat smaller, the strings which ran over the finger-board were, as in the ordinary Lute, arranged in pairs. Between the Theorbo and the Chitarrone was the Theorbo-Lute (see Fig. 346), in which the lower peg-box was bent backwards as in the Lute, while the upper one kept the same direction as the finger-board. The strings were arranged as in the Chitarrone. In

Fig. 346. Theorbo-lute. Painting by G. Terbore.

time—during the eighteenth century—the Theorbo also received double-strings on the finger-board, and the difference between it and the Theorbo-lute practically disappeared.

The Theorbo, which was invented in Padua in the sixteenth century, was the bass-lute and longest-lived, persisting until the middle of the eighteenth century. The Chitarrone, which is described as originating in Rome, was mentioned for the first time in 1524 (when the Duke of Mantua ordered the production of "alchuni Citaruni"); it disappeared round

411

about the year 1700. The Theorbo-lute is said to have been invented in 1594 by the Italian, Piccinini.

The Theorbo carried eight strings on the finger-board and eight at the side; in the Chitarrone there were six pairs and eight unstopped strings; in the Theorbo-lute seven or eight pairs and eight bass strings.

The offshoots of the Theorbo included: (1) the old Russian *Torban*, which was still very well known in Poland and the Ukraine in the eighteenth century, and continued until about 1825 as a popular Russian instrument; (2) the so-called *Angelica* (seventeenth to eighteenth century), with seventeen single strings tuned, like those of the harp, to a diatonic scale and was thus able to dispense with frets. It therefore quickly became fashionable as an instrument for amateurs, especially among ladies of the upper classes. Curt Sachs is of the opinion that the ancestor of this instrument was the strange Lute illustrated by Prætorius and which, according to his description, was "treated like a harp." The Angelica reproduced by Mahillon (see Fig. 347), on the other hand, resembles a Theorbo without frets.

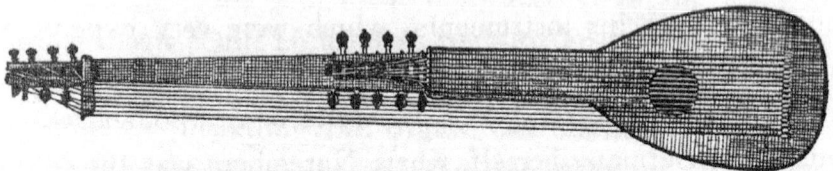

Fig. 347. Angelica (Mahillon).

In Literature. Famous Luthiers.

The reforms which gradually developed an instrument in Europe adaptable to the service of artistic music out of the Eastern lute, prove the existence of instrument-makers who studied their art and craft very thoroughly. From mere artisans these *luthiers* gradually became artists with a purpose.

It is probable that the first attempts at raising the status of the Lute were made in Italy. The talent of the Italian instrument-makers exhibited itself gloriously when they had brought the bowed instruments to their zenith. Originally the Lute and the Violin were made side by side by the same masters, a circumstance which explains the fact that the French instrument-maker is to the present day called a "luthier," i.e., lute-maker. If the names of the Italian lute-makers are now generally forgotten, it is due to the fact that their activity as makers of this popular instrument of ancient times, now dethroned, has been overshadowed by their world-renowned achievements as makers of the instrument which nowadays is the leading member of the orchestra. At any rate, it is a fact that large numbers of German lute-makers wandered into Italy in the fifteenth century in order there to learn the art. Several of them even settled in Italian towns where they established workshops. As the Amati of the Lute, the German, Lucas Mahler (1415), became famous, and is said to have altered the hitherto deep apple-shape of the Lute to the later flatter, broad-ribbed, and more sonorous, almond-shaped instrument. He lived at Bologna whence his instruments, which were very expensive, were sent all over Europe. Another well-known German emigrant was the lutenist, Max Unverdorben, who settled in Venice. In Germany herself, where Nuremberg was the centre of lute-playing, the Nuremberger, Konrad Gerle (1460), was famous among the lute-makers. His instruments also were in great demand abroad, and were known as "German" Lutes. Thus Charles the Bold ordered three Gerle Lutes through a German merchant in Nuremberg, for his "joueurs de Leut," and paid the large sum of forty-two livres, ten sols, for them. Konrad Gerle's descendants, too, the composers for the Lute, Hans Gerle (father and son) are also mentioned as famous lute-makers.

The Lute's Career in the Lands that Developed it (XIV-XVII Centuries).

Introduction. As we have seen, the Lute did not make its appearance in Europe until a rather late date, and only a relatively short epoch of its life fell within the Middle Ages. On the other hand, it was, as I have endeavoured to point out, just during this comparatively short space of time that it underwent the reforms in Europe which made it fit to serve artistic music.

The development of the Lute was naturally closely connected with the events which took place during that period in the domain of musical art. While music of the highest artistic value had from the beginning been given to the voice, the improvements which were introduced during the course of the fifteenth and sixteenth centuries at last drew these instruments also nearer to the service of the nobler music. The beginning was made by using the instruments for doubling or replacing the voice in the performance of the polyphonic vocal passages which predominated at that time. While the bowed and wind-instruments in the non-vocal reproduction of the sung polyphonic music could be used as parts of an ensemble of treble, alto, tenor and bass instruments, the Lute and the keyboard instruments (including the organ), as instruments capable of producing chords, possessed the qualifications necessary for reproducing polyphonic music, each by itself. Of these three chord-producing groups of instruments, the Lute, however, on account of the evanescent nature of its tone, was only able to a certain degree to carry on the threads making a piece of polyphony. This was so far important that at an earlier date than the other instruments it was compelled to free itself from vocal imitation in order to find new paths for itself. The first germ of independent instrumental music was to be found in the Lute music. Not until the Lute had shown the way, did the organ and the other keyboard instruments follow. The last to adopt an independent instrumental style were the bowed and the wind-instruments, which did not emancipate themselves until the invention of the Renaissance solo-song accompanied by instruments, had given them the initiative.

Fig. 348. The Lute as a domestic instrument. Photograph of a painting by Jean de Clouet. 16th cent. " Wiener Jahrbuch," 22.

If the Lute was so often described as "the Queen of Instruments," it was by no means only due to its merits in making instrumental music independent. In other respects the Lute was the leading instrument of the time. As will appear from what follows, the Grossgeige, Viola da Gamba, Guitar and Cittern, derived their tuning of Fourths and Fifths from the Lute; and from the Lute all the finger-board instruments borrowed the notation that carried the most ancient elements of their music down to the present time. Last but not least, French lute-music influenced the development of keyboard music.

The high position occupied by the Lute in the musical world of the past is tersely alluded to in an old German ballad:

> "Lautenschlagen ist eine Kunst,
> Wer es kann;
> Wer es nicht recht lernen will,
> Der lasse davon."

As will be seen, the Lute did not belong to the instruments that were easy to play. By its nature it could not be reckoned among the popular instruments, and in its completed, classic, form it belonged, as we have seen, to the realm of absolute and artistic music. In proof of this we have the very invention of their own notation by the lutenists, which enabled them to bequeath their compositions to posterity. The "natural" musician of the popular type, as a rule, hands down his music by tradition, whereby it gradually became corrupted, since every player usually altered it to suit his own taste and pleasure.

There is a great literature of Lute-music with contributions from most European countries, and the study of this literature is of the greatest interest in so far as it gives an insight into the activity of the Lute during the three centuries in which it took the lead in Euopean musical life, and when it was not only the central point in the music of the home, but also an important factor in cultural life. As the subject of this work is the history of musical instruments and not that of the art of music, there will only be room for quite a superficial valuation of Lute-music, after the necessary space has been reserved to deal with the fate of the instrument itself. A short account of the notation used for the writing of Lute-music will be found in the supplementary section.

A. THE LUTE IN GERMANY (XV-XVI C.).

In Germany the Lute is mentioned for the first time in 1404, in the list of contemporary instruments given by Eber-

hardus Cersne, of Minden, in his old German "Minneregeln."
Soon after, in 1413, the first German lute-master known to history was mentioned—Heintz Helt, of Nuremberg. The Augs-
burg master, Hans Meisinger, followed in 1447. A third
German lutenist, Johannes von Deutschland, was heard in the
royal palace at Milan in 1475. The most important fifteenth-
century German master of the lute, however, seems to have
been the blind Conrad Paumann, who was born in Nuremberg
in 1410 and died in 1473 as organist of the Frauenkirche in
Munich, where his tombstone may still be seen. As a virtuoso
on the lute, organ, fiddle, flute and trumpet, and as the inventor of the German Lute-tablature *(v. inf.)* he won so much
credit that he was celebrated in a poem by the Mastersinger,
Hans Rosenplüt:

> "Noch ist ein Meister in diesem Gedicht,
> Der hat ein Mangel an seinem Gesicht,
> Der heisst Conrat Paumann.
> Dem hat Gott solche Gnade gethan,
> *Dass er ein Meister ob allen Meistern ist.*
> Denn er trägt mit feinem List
> Die Musica mit ihrem süssen Tönen
> Sollt man um Kunst einen Meister krönen,
> So trug er wohl eine goldne Kron."

No lute compositions either by Paumann or by the other
lute-masters of the fifteenth century survive. Dating from the
sixteenth century, on the other hand, there are a number of
lute-books by such German lutenists as Hans Gerle (1552),
Hans Neusiedler (1536, in Nuremberg), Melchior Neusiedler
(1574 and 1596, Nuremberg), Sebastian Ochsenkuhn (1558,
Heidelberg), Wolf Heckel (1552 and 1562, Strassburg), Sixtus
Kärgel (1569, 1574 and 1575, Mayence), Hans Judenkünig, of
Schwäbisch Gmund (1523, Vienna), etc.

It is peculiar that the majority of these German masters
of the lute worked in the towns where the Meistersinger were
chiefly to be found. Nuremberg, Strassburg and Mayence
were the most famous centres of their art, and it cannot be
accidental that German instrumental domestic music found its

keenest cultivators in these very towns. The master-song infected the German amateur with a love of poetry and of the art of music; it was therefore quite natural that in Germany it was primarily the middle classes who took the initiative in furthering the cause of music in the home. In his lute-book Hans Gerle mentions the Nuremberg citizen, Franz Lederer, as one of the most distinguished lutenists; Hans Neusiedler is described as a master of the lute in Nuremberg, etc.

From the German lute-books we obtain the best idea of the kind of music performed on that instrument in Germany—i.e., dances, entrées (preludes) and transcriptions of polyphonic songs "which are most in use and heard with the greatest pleasure." In other words, the German lutenists adapted to their instrument all the music performed in church and in public, thus giving the lovers of the lute an opportunity of benefiting by it at home. Moreover, these lute-books were by no means content with merely giving the public a collection of pieces; in most cases they also gave elaborate instructions for tuning and playing the lute as well as instructions in the art of writing the tablature, in fingering, and in the placing of the frets, etc. The text is generally homely and intimate. The reader is always addressed with "thee" and "thou" (the familiar *Du*), and on every occasion he is admonished to listen carefully to what is said. The lute-books were also often used to perpetuate moral advice, and even questions of doctrine:

> " Hilff Gott und verlass mich nicht,
> Schön wär' ich gern, das bin ich nicht.
> Krum bin ich wohl, das hilft mich nicht.
> Jedoch tröste ich mich, dass auch das Geld,
> Wenn wir sterben bleibt in der Welt."

This verse, as well as many others in the same strain, are to be found in the copy of Hans Neusiedler's lute-book (1536) in the Royal Library of Copenhagen. In another verse, from a manuscript lute-book in the National Library at Berlin, the author gives his readers a piece of sound advice:

" Willstu schlahen die Lauten behend,
Schneid ab die Nägel, wasch die Hendt,
Dazu langsam zu schla'n übe dich,
Befleiss dich zu schla'n deutlic!..
Greif der Lauten woll ins Maul,
Sie soll nicht klingen träge noch faul.
Auch mustu den Tactum observieren,
Willstu schönen Mägdlein hofiren."

It is worthy of notice that none of these early German lute-masters made any pretence at professionalism. In the prefaces to their works, most of them declared with all modesty that they did not claim a place beside the recognised masters of the art of music, but that only love of art made them present their fellow-citizens with their collections of the most popular pieces current at the time. Nevertheless these German lutenists merit an honourable place in the history of music, for they were largely responsible for the first steps that were taken to give instrumental music greater freedom. In setting the common German dances and folk-songs, they broke with tradition for the first time by consistently placing the melody in the upper part, and combining the remaining parts into an accompaniment of chord sequences. At the same time they made much use of the Ionian mode (our major mode), which had hitherto been held in contempt by the writers of art music. Another step towards modernism was their habit of ending their dances on the tonic chord; and even when the first of the two repeated parts of a stereotyped dance-form ended on a modulation, the second section sought the original key and ended on the common chord.

B. IN ITALY (XIV-XVII C.).

While in Germany the lute found its main public among the middle classes, it was from the beginning, in Italy, the chosen instrument of the aristocracy and the artists. It was mentioned for the first time in Italian literature in the first part of Dante's "Divina Commedia," where the poet used it allegorically for his description of the deformed counterfeiter Adam of Brescia. Petrarch himself played the lute, and at his death in 1374 he left his instrument to his friend, Tomaso Bombasius, of Ferrara.

While the German lutenists of the sixteenth century, in spite of the merit due to them, went no farther than their ability allowed in setting the prevailing dances and songs for their instrument, the Italians at a comparatively early stage devoted the lute to the service of the imagination, and thus for the first time prepared the way for an artistic treatment of the instrument.

At the outset the lute was pre-eminently the vehicle for accompanying song. The so-called *Cantori a libri*, i.e., the trained vocalists who sang from book, were in the fifteenth century already rivalled by *i Cantori di liuto*, who sang solo to an improvised lute-accompaniment. What these accompaniments were, we do not know; but the high praise which the musical authorities of the time lavished on these improvisations, proves that they cannot have been anything but excellent. It was said of one of them, the celebrated artist, Leonardo da Vinci, that he was always greatly admired when he improvised a song and accompanied it on his lute.

A just valuation of the Italian lute-music was not possible until the invention of the Italian lute-tablature at length enabled players to reduce their compositions to writing. Simultaneously with the publication of the first printed editions of the classical vocal works from the Venetian music-printing press of Petrucci, the first printed Italian lute-books also appeared. Already in 1507 Francesco Spinaccino of Venice published two lute-books which were quickly followed by many others produced by the Venetians, Zuan Maria and Domenico Bianchini—called "il Veneziano"—by the Paduans Cesare Barbetta and Antonio Rotta, by the Milanese Pietro Paolo Borono and the famous Francesco da Milano, called "il divino," who was also an excellent organist. The most famous of them all, however, was Marco da Aquila, whose works crossed the Alps and reached as far afield as Nuremberg, where Hans Gerle, in his lute-book of 1532, gave him the proud translated name, "Max von Adler."

In addition to the dances destined for entertainment, these Italians in their lute fantasias cultivated a style which, by its improvisational character naturally recalled the song accompaniment of the "Cantori di liuto" mentioned earlier. Between passages of sonorous chords, in which the silvery ringing of the higher strings and the resonant tone of the bass were brought into effective contrast, there were in these fantasias interludes, sometimes consisting of rapid running passages, sometimes taking the form of an imitation of two or three of the voices in the counterpoint. In short, the player's imagination was allowed so much freedom that these compositions fully justified the modern interpretation of the name they were given. The germs of an independent instrumental style are here clearly discernible. Some of the fantasias take the form of "descriptive" music; in a little musical joke, "Gallus e Gallina," Vincenzo Bernio, for example, made a cock and a hen sing duets with each other; but martial themes were most popular. Side by side with these real fantasias, there were others which in a lesser degree correspond to the modern ideas attached to the name, for they exhibit rather the stricter polyphonic character of the "Ricercar" and therefore must be placed among the forerunners of the instrumental fugue.

C. IN SPAIN (XVI AND XVII CENTURIES).

Although the Spanish monuments prove that the lute was already used in the thirteenth century, and although it is mentioned in 1350 in a poem by Juan Ruiz, Archbishop of Hita, as one of the instruments used by contemporary jongleurs, it will be necessary to go as far as the sixteenth century before we find the first positive proofs of the artistic treatment of the lute in the country which, together with Italy, must have been the first to receive it from the Near East. The proofs are found in a large collection of Spanish lute compositions discovered recently, the musical value of which shows without a shadow of doubt that the lute in Spain, just as in Italy, must by the sixteenth century have already had behind it a long life as an artistic instrument.

As composers of this lute music (published in Paris by Count Morphy) we make the acquaintance of Louis Milan, Luis de Narvaez, Alonso de Mudarra, Anriques de Voldemabano, Diego Pisador, Miguel de Fuenllano, Luis Venzos de Hirestrosa, Esteban Daza, Hernando de Cabezon, who all lived in the sixteenth century. In the seventeenth century we meet Nicolas Doisi de Velasco, Lucas Ruiz de Ribayas and Gaspar Sanz. The masters belonging to an earlier period, and mentioned in Spanish literature from the sixteenth century, are Guzman, Martin de Jaen and his son Hernando Lopez, besides Baltasar Tellez.

The musical forms favoured by these musicians were almost identical with those cultivated at the same time in Italy, i.e., dances, that is to say, pavanes (sometimes with variations), galliards and fantasias. Sometimes we also find transcriptions of vocal works by foreign masters, among which are Josquin's "Mille Regrets," and a song by Adriano (Willaert ?), " Petite camusete." The style which interests us most at the moment from the historical point of view, however, is the song accompanied by the lute, i.e., Spanish and Portuguese *villanelle* and *canciones*, Italian *sonnets*, but principally the so-called *romances veios*, or mediaeval epic poems with their traditional melodies, as they were still sung in the sixteenth century together with their lute accompaniments.

While in the *villanelle* the lute only supported the sung melody note for note in arpeggiated chords, it was allowed sufficient liberty in the romances to introduce and conclude each line with short preludes and interludes, and to end the completed verse with a longer *ritornello*. About fifty years earlier Vincenzo Galilei, while attempting to revive the ancient Greek solo song accompanied by instruments, "invented" monody; but we already find examples of this style of composition in Spain.

The resemblance between the repertoire of the Spanish and the Italian lutenists naturally suggests the idea that the Italian *cantori di liuto* may also have used a monody provided with instrumental preludes, interludes and postludes. Galilei's so-called "invention" of monody was perhaps only the adaptation of the lutenist's fashion to serve Renaissance ideas. It is expressly stated that Galilei (like the famous *cantore di liuto*, Leonardo da Vinci) composed the melodies of the poems he sang and improvised an accompaniment on a stringed instrument, and that the musician Caccini, as an ardent partisan of the Renaissance movement, took up the idea and by composing a whole collection of monodies *(Le Nuove Musiche)* made this form of composition respected as artistic music; but he no longer improvised the accompaniment, and like the Spanish lutenists he preferred to write it down note for note.

D. IN FRANCE (XIV-XVII CENTURIES).

In France again the lute appeared at an early date as a distinguished instrument. On the monuments of the Middle Ages it found an honoured place in the celestial orchestras. It was played by kings, troubadours and ladies, but never by the popular minstrels. In the French mediaeval reproductions of the *danse macabre*, death makes use of it only when summoning noblemen, princes and nuns; never when fetching peasants or artisans.

The first French lutenist known to us by name was Henri de Ganière, "jouer de vièle et de lut," whom Louis of

Orleans rewarded in 1391. And since it was customary in the fifteenth century for the reigning princes of France and the neighbouring countries to entertain a larger or smaller orchestra of expert musicians, we find lutenists among them.

The first of the celebrated lutenists at the French court were Antoine Her, Pierre Yvert and François de Bugats. Among the members of the band of Francis I we find two famous foreigners: Pierre Paul Borono of Milan and Albert de Ripe (from Milan or Mantua), the latter serving the French king for twenty-five years and becoming so celebrated on account of his excellent performance that at his death poets vied with each other in writing French and Latin sonnets in his honour.

The first French lute book to be published appeared in Paris in 1529 from the press of Pierre Attaignant. In the fifties that of Adrien le Roy—"Instruction pour le Lut"—followed, a work now only known by an English edition published in London in 1574. Among the other important French lute works should be mentioned Besardus's "Thesaurus Harmonicus," which, though published in Cologne in 1603, contained lute music chiefly by French composers, and that of Antoine Francisque, the "Trésor d'Orphée," published in Paris in 1600.

With the seventeenth century began the period during which the lute was the fashionable instrument of the Parisian *salons*, when it was a necessary sign of good breeding to play the lute, when excellent performance on the instrument was the surest passport to success in the fashionable world. The mother of Louis XIV, Anne of Austria, having decided to take lute lessons late in life with the famous master Gautier, set an example which sent all the members of the court, headed by the redoubtable Cardinal Richelieu, to take up the instrument in the hope of thus ingratiating themselves with the queen. Instead of placing the lute in the heavenly choirs, the painters now introduced it into their "interiors" where it figured either in scenes of " music lessons " or of private music-making.

The seventeenth century on the whole, contained the palmy days of the lute. During this period the élite of the French lute composers lived, and during it were created the most important works in the voluminous French lute literature. Numerous collections came from the press every year, were received with enthusiasm by the distinguished amateurs, and found a ready sale. Many pieces of manuscript music also circulated from hand to hand.

Among the composers who provided lute-playing Paris with the most valuable part of its repertoire during this period, may be mentioned the great master of the lute, Saint Luc (perhaps the most distinguished of them all), and the two most celebrated members of the lutenist family of Gautier, Ennemond Gautier ("Le vieux Gautier") and Denis Gautier ("Le jeune Gautier"). The two Gautiers founded between them in Paris the famous Paris lute school, from which emerged in the course of time many famous performers and composers such as Mouton, Gallot, Du Bout, Du Faux and many others. Many of the lute compositions by these masters were of high musical worth, for they were the results of a thorough study of the natural capabilities of the lute, and their excellence was ensured by their suitability to the instrument for which they were intended. Thus, during this period, there is no question of transcriptions of contemporary vocal works, but of independent instrumental works conceived by artistic inspiration and a complete technical knowledge of the instrument.

A style which was taken up with enthusiasm by the French lutenists was that of the so-called *tombeaux*, compositions in memory of some honoured one departed. Every famous man and woman in seventeenth century France was honoured by the dedication of such a musical epitaph. Both the elder and the younger Gautier left several compositions of this kind. Gautier *père* was especially famous for a *tombeau* in memory of the lutenist Mezangeau, the fame of which even reached as far north as Denmark, where it appeared arranged for the keyboard in a manuscript book of keyboard music dating from the time of Christian IV ("Old Royal Coll.," No. 376, fol.).

Besides these occasional compositions, dances and fantasias, some of them "programme" music, occupied the most important place in the lute-books.

The numerous pupils of Gautier's school carried the art of the French lutenists all over Europe; but in France itself the lute began to go out of fashion towards the end of the seventeenth century. The decline is clearly noticed shortly after the death of Gautier *fils*. The amateurs now suddenly became bored with the difficulties connected with the instrument, and no longer took the trouble to learn the intricate lute notation. In the place of the lute, the *vielle* (i.e., the lyre, see Book II) now became popular, and later on the *lyre-guitar*. The expensive lutes were discarded or transformed into vielles or lyre-guitars. Mr. Brenet related the characteristic story of a young French lady who hesitated to sacrifice her costly lute, and who was upbraided by her teacher because she refused to follow the newer fashion. "The vielle," said he, "is now the grave of the lute."

E. IN THE REMAINING COUNTRIES OF EUROPE.

The fate of the lute in the other European countries can only be followed in the broadest outlines.

In England the instrument cannot be traced farther back than to Henry VIII who, together with his daughters, were said to have been ardent lutenists, and the Italian prince, Alfonso d'Este, presented the bluff Tudor with an expensive lute. In English literature, especially in Shakespeare, the lute is often mentioned, both generally (e.g., in "Julius Caesar" and "Henry VIII") and by direct reference (e.g., in "The Taming of the Shrew").

Among the famous English lutenists must be mentioned John Dowland, who for eight years served the Danish court (*v. inf.*), his son Robert Dowland (editor of the "Varietie of Lute-Lessons," to which his father prefixed some "Observations belonging to Lute-playing"), Robert Johnson and Dr. John Wilson. In Robert Dowland's "Varietie of Lute. Lessons" is to be found a galliard "commonly known by the name of the most high and mightie Christianus the fourth King of Denmarke, his Galliard." This was published, translated into Danish, by the present author in the "Aarbog for Musik," 1923.

The most important English work on lute playing was Thomas Mace's "Musick's Monument," published in 1676, when the lute was already going out of fashion in England. Mace therefore makes the lute lament, in a melancholy poem, that the public had now lost all interest in it and its music. (Mace blamed the "new violins" for the decline, not only of the lute, but of the viols also.—ED.)

The English lute music of the seventeenth century seems to have had a strong affinity with that of France. While a young man, Dowland went to France in order to study the instrument there, and the Frenchman, Jacques Gautier, generally known as Gautier d'Angleterre, served as lutenist for thirty years (from 1617 to 1647) at the English court. (Our authoress was apparently ignorant of several literary references to the lute in England when she said that the instrument could not be traced farther back than Henry VIII. My "Dictionary of Old English Music," s.v. Lute, gives a reference from the beginning of the fourteenth century, another from 1361-2; it is mentioned in Piers Plowman and by Chaucer and Gower. The reader is referred to this article for fuller information of an historical nature on the lute in England.—ED.)

Regarding the lute in Denmark, the earliest historical records date from the time of Christian IV, when the keyboard instruments had already begun to assert themselves in domestic use at the expense of the lute. At that time it was, however, by no means discarded. On the contrary, it still figured regularly in all festive music gatherings and was an instrument that it was considered necessary for the children of distinguished people to learn. In the court accounts of the seventeenth century there are several entries relating to purchasers of lutes and lute strings for the "little boys and girls" for whose lessons the king paid. It is well known that Christian IV himself, like the Swedish King Gustavus Vasa, played the lute.

Christian IV also invited several foreign lutenists to Copenhagen, among whom, as we have already seen, was the Englishman, John Dowland, and another countryman of his, Thomas Cutting. Among the Danish musicians, too, there were many instrumentalists who proved themselves to be clever exponents of the lutenist's art. Hans Nielsen, who was Danish court musician, and from 1623-4 vice-conductor of the court orchestra, studied lute playing at the king's expense with the prominent Belgian lutenist, Gregorio Howett, and for three years served as performer on that instrument at the Danish court.

The lute persisted longest in Germany where it was played for the greater part of the eighteenth century, although, it is true, in keen competition with the keyboard instruments. During its last days in Germany it was, however, chiefly used as a concert instrument, and its popularity as a domestic instrument had already waned. Nevertheless, both Bach and Haydn still added valuable contributions to the already great literature devoted to the lute. The last German lutenist and composer for the instrument was Scheidler of Vienna. His lute variations on a theme by Mozart formed the swan song of the lute in Germany.

2. INSTRUMENTS RELATED TO THE LUTE.

A. MANDORA OR MANDOLA.

The lute was preceded in Europe by the mediaeval mandora or mandola which, in its earliest known form, had the appearance of a sister instrument to the bowed European rebec developed from the Arabian rebab and the Byzantine lyra; but in the course of its further development it gradually acquired so many features in common with the lute, that the older

Fig. 349. Spanish Mandora. 13th cent. (Riano).

Fig. 350. Gamba from Borneo (Curt Sachs).

historians (Praetorius, Mersenne and others) described it as "a small lute." We must be careful not to confuse the mediaeval mandora with the eighteenth century instrument of the same name and which was in reality a modern mandoline of large size.

The principal characterising features of this mandora were its sickle-shaped peg-box crowned with an elegantly carved animal's head, the comparatively few strings it carried, and its having been played with a plectrum held by the right hand (see Fig. 349).

Basing his theories on this sickle-shaped peg-box, Curt Sachs thinks he is able to trace the instrument back to a kind of rebab still used in Borneo and Zanzibar, and which, contrary to the usual custom, is provided with a similarly curved peg-box with lateral pegs and an animal's head (see Fig. 350). In Borneo this instrument is called *gambus*, in Zanzibar *gabbus*, names which Sachs believes he can derive from the Arabic name *qobus*, which was also that of a lute-like instrument still in use in Turkey, Hungary, Russia, Roumania and several other places. Sachs supposes that this gambus or qobus came to Borneo with the Arabian culture that touched southern Asia, including the Malayan islands, and began as early as the seventh century, i.e., nearly a hundred years before the Arabs first set foot in Spain. It must therefore be assumed that both kinds of rebab were brought to Spain by the Moors at an early date. But while the ordinary rebab quickly allied itself with the bow, the other form remained a plectrum instrument. During their further development the two types of rebab evidently so far followed the same path that they gradually fell under the influence of the lyra and were changed into the European composite type known as the rebec.

Both in Fig. 349 and Fig. 351 the mandóra exhibits the form which characterises the bowed rebec. In Fig. 349 we even recognise the C-shaped sound-holes inherited from the lyra. In Fig. 351 on the other hand, we find the central rose, which naturally belonged to the rebab and the lute, and was far better adapted to a plucked instrument than were the C-holes.

When in the fourteenth century the lute came to Spain, the mandora received a rival against which it could hardly hope to hold its own. For with its hitherto primitive construc‧ tion the mandora could only satisfy very modest acoustical demands. The Arabian rebab was, like most primitive instruments of the fiddle type, simply made by hollowing a solid block of wood. In order to assert its position beside the sonorous lute, the mandora was therefore obliged to take its rival as its model. In the fifteenth century already a striking alteration was to be observed in the mandora, which decidedly became an instrument of the lute type. The mandora of that time thus borrowed from the lute the vaulted back made up of

Fig. 351. Spanish Mandora. 14th cent. (Riano).

ribs, the frets on the neck and the single beautifully carved circular rose. As reminiscences of the past, only the pear-shaped outline of the body, the four or five pairs of strings, and the sickle-shaped, but now far more elegant peg-box, remained.

The lute-like four stringed mandora was tuned to c, g, c, g', but its highest string was sometimes tuned down to f' or e'. Praetorius also gave two five-string tunings: c, g, c', g', c'', and c, f, c', f', c''. The strings were always made of gut.

In sixteenth century Germany the mandora was called the quinterne, a corruption of the French guiterne (guitar), a name that was transferred in the second half of the sixteenth and the beginning of the seventeenth century to the guitar with four or

five pairs of strings *(v. sup.)*. In the seventeenth century the
Germans preferred to call the mandora, mandürichen, mandör-
ichen, or pandurina. None of these meant a mandora of small
size, but referred to the size of the mandora when compared
with the large bass lute of the time, i.e., the theorbo and the
chitarrone *(v. sup.)*.

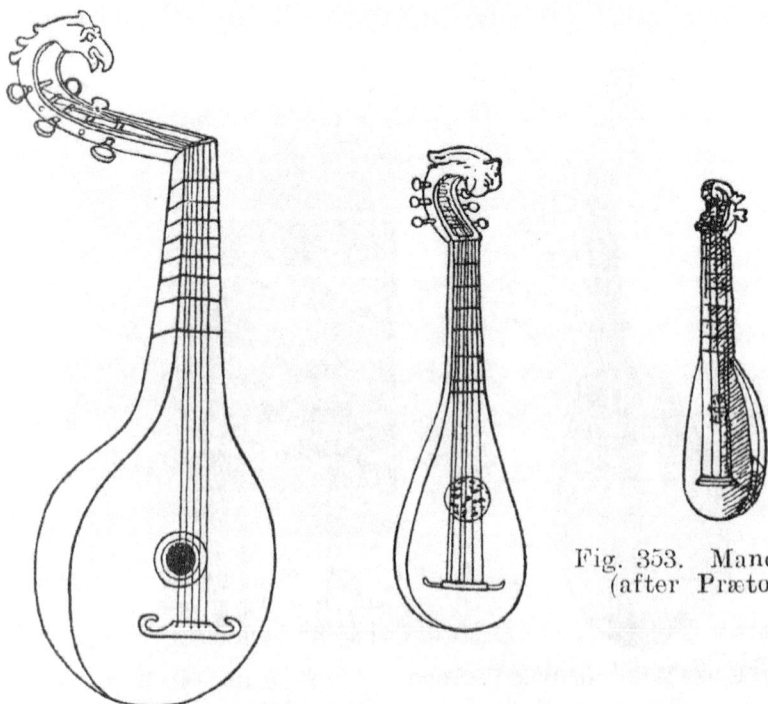

Fig. 353. Mandürichen
(after Prætorius).

Fig. 352. Mandora types. 15th cent. (Curt
Sachs).

In the seventeenth century the so-called Milanese mandoline
developed out of the mandora, which, unlike the ordinary
(Neapolitan) mandoline, had a comparatively shallow back, a
flat sound-board, a guitar tail-piece, a violin peg-box with
lateral pegs, six double (and from the eighteenth century,
single) strings of gut, and was plucked with the fingers.

B.   THE MANDOLINE.

The history of the Mandoline is rather complicated, for
there were in reality two types, which in all probability had
nothing whatever to do with each other. First, there was the

Milanese Mandoline which, as mentioned above, was descended from the lute-like mediæval Mandora or Mandola, just described, and secondly, the modern so-called Neapolitan Mandoline, which probably came from the East.

The modern (Neapolitan) Mandoline has the following distinguishing characteristics: a strikingly deep back, a sound-board provided with an oval rose and sloping evenly from the

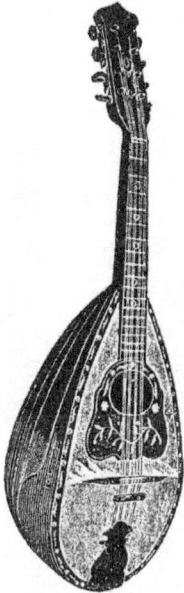

Fig. 354. Neapolitan Mandoline.

Fig. 355. Mandoline. Painting by Angelico, Fragment of Mary's Coronation (London). 15th cent.

bridge towards the tail-piece, a plate of hard wood inserted into the belly above the bridge and intended to protect the sound-board from being scratched by the plectrum, fixed metal frets across the finger-board, a slightly bent peg-board with pegs inserted from the back, and four double-strings made of steel and tuned like those of the violin. The strings cross a low bridge to a violin tail-piece or to a number of studs fixed in the base of the body, just beyond the sound-board. A short egg-shaped plectrum of tortoiseshell, horn, whalebone, or celluloid is used to produce a continuous *tremolo* from the short metal strings by means of a rapid movement of the hand backwards and forwards. With the best of the Italian virtuosi this *tremolo* almost resembles a violin vibrato.

433

This type of Mandoline may be traced back as far as Fra Angelico's famous painting, "Mary's Coronation," of the fifteenth century (see Fig. 355). Here already we find the method of fastening the strings, the four double strings, the backward bent peg-board with the pegs inserted from the back, the wooden plate and the plectrum of the modern Neapolitan Mandoline. Differing, however, from its modern descendant, this ancient example still has a flat sound-board and one large and one small sound-hole. Curt Sachs sees in this Mandoline an instrument invented by the Arabs in South Italy, as in all the Persian miniatures we may see instruments of the same construction.

From the moment that Fra Angelico painted this Oriental Mandoline, it disappeared totally from the pictures, not to emerge again until the middle of the seventeenth century, when it reappeared in the classic form in which it became a favourite Italian national instrument in the eighteenth century. In the history of the modern Mandoline there is thus a very large gap that still requires filling.

The Florentine, Genoese, Paduan, Roman, Sienese, and Sicilian Mandolines are all offshoots of the Neapolitan Mandoline, and cannot therefore be taken into consideration here, since they are all comparatively modern instruments.

C. THE NEAPOLITAN COLASCIONE.

The Neapolitan Colascione (in smaller form, *Colasciontino*) or *Coloscione* (French, *Colachon*; Germanised into *Galichon* and *Chalcedon*) was an instrument of the lute-type especially prevalent in southern Italy. Its comparatively small body was connected to an unusually long and slender neck ending in a peg-holder bent abruptly backward. The pegs were inserted from both sides. In its oldest known form it had but two or three strings fastened to a guitar tail-piece, and according to Mersenne (1636) it was tuned to: c', g', and to c', c'', g'' respectively, "but it might also be tuned in other ways." Mahillon gives a tuning in fourths: e', a', d'' (sounding two octaves lower).

The finger-board was provided with sixteen to twenty-four chromatically spaced frets which, as in the lute, consisted of lengths of gut wound twice round the neck. In a few examples the sound-board was made partly of parchment in the oriental manner, partly of wood; but generally, as the lute, made entirely of wood. The instrument was played with a plectrum. The Colascione was evidently derived from the long-necked *Pandouras* which may already in ancient times be found in Egyptian, Assyrian, Persian and Greek sculptures (see Figs. 154-172). It still exists in the *Tanburs* so widely distributed in the East. Differing from the south Italian Colascione, these instruments do not show the familiar guitar tail-piece, and the strings are fastened to studs beyond the sound-board, in the base of the body. The Colascione certainly received its backward bent head and its guitar tail-piece in Italy, where it may be traced back to about 1564. The two features just mentioned were probably derived from the lute, and in the seventeenth century the Colascione came even nearer to the lute by increasing the number of its strings from three to five or six, and by taking up the tuning of fourths and thirds used on the lute.

As the principal ground-bass instrument in chamber-music, the Colascione was mentioned as late as 1714 by Mattheson. When Bonanni *(Gabinetto armoniche)* illustrated and described it in 1722, he stated that it was still often heard in the kingdom of Naples and in Turkey, where under the name of *Dambura* it was especially played by women. The *Colascione Turchesco* illustrated by him had five single strings (which could be reduced *ad libitum* to two), but it was in other respects constructed like the Italian model of the instrument (see Fig. 357).

The Colascione was mentioned for the last time when the Brescian brothers Colla gave concerts in various towns of Europe in the second half of the eighteenth century, in order to popularise "two entirely new instruments," i.e., the Colas

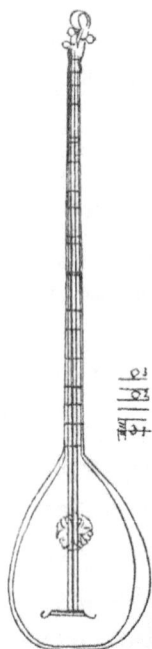

Fig. 356. Neapolitan Colascione (Mersenne).

Fig. 357. Turkish Colascione (Bonanni).

cione and the Colasciontino. In November, 1763, and in April, 1771, they performed at the Royal Theatre in Copenhagen (Overskou). By that time the instrument must have so far fallen into disuse that its previous existence had been forgotten.

B. WITH FLAT BACK AND RIBS.

I. THE GUITAR.

(The Characteristics of the two Classic Guitar-types: Chitarra
Battente and the ordinary Guitar.)

In the history of musical instruments a distinction is
drawn between two guitar-types: the Chitarra Battente, now
extinct, plucked with a plectrum (see Fig. 358) and the ordinary modern Guitar, twanged with the fingers (see Fig. 359).

In the Chitarra Battente the body, as will be seen in the
illustration, has a vaulted back with deep perpendicular ribs,
while the sound-board slopes down gently from the bridge
towards the rather lengthy neck. The strings, made of steel,
were arranged in groups of two or three tuned in unison, and
were fastened to pins inserted in the bottom rib at the lower
end of the body. The Chitarra Battente, like the violin, used
a bridge.

In the ordinary modern Guitar the sound-box is composed
of a flat back and a level table connected by means of comparatively shallow ribs. The gut strings are single and are
fastened to a fillet glued to the sound-board, which serves
simultaneously as bridge and tail-piece.

Both types have these features in common: (1) the gently
rounded sides of the body, (2) the metal frets on the finger-
board, (3) the large central round and, as a rule, open, sound-
hole, and (4) the slightly bent peg-board with the pegs inserted from the back. According to Curt Sachs, both types

437

were evolved from the Guitar-Fiddle known all over Europe from the twelfth to the fifteenth century *(v. sup.)*, and came into existence through the attempts of the South European nations to adapt it for the plucked method of playing which they preferred. This hypothesis is supported by the fact that the guitar-fiddle and the guitar in the pictures really resembled each other for a time so much that the observer could only decide by the manner of playing whether a given example was a bowed fiddle or a guitar. The fact, however, that the

Fig. 358. Chitarra Battente. Music Hist. Museum, Copenhagen.

Fig. 359. Modern Guitar.

guitar-fiddle of the ancient pictures was already fully developed in the twelfth century, while the guitar in its classic modern form and construction cannot be found before the fifteenth century in European pictures, proves that the adoption of the guitar-fiddle as the model for the guitar cannot have taken place until a rather late date, i.e., after various other types had been tried and discarded.

Precursors. a. The Primitive Guitar-type played with a Plectrum, in German Manuscripts from the Tenth Century Onward.

As the first primitive guitar I am inclined to select the instrument plucked with a plectrum and illustrated in a psalter preserved in the Royal Library at Stuttgart, dating from the tenth century (see Figs. 360 and 361). This instrument has the appearance of a large crudely made fiddle, produced by hollowing a wooden plank so that the sound-box and the comparatively broad and short neck form one piece. From a broad and in most cases triple tail-pin (see Fig. 361) which is fastened to the lower edge of the body, we see five strings that pass to the diamond-shaped peg-board at the end of the neck,

Figs. 360 and 361. Guitar Forerunners in a tenth-century Psalter (Stuttgart). After Heffner Alteneck.

where they are wound round the pegs inserted perpendicularly from the back. There is no bridge. When played, the instrument rested either horizontally across the chest of the player, or was supported in an erect position against the knee, so that the peg-board was raised well above the performer's head.

b. Square Guitar-types with Incurved Sides from Spanish, German and English Sources (XII-XIV Centuries).

Apparently closely related to the instrument last mentioned, were those reproduced in Figs. 362 and 363, which are seen so often in mediaeval pictures of the twelfth to fourteenth centuries that we are forced to the conclusion that they must have been widely distributed.

In common with the Stuttgart instrument these had the elongated form and the tail-piece divided into three lobes, almost always in the shape of a spear-head or a fleur-de-lis. What characterises this type is that the two long sides of the sound-box of the instrument, which is always played in a horizontal position, are slightly incurved so that it rests snugly against the body of the player and can thus be held firmly.

In its simplest form the type is seen in a Spanish sculpture (Fig. 362), in two statues in Cologne Cathedral, and a statue in Strassburg Cathedral. On another statue in the same place the corners of the sound-box are formed into round projections at one end, and into square ones at the other (see Fig. 364). As to the construction of the tuning mechanism, the sculptures give no particulars, because in most cases it is broken off. In order to clear up this point it will be necessary to examine the French and English manuscripts in which the instrument may be seen in an undamaged state. In the French picture seen in Fig. 365, the neck ends bluntly and the strings emerge from three pins which undoubtedly represent the shafts of three pegs inserted from the back. In the English picture, Fig. 366, the neck on the other hand ends in a large bent mandora pegholder crowned by a grotesque animal's head. Below the strings, on both pictures, may be seen the tripartite tail-pin, a bridge and a central circular rose.

It was evidently this type of guitar that formed the basis of the strange four-stringed instrument found in an English manuscript in the British Museum (see Fig. 367) and of which an original—belonging according to tradition to the Earl of

Fig. 362. Primitive Guitar on a Spanish sculpture in the Palacio del Arzobispo, S. Iago, Galicia. Photograph by Vernaccio, Madrid.

Fig. 363. Same instrument on a statue in Cologne Cathedral. Photograph by Deutsche Bilderstelle, Berlin.

Fig. 364. Modified model of the same instrument on a statue in Strassburg Cathedral. Photograph by Deutsche Bilderstelle, Berlin.

Fig. 365. Primitive Guitar accompanying the dance. From a French MS. After Violet le Duc.

Leicester, the favourite of Queen Elizabeth—is still kept at
Warwick Castle. Although the shape of the instrument is here
so far modified that the base of the body is rounded, and the
neck provided with a finger-board and frets, the main
peculiarities of the type have remained, i.e., the fleur-de-lis,
three-lobed, tail-pin, and the neck ending in a carved animal's

Fig. 366. Guitar-type in an
Oxford MS. (All Souls' Coll.).
Beginning of the 14th cent.
(Galpin).

Fig. 367. Guitar. Beginning of the
14th cent. MS. in the British Museum
(Galpin).

head, which in this case is continued in an animal's body that
occupies so much of the neck that only a small round opening
is left for the thumb, while the fingers press the strings on to
the frets. The instrument maker's taste in decoration is also
exhibited in other details of the instrument. The fleur-de-lis
of the tail-pin inspired him to decorate the corners at the

opposite end of the body, and the plectrum, with ornamentation to match.

Unusual Guitar-types in the Spanish Pictures (XIII Century).

The rounding of the lower end of the body, as in the guitar last mentioned, and the finger-board provided with frets, were already present in the thirteenth century and used in two Spanish guitars reproduced in the " Cantingas de S. Maria," which so far supplement one another that the details which have been omitted by the artist in one instrument, may be found in the other (see Fig. 368 and the instrument on the left in Fig. 369). Thus the existence of a round tail-pin of normal

Fig. 368. Spanish Guitar-type of the 13th cent. (*Guitarra Latina;* Riaño).

Fig. 369. Spanish Guitar-types of the 13th cent. (Riano).

dimensions, a bridge, a round rose in the centre of the sound-board, frets on the neck or on a finger-board continued from the neck across the sound-board, and the neck ending in a small beautifully carved animal's head, may all be proved. When played, the instrument rested, as was generally the case, before the breast of the performer, and was plucked with a plectrum. The position of the instrument in Fig. 368 is due to the fact that it is not being played, but tuned (note the left hand on the pegs).

The adoption of the Normal Guitar-Fiddle as a Plucked Instrument (XIV Century).

Not until the fourteenth century do the pictures show us a plucked finger-board instrument in the form of the guitar-fiddle, which is at once rounded and incurved.

The first attempts at using the bowed guitar-fiddle as a plucked instrument were perhaps followed by the guitar types reproduced in Fig. 370, from a fourteenth century manuscript in the British Museum.

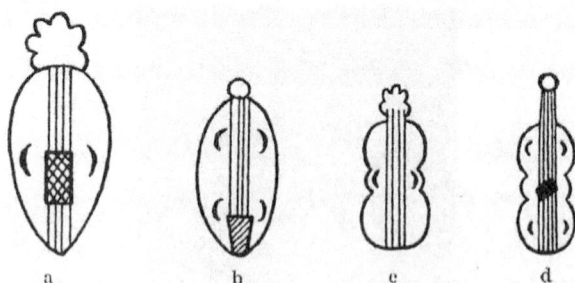

Fig. 370. Unusual Guitar-types of the beginning of the 14th century. Drawn from Add. 17333, Brit. Museum.

a.	b.	c.	d.
4 Strings.	4 Strings.	4 Strings.	5 Strings.
2 C-holes.	4 C-holes.	2 C-holes.	4 C-holes.

Here the body sometimes takes the form of an oval fiddle, sometimes that of a figure-of-eight fiddle; only in a single case (*d*) has it a neck. For fastening the four or five strings, type *b* probably used a tail-pin attached to a violin tail-piece, while *a*, *c* and *d* no doubt had the strings stretched over the sound-board and fastened to pins in the lower part of the back, below the table. It is not possible to make out the meaning of the square device placed on *a*, through which, or under which, the strings pass. At first glance it appears to be a violin tail-piece, but this idea has to be abandoned because the strings are continued on both sides of the square. Where the instrument is shown in use in the manuscript, it rests in a horizontal position on the lap of the player. The right hand is on the middle of the sound-board near the strings, the left is in the air above the strings ready to strike and produce a chord. Only in one case (b) the strings are stopped, but contrary to rule this is effected by the right hand. On closer examination this guitar-type appears to be a mysterious phenomenon which, in the history of the guitar, falls outside of the line of development and which, owing to its isolated position in the pictorial records, cannot have played a prominent part in the Middle Ages. With far greater certainty it is possible to follow the development of the modern guitar when we attempt to trace its evolution out of the guitar-fiddle.

Fig. 371. Transitional form between the Guitar-Fiddle and the Guitar. Painting by N. Pisani. Early 16th century.

The transition from the guitar-fiddle to the modern guitar first appears in the pictures in some intermediate forms, which in respect of the shape of the body, the stringing, and the form of the sound-holes, become modified and adapted for the new method of playing them which then became the guide to further development. Thus it is significant to see in a picture by Nicolo Pisani (early in the sixteenth century) an instrument which in spite of its viol-like curves, its viol-like C holes, and its violin scroll, is plucked by the fingers (see Fig. 371); and *per contra*, to meet on a French sculpture an instrument

445

provided with a beautifully cut rose as in the lute, a violin tail-piece and bridge, and played with the bow.

The Completion of the Chitarra Battente and the Modern Guitar (XV Century).

It cannot be determined exactly when the development of the guitar began and when it was definitely completed. It is in the first place difficult to follow the individual development of each of the two classic guitar-types which formed the final results of these two lines of development. The first was certainly the chitarra battente with its vaulted back, and which just as certainly emerged from the older fiddle made in one piece, its original form being possibly found in the figure-of-eight fiddle with a vaulted back.

The wide distribution of the lute in the fourteenth and fifteenth centuries which gradually made it an all-engrossing centre of interest to the instrument makers, played a definite part in the gradual reduction of the guitar-fiddle into a plucked instrument. Suggested by the lute, the oldest primitive guitar-types (see e.g. Figs. 365-367) were given large central roses instead of C-holes. As Figs. 367 to 369 teach us, the guitar at an early date took from the lute the idea of providing the neck with frets. Later the guitar also borrowed the backward turned peg-holder, the arrangement of the strings into unison ranks of two or three strings each, and their tuning in fourths and thirds. The last step towards the completion of the chitarra battente was made when it abandoned its gut strings and adopted the characteristic steel strings which, by the richness of the upper partials, to a certain degree compensated for the tone quality produced when the strings were vibrated by the bow. The resonant, plectrum-played, chitarra battente was then quickly adopted by the higher artistic circles and, as far as is known, it was used in Spain under the name of *vihuela* until the middle of the eighteenth century as a distinguished sister-instrument to the younger flat-backed guitar. It is now only known in Calabria, whither, in all probability, it made its way in the Middle Ages when Southern Italy, at the end of the thirteenth century, came under the sceptre of Aragon.

The Modern Guitar. Its Original Stringing and Tuning.

A much longer life was allotted to the flat-backed guitar which, according to Curt Sachs, cannot have come into existence until the fiddle had become an instrument with

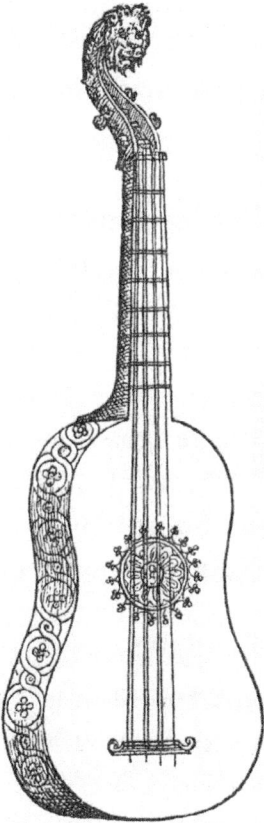

Fig. 372. F o u r - stringed G u i t a r : three double strings and one single (Mersenne, 17th cent.).

Fig. 373. Five-stringed Guitar (Curt Sachs). 18th cent.

vertical ribs, and the incurvity of the body had been made deeper. In following the lute, the guitar so far kept pace with the chitarra battente, that it took up the central large rose, the

447

double strings, the frets on the finger-board and the backward bent head of the lute; but by using the guitar-tail-piece of the lute, and by retaining its strings of gut, it came in reality still nearer to the lute than to its sister instrument.

The flat-backed guitar was not completed until the fifteenth century. Adapted to suit the convenience of the players, however, it was sought, thus differing from the case of the chitarra battente, to simplify its construction rather than to elaborate it. The oldest real guitar had only four strings (see Fig. 372) and was tuned like the oldest lute:

Not until the second half of the sixteenth century, when the lute had long since acquired six strings, did the Spaniard, Vincente Espinel of Madrid, give the guitar a fifth pair of strings, tuning it:

In France, Mersenne in 1636, gave the five-stringed guitar the following tuning:

i.e., he tuned the first string an octave higher than the Spaniards did, thereby making it higher than the third string. As he expressly said that this tuning "is peculiar to the guitar," there cannot be any misunderstanding. Only later on was this corrected by giving each of the first two strings a secondary string tuned to the octave above and below:

Very soon afterwards the addition of a sixth string followed, and the guitar was now tuned like the lute:

But this addition was only temporary; for when, in the sevententh century, all the strings were tuned a tone higher, it was found that the highest string could not easily stand the strain and a return was made to the older five-string arrangement, now tuned:

i.e., a tone higher than the older five-stringed guitar (*v. sup.*).

The sixth string was finally reintroduced after 1790 when the composer, J. G. Naumann, commissioned the German violin maker, J. A. Otto, of Weimar, to copy a five-stringed guitar which the Duchess Amalie of Weimar had brought from Italy, and provide it with six strings, for the older double stringing had in the meantime fallen into disuse.

In Literature. The History of the Guitar.

Though it may be proved by the instruction books and tablatures that the guitar was much used in Spain as early as the sixteenth century, and that it remained in favour there longer than in any other country, its palmy days as a fashionable European instrument did not come until 1650, to remain until 1840.

Among the early works for the Spanish guitar and its sister instrument, the following were the best known: Louis Milan, "Libro de Musica de Vihuela de Mano," Valencia, 1535; Alfonso Mudarro, "Les Tres Libros de Musica de Cifra para Viguela," 1546; the anonymous "Silva de Sirenos," 1547; D. Pisador, "Libro de Musica de Vihuele," Salamanca,

1552, etc. In the seventeenth century guitar books by Pietro Milioni and Lucas Ruiz de Ribayaz were published, the first in Rome, the second in Madrid.

In France the guitar enjoyed its greatest popularity in the eighteenth century. It is true that Mersenne already ("Harmonie Universelle") described its appearance and manner of playing, and that he mentioned some contemporary French guitar players and composers; but it did not become fashionable there until the difficulties connected with the tuning of the lute and the writing and reading of its notation caused amateurs to dislike it, though from an artistic point of view the latter was a far more satisfactory instrument. The French rococo artists, Watteau, Boucher, and others, simply outvie each other in reproducing the guitar, whether in the hands of a jester or an actor, or whether they use it as a becoming attribute to noble ladies and their cavaliers.

The guitar maintained its place so long in France that Paganini and Berlioz took it up with enthusiasm and utilised it as a virtuoso instrument. (Paganini was very fond of the guitar when a young man, long before he went to France and played in Paris. From 1801 to 1805 he neglected the violin entirely and only played the guitar. See my "Paganini, the Romantic Virtuoso," 1936.—ED.) But a reaction then followed. The growing need for music of a more sonorous type at length forced the guitar to recede into the modest position it now occupies everywhere as a practical accompanying instrument. The Portuguese designation for it—*viola francese*—still bears witness to its former popularity in France.

In Germany the passion for the guitar increased when the Duchess Amalie of Weimar, as mentioned above, had a five-stringed guitar brought from Italy and the instrument maker, J. A. Otto, added another string to it, winning still greater popularity for it. The six-stringed guitar with single strings penetrated everywhere very quickly on account of the greater ease in playing and tuning; and even in Italy and Spain the older, double-stringed, instruments with five strings were discarded.

In Denmark the guitar flourished until the nineteenth century when the father of Niels Gade still enjoyed some reputation as a prominent guitar maker, and when Henrik Rung succeeded in calling attention to the need for a more artistic treatment of the instrument, which was now only used by amateurs.

Names which have been applied to Instruments of the Guitar-type at Different Periods.

Guitarra (Spanish); *guiterre, kitaire, quitaire* or *guiterne* (French); *ghittern, gittern* (English). (In regard to the use of the names ending with an *n* for the true guitar, see my "Dictionary of Old English Music," under the heading "Gittern," page 95: " . . . when the instrument with the incurved sides arrived in England, it was called a gittar in a host of variant spellings; but in all of them the *n* is absent."— ED.).

Guitarra is met with for the first time in literary works in a Spanish list of jongleurs' instruments in "Libro d'amor," by Archbishop Juan Ruiz of Hita (1350) in which a *Guitarra Latina* and a *Guitarra Morisca de los voces aguda et de los puntos arisca* ("the Moorish guitar with its ringing tone and wild melodies") are mentioned side by side.

The same names are used in a French literary source at almost the same period, in the information that among the players of the Duke of Normandy there were a certain Jean Hautemer, who played the Guiterre Latine, and another named Richart l'abbé, who played the Guiterre Moreche. These names cannot thus have been chosen accidentally, and they prove that two different kinds of guitars, i.e., a Moorish and a Latin (Italian or foreign) type were used contemporaneously in Spain and France.

The Moorish guitar is believed to have been identical

with the instrument illustrated in Fig. 374 from the "Cantin-gas de Santa Maria," significantly played by an Arab; and in several respects, such as its half-moon shaped tail-piece and its large central lute-rose, it betrays its origin in the East. Through its shape the instrument recalls the ancient Egyptian *nefer* (see Figs. 162-168) and the Spanish almond-shaped plucked and bowed fiddle of the eleventh and twelfth centuries (see Figs. 311-313).

By Guitarra Latina was probably understood the guitar-type illustrated in Figs. 368 and 369 and possibly also the

Fig. 374. Spanish Guitarra Morisca 13th cent. (Riano).

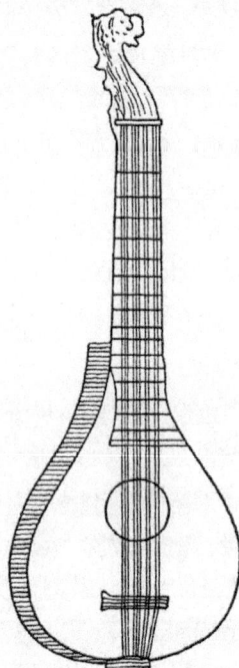

Fig. 375. The Cittern in its
classic form.

guitar forms that presumably led directly to them (see Figs. 362-367). Modern Spanish investigators maintain that the name Guitarra Latina in Spain, was originally used as a substitute for the Roman *fidicula*, but was later replaced by the Spanish alteration of this name into *vihuela* or *vigola* (corresponding to the French *viole* or *vièle*, the Anglo-Saxon *fithele*, and the Nordic *fidla*). The name may have been the natural consequence of the guitar gradually approximating to the bowed fiddle, which in fourteenth century Spain was already called *vihuela del arco* (bowed vihuela) with its counterparts in the *vihuela da penna* (plectrum vihuela) and the *vihuela del mano* (hand plucked vihuela). In the same way the lyre in France adopted the name vielle after it had acquired the form of the fiddle. When writing his musical dictionary, Tinctoris (1484) stated expressly "that the guitar invented in Spain" was called in that country, *vihuela*, and in Italy, *viola*.

At a later period in Spain and Italy, vihuela and viola were kept as special names for the aristocratic vaulted chitarra battente, while the old Spanish names, Guitarra or Guitarra Spagnole, were transferred to the popular flat backed guitar.

2. THE CITTERN.

Introduction.

The period of the cittern's greatest popularity falls between the years 1500 and 1800, and is thus in the main outside of the Middle Ages. Nevertheless, if it is dealt with here in connection with the mediaeval instruments, it is because there were literary references to it as early as the days of the troubadours, and because the mediæval pictures show us, in broad outline, several important moments in its early history.

Characteristics of the Cittern during its Classic Period (XVI-XVIII Centuries).

Viewed full face, the cittern somewhat resembles the lute; but its body had a flat back with ribs that diminished gradually in depth, thus bringing the table and back closer to each other.

The strings, which were of metal (steel or brass) and arranged in "ranks" of two or three strings tuned in unison, pass, like those of the chitarra battente, from a number of small iron pins fastened as a rule to a small projection attached below the base of the sound-board; proceeding over a relatively

Fig. 376.   Frontispiece to John Playford's "Musick's Delight on the Cittern," London, 1666.

high bridge on the table, over the finger-board and nut, to a peg-box of the violin-type.   In the centre of the table there is a circular rose often artistically designed, and on the finger-board a series of metal frets.   For plucking the strings a plectrum or the fingers of the left hand were used.

The Supposed Ancestor of the Cittern.

The cittern which in literary references may be traced back to the days of the troubadours, was not to be recognised with any degree of certainty in the pictures until the sixteenth century.   Historians are therefore ignorant of the nature of this original cittern *(cistole)* which is so often mentioned in mediaeval poems.

The points of resemblance between the classic cittern and the chitarra battente (i.e., primarily the fastening of the strings to the lower edge of the body, and the independent bridge) caused Curt Sachs to assume that these two instruments originated in the same source—i.e., in the bowed instruments of the earlier Middle Ages. If he sees in the Chitarra Battente a direct descendant of the mediæval Guitar-Fiddle, he as well as Galpin, is of the opinion that the Cittern was a descendant of the pear-shaped Lyre of the eleventh and twelfth centuries.

ON THE MONUMENTS.

Precursors.

Both of these authorities adopt as the earliest example of the mediæval Cittern, the small instrument seen in the frontis-piece of the Soissons Breviary, carried by several of the saints worshipping the Lamb (see Fig. 377).

It is, however, regrettable that the instrument is here reproduced on so small a scale that it is only possible at best to notice the existence of a round or oval body and a peg-holder with three pegs inserted from the side. Whether the sound-box was vaulted or possessed a flat back cannot be seen. In addition to this instrument, Galpin gives the "Lira" shown above in Fig. 163 the possible right to aspire to the name of Cittern, since it already possessed the double strings of the classic Cittern. Far more convincing is Curt Sachs's reference to the instrument carved in stone in Beverley Cathedral which, by its outlines and construction, points at once forward to the classic Cittern and backward to the Lira of the eleventh and twelfth centuries (see Fig. 378). An especially mediæval feature in this instrument is the perpendicular position of the pegs in the diamond-shaped peg-board, resembling that which is almost always found in the mediæval bowed instruments. In common with the sixteenth century Cittern, this instrument, on the other hand, has a flat back and four strings. The pear-shaped outline of the body and the strings running straight from the lower edge of the sound-board, finally, point in both directions.

Fig. 377. Part of the Frontispiece to the Soissons Breviary. 8th cent.

On a contemporaneous Italian sculpture an instrument may be seen reproduced in two different sizes, which approaches the more modern Cittern still more closely (see Fig. 379). Here may be clearly seen one single and four double strings, as well as five frets on the neck, which continues in a rather broad and backward-bent peg-board in which nine pegs are inserted perpendicularly in the mediæval fashion. The head ends in a finely-cut human effigy, such a one as originally only characterised the Mandora, but was in time indissolubly connected with both the bowed Rebec and the English and French Citterns. At the other end of the instrument, below the wrist of the playing angel, the projection from which the strings proceed, may be seen. A little farther forward the ends of a rather long bridge may be discerned. The narrow Rebec-like outline of the body of this Cittern may appear as a strange feature; but the keen observer will even here see an approximation to the classic Cittern; i.e., the germ of the beautiful curl which often embellishes the line of demarcation between the body and the neck (see Fig. 381).

Fig. 378. Early example of the Cittern. 15th century. Beverley, Yorks. (Galpin.)

Exactly the same type of Cittern is found in a painting by Giovanni Spagna (somewhat later), but the instrument is here provided with an ornamental rose, while the body and finger-board are of differing colour. There are also in this example four double strings (but no single string), played with a long quill and not plucked with the fingers.

According to Tinctoris, the classic Cittern came originally from Italy, and it is actually on an Italian painting that Curt Sachs shows the next and, to all appearances, last stage in the development of the modern Cittern before it was at length presented by Prætorius in its final shape. The Cittern-type

Fig. 379. Cittern carved on a pulpit in Florence. Luca della Robbia.
15th century. Photograph by Alinari.

Fig. 380. 16th century Cittern-type. Painting by Girolamo dai
Libri. Verona, 1526 (photograph, Alinari).

just described is found in a very modified form in this instrument (see Fig. 380). From an unusually broad base, the flat-backed body first curves inwards, but quickly bends out again, making an acute angle before gradually contracting to meet the rather short and broad neck. At the end of the neck is seen a round peg-board to which the nine strings are carried so that three of them on one side, and four on the other, are taken round small pins to side pegs, while the remaining two are taken directly to pegs which are inserted perpendicularly in the middle of the peg-box. On the finger-board, which projects over the sound-board, the frets are so arranged that only the first three groups (i.e., a single string and two double ones) may be stopped chromatically. Only every other fret extends as far as the last rank, so that there is a whole tone from each fret to the next. The usable compass on each string may possibly be indicated by the oblique line in which the finger-board ends, being shortest on the bass side.

The Cittern in its Final Classic Form. The Various Models and Tunings.

It is not known where or by whom the Cittern was given its final form. In the sixteenth century it was so widely distributed over Europe that tradition refers it, now to one country, now to another. While Tinctoris in the fifteenth century considered it an Italian instrument, Galilei, in 1582, looked upon it as English. At the same time it was described by some authors as a German, by others as a French instrument. The Portuguese even called it the "Flemish Guitar."

Several facts, however, referred to above, indicate that it was in the hands of the Italian instrument-makers that the Cittern passed through the last stage of its development. The Frenchman, Mersenne (1636) maintained that the Cittern in his time was used far more in Italy than in France, "where the Lute, on account of its perfection, now brings other instruments into contempt."

In 1618, Michael Prætorius enumerated five kinds of Citterns: (1) the ordinary four-stringed instrument which was tuned to:

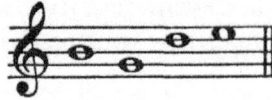

in Italy, and to:

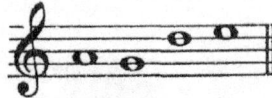

in France. (2) The "five-course" model tuned to:

(3) The six-stringed Cittern, the tuning of which varied. The early Italians tuned it thus:

while Sixtus Kärgel, of Strassburg, preferred:

(4) The larger six-stringed type, the sound-box of which was double the size of that of the ordinary Cittern, and which was consequently tuned a fourth lower; and (5) Prætorius finally mentioned Citterns with twelve strings (in pairs) "giving a wonderful resonance."

Prætorius especially alluded to a very small five-course Cittern which "nearly three years ago" was brought to Germany by an Englishman, "and which had the back left half open from the base upwards, and not glued, on which he could produce a strange, but very charming and beautiful harmony,

with fine and clean variations, and trembling hands
(tremolo?); so that it gave unusual pleasure to listen to it;
which can be performed also by excellent lutenists, etc."

In most cases the Cittern had twelve frets, occasionally
fifteen to seventeen, and they were generally, as in the Lute
and the Guitar, as long as the finger-board was broad, so that
chromatic stopping was possible on all the strings (see Fig.
375). The French four-course Cittern shown in Fig. 381 is an

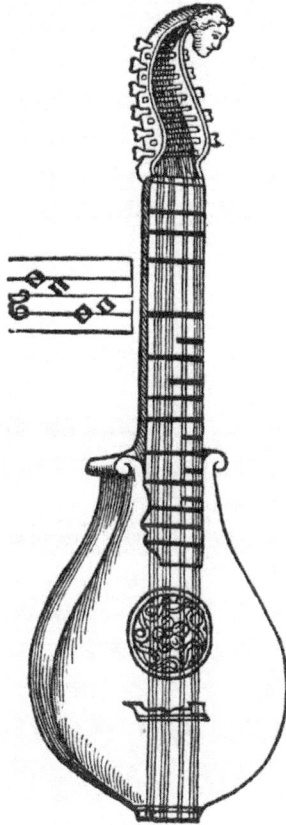

Fig. 381. French Four-Course Cittern (Mersenne).

exception. The arrangement of the frets is surprisingly like
that on the older Italian Cittern in Fig. 380, for here twelve
of the seventeen frets cover the whole breadth of the finger-
board and five only extend under the two foremost ranks of
strings. Consequently no more than the first two strings could
be stopped chromatically, while the rest permitted only of the

execution of a scale in which whole-tone sequences and semi-tones were mixed irregularly. In one case even the chromatic sequence was interrupted, for the third and fourth frets, which both extended under all of the strings, were placed a whole tone from each other.

The Mediæval Names of the Cittern.

While the name Cittern (Italian *Citra*, Spanish *Cedra*, French *Cithre*, Danish *Cister*) was traced by the older historians to the Latin *Cistella* (i.e., a small box), and therefore taken by them to mean a kind of Psalterium, more recent investigators agree in deriving it from the late Latin *Chitarra*. The Spanish author, Cerone, who lived in Italy at the end of the sixteenth century, stated definitely that Cittern was synonymous with the mediæval *Citole*, one of the instruments which were played by all the jongleurs in the thirteenth century. The final syllable, *-ole*, indicated that the instrument was small and that it was in all probability originally called *Citarole*, a name that the Italians later contracted to *Citola*, the Spaniards to *Cetola*, the French to *Citole* or *Cuitole*, and the mediæval (High) Germans to *Zitole*, *Cistol*, or *Sistole*. Later on the Germans employed the names *Cither* and *Zither*, also *Cister*, and, in the eighteenth century, *Sister*, which was a variation of the French *Cistre*. Nowadays the name *Zither* is used particularly for the so-called "Mountain-Zither," belonging to the instruments descended from the Balk Monochords (Scheitholt, Langeleg, Humle, etc.), and thus having nothing to do with the Cittern.

In the thirteenth, the fourteenth, and the beginning of the fifteenth century, the Citole was frequently mentioned by English and French writers (e.g., Guill. Guiart, 1214; Guill. Marchaud, fourteenth century; and several others). (In England a "Citoler" was mentioned in 1306; Wiclif, Gower, Chaucer, and Lydgate, all refer to the instrument as Sitol, Cythol, Cytole, Sytholle, as well as Citole.—Ed.)

In German poems of the thirteenth and fourteenth centuries, too, the *Zitole* or *Citole* was mentioned: "Zitol und orgelclanc" (Frauenlob), "Citolen und Saitenspiel" (Erlösung), and "ein Herplin (little harp) und ein Citolen" (der Renner).

The Cittern in the Eighteenth Century.

As far as its shape was concerned the Cittern really never settled down. Side by side with the classic form (Fig. 375) many variations were still used in Europe during the eighteenth century. Only the two most important can be mentioned and illustrated here; the so-called English Guitar and the bell-shaped *Hamburger Citrinchen*, invented in Hamburg at the end of the seventeenth century (see Figs. 382 and 383).

At the end of the eighteenth century attempts were made to provide the Cittern with bass-strings alongside the fingerboard, and thus a Theorbo-Cittern or an Arch-Cittern arose with the following tuning:

(See Fig. 384.)

Another improved variety of the Cittern that should be mentioned, was the English Key-Cittern invented in 1783 by Chr. Clauss in London (see Fig. 385), the object of which was to protect the delicate finger-tips of the ladies who used the instrument. Over the sound-board and near the base of the instrument, a short keyboard was attached, which was connected with a hammer mechanism hidden in the body. When the fingers depressed the keys, small hammers rose through openings in the rose and struck the strings, causing them to sound. (The left hand performed the fingering as usual.— Ed.)

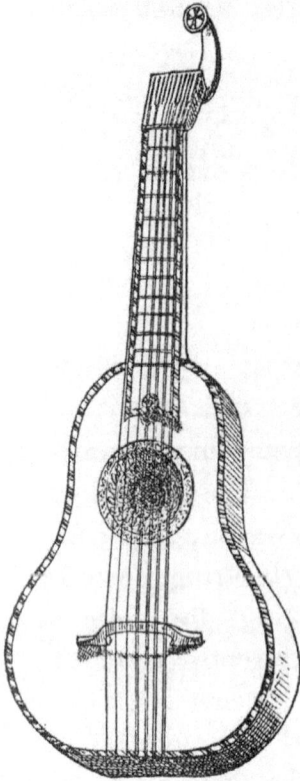

Fig. 382. Cittern made at Dunkerque (1779) with an unusual tuning mechanism (Mahillon).

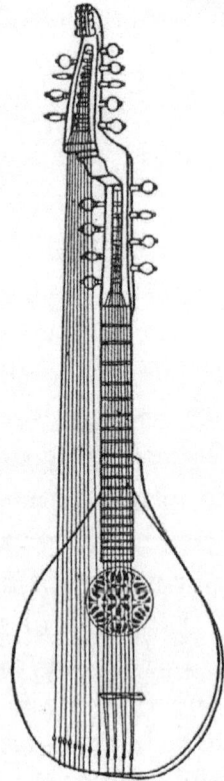

Fig. 384. Theorbo-Cittern (Curt Sachs).

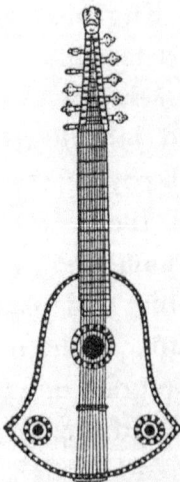

Fig. 383. Hamburger Citrinchen (Curt Sachs).

Fig. 385. Keyboard Cittern (Galpin).

Another attempt to study the convenience of the ladies was the introduction of an ingenious tuning mechanism by means of which the strings could be tightened and eased by means of a watch-key (see Figs. 382 and 385). (Preston, of London, also used this tuning mechanism, and an excellent example of the device may be seen on an instrument in the Victoria and Albert Museum, London. It was introduced more probably to ensure greater accuracy in the tuning of the hard metal strings than to please the ladies.—Ed.)

While these improvements were being made, however, the days of the Cittern were numbered. The campaign of the Guitar against its rival was in full swing and its effects were felt in the gradual substitution of single strings for the double strings, and that of covered gut strings for those of solid metal. During the course of the eighteenth century the Cittern withdrew completely from the field; first in Italy, then in Holland. In the north of France and in England it clung to life for some little time longer as the instrument of gentlewomen, but with the dawning of the nineteenth century its reign ended. It persisted longest in England for the entertainment of waiting customers at the hairdresser's, before newspapers served that purpose. ("The Barber's Cittern" was a common feature of Elizabethan England, and was played by any customer who felt disposed to while away the monotony of waiting by its help. It was mentioned as such—and very humorously—by Ben Jonson and John Ford.—Ed.)

Conclusive proof of the earlier popularity of the Cittern as a domestic instrument will be found in the very extensive collection of cittern-music which was accumulated; considerable quantities being still preserved in public and private libraries in printed as well as manuscript form. Adrien le Roy and Robert Ballard, of Paris, issued collections in 1565 and 1572, Peter Phalesius, of Leyden, published works for the instrument by Friedrich Viaera, of Friesland (1564), Sebastian Vreedmann (1568), and the cittern-book, "Hortulus

Cytharæ" (1570), Hadrian Valerius, in Haarlem, printed the "Nederländische Gedenk-Clanck" in 1626, and Bernhard Jobin, of Strassburg, printed the Tablature-Books for the Cittern by Sixtus Kärgel and J. D. Lois (1578).

England was especially interested in the publication of works for this popular instrument, and among others there appeared: Holbourne's "Citharn Schoole," in 1597, Thomas Robinson's "New Citharen Lessons" in 1609, John Playford's "A Booke of New Lessons for the Cithren and Gittern" in 1652, and "Musick's Delight on the Cittern" in 1666.

SUPPLEMENTARY CHAPTER.

THE BOWED INSTRUMENTS OF THE RENAISSANCE.

KLEIN AND GROSSGEIGEN.

When instruments were first employed in the sixteenth century for the production of artistic music, they had no music of their own. They were first used to increase the volume of the vocal music and to double the singing voices in polyphonic compositions. While the instruments hitherto used were chiefly the smaller and medium-sized types (i.e., instruments of treble and alto pitch), it was now found necessary to produce instruments capable of taking the tenor and bass parts. At the outset this difficulty was overcome by making the instruments already existing, in four sizes, without changing their form or construction in the least. The main types among the bowed instruments so treated were, on the one hand, the vaulted Rebec, and on the other, the Fiddle with the flat back and the incurved sides. Thus were created the four quartets which were described and illustrated in Martin Agricola's " Musica Instrumentalis " of 1528.

The first of these quartets, which Agricola called the " Three-stringed unfretted *Kleingeigen,*" or " Polish Fiddles," consisted of four vaulted instruments of the rebec type, i.e., a *Discantgeige* tuned to g, d', a', an Alto and a Tenor " Geige " tuned to c, g, d', and a Bass Geige tuned to

F, c, g, i.e., in Fifths like the modern violin (see Fig. 386). The other three quartets were composed of flat-backed Fiddles.

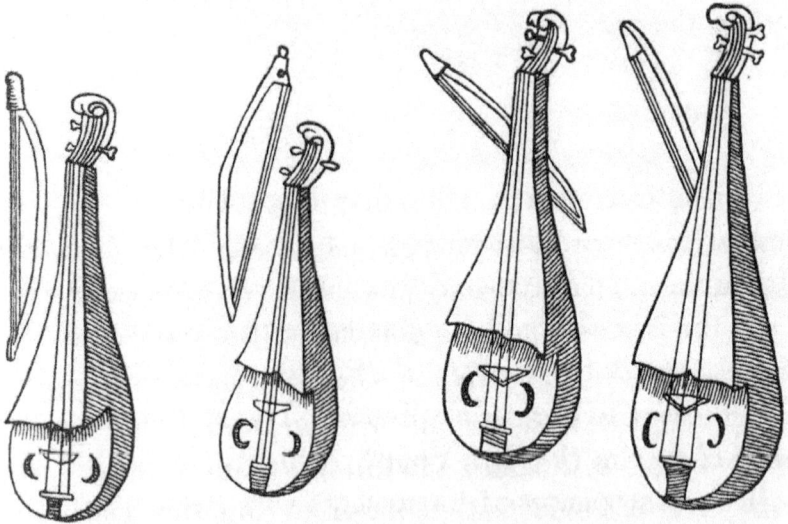

Fig. 386.   Treble, Alto, Tenor and Bass unfretted Fiddles. (Agricola, 1528).

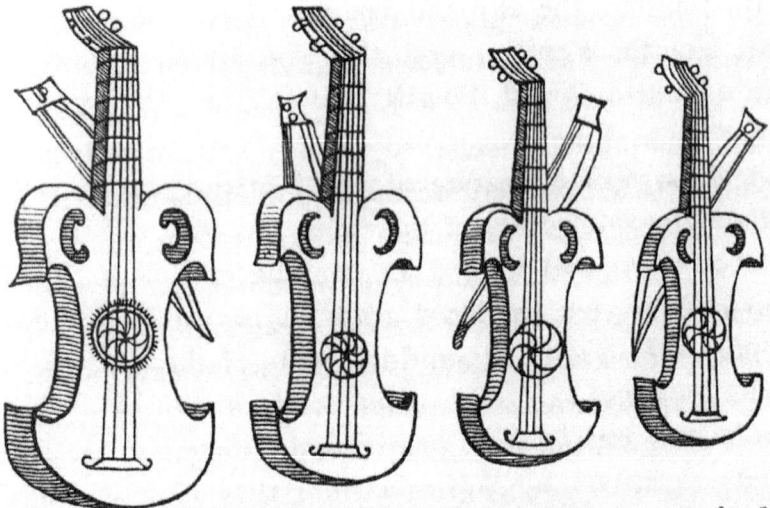

Fig. 387.   Bass, Tenor, Alto and Treble fretted Fiddles (Agricola, 1528).

These, according to Agricola, were the "Three-stringed *Kleingeigen*," the "Four-stringed *Kleingeigen*," and "Five and Six-stringed *Grossgeigen*" (*Kleingeigen* were "small" fiddles, and *Grossgeigen* "large" fiddles.—Ed.).   They resembled both the Lute and the Guitar-Fiddle, for they borrowed from the lute, the guitar tail-piece, the large central round rose, the frets tied round the neck, and the peg-holder with pegs inserted from the side; from the guitar-fiddle they inherited the curved body and the two C-shaped sound-holes cut in the upper bouts (see Fig. 387).

The instruments in the first of these three quartets, i.e., the guitar-shaped three-stringed *Kleingeigen* with frets, were tuned in Fifths like the vaulted instruments. The two other groups were tuned on the lute-principle and favoured Fourths and Thirds.

Of the four-stringed *Grossgeigen* (see Fig. 387) the treble was thus tuned to g, c', f', a' (Fourth, Fourth, Third), the alto and tenor to c, f, a, d' (Fourth, Third, Fourth), and the bass to G, c, f, a (Fourth, Fourth, Third).

In the last quartet of instruments with five and six strings, the treble, alto and tenor had five, and the bass six, strings. The treble Geige was tuned to f, a, d', g', c'' (Third, Fourth, Fourth, Fourth), the alto and tenor to c, f, a, d', g' (Fourth, Third, Fourth, Fourth), and the bass to G, c, f, a, d', g' (Fourth, Fourth, Third, Fourth, Fourth), i.e., the regular lute tuning (*v. s.v.* Lute).

A characteristic feature of the *Grossgeige*-type was the strikingly long incurvity of the sides, for they did not curve gently outward and inward as was the case with the older Guitar-Fiddles, but produced acute angles which gave for the first time the idea of the middle bouts of the modern violin with its "corners."

The two types which provided the material for the four quartets described by Agricola were thus closely connected with the mediæval Rebec and Fiddle types. If we now glance at the work in which the bowed instruments are next exhaustively dealt with, i.e., Prætorius's "Syntagmatis Musici," we shall be astonished at the long step we have suddenly made in the direction of the bowed instruments of modern times. The vaulted *Kleingeige*, which in Agricola's time was used to provide one quartet only, while the flat-backed Fiddles supplied materials for three, recedes in Prætorius's work into an Appendix as a "*gar kleine Geig*," or *Pochette*, while the guitar-shaped *Grossgeige*, under the name "*alte Fidel*," is relegated into the background by being mentioned at the end of the book with the discarded instruments of the past. Prætorius no longer refers to the bowed instruments in German as *Fidel*, but gives them the Italian name of *Viole*, and as such divides them into two categories: the *Viole da Braccio* (arm-viols), and *Viole da Gamba* (leg-viols). Only colloquially were the arm-viols still called *Geigen*.

That the bowed instruments had now been given Italian names was the natural consequence of the assumption by the Italians of the leading rôle in the domain of violin-making, and the advance made proves that they were the best persons to take up this task. By means of the Italian paintings it is possible to follow the development of the bowed instruments step by step during this interesting period when violin-making, after having been a mere handicraft, was gradually developed into a science based upon elaborate acoustical researches that did not evade the labour of experimentation in order to make of the bowed instrument a suitable vehicle for the interpretation of artistic music such as the period commencing with the Renaissance provided for it.

As the ancestor of the modern violin-type which forms the basis of the present-day string-quartet—the Violin, the Tenor or Viola, and the Bass or Violoncello—A. Haidecki ("Die italienische Lira da Braccio," 1892) selected the Lyra da Braccio, i.e., an arm-viol discovered as early as the fifteenth century.

Prior to the modern violin-shaped leg-instrument (the modern Violoncello), there was an independent family of leg-viols—the *Viole da Gamba*—the development of which may be traced farther back than that of the violin, but which, on the other hand, persisted for a while even after the modern violoncello type had been evolved from the violin. During the Renaissance, however, the development of the arm and leg viols ran parallel.

The Lyra da Braccio.

The presumed ancestor of the modern violin was in many ways still so closely connected with the mediæval Fiddles that it has been accepted without hesitation as an improvement on them. Like the mediæval oval fiddle, the Lyra da Braccio still had five strings over the finger-board and two at the side of it (Bourdons). The shape of the peg-box at the end of the neck and the pegs inserted perpendicularly, were similarly mediæval features. In an Italian painting the construction of this peg-box may be clearly seen, and it will by this means be possible to examine all the details of this important part of the bowed instrument which in the mediæval pictures is generally so indistinct (see Fig. 388). As will be seen from the painting, the peg-box, now developed into an elegant heart-shape (see also Fig. 338), was open at the back and the pegs were inserted from the front (see Figs. 389 and 390), so that the heads of the pegs projected above the face of the box, while the shafts on which the strings were wound, were hidden in the interior. In order to reach the holes in the pegs, the five main strings, after having passed over the saddle or nut, were drawn through holes in the box, while the two bourdons which lay beyond the finger-board, were carried over or through a nail which projected from the left side of the box in order thus to be taken to the holes leading to their respective pegs.

In the Lyra da Braccio type illustrated in Figs. 389 and 390, the form of the body is new, for it already has the upper and lower bouts of the modern violin. The sound-holes

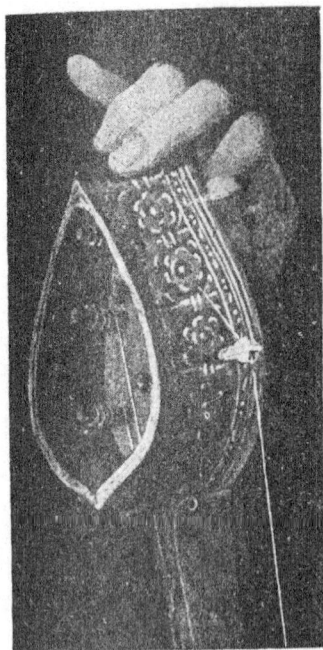

Fig. 388. Interior of Lyra
da Braccio Peg-box.

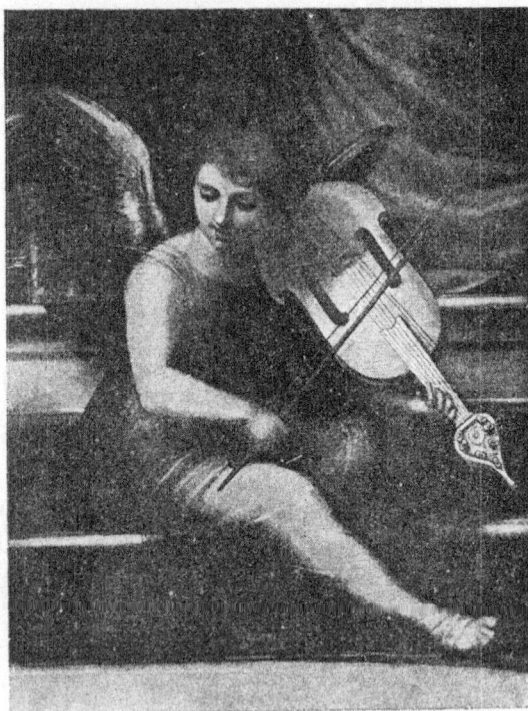

Fig. 389. Lyra da Braccio in its original
form. *Ca.* 1500. Painting by Fra Bartolomeo.
(Photograph, Alinari.)

Fig. 390 Lyra da Braccio. Painting
by Carpaccio. (Photograph, Alinari.)

Fig. 391. Apollo. Giov. Spagna.
Circa 1530.

which in Fig. 389 were disproportionately broad and long, still had the C-shape of the Middle Ages.

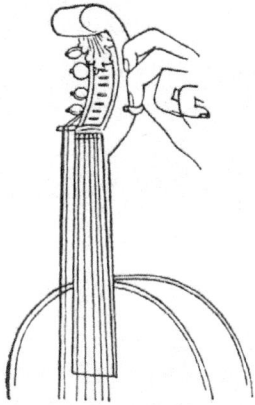

Fig. 392. Neck of Lyra da Braccio with rudimentary scroll and lateral pegs.

Fig. 393. Twelve-stringed Lyra Perfetta (Prætorius).

On the Lyra da Braccio drawn by Giovanni Spagna (Fig. 391) the sound-box has already been corrected to an almost regular violin body with upper, lower, and middle bouts, while the sound-holes and the peg-box still retain the old shape and construction.

In Prætorius's "Syntagma" (1618) the C-holes were at last replaced by f-holes, and in the example shown in Fig. 392 the heart-shape peg-box was finally removed to make room for an approach to the modern scroll and a peg-box with lateral pegs, only the bourdons remaining as survivals from the past. The last step was the removal of the bourdons and the reduction of the number of strings to four. The modern violin at length came into existence with the appearance of the instrument illustrated in Fig. 394.

In spite of the improvements which the old Lyra da Braccio introduced, and which gradually led to the modern violin-type or Viola da Braccio, the older instrument (the Lyra da Braccio) in its original form was still used side by side with the violin for nearly a hundred years. Like the violin (*v. inf.*) it was in the course of time even made the prototype of a whole family, completed by a tenor instrument, the Lyra da Gamba (also called *Lirone* or *Lyra Imperfetta*), with nine to thirteen strings on the finger-board and two bourdons along-side, and a bass instrument, the *Lirone* or *Lyra Perfetta*, which was played standing and which, besides the two bourdons, had ten to fourteen strings on the finger-board (see Fig. 393).

THE VIOLA DA BRACCIO.

(THE MODERN VIOLIN-TYPE; *i.e.*, THE FORM WHICH BECAME THE MODEL FOR THE INSTRUMENTS FORMING THE PRESENT-DAY STRING-QUARTET.)

The earliest Viola da Braccio was an alto instrument and corresponded to the modern Viola. With this as a model, a smaller treble Viola da Braccio (also called *Violino Piccolo alla Francese*), was made, to be followed later by two larger ones, the tenor Viola da Braccio (now obsolete) and the Bass-

Viol (also called *Violoncino*), the leg-viol which became the barytone of the modern string-quartet, and at the beginning of its career a keen competitor of the tenor Gamba *(v. inf.)*.

Fig. 394. The Viola da Braccio.

The name "Violin," when it first appeared in the "Sacræ Symphoniæ," by Giovanni Gabrieli, in 1597, was applied—as the alto clef proves—to a Viola. Seven years later, on the other hand, Valentin Haussmann deliberately wrote "Violin" over the treble part of his "Neue Intrada." Originally, then, this name was applied to the Violin as well as to the Viola. In 1607 (three years later) Monteverdi called the Violin the *Violino Piccolo*, and the Viola the *Violino Ordinario*. The tenor Viola da Braccio, mentioned above, was, according to Hizler ("Neue Musica oder Singkunst," Tübingen, 1628), tuned to: *F, c, g, d'*, and must not be confused with the Viola which was later, as a rule, called the tenor Viola da Braccio (the German *Bratsche*), and which was tuned to: *c, g, d', a'*. The Violoncello did not come to the fore until the eighteenth century. Up to that moment it had to be content with its part in the thoroughbass accompaniment in orchestral and chamber music.

The other modern leg-viol, the Contrabass Viol, which was originally called the Violone or Contrabass Violone, can only be classed among the violins conditionally, for in its form it comes nearer to the Viola da Gamba and must, if anything, be considered as a descendant of the *Gross-bass Viola da Gamba* (*v. inf.*, *s.v.* Viola da Gamba family).

While the Viola da Braccio family is now only represented by two instruments—the Violin and the Viola—it originally, according to Prætorius, numbered six: (1) "Gar kleine Geige" (the *Poche*), which had either the form of the Rebec, the Guitar-Fiddle (see the Poche in Figs. 303 and 304), or a Violin; (2) "Kleine Diskantgeige," which, together with the preceding, disappeared long ago; (3) the Treble Viol, i.e., the modern Violin; (4) the Tenor Viol, i.e., the modern Viola; (5) the Bass-Viol (obsolete); and (6) "Gross Quint Bass" (with five strings). With the exception of the first, which could have three or four strings, the arm-violins only had four strings, which were tuned as they are now—in Fifths.

Postscript. In the light of more recent research, the assertion of Haidecki that the Viola da Braccio developed out of the Lira da Braccio can no longer be maintained in the original and strict meaning of the words. Curt Sachs draws attention to the fact that while the Lira da Braccio was beginning to change little by little into an instrument of the violin-type, we find two Fiddles in a painting by Lorenzo Costa which deviate from that type only in their possession of C-holes, five strings, and the absence of the middle bouts. The Lira da Braccio could therefore not alone have prepared the way for the violin. "About the year 1500 the conditions affecting instrument-making were completely revolutionary," he wrote; "the obstinate clinging to inherited principles was suddenly ended. Instruments which for hundreds of years had been kept distinct from one another, now relinquished their jealously guarded peculiarities in order to blend them with those of others and bring forth bastards. Lira, Viola da Gamba, and Viola da Braccio, can thus only be understood as crystallisations of a confused multitude of Gigues, Fiddles and Lute-instruments."

THE VIOLA DA GAMBA.

At the period during which the alto Viola da Braccio or arm-violin was separated from the Lyra da Braccio of the sixteenth century and made the model for a quartet of its own kin, conditions also forced the tenor and bass Viole da Gamba to enter new paths.

The mere increase in the bulk of the instruments from the treble and alto size to the tenor and bass, was soon shown, as far as the bowed instruments were concerned, to be unpractical and inefficient, unless changes in the construction were made at the same time. What was primarily troublesome to the player accustomed to the treble and alto fiddles, was the altered measurement of the stop. In order to fill in the Fifth which in the Fiddle normally separated the notes of the open strings, the stopping fingers on the larger instruments had to stretch considerably in order to reach the required points. To facilitate the playing of passages on the instruments with the longer stop, the first step was therefore to tune the open strings to smaller intervals by replacing the tuning in Fifths by that of the Lute in Fourths and Thirds. In consequence of this, however, the compass was reduced, a circumstance that immediately compelled an increase in the number of strings from four to six or seven. In order further to facilitate the management of the larger stops, the player, again taking the Lute as his model, was finally obliged to determine the stopping points by means of frets.

All these reforms were already effected in the four, five, and six-stringed "Grossgeigen" *(v. sup.)*, but even further steps were soon taken. To enable the bow to work on each string separately with greater ease, the comparatively short but deeply cut middle incurvity was first introduced; and it is this feature which distinguishes the modern violin-body. It appeared earlier in the Gamba than in the arm-viols (see Lyra da Braccio; Fig. 391 and cf. Fig. 395). At the same

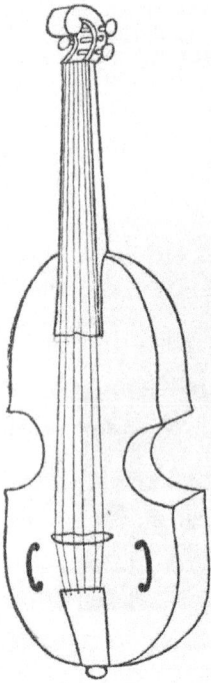

Fig. 395. (Curt Sachs.) Fig. 396. (Curt Sachs.) Types of Viole da Gamba.

time the table was moulded while the back remained flat and was sloped off in the upper part to facilitate the placing of the instrument between the knees. Later on the attempt was made to give the left hand more latitude by narrowing the upper part of the body where it joins the neck (see Fig. 396). The numerous and heavy strings of the Gamba, in addition, necessitated the introduction of a different tuning mechanism, better able to withstand the increased tension of the strings. Like the arm-violins, the Gamba therefore borrowed the backward turned head with pegs inserted from the sides—the Rebec head, which could be terminated in a scroll or—as in most cases—in a carved human head. The last change made was to shift the sound-holes from their old position in the lower half of the table near the bridge to a new one in the middle bouts. The holes were then cut in the reversed sense so that the open side of the C was parallel with the curve of the "waist" (see Fig. 396).

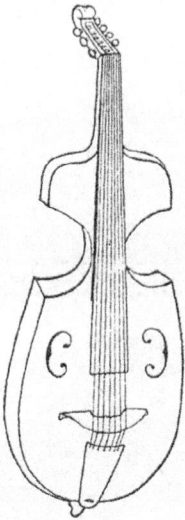

Fig. 397. Viola da Gamba in Grünewald. The Isenheimer Altar.
(Curt Sachs.)

It is interesting to notice how the desire for "improvements" led to exaggeration, such as making the incurvity of the sides so deep that it often reached as far as the fingerboard (see Fig. 397) or placing indentations in the shoulders to give the stopping hand freer access to the strings (see Fig. 398).

When a norm was at last reached, the Viola da Gamba and the Viola da Braccio, in spite of their many points of resemblance, remained distinct and independent types.

Fig. 398. The same in Burgk-mair: Maximilian's triumphal march. (Curt Sachs.)

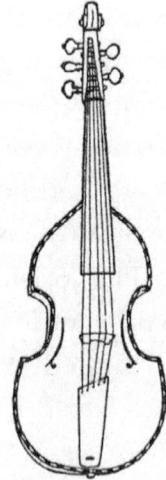

Fig. 399. Pardessus de Viole. (Curt Sachs.)

Points of Difference between the Viola da Braccio (the Violin-type) and the Viola da Gamba (the Gamba-type).

In the violin family (Violin, Viola and Violoncello) the shoulders of the body emerged almost at right angles from the neck; in the Gamba the sound-box, on the other hand, had sloping shoulders, the body running up to the neck almost in a point.

No frets are used on the violins, and the sound-holes are f-shaped; in the Gamba the neck was provided with frets and the sound-holes were C-shaped. In the Violins the back is moulded; in the Gamba the back was perfectly flat.

The ribs of the violins are much narrower than in the Gamba. In the violins the neck ends in a scroll; in the gamba the crowning feature was generally of the rebec-type, with a carved animal or human head. The violins in their final state have only four strings, while the gamba had six or seven.

Just as the alto Viola da Braccio was the germ from which the violin family grew, so was the alto (and tenor) Viola da Gamba the origin of a whole family of *Gambe*. Gerle in 1532 thus presents them in three sizes: (1) the Treble Gamba, (2) the Alto and Tenor Gambas, and (3) the Bass Gamba. By 1600 the family had increased to six members—the Treble, the Alto or Tenor Gambas, the "Kleinbasgamba," "Grossbasgamba," and "Sub-basgamba." With the exception of the five-stringed "Sub-basgamba" all these instruments had six strings tuned in the Fourth-Third accordance of the Lute. Only the large Viola da Gamba ("Gross-Bass-Viola da Gamba" was tuned entirely in Fourths.

During the course of the seventeenth century most of these Gamba types disappeared, so that until the end of the eighteenth century the Tenor Gamba was the only competitor of the Violoncello. Shortly before the Tenor Gamba also vanished, the treble variety was revived for a brief time in France, without its lowest string, under the name of *Pardessus de Viole* or *Quinton* (see Fig. 399).

The newer varieties of the Viola da Gamba, such as the Tenor Gamba invented in England and provided with additional sympathetic strings of metal, occurred too late for inclusion here. These instruments were the *Viola Bastarda* and such of its variations as the *Barytone* or *Viola Bordone* of tenor pitch, and the *Viola d'Amore* to serve as the alto of the group. The *Viola Bastarda* may be traced in literary references back to 1589. The period of the *Barytone* fell in the eighteenth and nineteenth centuries, while the *Viola d'Amore* was invented towards the end of the seventeenth century, and fell into disuse at the end of the eighteenth century. (All these variations and hybrids are of far too recent development to justify their inclusion in a work dealing with the instruments of the Middle Ages and, at the latest, the Renaissance. It may be of interest to note that I possess an original Tenor made by William Turner in London (1652; six-stringed) and a modern replica by Saint-George of an old Italian Viola d'Amore, both of which I frequently played to illustrate the lectures of the late Sir Frederick Bridge at Gresham College and the University of London.—*Ed*.)

With the final settlement of the violin-type, the development of the bowed instruments came to a close. What improvements still remained to be effected were only the subtleties and niceties noticed by connoisseurs, but which are of little interest to the historian. These last touches were given by the famous violin-makers of Brescia and Cremona—Gasparo da Salo, Maggini, and the Amati, Stradivari, and Guarneri families. All later attempts at making new violin-types to "improve" or supplant the classic ideal, have failed.

THE HARPSICHORD.

As a keyboard instrument which competed for centuries with the Clavichord (see Book II), the Harpsichord may, in its completed form, be looked upon as a Psalterium with a keyboard (see Book I, 146 *ff*.). Like the Psaltery, it had strings of unequal length and was played, also like the Psaltery, by plucking the strings.

The means for plucking the strings of the Harpsichord was supplied by a rather neat little piece of appartus called the *Jack*, a light wooden rod at the upper end of which was hinged a small movable tongue provided with a spring (see Fig. 400). (On this tongue a quill, a slip of leather or metal was fixed. *Ed.*) When the finger struck the key and depressed it, the Jack, which stood perpendicularly at the extreme rear end of the key, was raised past the string and plucked it. When falling back, the spring prevented the quill from again twanging the string, and at the same time two small pieces of cloth fastened to the Jack, one on each side of the tongue, came in contact with the vibrating string and immediately damped it.

Like the Psaltery, the Harpsichord was made in many different forms. When made in a small size it generally took the form of an oblong box in which the strings were stretched in the direction of the longer sides, so that the shafts of the keys in this type of instrument passed under the strings. The length of these shafts varied according to the distance of the string which each was to serve. In these small instruments the strings were, as a rule, single.

In Germany this small keyboard instrument was called the *Virginal* or *Spinet*; in France, *Épinette*; in Italy, *Spineto*; in England, *Virginal*. *Spinet*, *Spineto*, and *Épinette* refer to the plectrum which plucked the strings (Italian, *Spino*; French, *Épine*, a thorn). The name *Virginal* may be explained in two ways: one derivation sees in the rod of the Jack *(Virga)* a source for the name; the other (English) etymology connects the word with *virgin* because this type of instrument was generally played by women (see Fig. 401).

In the large size, on the other hand, the Harpsichord was made in the shape of a grand pianoforte and, in this case, the strings ran in the same direction as the keys. The Jacks were arranged in a row and stood sideways on the rear extremity of the keys, so that they plucked the strings from the side. As a rule, the strings were trichord, so that for each note a rank of three strings tuned in unison was required, each of which had to be plucked by its own Jack. The name of this grand-pianoforte shape was *Kielflügel* in German, Harpsichord in English, *Clavicembalo* in Italian, *Clavecin* in French.

Kielflügel and Harpsichord both refer to the quill *(Federkiel)* of the Jack, and to the harp-like plucking of the strings.

The unequal length and pitch of the strings enabled the Harpsichord—unlike the Clavichord—to produce every possible harmony. On the other hand, the Harpsichord lacked

Fig. 401. Virginal in Berlin Collection of Instruments, 1657. (Curt Sachs.)

Fig. 400.
Jack.
(Curt Sachs.)

the Clavichord's power to modify the tone-volume by varying finger-pressure. If the quill and the spring were to act, rather firm pressure on the key was required. If the pressure was too slight, the quill did not pass and twang the string. Differences between *piano* and *forte* had therefore to be produced by artificial means : either by a " stop " which, when drawn, shifted the whole of the spring-mechanism and permitted only one of each trichord group of strings to sound (cf. the " soft " pedal of the grand pianoforte), or by using two keyboards, one of which was connected in the normal way with the complete trichord stringing, while the other was connected only with one string of each rank.

The inability of the Harpsichord to modify the volume of its tone, gave rise to the invention of a large number of devices which, by using various stops, changed the *timbre* of the tone. Among these the "Harp-stop," in which brass was used for the plectra, imitating the harp-tone, and the "Lute-stop," in which slips of leather or hard felt were employed in conjunction with a damping device, were very popular and frequently used.

Since the strings of the Harpsichord could vibrate throughout their entire length, it was a far more sonorous instrument than the Clavichord, and therefore played a highly important rôle, not only as the chief "general-bass" instrument in the orchestra and chamber-music, but also as a solo-instrument on the concert-platform during the sixteenth, seventeenth and eighteenth centuries. Indeed, it did not disappear until some time after the pianoforte had become the prevailing type of keyboard instrument.

Though it seems established that the Harpsichord was invented in Germany, England undoubtedly enjoys the honour of having further developed it. The earliest representation of the instrument is to be found on a wood-carving in Manchester Cathedral (see Fig. 403).

In literature the Harpsichord may be traced in its two forms under the names of Schachbrett and Clavicymbalum to the fourteenth century, and Cersne von Minden's "Minne-regeln" are our chief source of information in this connection. In that list of the instruments popular at his period, Cersne, besides mentioning the *Schachbrett* and the *Clavicymbolum*, names the *Psalterium* and the *Cymbel*, which belonged to the families of the plucked Psalteries and the instruments played with beaters or hammers, and called *Hackbrett* in Germany, *Salterio Tedesco* in Italy, and *Dulcimer* in England (see Book

I, p. 155). As a keyboard instrument we do not find—as we might expect—a "Clavipsalterium," but a "Clavicymbolum," i.e., a *Cymbel* provided with a keyboard. The conclusion arrived at therefore has been that the Harpsichord, in its original form, must have been an instrument played with

Fig. 402. The Harpsichord in grand piano form. Paul de Wit, "Perlen der Instrumentensammlung P. d. W's."

hammers, and that the Harpsichord provided with Jacks, quills and springs was a later stage in the development of the instrument. Whether this change had already been made when the Harpsichord was mentioned in the "Minneregeln" cannot be determined. The accomplished fact cannot be proved with certainty until we reach the description of the Harpsichord given by Virdung in 1511 ("Musica Getutscht.")

Positive proof of the application of the spring mechanism to the keyboard-instrument is found, as we now know, in the *Schachbrett* mentioned in the "Minneregeln," which is rightly identified with the *Echiquier*, *Exchequer*, and *Exaquir* men-

Fig. 403. Oldest known illustration of the Harpsichord in "Grand Pianoforte" shape. (Galpin.)

tioned at an early date in the French, English, and Spanish literary sources. These names in ordinary usage mean a chess-board; but they are also clearly applied to a stringed instrument with a keyboard. How and why "Chess-board" was adopted as the name of such an instrument, was a mystery for a long time, and research-workers vainly endeavoured to solve it. The result was a large number of fantastic and totally unsatisfactory hypotheses, which were all rejected when Curt Sachs, in the "Sammelbände der I.M.G." (1912) advanced a theory which in the most natural manner explains the connection. He proves that the West European description of the instrument as "Chess-board" was due to an erroneous trans-

487

lation of the word *Schachbrett* when it made its appearance in the manuscript of Cersne von Minden as the name of an instrument. In mediæval Germany a chess-board was not called *Schachbrett*, but *Schach-Zabel*. *Schacht* is a Dutch word meaning a spring or a quill, and has nothing to do with Chess or the Chess-board. Cersne von Minden, living in Westphalia, borrowed this name in all probability from the Netherlands, a land enjoying a high reputation at that period for the excellence of its musical culture, and where the Harpsichord of small size was probably then called the *Schachtbrett*.

3. INSTRUMENTAL NOTATION.

A. THE GERMAN ORGAN TABLATURE.

This notation originated in the letters of the alphabet in the mediæval script, the first seven of which were used to designate the different notes. The lowest octave was distinguished by the employment of capitals, the second octave by " lower case " letters, the third by the same with a line above them, and so on.

When the German organists commenced to use the letter-notation for writing keyboard-music (i.e., about the year 1500), the keyboard already presented its modern appearance with alternate groups of two and three upper keys arranged between the seven lower keys, so that the succession of the notes in each octave was then, as now: *c, c-sharp, d, d-sharp, e, f, f-sharp, g, g-sharp, a, b-flat, b*. These letters appeared as follows :

$$c \; g \; d \; d_{\!\!\!/} e \; f \; f_{\!\!\!/} g \; g_{\!\!\!/} a \; b \; h$$

Instead of referring to the semitone above *a* as *a-sharp*, the letter b *(b-rotundum)* was employed, while the square b (♭, or *b-quadratum*) was used for *b-natural*. By omitting the baseline in the square *b*, it was made to resemble an *h*, ⊢ and *b-natural* soon acquired the name *h*. This error has persisted to the present day in Germany and the Scandinavian countries, and our *b-flat* is there called *b*, while our *b-natural* is known as *h*.

Above each letter a sign was placed to indicate its duration:

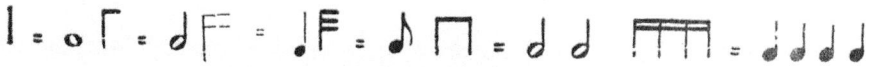

Such a sign placed where there was no letter, indicated a rest of the same value. The different parts were arranged in score, and in a passage for three voices, six signs had to be read at a time; in a passage of four parts, eight signs, etc. Bar-lines were used to divide the phrases into smaller units.

A short Example of German Organ-Tablature.

Translation:

From Ammerbach's Clavier-Book, 1571.

B. THE LUTE-TABLATURES.

The object of all these methods of notation was to give the fingers some visible directions as to their proper places on the finger-board, though the lutenists of Germany and the Romance countries used different systems.

I. THE GERMAN LUTE-TABLATURE.

When this system was invented, the Lute had only five strings and five frets. The notes produced by the open strings were indicated in the Tablature by the figures 1, 2, 3, 4, and 5, so that 1 stood for the lowest string, 2 for the next above it, and so on. The notes produced by placing the fingers at any of the twenty-five points at which strings and frets crossed, were designated by the letters, arranged alphabetically. The points at which the first fret crossed the strings were named *a*, *b*, *c*, *d*, and *e* respectively; the notes on the second fret were, similarly, indicated by the letters *f*, *g*, *h*, *i*, and *k*, and so on; the notes on the third fret were named *l*, *m*, *n*, *o*, *p*, those on the fourth fret, *q*, *r*, *s*, *t*, and *v*, and those on the fifth fret, *x*, *y*, *z*, *ʒ* and *9*. The letters *j* and *u* were not used, as they were considered identical with *i* and *v* respectively. In order to find signs for the twenty-five notes on the frets, the other form of *z* and the sign *9* were used, which were the common abbreviations of the Latin *et* and *con*.

Since the five-course Lute was normally tuned to: *d*, *g*, *b*, *e'*, *a'*, and since the frets followed each other chromatically, the note *d-sharp*, for example, was produced by placing the finger on the first fret and the first string; the note *b-flat* was obtained at the point *m* (where the second string crossed the third fret); *d* was produced by touching the point *n* (where the third string crossed the third fret), and so on.

9	*3*	*7*	*y*	*x* Fifth Fret.
v	*t*	*s*	*r*	*q* Fourth Fret.
p	*o*	*n*	*m*	*l* Third Fret.
k	*i*	*h*	*g*	*f* Second Fret.
e	*d*	*c*	*b*	*a* First Fret.
5	*4*	*3*	*2*	*1* Open Strings.
a¹	*e¹*	*h*	*g*	*d* Tuning,

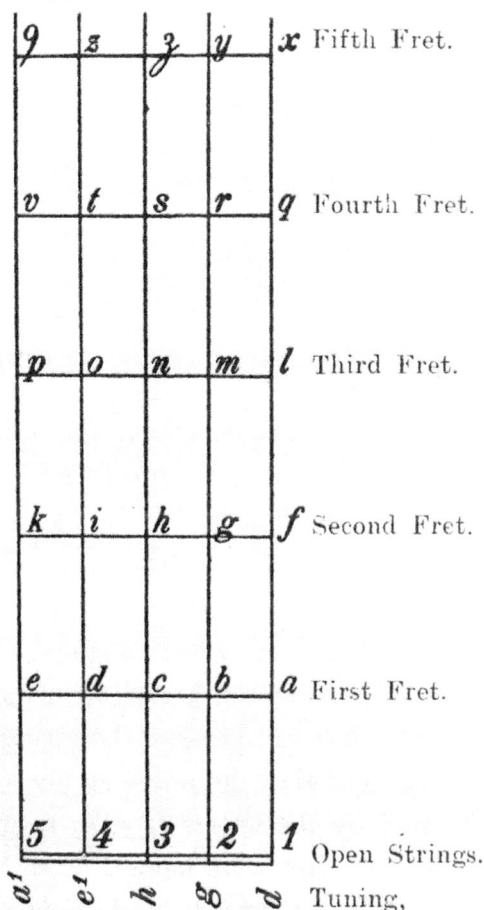

When the number of the frets was increased (up to eight),
the new notes were named by doubling the letters: *aa, bb, cc,*
etc. After the Lute was given more strings, the old method
was retained for the five original strings. For indicating the
notes on the added strings, the German lutenists employed a
different method. The open sixth, seventh, and eighth strings
were generally noted as ⨍ ⨍ ⨍ respectively; the naming
of the points at which these strings were crossed by the frets, on
the other hand, was subject to some variation. While some
named the points of crossing on the sixth string after
those on the neighbouring string, using the capitals,
A, F, L, Q, X, and for the parallel points on the

seventh and eighth strings by the same letters traversed by one or two lines: *A F L O X* and *A F L O X* others preferred to designate them by a new alphabetical series in capitals: A, B, C, D, E, etc., and yet others continued the example of the open strings *1 1 1* by using the succeeding figures, again with one or two lines drawn across them: *2 3 4 5*, and *2 3 4 5* etc.

The rhythm was indicated in the German Lute-tablature as it was in the German Organ-tablature, by placing the usual notational signs of duration above the notes.

Example of a Melody noted in German Lute-Tablature.

The German Lute-tablature was not only used for the notation of lute music, but was also employed for the *Grosse* and *Kleine Geigen* tuned like lutes. Examples may be seen in Hans Gerle's "Musica Teutsch auff die Instrument der grossen vnd kleinen Geygen, auch Lauten," and "Musica vnd Tabulatur auff die Instrument der kleinen vnd grossen Geygen," published at Nuremberg in 1532 and 1546 respectively.

2. LUTE-TABLATURES OF THE ROMANCE COUNTRIES.

These were of far more practical use than the German tablature, since they used lines to designate the strings and figures or letters to indicate the frets.

Thus in the Italian and Spanish tablatures a zero (o) meant the open string, the figure 1 the first fret, the figure 2 the second fret, etc. In the French tablature the letter *a*, on the other hand, always meant the open string, *b*, the first fret, *c*, the second fret, etc. What renders the reading difficult (to modern musicians.—*Ed*.) is the practice of the Italians and Spaniards to consider the lowest of the lines as the highest string, numbering the strings from the top downwards, while the Frenchmen more logically looked upon the lowest line as representing the deepest string (see examples below).

The Italians and Spaniards, and, as a rule, the Frenchmen also, used the ordinary mensural notes as signs of length:

While the indications for the notes and the signs of duration were given together in each part of a polyphonic composition in the German organ-tablature, so that each part could be followed independently, the lutenists were content to place the signs of time-value above the stave once only (see example 3 below). Furthermore, they never repeated the duration sign if the following notes had the same value, changing the sign only when the length of the note changed. As long as the notes retained the same value, the succeeding spaces were left empty until a new value replaced the old (see below). While the reading of the signs themselves, in all Lute-tablatures, occasions but little difficulty, considerable theoretical knowledge is necessary when translating polyphonic music in lute-tablature correctly. This has been the cause of many a translator landing himself into difficulties; for he has probably only considered the notes and allowed himself to be misled by the general rhythmic indications set roughly at the head of the tablature. It must not be forgotten that the lutenists of the past were, before all else, excellent musicians and thoroughly educated in the hard school of the polyphonic era.

By transferring this style to their instruments, they wrote and played, as far as was possible, in such a way that the ear (despite the short duration of the individual notes) was able to hear and follow the weaving of the counterpoint. Only with this knowledge, and under these conditions, will the translator be able to arrive at the correct interpretation of music written in Tablature.

Some occasional guidance was afforded by the examples of fingering now and then occurring in the Lute-books, and by the marking of long notes, where the finger, in order to hold the melody, had to sustain a note beyond the time indicated. For this purpose the German lutenists, when writing for beginners, placed a small cross before the sign in question. The French writers, on the other hand, used an oblique line or a slur extending from the beginning of the note to the end. It was, however, only in exceptional cases that such means were employed. As a rule, composers took for granted that the advanced player knew where to allow his fingers to remain in position and where they could be released. These precautions were unnecessary in the case of the open strings, for they continued to sound of themselves.

Keys for the solution and translation of the Italian, Spanish, and French Lute-tablatures:

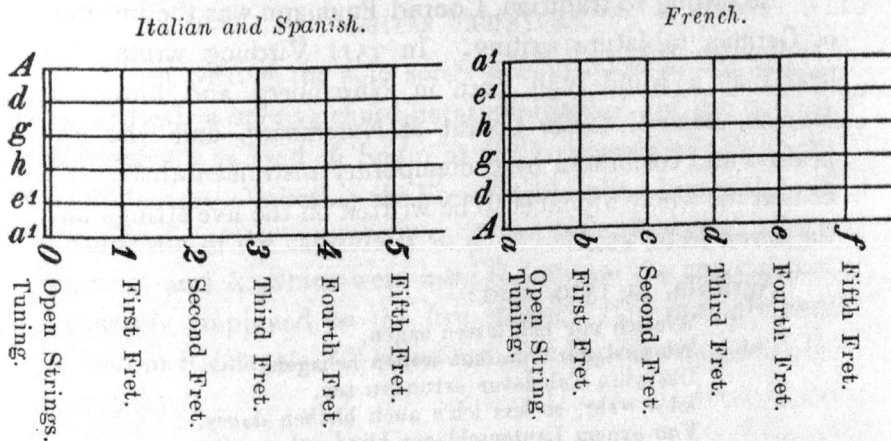

Italian and Spanish.

French.

The melody last given above:

1. In the Italian Tablature:

3 2 3
0 1 1 0   3 1
                1 1 0   1

2. In the French Tablature (time-values as above):

a   b b a   b b a   b
d c d   d b

3. Example in French Tablature of the polyphonic passage given above in Organ-tablature:

a   b   b a   b b a   b
d c d b   b   b a d   b   b   b
d   d b   d   d b   d f
d c d   d   c d f   d
f a f d   a c   d f d
        b a   b

According to tradition, Conrad Paumann was the inventor of German tablature writing. In 1511 Virdung wrote: "I hear that a blind man, born in Nuremberg and buried in Munich, named Master Conrat of Nuremberg, and who was praised and celebrated by contemporary instrumentalists. He caused the whole alphabet to be written on the five strings and the seven frets, etc."

Agricola, in 1529, said:

"Wie ich mir hab lassen sagen,
Wiewohl mir's nie hat wollen behagen.
Das yhre Tabulatur erfunden sey,
Ist's wahr, so lass ich's auch bleiben dabey,
Von eynem Lautenschläger blind geboren." . . .

Hans Judenkünig (1523) expressed himself more vaguely: "It is generally known that in recent years within the memory of man, the Tablature for the Lutes was discovered."

The period of the invention was undoubtedly round about 1450. German Lute-tablature remained in use for about a century and a half. When, roughly at the opening of the seventeenth century, the Hispano-Italian and French Lute-tablatures made their way towards the north, the days of the German system were numbered. One lutenist after the other deserted the old manner of writing. Already in 1529 the German system was ridiculed by Agricola, who declared that the blind lutenist (Paumann) had led his pupils on a false path and had also made them blind, so that it was not strange that people laughed at them.

It cannot be decided when or by whom the lute-notations of the Romance countries were invented. The Hispano-Italian Tablature was in all probability invented in *ca.* 1500, i.e., shortly before the first Spanish and Italian lute-books were made public in manuscript and printed form. The French system probably arose somewhat later, but was, on the other hand, retained in use until the eighteenth century.

3. GUITAR TABLATURE.

When writing the solo songs accompanied by the Guitar (monodies), a special chord-notation adapted for use on that instrument was used in Spain at the beginning of the seventeenth century. Imitating the French and Italian lute-tablatures it made use of the capitals A to Z and four additional signs: +, 2, 9, and ℞, which were used to indicate the chords most frequently employed on the five strings. (An example may be seen in Riemann's " " Handbuch der Musikgeschichte," II, 2, 359 *f.*)

4. CITTERN TABLATURE.

For writing the music of the Cittern, the French lute-tablature was generally used, employing four or six lines according to the stringing of the instrument: four lines for the four-stringed, and six for the six-stringed Cittern.

Printed in Great Britain
by Amazon